Effective management
People and organisation

SECOND EDITION

DEREK TORRINGTON

and

JANE WEIGHTMAN

PRENTICE HALL

New York   London   Toronto   Sydney   Tokyo   Singapore

First published 1989
This edition published 1994 by
Prentice Hall International (UK) Limited
Campus 400, Maylands Avenue
Hemel Hempstead
Hertfordshire, HP2 7EZ
A division of
Simon & Schuster International Group

© Prentice Hall International (UK) Limited 1994

Typeset in 10/12pt Times
by Keyset Composition, Colchester, Essex CO1 2LP
Printed and bound in Great Britain by T. J. Press (Padstow) Ltd

---

Library of Congress cataloging-in-publication data

Torrington, Derek, 1931–
    Effective management: people and organisation / Derek Torrington
and Jane Weightman. — 2nd ed.
        p.   cm.
    Includes bibliographical references and index.
    ISBN 0-13-202202-8
    1. Management. I. Weightman, Jane. II. Title.
HD31.T6415 1993
658—dc20   93-38217
                                                            CIP

British Library Cataloguing in Publication Data

A catalogue record for this book is available from
the British Library

ISBN 0-13-202202-8

---

1 2 3 4 5   98 97 96 95 94

Contents

Preface

This book is a second edition of *Effective Management* by Derek Torrington, Jane Weightman and Kirsty Johns, which Prentice Hall published in 1989. The first edition was a successor to *Business of Management* by Derek Torrington and Jane Weightman, which Prentice Hall published in 1985. The previous books were satisfying ventures, but we felt that changes beyond simple updating were needed when the time came to consider a second edition. Those familiar with the previous books will find much that is little altered, some new material, some radically altered and some omitted.

Our objective remains that specified in our 1985 preface:

> Management textbooks do not impress students unless they seem practical, but practical books are of little value without a satisfactory theoretical framework. We have tried to write a practical book that will gain the assent of practising managers as a realistic explanation of what they are doing, but which will also be convincing to students: 'this could be your life'. We have been careful to examine not *management* but *managing*, seeking not detachment from, but identification with, the life that managers lead and the problems they face.

Our colleague Kirsty Johns who joined us for the 1989 version of the book has now left for tropical climes so we are back to writing as two.

Completely new chapters are: 8 Corporate governance and individual responsibility, 10 Management in an international organisation, and 13 Equal opportunities and the management of diversity. Most of the others have undergone varying degrees of development, including some amalgamations, some splittings and much retitling. We have also reorganised the book around the five sections Goals, Responsibilities, Organisations, Uncertainties and People, which gives our mnemonic GROUP representing the main work of management.

We trust the text will prove relevant and readable to those facing the problems and opportunities of managing into the next millennium. We have included a number of practical examples of named individuals. These are actual incidents we have encountered, but we have excluded the name of the organisation, partly because most of the individuals were anxious to remain anonymous and partly to avoid the distraction from our discussion that naming the organisation could introduce.

Our thanks go to Julia Helmsley, Louise Wilson and others at Prentice Hall for their unwavering support and efficient production. We also very much appreciate the comments of those who have used the book, whether as students, tutors or practising managers.

Finally we would like to thank the following authors and publishers for permission to reproduce figures from their books: M. E. Porter and Free Press for Figure 4.2; R. Collard and IPM for Figure 7.1; M. E. Reid, H. Barrington, J. Kenney and IPM for Figure 23.5; J. McCalman, R. A. Paton and Paul Chapman Publishing for Figure 9.2; and The Employment Department for Figure 23.2. Every effort has also been made to contact the authors and publishers for the following figures: A. A. Thompson, A. J. Strickland and R. D. Irwin publishers for Figure 4.1 and R. A. Burgelman, L. R. Sayles and the *Administrative Science Quarterly* for Figure 9.4. If anyone feels that due acknowledgement has not been made then we would be pleased if they contacted us so we could do so in the future.

School of Management   Derek Torrington
UMIST   Jane Weightman
PO Box 88   *October 1993*
Manchester M60 1QD

Part I

Management and the manager

Managers of the late 1990s looking towards the twenty-first century have a job to do which is both considerably different from that of their predecessors and at the same time basically the same. This introductory section of the book sets management and the manager in their contemporary context, as well as tracing the development of management ideas from antiquity to the present. The reader sees the unchanging nature of the management role as well as the changes it has undergone. There is also an analysis of how management work is constituted, how management functions and managers' jobs differ, and what they all have in common.

Chapter 1

Introduction to management

The human race survives and operates through organisation and organisation has to be managed, controlled and developed. Organisation is needed to provide us with our motor cars and cultural amenities; our health care and education; our consumer goods and information services. For all these things we have to work together – to organise and to be organised.

Organisational life is the setting in which most of us spend our working hours and at least part of our leisure. A day at the office may well be followed by an evening with the amateur dramatic society or a weekend with the hockey team.

This book concentrates on the role of manager in contemporary organisation. It is about management as a job to be done by people with a wide range of specialist responsibilities, not just about those who are ultimately in charge, but mainly about those who cope with bits of the organisation rather than with the grand design. We try to get inside the mind of the individual manager and answer questions like: How do I understand what is going on around me? Why do people behave this way? Why is my undertaking organised differently from the one in which my neighbour works? How do I cope with this situation? Do I understand the structure properly? Can I make a better contribution? Am I secure? How do I resolve this problem? How do I get things done? How do I meet my responsibilities?

In recent years there has been some reaction against very large-scale, impersonal and bureaucratic organisations, but working together with others rather than working alone continues to be our conventional idea of 'a job'. The extraordinary achievements of people doing things on their own, like Francis Chichester or Terry Waite, are famed because of the courage and skill of individuals triumphing over formidable obstacles, but when Neil Armstrong walked on the surface of the Moon it was the triumph of thousands who had contributed to the cooperative venture of the NASA space programme. Marie Lloyd or Harry Lauder were solo performers of

3

great popularity, but the contemporary rock star travels with an entourage of dozens or hundreds of people, all of whom are needed to put together the eventual performance. Individuals will continue to make great contributions to society on their own, but the major achievements that are often needed come from managed organisations; not only factories, offices and commercial undertakings, but hospitals and research centres, government departments and charitable bodies, schools and colleges.

Management is not just a job done by people called 'managers'; it is an aspect of the job done by all those who have to cope with the problems and opportunities of organisation.

There are many challenges to mankind that require a management contribution for their resolution. We have to learn to manage problems such as atmospheric pollution and the shortage of energy; technological innovation and the obsolescence of traditional skills; poverty in the Third World and unemployment in the West. Few of these problems have a simple solution requiring no more than the necessary political will, and few of them depend on the intuition or insight of an individual. Managed activity is needed both to produce the solutions and to implement them.

Trewatha and Newport (1982, p. 21) quote the late President J. F. Kennedy, writing in 1963:

> Much of the free world's success in using its human resources fully and with dignity can be laid to enlightened and progressive management . . . It is to managers who grow with the needs and resources of their time that we must continue to look for the new ideas and their implementation to meet the challenges of the future.

The background to contemporary management

Aspects of the setting of contemporary management are set out now as a preliminary to a historical review.

Managerial confusion

Many of the people with management jobs, or jobs with a management component, are uncertain of what they are doing. For some this stems from disappointment on finding out how little managers can achieve. Believing that managers make decisions, solve problems and shape the future, they find in practice that their scope is limited and that only a portion of their time is spent in these exciting activities: mostly it is keeping things going, picking up the pieces after a calamity, trying to change things that have been the same for as long as anyone can remember, and coping with muddle. Other people are frustrated by problems of structure or policy within their organisation that they feel helpless to remedy. We have, however, found the most common reason to be uncertainty about simple things, like the nature of managerial work, the basic methods of working that are available, and the difference between different types of managerial role. In reading books about organisation, or participating in management courses, managers and aspiring managers frequently find the material fascinating but insufficient, as it deals with what they see that others ought to do rather than what they personally can do.

| REVIEW TOPIC 1.1 |

To what extent are managers in control of the areas of the organisation for which they are responsible, and to what extent are they at the mercy of external factors?

The numbers and changing circumstances of managers

Over 10% of the working population are now in management jobs. This does not include the many more who have a management dimension to their work without their being regarded as managers. Managers are therefore now one of the most numerous groups in the country.

The management career is changing also. In the expanding organisations that were the norm of industrialised societies until the middle 1970s, there was the assumption that most managers would eventually be promoted to senior posts, and middle management positions were used as training posts for senior management. This was never really true, but it was believed widely enough for it to become a valid operating assumption. Increasingly middle management is a whole career for many people, although it is more likely to be pursued across several different organisations, rather than being concentrated in one. Also middle managers seldom describe themselves that way: middle managers are now managers with less emphasis on the level and greater emphasis on the role.

Another twist to this situation is the age at which people are put in management posts. No longer do young people graduating from university, for instance, aim to be in a management position by the time they are thirty; they expect it within months. Any visit to a supermarket will confirm the number of people holding significant management responsibility in their early twenties, so the time spent 'in the middle' may well be increasing for many people.

Throughout the 1990s we have seen a further development in the compression of hierarchies. Management levels are no longer as clear-cut as they used to be; many large organisations have taken out one or two tiers in the hierarchy in the process of becoming leaner and fitter, while others have flattened their hierarchies in order to put more emphasis on performance and less on status. Associated with all of this has been an increasing insecurity in management posts, as few remain in the same organisation for all their working lives and managers have needed to broaden their skills so that they are better equipped to change jobs between companies as well as within them. We have acquired the strange euphemism of 'outplacement' to describe trying to help people find other employment rather than simply dismissing them.

Organisational size

Management and management ideas both developed up until the 1970s against a background of increasing organisational size and an expanding number of jobs classified as managerial, bringing greater problems of coordination and communication and an emphasis on the administration of stable environments rather than dealing with the risks and uncertainty which are the reality of the modern organisation. Middle managers have been identified as the administrators of the stable state and with a vested interest in resisting change. White (1981) conducted a study in a south coast electrical company and explained middle managers' resistance to innovation by the fact that they were structurally dissociated from the satisfactions of ownership, technically dissociated from the process of production and socially dissociated from the workforce. Over ten years later middle managers are still often held to be the scapegoats for organisations failing to innovate, as new initiatives such as TQM or performance management are seen by them as threats to their increasingly insecure situations.

The move to ever-increasing size has halted and reversed, especially in the number of people employed. Most large organisations have reduced the number of employees and many have decentralised their management operations so that only a small number of matters are reserved for resolution at the centre while operating units are managed with increased autonomy. A further aspect of this trend is that managers are finding their sphere of operations to be more compact. Some forecasters also think that the number of small, independent companies will increase. At the same time there is the growth of the employment complex, like the airport, shopping centre, construction site or science park, where a large number of independent organisations share a common location and facilities and some aspects of coordination.

The flight from specialisation

As organisational size increased, managerial specialisation increased as well, much encouraged by two sets of interest groups: professional bodies and academic institutions. Professional bodies exist to serve the interests of those who share a specialised bit of the management action, such as purchasing or personnel. Once created, the professional body then has to strengthen and expand that specialised interest in order to exist itself.

Higher education adopted management with enthusiasm during the 1960s and 1970s in order to meet the demand from large numbers of students seeking entry to the apparent joys of managerial life and a company car. The essence of academic study is specialisation within academic disciplines, so both universities and the professional bodies have an interest in the specialist manager. Between them they provide the most common entry ticket: qualification, so that people coming in to management have a developed specialisation.

One of the effects of the economic recession in the 1990s has been a move away from specialisation towards flexibility. The self-justifying specialised function that Parkinson (1957) caricatured so vividly is losing ground so that individual managers are rediscovering a need to operate in all areas of the business, which was regarded as the prime attribute of those who first experienced business school training. This move has been stimulated by the introduction of National Vocational Qualifications (NVQs), which set out to provide a vocational alternative to the academic route towards qualification (Fletcher, 1991). NVQs also reduce artificial barriers to qualification, such as the need to join a professional body as a prerequisite to qualification. In that way they modify the significance of both universities and professional bodies.

| REVIEW TOPIC 1.2 |

Think of one or two methods of managing that are *only* academic and one or two that are *only* practical. What are their shortcomings?

Management as part of human history

Having looked briefly at the prevailing situation we take a glance back towards antiquity, as management is no more than one facet of the long-running saga of human organisation. Our understanding of contemporary management phenomena is enlightened and placed in perspective by looking for some of the ways in which the process evolved.

The Egyptians

The modern nation state evolved 4,500 years ago and was brought into being by the building of the great pyramids at Giza, near Heliopolis in Egypt. Mendelssohn (1974) has argued that the great pyramids were built as a method of creating an integrated human community the size of a state. Previously man had lived in communities no larger than a tribe or village, but the increasing size of the Egyptian population required a larger-scale pattern of organisation in order to make optimum use of the resources of the Nile, the sole source of water to irrigate the land on which the food was grown. Not only was the water seasonal, with inundation followed by drought, but the level varied from year to year.

For the people to be fed there had to be co-operation, not just between families and within the local village, but between villages that were widely dispersed. That sort of cooperation depends on social organisation to bring about commitment, obedience and sacrifice for the sake of benefit.

For three months each year 100,000 to 120,000 men were gathered together on the Giza plateau to cooperate on this immense task. These men left their families and their homes for three reasons. First, the pyramids were great projects on which to be engaged, providing an experience quite different from the limited routine of village agriculture. Secondly, the resurrection of the pharaoh, after a suitable burial, was essential to the afterlife of the common man. You ensured your own afterlife by contributing to the appropriate interment of your pharaoh. Thirdly, the surrounding system of social organisation provided the pharaoh with centralised stocks of grain for distribution during the lean years.

This project achieved a number of outcomes:

A civil service infrastructure.   If 100,000 men were to work on the arduous physical labour of cutting and manhandling blocks of stone weighing fifteen tons each, they had to be not only organised, but fed and housed. This required a large number of administrators and a bureaucratic system.

A sense of nationhood.   The workers developed a sense of commitment to, and membership of, the nation as well as their family and village, because of the common task on which they were engaged. Patriotism was born.

Dependence on the centre.   The pharaoh had the grain, so the common people were economically dependent on him for survival, and the central administration acquired a steadily increasing hold over the population as a whole.

Hierarchy.   The organisation and coordination of such a large labour force produced a hierarchy of authority as the logical means of integrating dispersed effort.

The pyramid project provided the pattern for the nation state, which was not only successful in Egypt, but was taken as the pattern for succeeding nations and other large-scale organisations like armies and the Roman Catholic Church. In turn it became the pattern of schools, hospitals, local government and business.

The principle was simple and logical, and it worked because the task facing the organisation was relatively simple once the original design and technological work had been done. After that the project required small expertise and huge labour.

The main features of the pyramid organisation are to be found in all large-scale contemporary enterprises. The hierarchy and the 'civil service infrastructure' of central administration binds the dependent employee to the corporation. Wages, salaries and fringe benefits have replaced the stock of corn, and the employing organisation may well be one in which the employee takes great pride, but the company pension scheme for support in the afterlife of retirement is a poor substitute for the eternity with Osiris that the pharaoh could offer. Furthermore the modern-day corporation will seldom have a single undertaking for its employees of the simplicity of pyramid building. So the pattern of human organisation that has been with us since antiquity is no longer sufficient.

The Sumerians

The earliest civilisation known in the fertile crescent of the Middle East was that of the Sumerians, slightly before the early Egyptians. Their main contribution was to invent writing, because their priests kept business and legal records on clay tablets.

Woolley (1963) excavated extensively in the area of Ur of the Chaldees and demonstrated how priests in Sumer achieved great power. The ordinary Sumerians did not anticipate the blissful afterlife that was the expectation of the Egyptian pyramid-builders; they expected it to be at best a dismal reflection of their time on Earth and their apprehension led them to offer constant propitiation to the gods. The priests were the only ones able to carry out the ritual, which involved sacrifices with the quality of the propitiation being related to the volume of sacrifice that had been made. It was also the priests who kept the records of what sacrifices had been offered and by whom.

Records were the basis of control and became the avenue to an elite position of power. As organisations have developed and evolved, the need for centralised information has remained and carried with it the power to control. The main contemporary examples are the accountancy profession and the computer, which are used to control complex organisations, and which are shrouded in mysteries which their practitioners use to maintain their exclusive access to the data banks.

The Florentine

A novel and original contribution came in the writings of a disgraced Florentine civil servant of the late fifteenth century. Niccolo Machiavelli served as secretary to the Florentine Republic from 1498 until 1512, when he was dismissed and imprisoned on the charge of conspiring to overthrow the Medici family, who had returned to power. When he was released he started writing, but his classic *Il Principe* was not published until 1532, five years after his death. In this book Machiavelli makes a clear distinction between ethics and politics, which brought him long-running notoriety, although many statesmen have followed the spirit of this concept by not allowing objection on ethical grounds to interfere with political and diplomatic goals. It is an easier notion for managers to accept, as they can argue that social responsibility is drawn from them by legislation, government policy, employee resistance, union power or consumer choice, so that their task is to get on with running the business as effectively as possible within those constraints.

The main interest in Machiavelli's ideas lies in his analysis of how the prince (or leader, or manager) meets obligations. These have been resurrected for the management audience by Jay (1967), but the original in modern translation (Machiavelli, 1981) is so lucid and so constantly relevant that it is eminently accessible, as well as short. The main points are:

Cohesive organisation.   The prince should maintain the cohesiveness of his organisation by binding to him his friends and those on whom he will depend. This will involve giving them rewards for their contribution and making sure that they know what the prince expects and what they can expect from him.

Mass consent.   However cohesive the power structure of the organisation, the prince has to maintain the consent of the governed, as this is the source of his authority. Not only does it give him authority over the governed, it also gives him authority over his 'courtiers'.

Leadership.   Cohesive organisation and mass consent can only be achieved if the prince is a leader and example-setter for his people, being wise and tempering necessary justice with mercy.

Toughness.   There will be attempts to unseat the prince, so he must have the toughness to resist any such attempts and be ruthless with the instigators.

| REVIEW TOPIC 1.3 |

Think of contemporary examples of cohesive organisation, mass consent, leadership and toughness, as defined by Machiavelli.

This cool appraisal of what is involved has given our language the word Machiavellian, to mean cunning, amoral and opportunist.

The Industrial Revolution

Slowly the patterns of human organisation began to evolve and the role of the leader was clarified, but then came the watershed of the Industrial Revolution which was to transform first Britain and then the rest of Europe and the United States into industrialised nations. Hitherto the practice of management had been confined to church, state and army; the job of prelate, prince or officer. Now the great institutions of commerce and industry were born, and the traditional leaders of society had no place in them – wanted no place in them – so we acquired a new occupation and a new class, the *bourgeoisie*:

> The bourgeoisie has created more massive and more colossal productive forces than have all preceding generations together. Subjection of nature's forces to man, machinery, application of chemistry to industry and agriculture, steam navigation, railways, electric telegraphs, clearing of whole continents for cultivation, canalization of rivers, whole populations conjured out of the ground – what earlier century had even a presentiment that such productive forces slumbered in the lap of social labour? (Marx, 1848, p. 147)

The wealth of technological innovation at this time brought great economies of scale, and the invention of power-driven machinery transformed the production process. The capital cost of the new equipment was beyond the individual worker, who was therefore obliged to move out of the home and into the factory, where the machines could be economically located under one roof and efficiency could be enhanced by skilled coordination of employees' work.

Marglin (1971), using extensive examples from the weaving industry, argues that it was the discipline and supervision of the labour force in the factory that was most important in reducing costs as there was greater labour input and less embezzlement and patents were easier to monitor. Also by increasing the division of labour the entrepreneur had an essential role as integrator, controlling the process and quantity of output, as workers were now selling their labour rather than selling a product.

In 1800 James Watt and Matthew Boulton built a new factory to make steam engines and introduced practices that were to form the basis of production organisation for more than 150 years:

Flow of work. Having estimated the demand for their engines, Watt and Boulton laid out their factory for a smooth flow of work between the various operations and equipped it with machines that were timed so that the expected output would match as closely as possible the anticipated demand. At the same time the jobs of individual employees were broken down and analysed to estimate their contribution – the beginning of time and motion study.

Wages. Wage payment arrangements were developed to be consistent with the requirements of each job. As many jobs as possible were paid on a piece rate basis so that income was linked to output, and weekly rates were paid for those jobs where such measurement was not feasible.

Records. Detailed records were developed for cost accounting, so that there was control of direct and indirect costs, enabling the managers to identify areas of inefficiency and high productivity. With this information the managers were able to control the operation by trying to raise the efficiency of those areas where it was defective and adjusting the payment system.

The flow of work had been one of the organisational problems of the early Egyptians, the keeping of records for control had been developed by the Sumerian priests, but the elaboration of wages as an impersonal means of motivating employees rather than the leadership ideas of, for instance, Machiavelli, was a new departure and a new breeding ground for the development of middle management expertise.

The philanthropists

At the close of the nineteenth century developments in management were much influenced by the non-conformist conscience. Seebohm Rowntree was a renowned sociologist and was also chairman of the family confectionery company for sixteen years. Together with several other wealthy and influential entrepreneurs, he began innovations in management practice that were in reaction to the brutal conditions of most factories. Welfare officers were appointed, canteens and social clubs were introduced and a range of employee benefits provided. Lord Leverhulme built Port Sunlight for his workers in Ellesmere Port and introduced a wide range of welfare measures.

These men set a pattern of benevolence combined with prosperity, but there are two aspects of this era that are especially relevant today. First, they concentrated on the context in which people worked rather than on the work itself. Secondly the innovations were those of paternalists, who knew best. When introducing a profit-sharing scheme that few businesses could match eighty years later, Lord Leverhulme wrote in 1913:

> Seven pounds is a lot of money, and it will not do you much good if you send it down your throats in the form of bottles of whisky, fat geese for Christmas and sweets for the children. If you leave the money with me, I will use it to provide those things that make life pleasant, houses, schools and hospitals. Anyway I am not disposed to allow profit-sharing in any other circumstances.

| REVIEW TOPIC 1.4 |

Why have we said that these two aspects (concentrating on the context and being paternalist) are especially relevant today?

Twentieth-century developments

Through the first three-quarters of the twentieth century there were a number of new ideas or schools of thought that can be summarised as follows.

Scientific management

This was the formula of F. W. Taylor, who tried to find the 'one best way' of working. Some of his key innovations – selection, training and job analysis – still form the basis of modern personnel management, even though he is always associated with the emphasis on productivity that led to mass production and Fordism.

Taylor is a figure of overwhelming importance in the development of management. He was an American working at the turn of the nineteenth century, as were the other pioneers associated with scientific management: Henry Ford, Henry Gantt, and Frank and Lillian Gilbreth. At that particular time the United States was entering upon that extraordinary period of economic growth and political self-confidence that was to make it the world's leading industrial power by the beginning of the twentieth century. The Wright brothers made the first powered flight, industrial expansion moved at unprecedented speed following the development of popular capitalism and, on 7th October 1913, Henry Ford introduced the first moving assembly line, reducing the number of man-hours required to produce a Model T chassis from fourteen to two.

Taylor was the theoretician who created management as a job to do and helped develop a culture in the United States that gave management a degree of respectability, separate identity and status in that country that has yet to be matched in European countries. It was also the beginning of an era in industrial supremacy for the Americans that continued until the Japanese challenge of the 1970s.

Administrative management

The development of a theory of administrative management came initially from the Frenchman, Henri Fayol, who defined the five functions of management as planning, coordinating, organising, commanding and controlling. Whereas Taylor's work was a theory of supervision, Fayol produced a conceptual framework for management as a whole. Working in the same mode of thinking were Mary Parker Follet and Lyndall Urwick.

| REVIEW TOPIC 1.5 |

Lyndall Urwick wrote in 1974: 'No executive should attempt to supervise directly the work of five, or at the most six, direct subordinates whose work interlocks.' What are the weaknesses of that point of view?

Although no disciple of Fayol, the German sociologist Weber influenced this school of thought by his analysis of bureaucracy. He argued that the market structure of Western societies required business organisations to be highly structured, or bureaucratic, with the following qualities:

Role definition.   The duties and responsibilities of organisation members are clearly defined.

Hierarchy/authority.   There is a clear chain of relationships with all members knowing precisely to whom they are responsible and who is responsible to them.

Rules and procedures.   The organisation operates according to an elaborate system of rules determining the way in which each member should perform. Records should provide precedents to be followed so as to ensure consistency.

Qualification for office.   People are appointed to positions on the basis of merit that is formally attested and subject to systematic selection and training.

Impartiality.   Members of the organisation discharge their duties without heat or partiality, motivated by the prospect of moving up the hierarchy, as well as by a sense of duty.

This has proved to be a very accurate account of how many organisations have functioned, especially the large and complex, but there is a tendency for rules to become an end in themselves and for personal initiative to be discouraged.

The Human Relations movement

A number of researchers set out to redress what they saw as an imbalance in the work of Taylor and Fayol, by taking greater account of the mind as well as the body of the employee. The most famous member of what came to be known as the human relations school of management thought was Elton Mayo, who conducted experiments to demonstrate the limitations of the precision of F. W. Taylor. Workers were no longer the extension of the machine responsive only to the electric current of financial incentives; instead they were seen as individuals and members of a social group, with attitudes and behaviours that were the key to effectiveness.

The management theory jungle

Recently there have been fewer attempts to produce a total theory of management. Social scientists in the field have often divided problems into manageable units so they can carry out an academically viable study. The quantitative approach has developed techniques of operations research that have had great success in dealing with problems of production planning, warehousing and materials. The advent of the computer has boosted this field of work in defining objectives and constructing models for the solution of complex problems.

The contingency approach to management was developed as a result of researchers trying to understand why management methods that appeared to work well in one situation failed in another. The logical conclusion was that success depended as much on the situation as on the method, so the task of the manager was to decide not which was the best method, but which method would work best in a particular situation.

The behavioural approach has moved in so many directions that it is difficult to contain it under a single, general heading. The main thrust is obviously in studying how managers get things done through people, but some advocate an understanding of the individual as a means towards more effective management, while others see management as a social system of interdependent groups.

In the United Kingdom the development of industrial relations activity since the 1950s has had two main effects on the work of managers. First, the plurality of legitimate interests in the organisation has been recognised to the extent that management was seen as a process through which managers and others seek to bring those varied interests into balance. This led to the second effect, the extended use of procedures: not simply administrative procedures as ways of obviating decision-making for situations where a formula has already been worked out, but also control procedures, like grievance and discipline, whereby management and employee delimit the scope of each other's activities by specifying the range of freedom of action each has. Since the middle 1980s there has been some reaction against that, partly because of the degree to which unions have been marginalised in most organisations, but also because of the extent to which control procedures have been seen to slow down necessary change and concentrate on internal matters rather than the interaction between the organisation and its environment – especially the customer.

The concept of excellence and the focus on strategy

The most recent developments have concentrated on the idea of excellence and the importance of strategy, the first following a recent study by two American consultants, Peters and Waterman (1982). After studying 43 companies that were 'excellently managed' according to a range of criteria, Peters and Waterman concluded that the success was not due to anything more elaborate than being 'brilliant on the basics' and working hard at fundamental aspects of management. Academics immediately found fault with their analysis for all manner of reasons, but the authors remained undeterred as their book sold over one and a quarter million copies. This does not prove them right, but it does make them convincing, and managers, like everyone else, model their actions on prescriptions which they believe will help them rather than on analyses which do not convince.

Peters and Waterman derived eight attributes of the management style of their 'excellent' companies, as follows:

Bias for action.   A preference for doing something rather than waiting for further analysis.

Keeping close to the customer.

Autonomy and entrepreneurship.   Breaking a corporation into small units, each thinking independently and competitively.

Productivity through people.   Enabling all employees to appreciate the importance of their personal participation and enabling them to share success.

Hands on, value driven.   Keeping everyone in touch with the main task of the business.

Sticking to the knitting.   Remaining in a line of business that the people are good at.

Simple form, lean staff.   Uncluttered organisation charts, with the minimum number of levels in the hierarchy and few people at the upper levels.

Simultaneous loose–tight properties.   A climate in which there is dedication to the central values of the company combined with tolerance for all employees who accept the values.

The attractiveness of these ideas has been their simplicity and their realism, although the subsequent performance of some of the studied companies has not necessarily confirmed the unfailing accuracy of the diagnosis.

| REVIEW TOPIC 1.6 |

In what way is your organisation 'brilliant at the basics'?

Partly in reaction to the iconoclasm of the excellence movement, there has been an increasing emphasis on strategy:

> . . . concerned with the future direction of the business as a whole . . . long term in nature and bound to have far-reaching implications on employment, the financing of the business and the types of product manufactured.
>
> (Johnson and Scholes, 1989, p. 3)

Rose (1975) has argued that the various schools of thought on management have continued to develop in an evolutionary manner. This has the attraction of integrating everything currently known, implying that the latest product is the best. However, there seem to be fundamental differences in the basic assumptions of some schools that have not yet been reconciled or integrated. This has been well described by Burrell and Morgan (1979) who argue that some contrasting assumptions could never be reconciled.

All these issues are explored more fully in the following pages, especially in the next two chapters. We conclude this introductory chapter by offering a definition of what we mean by management.

A working definition

Probably the best-known definition of management is that of Mary Parker Follet, who described it as 'The art of getting things done through people'. This is neat but insufficient, as the emphasis is solely on getting other people to do things, without giving due weight to other tactics and resources. It also implies that the 'other people' are subordinates, although they are frequently peers, outsiders or superiors in a hierarchical sense. The sales manager aiming to increase sales may achieve that by getting the salespeople to work harder or more effectively, but it may also be achieved by altering the advertising policy. We suggest five headings for the dimensions of management as a job to be done:

1. Managers have conflicting **goals**. They have to meet production targets at the same time as keeping costs down. They achieve profit margins but also satisfy the needs of subordinates. They seek to use economic methods of production but also need to meet environmental criteria. They are always seeking for a balance to ensure that one goal is not attained at the expense of another.
2. Managers are held **responsible** for results, not only their own results, but also the results of others. The branch bank manager is held responsible for everything that happens on branch premises. If there are mistakes, it is the manager who takes the blame from superiors in the bank, from staff in the branch and from the customers, all of whom have a touching faith in the manager's ability to satisfy their various expectations.
3. Managers work in and around **organisations**, with all the resources, opportunities and frustrations that such settings provide. The complexity of the organisation provides a wide range of skills and facilities that can be deployed, but it also requires cooperation, synchronisation and communication. Enabling the complex organisation to perform is a crucial part of the manager's job that makes it distinctive from some other leadership functions like, for instance, captaining a cricket team.
4. The stable state for managers is **uncertainty**. There will be planning and procedures to reduce the level of uncertainty, but the unexpected problem, the unprecedented situation, the need to change the familiar, is the realm of the manager. Generally the members of an organisation with clearly defined jobs and roles are able to cope with predictable situations as a result of their training, information and authorisation, but have to call on managerial assistance to deal with the unfamiliar, either because

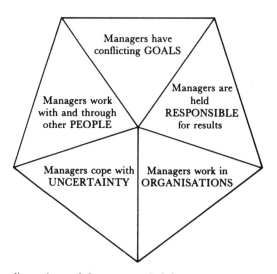

Figure 1.1 Five dimensions of the manager's job.

the manager has more technical understanding and experience or because the manager has an element of hierarchical authority to take certain decisions which have not been delegated to others. Managers are at the heart of every change.

5. Managers work with and through other **people**. Here we are not quite back to Mary Parker Follet, because the people are not only subordinates but also organisational peers, customers, clients, suppliers and many other outsiders who make up the network of contacts that the manager uses to make the job effective. In the 1990s it is a very varied, changing constituency that the manager has to manage.

The initial letters of the key words above produce the mnemonic GROUP, and increasingly managers find all those five aspects of management are being mediated through groups or teams (see Figure 1.1). There is the group decision-making of boards of directors and senior management teams, planning conferences in advertising and the media, autonomous working groups and total quality management teams in factories, team briefing, selection panels, suggestions, committee meetings, staff meetings, job evaluation panels and all the other ways in which managing becomes a corporate activity rather different from the emphasis on individuals that until recently was the sole focus for management work.

──┤ SUMMARY PROPOSITIONS ├────────────────

1.1 Although managing the work of organisations is a widespread activity, many managers lack understanding of their role and knowledge of simple methods that can be used in managerial work.

1.2 The main dimensions of the manager's job are that they have conflicting goals, are held responsible for results, work in organisations, cope with uncertainty, and work with and through other people.

1.3 Management is just one aspect of human organisation, which can be traced back to the beginning of civilisation.

References

Burrell, G. and Morgan, G., 1979, *Sociological Paradigms and Organisational Analysis*, Heinemann, London.

Fletcher, S., 1991, *NVQs, Standards and Competence*, Kogan Page, London.

Jay, A., 1967, *Management and Machiavelli*, Penguin Books, Harmondsworth, Middlesex.

Johnson, G. and Scholes, K., 1989, *Exploring Corporate Strategy*, Prentice Hall, Hemel Hempstead.

Machiavelli, N., 1981, *The Prince*, Penguin Books, Harmondsworth, Middlesex.

Marglin, S., 1971, *What Do Bosses Do? The Origins and Functions of Hierarchy in Capitalist Production*, Harvard University Department of Economics.

Marx, K., 1848, *The Communist Manifesto*, quoted in Bottomore, T. B. and Rubel, M., 1979, *Karl Marx: Selected Writings on Sociology and Social Philosophy*, Penguin Books, Harmondsworth, Middlesex.

Mendelssohn, K., 1974, *The Riddle of the Pyramids*, Thames & Hudson, London.

Parkinson, C. N., 1957, *Parkinson's Law*, John Murray, London.

Peters, T. J. and Waterman, R. H., 1982, *In Search of Excellence*, Harper & Row, London.

Rose, M., 1975, *Industrial Behaviour: Theoretical Developments Since Taylor*, Allen Lane, London.

Trewatha, R. L. and Newport, M. G., 1982, *Management*, 3rd edn, Business Publications, Plano, Texas.

White, O., 1981, Why won't managers cooperate?, *Industrial Relations Journal*, March/April, pp. 61–72.

Woolley, L., 1963, *Digging up the Past*, Penguin Books, Harmondsworth, Middlesex.

Chapter 2

Management work

In this chapter we examine what managers actually do, and especially what different types of manager have in common. In the next chapter we distinguish between different types of management job.

The work of management has to be assumed from the activities of managers, which are mainly talking, reading, writing, telephoning, using electronic hardware, driving cars, waiting for aircraft, attending meetings and so on. We have to infer the nature of management work from these activities, as well as distinguishing it from the work of people not called managers; and distinguishing it from other work done by managers that is technical, such as selling, budget preparation, design engineering or whatever their specialist area happens to be.

There are five main ways of trying to understand management work. First one can study the behaviour of managers by asking them to fill in detailed *diaries* of how they spend their time or by observing their behaviour over a period. Classic examples of this type of study are Carlson (1951), Stewart (1967) and Mintzberg (1971). Secondly, one can read the *autobiographies* of successful managers and leaders who try to pass on what they found worked in their experience, their prescriptions of how others can replicate the success that they have enjoyed. Statesmen and generals are the best known providers of this type of material, but examples of successful managers' writing are Sloan (1967), Forte (1986) and Harvey-Jones (1988). A slightly different version of this is where a person with a successful business career attempts an explicitly management book. Examples are Barnard (1938), Brown (1971), Townsend (1970) and Harvey-Jones (1992). A third method is to *interview* managers about what they do. Examples of this approach are Marshall and Stewart (1981), Kotter (1982), Scase and Goffee (1989) and Torrington and Weightman (1982, 1987).

Fourthly one can look at *management textbooks*. These make implicit assumptions about the nature of management work by choosing to include some subjects but not others, partly because some aspects of management are more suitable for written treatment than others. Most textbooks employ the conventional categories of management work suggested by Fayol: planning, organising, controlling, commanding and coordinating. The fifth method is a detailed, *empirical study* of a particular area of management, which can provide a great deal of information about specific aspects such as motivation or leadership.

None of these is sufficient alone. Diaries are very revealing, but many managers are reluctant to compile them and to reveal themselves in what they regard as an unfavourable light. The problem of objectivity is also present with autobiographies, together with the fact that the very successful usually have the benefit of some exceptional personal qualities or good luck that were the main determinants of their success, and enabled them to operate in an idiosyncratic way that others would find hard to emulate. Interviewing managers introduces the detachment of the interviewer to achieve a more objective account than simple self-reporting, but the manager being interviewed is the sole source of information. Textbooks have the drawback that their purpose is to provide appropriate material for study, so there will always be an emphasis on that which is easiest to handle in written form. This is one reason why textbooks have always had such a large proportion devoted to decision-making. Empirical study is always partial and tends to isolate the subject being examined from the context in which it was undertaken.

The most fruitful way of trying to understand management work is to blend insights from all these sources.

What image of the organisation does a manager have?

Managers will do different work even in similar situations because they will interpret their role differently depending on their underlying beliefs about what the organisation is for and what model of management they hold dear. Gareth Morgan (1986) in his excellent book *Images of Organisation* describes various theories of organisational analysis: see Figure 2.1. He also makes the point that effective managers need different strategies to 'read' the organisation and the various situations which occur. This is partly because some models are more powerful at handling some situations whereas other models are better for interpreting other issues. It is also very useful for a manager to have a variety of models available when the first thoughts have not worked.

Different theories of organisational analysis provide these different strategies, so it is useful for managers to have a variety of models to hand so they can try something else when the first idea has not worked. Because organisations are complex, and consequently so is managing them, they can be understood in different ways. For example, Eddie is in charge of a team whose function is to produce the heavy parts to go into a gas turbine for

1   Organisations as machines
    With orderly relationships
        clearly defined parts
        determined order
2   Organisations as organisms
    With adapting to the environment
        life cycles
        dealing with survival
3   Organisations as cultures
    With patterns of belief
        daily rituals
        own language
4   Organisations as political systems
    With authority
        power
        right to manage or individual rights
5   Organisations as brains
    With think tanks
        strategy formulation
        corporate planning teams
6   Organisations as psychic prisons
    With trap of one way of thinking
7   Organisations as instruments of domination
    With some having influence over others
        work hazards

Figure 2.1   Some ways of looking at organisations (based on Morgan, 1986).

electrical generation. He feels the engineers are not as productive as they should be. If he takes a machine model, see Figure 2.1, he is likely to look for answers by specifying the work more carefully. If he looks for answers through culture he will spend time encouraging a more integrated workforce. If he takes a political view he might be concerned with his right to manage. If he takes the psychic prison model he might want to generate quite different modes of working. Which model Eddie takes first will depend on his nature and which he considers is most cost-effective in the circumstances. There is not just one simple solution to organisation and management – if one believes that one is very susceptible to the latest fads and fashions. So what do managers actually do?

How managers spend their time

In 1981 Roger Mansfield and his colleagues reported on a detailed survey carried out in the previous year among 1,058 British managers, widely spread geographically and between different types of organisation. One question to the respondents was the amount of time spent on work each

Table 2.1 Weekly hours spent working by British managers in 1980

Hours per week	Percentage of sample
less than 30	0.7
31–40	14.1
41–50	44.3
51–60	27.7
61–70	10.5
more than 70	2.7

(Mansfield *et al.*, 1981)

week. Remembering the problem of self-reported information that has already been mentioned, the figures suggest that managers work about the same amount of overtime as manual workers: see Table 2.1.

Other evidence suggests that managers at middle and lower levels spend less time on work (Horne and Lupton, 1965) and chief executives seldom stop thinking of their jobs (Carlson, 1951). This can, however, give no more than a very general picture as these replies are affected by some uncertainty in the minds of the respondents regarding what does and does not constitute management work. Is reading the *Financial Times* work or pleasure? Undoubtedly the activities of most managers are characterised by brevity, variety and fragmentation. For example, Mintzberg (1973) found that the chief executives he studied made contact, on average, with 52 people each day. Only 10% of tasks took an hour or more and more than 50% of tasks took less than nine minutes. This differs sharply from the specialisation and extended periods of application to a single task that characterise most non-managerial jobs. Doktor (1990) found that Japanese and Korean chief executives had a much less fragmented pattern than American ones, possibly because hurried contacts are felt to be impolite in these societies; also they tend to have fewer and longer meetings. But it is interesting to speculate what the relative effects on effectiveness might be of having a fragmented or a non-fragmented day.

Managers spend much of their time, between 50% and 80%, in conversation with others (Guest, 1955; Stewart, 1967; Mintzberg, 1973). Stewart found that they spent an average of 41% of their time with subordinates, 12% with superiors and 47% with others. Mintzberg has similar results and suggests a preference among managers for spoken rather than written material and for current information and live action rather than considered reports.

- With how many people do you make contact in each working day?
- What percentage of your daily tasks take more than one hour?
- What percentage of your daily tasks take less than nine minutes?
- How much of your time do you spend with subordinates?
- How much of your time do you spend with superiors?
- How much of your time do you spend with others?
- Are there any of those numbers or percentages you would like to change?
- If so, why?

Mintzberg (1975) uses this sort of evidence to argue that managers are not in fact devoting their time to planning, decision-making and the other types of reflective activity which the textbooks suggest. If, however, we take account of what is being said in all these face-to-face encounters and telephone conversations, often decisions are being taken and plans being laid, although the independent observer may regard the process as lacking system and thoroughness. Similarly the business lunch or game of golf has considerable potential content in terms of information exchanged, discussion and agreement on actions to follow, even though some may consider them a wasteful and self-indulgent method for managers to conduct their affairs by.

These studies tell us that managers spend much of their time in conversation with a variety of people and they are frequently interrupted, but why do managers work in this way?

Different types of management work

There are three distinct strands in the work that managers do: technical, administrative and managerial. The technical work of a manager is that work done not because of being a manager, but almost in spite of that fact: work concerned with the main task of the organisation, section or department, which is probably the work of at least some subordinates as well. It is the head teacher teaching children in the classroom, the chief designer working at a drawing board, the sales manager visiting a customer, the nurse manager discussing infection control, or the garage proprietor tuning the engine on a customer's car.

This technical work involves the manager using the skills and knowledge acquired through qualifications, training and experience. Many of these technical skills could be transferred to all other organisations where they are used, like the examples quoted in the last paragraph, or they may be specific to the particular organisation in which the manager works, such as understanding precisely how Shell's polymer functions in practice, or how Coca-Cola is made. We suggest in Chapter 3 that managers abandon these skills at their peril, as they can then lose touch with the main task of the department or organisation, although the management development process in many British organisations appears to encourage managers to let their technical skills atrophy.

Administrative work is concerned with organisational maintenance, while managerial work is taking initiatives. The one is carrying out official, often regular, duties authorised by others, such as the organisational superior or a committee; the other is conducting and controlling organisational affairs with the freedom to create precedents. Much of management literature is about administrative activities with its emphasis on administering the stable state rather than the unstable, uncertain world faced by many managers.

One aspect of the managerial/administrative distinction is intuitively described by many managers when they talk about the scope that a person has to make mistakes or exercise discretion. The greater the discretion, the greater the managerial content of the job and the more one is setting rather than following precedents. This is reflected in the timespan theory of discretion advanced by Elliott Jaques (1970), who postulated that all jobs have a prescribed content and a discretionary content. The first comprises those elements of work over which the job holder has no authorised choice, while the second is that area of work where the job holder chooses how to do the work. Jaques used this to describe all work, not just managerial work, and devised the concept of the timespan of discretion:

> The maximum period to time during which the use of discretion is authorised and expected, without review of that discretion by a superior.
>
> (Jaques, 1970, p. 21)

It is the greater range of discretion open to managers, and especially the greater length of time that will elapse before the effect of mistakes is known, that is one of the distinctive characteristics of management work.

This administrative/managerial distinction can also be expressed in terms of novelty and comfort. Like many human activities, managerial work is active, extrovert and novelty-seeking, concerned with initiating and taking risks by setting precedents. Administrative work is a quieter activity, introvert and providing the comfort of familiarity and dealing with what is known. It keeps the system going by maintaining things in working order. Scitovsky (1976) discusses how a number of psychologists have offered the opinion that the novelty/comfort balance in human beings is always in a state of change, according to the situation in which they find themselves. The behaviour of those facing bereavement is often characterised by actions that are so prosaic as to seem bizarre, like needing to go to the hairdresser or to go shopping, and deciding to decorate the back bedroom or work on the car. This is not callousness but seeking the comfort of the familiar at a time when the crises are too great to bear.

When managers are faced with too many difficult problems and are uncertain about what to do, they may take great comfort in filling in timesheets, record cards or other routine administrative tasks. The executive briefcase is partly a badge of office ('I am important') but also contains a supply of administrative comforters to go with the indigestion tablets. The first-class compartments of intercity trains are full of managers travelling to meetings and passing the time by 'catching up on their reading' or 'checking through the figures'. On the other hand, when the routine paperwork becomes too oppressive a manager may seek some stimulus to get the adrenalin flowing: they go looking for novelty or excitement. Much of the by-play of organisational politics described in Chapter 18 comes from this need for challenge.

Using STAMP

Over the last fifteen years we have done various studies of managers. The first study, during 1980–1981, was of ten middle managers in various organisations (Torrington and Weightman, 1982). We then, during 1982–1985, looked in more detail at 52 senior and middle managers in sixteen different organisations (Torrington and Weightman, 1987). Thirdly, as part of a large study of school management during 1986–1988, we looked at the work of the senior staff in 24 schools (Torrington and Weightman, 1989). In 1989 we used STAMP as part of a study of the work of 31 senior and middle managers within a Health Authority District.

Throughout this period we have developed our STAMP device using the following definitions:

Social everyday social interchanges of organisational life. Things like talking about the TV programme we saw last night, asking about the football and talking about the weather.

Technical work done because of profession, experience or qualification. This may be doing the work or advising and discussing things technically. It is the head teacher talking to children, the sales manager going to see customers, the engineer discussing how the software can be improved.

Administrative concerned with organisational maintenance, official often regular duties authorised by others, usually clerical work. It includes photocopying, trying to get through on the telephone, filling in holiday rotas.

Managerial setting precedents which usually involves influencing others to some non-obvious action. It is getting things done that would not have been done otherwise. It is usually the small influencing actions such as saying 'Yes, that sounds a good idea', or 'Well . . . if I were you I'd go and see Susie as I'm sure she has done something along these lines', or 'I think if you wait a week or two you'll find that we will have got more interest in the topic'.

1987 STAMP distribution by proportion of time for six managers

	T%	A%	M%	S/P%
Range	0–30	13–55	16–63	2–50
Mean	10	32	41	16

1989 STAMP distribution by proportion of time for 70 school managers

	T%	A%	M%	S/P%
Range	0–67	2–77	4–82	0–27
Mean	34	24	35	5

1990 STAMP distribution by proportion of time for 31 health managers

	T%	A%	M%	S/P%
Range	0–78	7–66	0–86	1–11
Mean	24	32	39	6

Figure 2.2   Observation of managers using STAMP.

Personal   sometimes personal matters have to be dealt with at work. This includes such things as phoning home to sort out child care, making a doctor's appointment, or taking the car to be serviced.

This gives us the mnemonic STAMP. Figure 2.2 gives a summary of our findings on the proportion of time different managers spend on these various types of work. The range of figures shows how widely individual managers differ from each other, whereas the averages inevitably tend towards an even distribution. We argue that many managers are uncertain about the nature of their managerial work, so do more administrative work than is appropriate because it is identifiable and comforting. This means the managerial work does not get done. We also argue that managers need to keep up with technical work and involvement in order to stay in touch with the organisation or section. So what would we recommend as a suitable balance for effectiveness and satisfaction?

We would suggest that managers usually need to reduce the time and effort they spend on administrative activities by delegating them, not doing them at all and reviewing the nature of the administration. The time saved from this should normally be spent on really coming to terms with their managerial work. This will mean being in touch technically with the section, so may involve more technical work. It may also require negotiating with their own boss to permit more managerial work being delegated. The conclusions this has led us to are also discussed below in the section on credibility.

─┤ REVIEW TOPIC 2.2 ├─────────────────────────────

In your job have you got the balance right between technical, administrative and managerial work?

Credibility

All managers are people with authority, stemming from the position they hold with all the formal power that the position confers. Successful managers have something more: they possess skill, knowledge and expertise that others consult willingly. Credibility is the word used in organisations, particularly amongst professionals, to describe this prerequisite ability that someone needs in order to get things done. In the increasingly informal workings of organisations, people have to earn and maintain credibility for themselves. The job title and organisational position will help, but will not be sufficient.

People with credibility are worthy of belief, trustworthy, convincing and respected. They are listened to and can get things done willingly, whereas their colleagues who lack credibility meet resistance and have to rely more heavily on the glacial speed of formal mechanisms. The difficulty for managers is their need to maintain credibility with several constituencies, as their work impacts all parts of the organisation.

We have found the following are important for maintaining credibility:

1. *Keeping in touch with the main task.*   It is only by keeping in touch with the main task of the organisation as a whole and the section in which the manager is located that new ideas can be based in reality. Managers who lose touch with their operational expertise risk losing credibility with their colleagues.
2. *Legitimacy.*   Those on the receiving end of managers exercising authority will only respond readily when they perceive the authority as being legitimate. The formal organisation charts, job titles and pay structures provide such legitimacy, but Western society and its organisations have developed a taste for informal means to supplement these. Keeping in touch with the main task and maintaining technical competence is the main feature, but managerial authority is also legitimised by such personal characteristics as willingness to do things, working hard and demonstrating enthusiasm.
3. *A network of contacts.*   Having a wide network of contacts both inside and outside the organisation enables a manager to consult about new projects effectively and to hear and understand when things begin to start going wrong rather than having to wait until they have gone wrong. Managers who rely on formal relationships will only be told what they expect to hear and when they have to be told.
4. *A clear role.*   It is important to ensure that everyone has a real job to do. Particularly when there is a reorganisation at one level, it is vital to ensure that those holding posts on the next tier have real, clear roles and responsibilities.

| REVIEW TOPIC 2.3 |

What do you have to be, or know, or be able to do, to be credible in your role with:

- your boss?
- your colleagues?
- your staff?

The soft dimensions of management

The study of management work in the 1980s and 1990s has been much concerned with the soft dimensions of management. For example, culture, style, people skills, leadership, empowerment, enterprise and flexibility are all part of new thinking which has been influenced by competition from Japan. See, for example, *Thriving on Chaos* (Peters, 1988), *The Age of Unreason* (Handy, 1989), *The Art of Japanese Management* (Pascale and Athos, 1982), *When Giants Learn to Dance* (Kanter, 1989), and the explosion of books on organisational culture which typified the mood of the 1980s. Typically these books emphasise the informality of relations between people in work organisations. For example, in Kanter's *When Giants Learn to Dance* she emphasises working together with memorable phrases such as 'Becoming PALs through Pooling, Allying and Linking across companies'.

We specifically deal with each of these elsewhere in the book – see for example Part V – but this sort of approach has influenced people away from thinking of management work as merely hierarchical control towards more informal methods of influencing events. This is also sometimes expressed in a desire for devolution, decentralising and the flattening of hierarchies. The difficult thing to judge is how much of this thinking is really being practised in organisations rather than being just a change of vocabulary. Another question is to see whether the pendulum starts to swing back towards more tightly controlled, centralised, 'European-wide' organisations, with the economic changes of the 1990s after the prosperity of the 1980s.

The distinction between management and other work

Most other jobs have an immediate inbuilt purpose and logic. The schoolteacher faces the classroom of children waiting to be occupied, the machinist has a pile of cloth waiting to be made into shirts, the chef has customers waiting for food to be cooked, and the postman has a satchel full of letters to deliver. The job is clear in its logic, which is to translate a demand from the system of the organisation into activities or tasks to be undertaken by the job holder.

Managers have some aspects of their jobs that are like this: the in-tray full of papers, the incoming mail to be dealt with, the outgoing letters to sign, the telephone to be answered. These are responses, mainly administrative, to demands from the system of the organisation. An activity of a manager is to read letters that arrive in much the same way as the activity of a postman is to deliver the letters in the first place. How the manager responds to the letter will be one aspect of how management work differs from other work, as it is likely to involve some aspects of problem-solving and decision-making with features of coordination and command. It is still, however, reacting to a situation and responding to the initiatives of others. Managers we have studied usually describe these activities – mail, paperwork, answering the telephone, dealing with enquiries – as time-consuming and unsatisfying. They prefer those activities where they impose their own logic on a task rather than the task having its own logic which is imposed on the manager. They prefer 'making things happen' or being proactive instead of reactive.

Managers enjoy being able to control the details of their working programme, and demonstrating if only to themselves the degree of autonomy they have, by the use of their personal diary. Every Christmas one of the favourite 'executive presents' is the desk diary in hand-tooled leather, which is a status symbol because it declares the flexibility that managers have. Not for them the precisely controlled and timetabled day: they organise their own daily and weekly programme. Although many demands are made on their time, the individual manager usually reserves the right to agree that something can be 'fitted in' to the schedule, on which much time is spent reviewing, reordering and projecting. Most other workers have a daily schedule or just do what they are asked to do as it occurs, but managers have a greater range of discretion, so that they exercise choice not only in what they do and how they do it, but also when they do it.

Another aspect of this range of choice is the degree of responsibility which managers carry. 'That is my decision . . .' is a typical statement by managers asserting and taking pleasure in their power. 'That is my responsibility . . .' is the statement of managers asserting their duty, but also declaring their status by setting themselves apart from the ordinary people who merely hew wood and draw water, leading simple lives unburdened by any sense of duty. The responsibility may be for the results achieved by subordinates, for the decisions reached by the manager or for other aspects of the quality of work, like the satisfaction of colleagues with their performance and contribution. The managers certainly have more scope than others for organising their own work and changing the nature and direction of these activities, either through delegation or through initiating changes vis-à-vis other members of the hierarchy. This contrasts with non-managers, who have virtually no choice, despite the programmes of empowerment, job enrichment and job enlargement that have been popular.

In different ways managers assert and cherish their independence and autonomy, being free from close supervision, having duties that are not repetitive and not too specialised.

The core behaviour of management

Can we now produce a list of job dimensions that can characterise a job as managerial, no matter what title it carries?

Several systems have been developed to grade jobs within organisations. One that is highly regarded is the Hay-MSL system of job evaluation, which is based on an assessment of three elements in a job: knowhow, problem-solving and accountability, each with subdivisions, as can be seen in Figure 2.3.

The purpose of this and similar systems is obviously to determine which jobs are the more valuable to the organisation and therefore which merit a higher level of pay. This approach has the value that it indicates some of the areas of work that are widely accepted in organisational circles as being managerial. The system defines what management is and then makes possible the assessment of individual jobs to determine how they compare with the model.

An attractively simple approach to defining the core behaviour of managers has been provided by Kotter (1982). In a study of general managers in the United States he concluded that they all had two activities in common: setting agendas for action, and setting up networks to implement those agendas.

He used the word *agenda* in the sense of a list of items to be dealt with, so that it becomes a way of putting into practice the whole range of decisions that are made, such as policy, plans, strategies and agreements. Each of those is an occasional, cerebral act. Setting agendas is the constant activity of managers as plans and ideas are put into operation. 'Increase sales turnover

1. Knowhow
   (a) Technical, professional.
   (b) Managerial.
   (c) Human relations.

2. Problem-solving
   (a) Environment in which the thinking takes place;
       from routine to completely unstructured.
   (b) Challenge; from repetitive to creative.

3. Accountability
   (a) Degree of discretion; freedom to act.
   (b) Value of the areas affected by the job.
   (c) The directness of the impact of the job.

Figure 2.3 The Hay-MSL system for assessing the content of management jobs.

by 25% over the next twelve months' is a splendid general statement of policy, but the manager responsible will set up a series of agendas to bring out the desired result. Some hard bargaining with union officials may produce an agreement 'to introduce a new scheme of job evaluation', but that will be no more than a general declaration of intent until a manager puts together an agenda of what to do, what to do first, what to check, whom to deploy, whom to ask, when to aim for as a completion date, and so on. The organisation may have a corporate plan, but the individual managers responsible for achieving the results of the plan will each have a series of agendas, evolving, developing and extending, as the plan becomes a reality.

These variegated frameworks for action are created by a process of thinking out possibilities, constant questioning and aggressively gathering information, with the questioning aided by a shrewd knowledge of the business. Choices are made both analytically and intuitively as careful calculation is combined with skilled guessing to move into action. The agendas are seldom written, although many lists are jotted down on the backs of envelopes, and may be either vague or specific, according to the subject matter.

Agenda-setting is one way in which managers impose their will on the situation around them; the other is by setting up and maintaining *networks* through which the agendas are implemented. These are quite different from the formal structure, although no substitute for it. Networks are a reflection of the need for political activity that is discussed in Chapter 18. The individual manager identifies a large number of people, both inside the organisation and outside, who will help in implementing agendas, as well as being sources of information to go into agendas. The popular picture of the manager constantly making telephone calls is an expression of the network process of 'having a word with' contacts: the people who help to get things done by speeding something up, providing information, jumping a queue, endorsing a proposal in committee, checking data, arranging for the manager to meet someone and – of course – doing jobs. Networks are peopled partly by subordinates, but by a large variety of others, including those who have some respect for the manager, those who are dependent on or under obligation to the manager. Position in the hierarchy is crucial to having a good network, but so is expertise and social skilfulness. Methods used to set up networks include using disarming candour, doing small favours for others, being a 'nice guy', building a team of willing subordinates and generally shaping the relationships among the people in the network.

| REVIEW TOPIC 2.4 |

What agendas and networks are you currently operating? Is there any way in which you could extend and improve any of your networks?

Enterprises often begin life as a partnership between two people, one of whom is better at agendas and another who is better at networks. Henry Royce was a brilliant engineer who could see clearly the 'agenda' of what was needed to create high-quality motor cars, but it was Charles Rolls who was able to set up and sustain the 'network' of business contacts that was to make Rolls-Royce a long-running success story. One activity emphasises analysis, imagination and planning; the other emphasises social skill and political judgement. All managers do both, but the most effective are those with equal skill in both areas.

The current approach to management training and development is to develop lists of competences which managers need to be effective and then train or develop these. The current interest in competences was developed by Boyatzis (1982) and the term includes not only skills but also mind sets and personal attributes. The lists are usually generated by committees of experienced trainers and practitioners debating what should be included. We discuss competences in more detail in Chapter 23.

In Britain the government has spent a lot of money developing National Vocational Qualifications, one of which is a set of management standards, or competences, known as MCI (Management Charter Initiative). Table 2.2 lists the competences included in MCI standards I and II aimed at junior and middle managers. Managers acquire these competences through experience as well as through formal training.

The management job

We have been describing various ways of classifying managerial work as a means of understanding the range and variety of the managerial role. We have carefully avoided a definition of management or of manager because any definition tends to exclude as many jobs as it includes. Perhaps the most realistic approach is that of Rosemary Stewart in starting her research:

> We used the word 'manager' very broadly to include anyone above a certain level, roughly above foreman, whether they were in control of staff or not. There was no need to be more precise because we were interested in studying the jobs that our companies called managerial, and which formed part of the management hierarchy for selection, training and promotion.
>
> (Stewart, 1976, p. 2)

Her investigation included jobs with titles like mill accountant, assistant treasurer, chief draughtsman, nutritionist, deputy chief architect, veterinary officer, and buyer. This is not because some jobs were included incorrectly, but because the essence of management appears in so many different jobs. This is still the case over twenty years later.

Some jobs have all the elements of management that have been considered in this chapter, yet the job holders are never described by that

Table 2.2   MCI standards, 1991

Manage Operations

Maintain Operations
1.1 for quality
1.2 for productive
work

Contribute to Change
2.1 Evaluation
2.2 Implementation

Manage Finance

Expenditure and
Resources
3.1 Recommendations
3.2 Monitor and
control

Manage People

Recruitment
4.1 Define
requirements
4.2 Selection

Develop People
5.1 Teams
5.2 Individuals
5.3 Oneself

Plan Work
6.1 Set objectives
6.2 Plan work methods
6.3 Allocate work
6.4 Provide feedback

Enhance Relationships
7.1 with subordinates
7.2 with manager
7.3 with colleagues
7.4 Minimise conflict
7.5 Discipline/grievance
7.6 Counsel staff

Manage Information

Evaluate Information
8.1 to aid decisions
8.2 Record and store it

Exchange Information
9.1 Lead meetings
9.2 Contribute
9.3 Advise and inform

Knowledge and Understanding

*(a) Purpose and
Context*
*(b) Principles and
Methods*
(c) Legislation
(d) Defining
competences
(e) Recruitment
(f) Motivation and
delegation
(g) Working with
others
(h) Staff development
(i) Teams

(j) Operations
(k) Change and
innovation
(l) Marketing (Std II)
(m) Finance
(n) Accessing and
storing information
(o) Evaluating
information
(p) Organising and
presenting
information

Figure 2.4 Managerial work and the core of management behaviour.

term and would probably not welcome its use about what they do. Only recently have head teachers begun to describe themselves, on occasions, as managers and the use of management ideas is quite widespread in nursing, but town clerks, solicitors, estate agents, orchestral conductors, film directors and choreographers are just a few of the job titles that carry a large management element; so there are some managers who are not called managers.

We have seen so far that managers, whether with that title or not, have a subtle and varied job, although the core behaviours of making agendas and operating networks are so simple that the detractor is inclined to say that the manager's job has been inflated out of all proportion and that any subtlety and complexity is around the job rather than in what managers actually do (see Figure 2.4).

In the remainder of this work we set out the details of what makes the management job so much more demanding and rewarding than it first appears, as those with the flair, common sense and experience to be in management positions combine the elements we have described to achieve equilibrium by getting all the components into a degree of balance. This is summarised in Figure 2.5.

In understanding management work, however, we must always re-member:

> Management is a much less tidy, less organised, and less easily defined activity than that traditionally presented by management writers or in job descriptions.
>
> (Stewart, 1976, p. 125)

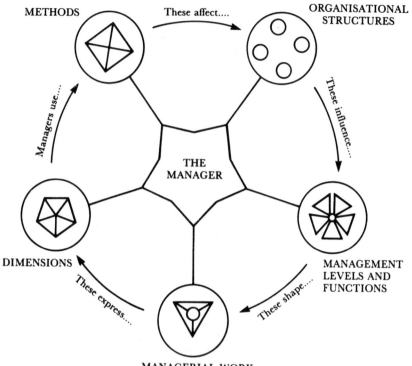

Figure 2.5 The dynamics of management.

SUMMARY PROPOSITIONS

2.1 Management work differs from most other types of work in being more varied and staccato, involving extensive interaction with others and responsibility for initiating change.

2.2 The work managers do has three distinctive strands: technical (which is non-management), administrative (which is maintaining the system) and managerial (which is being able to change the system).

2.3 Compared with most other jobs, managers exercise choice in what they do, how they do it and when they do it.

2.4 The core behaviour of management is setting agendas for action and setting up networks to implement the agendas.

2.5 Some jobs have all the hallmarks of being managerial, but are never described in that way.

PUTTING IT INTO PRACTICE

Administrative drill to determine management content of one's own job

This is a simple method to analyse the management elements of one's job and the frequency with which they occur. This can help with understanding the demands of the post and modifying those aspects that can be improved.

Account for time spent.

1. Keep a diary for at least one week of exactly how time at work is spent. See Table 2.3 for a sample diary sheet.
2. The form is a basis that could be modified to your personal situation. Fill it in as events take place, rather than by recalling what has happened. Every time you switch attention from one subject to another, or from one person to another, that is a change of activity, and you start a new line. A meeting counts as one activity.
3. Read through the notes about how to analyse the results before starting to record.

Analysis of diary.

This record of exactly what you have done can be used in a number of ways. Here are some suggestions:

1. How many hours did you spend working each day and in the whole week?
2. What percentage of your time is spent with people?
3. How much of this time is spent with superiors, subordinates, others inside the organisation, people outside the organisation?
4. What is the average length of time you spend on an activity and, on average, how many activities do you have in a day? To what extent is your work characterised by brevity, variety and fragmentation, as suggested by Mintzberg?
5. What percentage of your activities is initiated by yourself, your boss, subordinates, others in the organisation, outsiders, or standard procedures? What proportion of your activities are you initiating?

Table 2.3 A sample diary sheet

Time	Activity	Who with	Who initiated	STAMP

6. What do you do most and least?

Outcome of analysis

By looking at the descriptions, sort the activities into categories, viz:

1. Mainly technical.
2. Mainly administrative, e.g. routine paperwork, getting typing done.
3. Mainly managerial, e.g. influencing others, resolving conflict.
4. Mainly social.
5. Mainly personal.
6. Others, e.g. don't knows, mixture.

How satisfied are you with the distribution? What can you do to improve it?

References

Barnard, C. E., 1938, *The Functions of the Executive*, Harvard University Press, Cambridge, Mass.

Boyatzis, R. E., 1982, *The Competent Manager: A Model for Effective Performance*, John Wiley & Sons, Chichester.

Brown, W., 1971, *Organization*, Heinemann, London.

Carlson, S., 1951, *Executive Behaviour*, Strömberg, Stockholm.

Doktor, R. H., 1990, Asian and American CEOs: a comparative study, *Organizational Dynamics*, Winter, pp. 46–56.

Forte, C., 1986, *The Autobiography of Charles Forte*, Pan Books, London.

Guest, R., 1955, On time and the foreman, *Personnel*, no. 32, pp. 478–86.

Handy, C., 1989, *The Age of Unreason*, Business Books, London (second edition, 1991).

Harvey-Jones, J., 1988, *Making It Happen: Reflections on Leadership*, Collins, London.

Harvey-Jones, J., 1992, *Troubleshooter 2*, BBC Books, London.

Horne, J. H. and Lupton, T., 1965, The work activities of middle managers, *Journal of Management Studies*, vol. 2, February, pp. 14–33.

Jaques, E., 1970, *Equitable Payment*, Heinemann, London.

Kanter, R. M., 1989, *When Giants Learn to Dance*, Unwin, London.

Kotter, J., 1982, *The General Managers*, Free Press, New York.

Mansfield, R., Poole, M., Blyton, P. and Frost, P., 1981, The British manager in profile, *BIM Survey*, 51, British Institute of Management, London.

Marshall, J. and Stewart, R., 1981, Managers' job perceptions, *Journal of Management Studies*, vol. 18, nos 2 and 3, pp. 177–90 and 263–75.

MCI, 1991, *Management Standards*.

Mintzberg, H., 1971, Managerial work: analysis from observation, *Management Science*, vol. 18, pp. 97–110.

Mintzberg, H., 1973, *The Nature of Managerial Work*, Harper & Row, London.

Mintzberg, H., 1975, The manager's job: folklore and fact, *Harvard Business Review*, July/August, pp. 49–61.

Morgan, G., 1986, *Images of Organization*, Sage Publications, Beverly Hills, California.

Pascale, R. and Athos, A., 1982, *The Art of Japanese Management*, Penguin Books, Harmondsworth, Middlesex.

Peters, T., 1988, *Thriving on Chaos*, Macmillan, London.

Scase, R. and Goffee, R., 1989, *Reluctant Managers: Their Work and Lifestyles*, Unwin Hyman, London.

Scitovsky, T., 1986, *The Joyless Economy*, Oxford University Press.

Sloan, A. P., 1967, *My Years with General Motors*, Pan Books, London.

Stewart, R., 1967, *Managers and Their Jobs*, Macmillan, London.

Stewart, R., 1976, *Contrasts in Management*, McGraw-Hill, Maidenhead, Berkshire.

Torrington, D.P. and Weightman, J.B., 1982, Technical atrophy in middle management, *Journal of General Management*, vol. 7, no. 3, Spring, pp. 5–17.

Torrington, D.P. and Weightman, J.B., 1987, Middle management work, *Journal of General Management*, vol. 13, no. 2, Winter, pp. 74–89.

Torrington, D. P. and Weightman, J. B., 1989, *The Reality of School Management*, Blackwell Oxford.

Townsend, R., 1970, *Up the Organization*, Michael Joseph, London.

Chapter 3

Management jobs

Management covers a range of jobs more diverse than many other general occupational titles. The title 'doctor' or 'teacher' describes a job where all job holders have a common core of activity that is substantial and generally acknowledged, no matter how varied the specialisation. Managers have a common core to their activities that is more vague: a general concern with directing and controlling affairs lacking a clear knowledge base, the mastery of which enables the job holder to produce acceptable performance. The uncertainty is increased by the range of activities in which management is undertaken. The combination of an imprecise core of activity and knowledge and such a diversity of applications make categorisation difficult. The most familiar and traditional methods of differentiating between management jobs are to classify them according to function or level, and a consideration of those methods forms the bulk of this chapter.

All these classifications are really only appropriate to large organisations. In small organisations, for example the many small software companies that have developed in the computing business, individuals will work closely together and many will share both technical and managerial responsibility. Some aspects of these ways of working in small businesses have been imported to large organisations through the use of devolved business teams, autonomous directorates and work groups. Small businesses are also more likely to have managers who emphasise enterprise and working closely with their customers. Both of these have been taken on by large organisations; see, for example, the Total Quality Management material we discuss in Chapter 7. But usually there is still some formal distinction made between management jobs in large organisations and we concentrate on these in this chapter. However, it is also useful to look at differentiation by activity and we start with various ways of doing so.

Differentiation by activity

When we studied the work of managers in a health authority we found that we could group them into four types of management job: Strategic, Operational, Technical and Systems. We describe these below. We also give an account of Mintzberg's method and the alternative method of Rosemary Stewart.

Management jobs seem to involve one of four kinds of work: running something or 'strategic' jobs, managing people or 'operations' jobs, technical work or 'professional' jobs and 'system' jobs. We do not see these jobs and their attendant work as being in any sense hierarchical. All of them need doing within the organisation and we found people at different points in the hierarchy in each of our four categories. What distinguishes the categories is the sort of work that has to be done and the types of credibility required to do them.

Strategic jobs

Jobs in this category were about making things happen, to use Harvey-Jones's (1988) phrase. They had particular areas to promote within the organisation and were involved in understanding how to promote change. They were constantly scanning to see what new trends, demands or initiatives were coming along that the organisation or section would need to reply to, implement or capitalise on. They were closely involved with policy-making and getting decisions both made and implemented. People in this group felt they had the autonomy to get on with things and did not need to constantly refer to their boss.

Jobs in this group are about understanding and influencing a wide group of people. For a health manager, for example, this would include people within the District or Trust or Regional Health Authorities, as well as representatives from a large number of outside agencies, from Local Authorities to Rotary Clubs. For managers in other types of organisation the group may include professional bodies, employers' organisations, government bodies, overseas customers and other associated companies. Many of these interactions require an understanding about power. As organisations increasingly depend on less formal forms of influence it becomes increasingly important for managers with this type of job to understand power and the use of it. Those who understand the subtleties of power in relationships are better able to get things done than those who ignore them.

This group usually had several constituencies to work to, for example their own bosses in the Health Service, the Regional Health Authority, the various coordinating committees to which they belonged, their subordinates and other professionals. Maintaining credibility within such a wide network usually requires keeping up to date on current initiatives, being seen to have a particular contribution or point of view to make and getting on with it. There was less dependence in this group on technical expertise as the basis for credibility. They seemed to rely more on personal qualities, such as wanting to be involved, devoting their time (they often put in very long days), and a willingness to take things on.

People in this group were doing more managerial work (see Chapter 2) than we found in other groups and more than was found in middle and senior managers elsewhere (Torrington and Weightman, 1982, 1988). This emphasis on managerial work seemed appropriate to their jobs of keeping things running and bringing in new developments. Most had reasonable clerical and secretarial assistance, so did not get bogged down with simple administration. They had very little, if any, clinical or technical involvement, so their credibility was dependent on getting things done.

Operations jobs

Jobs in this group are really the other side of the coin to those in the strategic group. Operations jobs are about 'keeping the show on the road'. Day by day, hour by hour, people with operations jobs make it all work, whereas those with strategic jobs are constantly scanning the horizon, to see what is coming along that will need dealing with. There is a logical distinction between the two jobs. The skills and competencies required in the two groups are really very different; consequently it can be very difficult, nay impossible, to go directly from a job in one group to one in the other.

The usefulness of this type of job is the picking up on the differences between plans and reality. All the day-to-day problems need someone to deal with them. There are all sorts of uncertainties, such as staff absences, leaking boilers, supplies not being delivered and, in a hospital context, patients getting confused. All of these need attention quickly.

Many of the job holders in this group see their work as managing people. They were often engaged in recruiting, disciplining and working out rotas. Additionally they may be picking up on the stress of those in their sections by being available for a 'chat'. Managing people cannot really be divorced from other aspects of operations, such as dealing with difficulties, resources and budgets.

For people with jobs in this group there are two main issues. First there is the tension between how much autonomy to give to their subordinates and the degree of central control: for example, who should decide such things as rotas, resources, patient care, or training. The second issue is whether the job is interpreted as mostly about nurturing relationships of high trust and consensus, or whether it is mostly about dealing with the different groups whose interests conflict. Decisions on these two issues will affect the nature of the organisation, the climate of the department and how people work together.

The main constituency for people with this type of job is the group of people they manage. Operations job holders can only get things done if they have credibility with those who work for them. Only by keeping in touch with the day-to-day activities, problems and tasks can these managers expect to be able to take suitable action when things inevitably do not run to plan. Equally they need to be in close contact with the details of their section if they are to provide suitable advice and comment to people in other positions when new initiatives are suggested.

There are two ways for operations managers to keep in touch. First, they can keep some technical work of their own. By actually doing some of the work of the section or department they keep up to date with how things are done, what current issues are being presented, and how equipment, systems, etc., work in practice. This can be a source of continuing expertise which allows others to seek their advice as an expert. It can inform the decisions that are taken because they are based on current experience. It also ensures that the only managerial work done is that which really needs doing.

Second, operations managers can keep in touch by keeping close contact with their staff. This is probably most easily done where there has been an internal promotion or where the manager has a technical expertise that staff will consult for expert advice. It is very difficult to keep in touch with staff just by being pleasant to them. Although we all need to have some social exchange at work, most people are far too busy and can resent their boss if it is felt they are just filling time with idle chat. Credibility can easily be eroded if the boss is seen to have nothing to do and no expertise.

This group had more technical work than those in the strategic group, but more managerial work than those in the systems group described below.

Professional jobs

We have included in this group a variety of technical and professional jobs which involve the job holder in using their expertise to provide a service or policy for the whole organisation or relevant parts of the organisation. Some of the job holders in this group in our study were surprised to be included in a management project as they did not see themselves as 'management'. In the sense of being the controlling body of the District, they probably were not management, and their focus on their technical expertise was entirely appropriate. But in terms of the work they did there were some parts of that work that can be appropriately included with management, particularly the strategic work associated with developing the service. This was in addition to the particular management responsibility of some who were responsible for running a department.

Although the main part of the work of these people is technical, they also have managerial work to do in the sense of influencing the rest of the organisation to use the service, or put into practice, or accept, the policies and procedures commensurate with their technical expertise. This requires a great deal of lobbying for interest, negotiating for resources and communicating with a wide group of people. It is trying to change people's behaviour by demonstrating expertise.

The management side of these people's jobs often involves innovation. This might be some new procedure, policy, equipment or behaviour. To do this effectively professional job holders need to understand the sequence of innovation. Having the new idea is only the beginning. Most energy is expended in disseminating and developing the innovation to fit the particular circumstances. It is also important to deal with all the consequences of innovation, including those that are unintended.

Another important managerial issue for those with professional or technical jobs is developing and maintaining a suitable network of contacts. This will include other professionals, usually outside the organisation, to keep up to date. Within the organisation a variety of relationships need to be maintained so that information, resources and ideas can be exchanged. Many of the people in this group were in contact with a surprisingly large number of people within the organisation as their services, or policies, affected cross-sections of the organisation.

The most important aspect of credibility for people with these types of job is their professional or technical expertise. Without that they really cannot begin to influence others. If they are seen as being out of touch with current trends or the reality of the organisation, no-one will be very impressed and issues will be dealt with unilaterally rather than having some coordination. This technical expertise has to be sufficient that others can consult the expertise confidently. It also requires the job holder to be sufficiently accessible, and at least adequate at communicating, if they are to be influential. For those with departments to run this professional expertise is also important for credibility with their subordinates.

System jobs

This group also included several people who did not see themselves as managers. They may have been included because they were seen by their bosses to have the potential for management, or it may be that those selecting were unsure of the work these jobs involved, or because the job had changed dramatically recently, or because these people were included in management for salary purposes and consequently it was felt appropriate to look at their management training needs. However, these jobs were well worth looking at in order to clarify the distinction between managing and administration. The first is about policy making, setting precedents, being the boss. The second is about knowing how the procedure or system works and trying to get people to use it.

These jobs are about organisation maintenance. Whereas the operations jobs are about making it happen day by day, hour by hour, these system jobs are about keeping things going by looking after all the housekeeping-type jobs. If these bits and pieces were not done everyone would be most irritated, but they are rarely noticed when done well. System jobs are primarily about systems, procedures and monitoring. These are usually agreed and laid down by other people. In the Health Service this can be at National, Regional, District or Trust level.

The system job holders are not primarily involved in initiating procedures. However, they are involved in putting them into practice and using them. Above all, job holders in this group need to know the minutiae of the systems they are using. This often involves experience and good contacts with other people to make them workable. For example, some of the people we met in this group were responsible for servicing meetings. This required them to know exactly who to invite, who to consult over the agenda and minutes, and how to determine the most appropriate venue for the meetings. But they were not personally involved in taking decisions at these meetings, although they were present.

Knowledge of the system, procedure or monitoring device was the basis of credibility for most job holders in this group. They also needed to explain this to others sufficiently well for them to understand the purpose and benefits of the devices.

Mintzberg's and Stewart's classifications

Mintzberg (1973) studied management job holders in North America and subsequently listed ten management roles (see Figure 3.1) that were present in the jobs of all managers, although the proportion varied with different jobs.

He argues that managers derive status from the formal authority they have over the units, departments or activities with which they are identified. Because of this position they are involved in interpersonal relations with subordinates, peers and superiors, who provide the manager with the information he needs to make decisions.

Interpersonal roles

These help keep the organisation running smoothly. The *figurehead* role is where the managers have certain ceremonial duties to perform, like taking a customer to lunch or greeting a visitor, where they represent the unit or activity for which they are responsible. As *leaders* managers are dealing with subordinates and enabling them to perform well and meet objectives, while the *liaison* role requires them to deal with people outside the unit, either peers within the organisation or customers, suppliers and others outside.

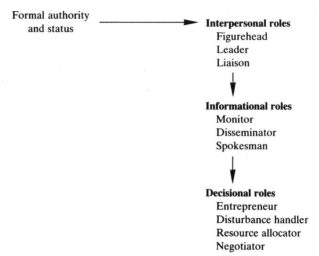

Figure 3.1   Mintzberg's managerial roles.

Informational roles

Mintzberg regards, as the most important aspects of the manager's job, those activities which are concerned with giving and receiving information. As *monitors* managers seek to be well informed about events relating to this section of the organisation. They gather and store information that will be useful, by questioning subordinates, tapping a personal network of contacts and scanning unsolicited information that comes in. As *disseminator* the manager distributes information to subordinates that would otherwise not be available to them. This, of course, is a crucial aspect of the manager/ subordinate relationship and the main source of the trust or mistrust existing in that relationship. As *spokesperson* the manager passes on information collected to people outside the unit or outside the organisation. A large part of this role is keeping the boss informed, but other aspects might be advice to a customer about a product or information to a supplier about modifications that are required before delivery.

Decisional roles

In these cases the manager makes use of the information received to make decisions. The *entrepreneur* is trying to make changes because a new idea is worth pursuing, that it will develop the area of activity and responsibility. *Disturbance handler* is not initiating change but coping with the result of situations that cannot be controlled: a customer goes bankrupt, the warehouse is burned down, someone is away sick, or any one of the thousand situations that have to be managed to prevent the disturbance reducing the effectiveness of the unit. The role of *resource allocator* is when the manager decides where and how the resources of the unit, including managerial time, will be deployed. The final decisional role is that of *negotiator*, where the manager is doing deals with those people and interests whose consent and/or cooperation are needed by the manager's organisation but where there is no formal authority over them: union representatives, suppliers wanting to change their pricing, local authority officials seeking better employment opportunities, and so forth. Negotiating is an important activity for managers, as only they have the information that negotiating requires and only they have the necessary scope of authority to make realistic decisions about progress in negotiations as the information available to the two parties separately is gradually exchanged and organised. As the proportions of the roles varied from job to job, Mintzberg (1973, pp. 126–9) concluded that there were eight types of managerial job:

The contact manager, who is a figurehead and liaises with outside agencies.

The political manager, who spends a lot of time outside the organisation trying to reconcile conflicting forces that affect it.

The entrepreneur, who seeks opportunities and implements change in the organisation.

The insider, who tries to build up and maintain internal expectations by 'fire-fighting'.

The real time manager, who tries to build up and maintain a stable system over time.

The team manager, who is preoccupied with the creation of a team which will operate effectively as a cohesive whole.

The expert manager, who advises other managers and is consulted on specialised problems.

The new manager, who so far lacks the contacts and information to be any of the other seven.

The Stewart method of classifying management jobs

Rosemary Stewart is a British research worker who has spent twenty years studying management work and who produced an original classification method in 1976. She regarded the main weaknesses of the function/level mode of classification as being the assumption of similarities rather than a search for differences. She studied the behavioural rather than the technical content of managers' jobs and asked questions about the demands that the job made on the manager's behaviour. After detailed examination of the demands made by 253 jobs she produced a novel typology, the bare outline of which we reproduce here (see Figure 3.2) as it enables the readers to

Hub jobs have necessary contact with subordinates, superiors, peers and others above and below them in the hierarchy. This was the most common type of job among the managers studied and had a dominant people-management component. (116 jobs)

Peer-dependent jobs were those where there was less 'vertical' demand and much dependence on winning the cooperation of peers. They were much found at the boundaries of the organisation. (63 jobs)

Man-management jobs were those concerned primarily with the vertical type of working relationship, having contact mainly with superiors and subordinates. (52 jobs)

Solo jobs were those of managers who spent a large proportion of their time working alone on assignments. (22 jobs)

Figure 3.2 Breakdown of the demands made by 253 management jobs studied by Stewart (1976, pp. 15–16).

think about their jobs in a fresh way, and to understand better the constraints and opportunities available to them.

Stewart's continuing interest in the differences between managerial jobs has led to her looking at the differences in general management jobs (Fondas and Stewart, 1992) where she gives a guide to the differences between jobs. She suggests that there are differences in the job context; in the scope of the job in terms of responsibility, domain of activity and independence from others; in expectation of others; and in which tasks are important.

The full account of Rosemary Stewart's work and results of her early investigation are to be found in her book *Contrasts in Management* (Stewart, 1976). Her methods and ideas are developed further in *Choices for Managers* and *Managing Today and Tomorrow* (Stewart, 1982, 1991).

─┤ REVIEW TOPIC 3.1 ├──────────────────────────────

Of the eight types of managerial job listed by Mintzberg, which is most like the one you have now? Which would you like to be? What are your reasons?

───

Differentiation by function

One of the most familiar ways of organising management jobs in large organisations is to label them according to function, so that the prefixed title indicates the area of the organisation's activities in which the manager specialises, e.g.:

- General Manager
- Operations Manager
- Marketing Manager
- Personnel Manager
- Accounting Manager

There are many other specialisations; we find managers of purchasing, research, management development, distribution, data processing, public relations, warehousing and so on. This method is extensively used, even in situations where the fundamental activities of production and marketing do not exist. The different units of the British National Health Service, for instance, have been in the charge of management teams with the following membership:

- Medical Director
- Nursing Director
- Finance Director
- Operations Manager
- Estates Manager

This method is designed to fit the classic methods of functional organisation that we consider in Chapter 14, but functional labels are also used in matrix and other types of organisation, although the emphasis will differ.

This method of labelling assumes that a job holder is a specialist first and a manager second, so that a nursing director qualifies as a nurse and works in that specialism before becoming a director and controller of nursing affairs. Management is represented as an aspect of a wide variety of jobs which have their main substance and justification in an area of specialised knowledge or skill that is deployed within the employing organisation. The method also links the activities of the manager with those other employees who share the specialised knowledge. The marketing manager is a linking pin between all marketing personnel and other organisational members: this is the voice of marketing and responsible for its people. It is this sort of classification that makes sense of management education, in which students typically study functional areas, and is sustained by professional bodies. In the United Kingdom there are institutes that act as qualifying associations for specialists in accounting, marketing, operations, personnel, purchasing and other functions. The degree of control these bodies exercise over their professions or quasi-professions varies, but they all represent a vested interest in functional affiliation by individual managers.

In the first example we gave of functional management, the general manager was the odd man out: this specialisation is in coordinating affairs in general, acting as a mediator between the specialisms. Some methods of organisation have a number of general managers who act as the only manager in relatively small units, sometimes as a result of geographical distribution of activities. The picture of functional management is therefore only complete when we include the non-functional manager. The retail bank has a single manager, as do many shops, distribution depots and small factories. The project manager in a matrix organisation is a form of non-functional manager.

Differentiation by level

A more significant form of management differentiation in large organisations is that of the level at which the manager operates, because we now see
the effect of the hierarchy. There may be any number of levels in a
hierarchy, but we can identify four levels at which the nature of the
management job differs: top, senior, middle and supervisory (see Table
3.1). Some readers may feel that this labelling is no more than attributing
different amounts of status to people, but we will see that there are
substantive differences in the type of jobs done by incumbents.

Received wisdom in management literature and at conferences in the
early 1990s is that understanding level and hierarchies is increasingly
irrelevant as management structures are flattened. The argument continues
that as the softer aspects of management such as empowerment and
autonomy are encouraged there is less need for management hierarchies.
Our travels around organisations suggest that the reality is not always the
same as the rhetoric; indeed in 1993 many large organisations seem to be
increasing their management layers. For example, in a petrochemicals
company a new layer of management has been introduced to coordinate the
business across Europe. There are three levels of management in this
structure in addition to those already existing in the operating companies
within each country. Another example is within the Health Service where
the reorganisations have led to increased management structures within

Table 3.1 Management jobs classified by level

Level	Main characteristics
Top managers	Relatively detached from the organisation; few, but very important, responsibilities; spend most of their time with outsiders and with peers, very little with subordinates.
Senior managers	Head up functions or operations; concerned with policy formulation and implementation; work tends to be hectic and frequently interrupted; often out of the office; spend time dealing with outsiders, peers and subordinates.
Middle managers	Work mainly within the organisation and are concerned with making the organisation work; can be line or staff; work mainly with peers and senior managers.
Supervisory managers	Relatively detached from the management hierarchy, but vitally concerned with the main activities of the organisation; busy, frequently interrupted and constantly switching between jobs; spend most time with subordinates, some with peers and little with superiors or outsiders.

hospitals and Trusts. For example, most have established the new post of Clinical Director responsible for discreet patient services such as surgery. But the old Unit, District and Regional management structures still continue, albeit with different titles and tasks. In the Education Service in England and Wales there is now a new layer of managers in agencies to coordinate the work of opted-out schools in addition to the existing Local Authorities and central Department for Education. If anything, there are now more layers of management between those doing the work of the organisation and the chief. So we make no apologies for continuing to include the following section about differentiating the jobs of managers by level.

Top managers

Many top managers are senior managers as well, so our account in this section includes only part of the work of such executives, the other part being set out in the next section. Top managers have few, but enormous, responsibilities, such as occasional major changes in direction: to introduce a new product, or not; to export to Chile, or not; to opt out or not; to close a factory, or not; to dismiss the chief executive, or not. These activities are usually undertaken by the Board of Directors or comparable body with a broad legal responsibility in commercial companies to safeguard the shareholders' interests and the long-term interests of the company.

The principal top manager is the chair, who has the most important task of appointing, with directorial colleagues, the managing director or chief executive and other key senior appointments. When *The Times* and *Sunday Times* newspapers were bought in 1981 by the Australian entrepreneur Rupert Murdoch, quite elaborate arrangements were made to vest the authority of appointing the editor in the hands of external, independent directors. The editor could not be dismissed without their concurrence, although they could not stop the editor from resigning. A director is not, as such, an employee or servant of the organisation. Their accountability is to the shareholders or owners in commercial companies and to those they represent in public sector organisations. Top managers are not, however, precluded from holding employment in the company by this directorship, and many board members are also full-time employees, discharging duties of senior managers, which we come to shortly. Also, a very small proportion of directors are employees holding more humble positions in the hierarchy, usually termed worker directors.

The value of top managers lies in their relative detachment from the organisation and its employees. They will probably be involved with several organisations, giving them a range of current operating experience that full-time employees in a single undertaking will lack. This relative detachment and independence will also enable them to handle more easily some of the difficult decisions that have to be made. If a project has to be discontinued because it is no longer viable, many senior managers will be so involved with that project, for sentimental, career or status reasons, that they will be committed to protecting it. But an independent director could view it more dispassionately. Many organisational changes involve making employees redundant. Senior managers frequently know the employees personally and have great difficulty in facing up to this operational necessity, so that the detachment of the top manager can be an invaluable element in the discussions that have to take place. Governors of maintained schools have increasingly played this role.

Top managers spend most of their time with outsiders and with peers, and very little with subordinates.

Senior managers

Senior managers are those who head up functions, such as marketing or personnel, as we saw at the beginning of the chapter; or they head up operations, factories, branches, depots or other units that are relatively self-contained with a number of functions being coordinated. While it is important to distinguish between top managers and senior managers, any neat distinction is made difficult by the fact that so many top managers are also senior managers. A way of clarifying the distinction is to say that senior managers are concerned with both policy formulation, in conjunction with top managers, and policy implementation, in conjunction with subordinates.

Defined like this, policy formulation is a collective activity where senior managers with specialist responsibilities and interests meet with each other, and with top managers who do not hold specific portfolios, to decide matters that can best or only be satisfactorily determined by consensus between them. A policy to resist the use of consultants, for instance, might be an aspiration of the personnel managers, but they could not make that effective unless they could obtain the understanding and consent of senior management colleagues to make it work. A plan to change advertising policy away from national newspapers to television would be for the marketing managers to devise, but they too would need to convince colleagues of its wisdom.

Policy formulation has the predominant emphasis on decision-making but includes the element of control to ensure that decisions are being put into operation.

In policy implementation the senior manager changes activity away from deciding what should be done towards putting the decisions into practice: they become executives working with those who share specialist concerns, knowledge and skills, whether that specialist interest be in a function or an operation. Implementation also involves constant activity in a boundary role on behalf of members in the specialist group, as the senior manager enlists the help of people elsewhere in the organisation or outside it, seeks clarification from other specialists, and mediates demands on the specialist area from outside.

Studies of the work of senior managers in Western societies (for instance, Carlson, 1951; Copeman *et al.*, 1963; Mintzberg, 1975) all confirm that the senior manager's job tends to be a very hectic one, dealing with peers, outsiders and subordinates. Many of the matters to be dealt with are urgent and there are frequent interruptions: Copeman and his colleagues found an average of three visitors and four telephone calls each hour. Senior managers are frequently out of the office and spend the majority of their working time talking to people.

Middle managers

Middle managers are creatures of medium to large organisations, as only in those situations are there enough people to generate hierarchical layers between senior managers and supervisors. This tends to be a difficult role because of its potential artificiality. It is not sufficiently senior to have a broad task of coordination nor significant decision-making powers, and it is not closely in touch with the urgencies of the organisation's main activity, like making machine tools in a factory or caring for patients in a hospital.

The basic artificiality of their management work provides the main problem, not only for many middle managers, but also for their organisations. It is the organisation and its bureaucracy that 'feed' the middle managers. Too few of them can enjoy the satisfaction of bringing off a sale, or manufacturing an excellent item, or acquiring a useful subsidiary, even though they may help towards such achievements. Many middle managers find their satisfactions within the organisation and its operating complexities.

In 1956 William H. Whyte coined the term 'organisation man' to describe people who became over-preoccupied with, and dependent on, the organisation of which they were part. The following year Parkinson (1957) produced his devastating critique of administration, with particular reference to the British civil service. Both pointed to the way in which those holding middle management roles live in a world which takes on a life and purpose of its own, quite distinct from the purposes of the undertaking in which they are supposed to be engaged. Some discussion in the United States even reached the point of regarding organisational growth as a denial of individual freedom. The worst predictions of the organisation man syndrome have not been realised, but middle managers remain more concerned about organisational mechanics and process than products. This makes them vulnerable when the foundations shake. If an organisation goes out of business or sheds personnel, displaced middle managers frequently find that their chances in the labour market are poor because all their expertise has lain in making one organisational system work and knowing how to get through the particular administrative jungle. Scase and Goffee's (1989) study of middle

Table 3.2 Horne and Lupton's analysis of the working lives of middle managers

Activity	Percentage of time
Giving, seeking information	42
Giving, seeking advice	6
Giving, confirming, reviewing decisions	8
Giving, receiving, confirming instructions	9
Coordinating, reviewing plans	11
Seeking, preparing explanations	15
Other activities	9

managers in large British organisations found that they were reluctant managers and sought their main attachments outside organisations as the previous rewards of promotion, security and status have been eroded with the recent economic pressures.

Middle managers have a wide variety of jobs and roles. Some have large numbers of subordinates, while others have none. In one research investigation we spoke to an army major with 130 subordinates, but we also spoke to a management services consultant, a project manager and a senior nursing officer who did not have any subordinates. Some will share the same work as their subordinates, but have additional administrative duties, such as heads of departments in schools. Others will do quite different work, like the project manager mentioned above, who coordinates the work of engineers, designers, suppliers and customers. Middle managers of all types spend a great deal of their time operating procedures and responding to the requests, queries, demands and initiatives of others rather than generating their own work.

Horne and Lupton (1965) analysed the working lives of 66 middle managers and found that they spent most of their time exchanging information (see Table 3.2).

The promotion to middle managemeent often leads to people allowing their previous, technical expertise to wither. The salesman gives up seeing customers, nurses no longer give bedside care and engineers leave technical problems to others. This is because they are 'too busy' with meetings, paperwork and other administrative tasks; learning the way of life that Mant sceptically calls 'clean and gentlemanly'. There are problems in abandoning previous expertise or involvement with the main task of the organisation; problems for the individual managers, for their subordinates and for the organisation.

Early in their careers middle managers acquire a body of knowledge and technical skill to qualify and practise as pharmacist, engineer, teacher or whatever specialist career was followed. The jobs could not be done without that knowledge, and more specific information could always be obtained to solve an unexpected problem so that an answer could always be found.

When they cross over to the better paid, higher ranking (and logically more skilful) activity of managing, they expect the new activity to have a similar body of expertise: reliable, explicit and accessible. All they find is a ramshackle collection of humdrum tasks that any literate school-leaver could easily accomplish, but their earlier training makes it almost impossible for them to believe that there is not more to management than this, so they look for the solution to a non-existent mystery. To some extent they find what they are looking for in management development. The constant stream of books, lectures, seminars and symposia from the behavioural science entrepreneurs offer neat packages of answers, rapidly replacing one management myth with another, and the clientele for such placebos is almost exclusively middle management.

As few middle managers are lazy they often set up activities to justify their positions, producing administrative controls, internal coordinating meetings and requests for information that are not needed other than to build the individual middle manager more securely into the administrative system of the undertaking. Thus begins the political activity of the middle manager, that is discussed more fully in Chapter 18.

The problems for the subordinates of these middle managers are expressed in the complaint heard frequently in organisations that the manager has lost touch with the task and is making unrealistic demands and unreasonable decisions which are out of date with current problems. Although much of this grumbling will be no more than the jaundiced view of those who resent the greater privilege of those immediately 'above' them, the loss of technical skills by a middle manager does not help and leads to a situation in which subordinates are expected to comply with managerial requests on the basis of the manager's position of authority, whereas compliance based on experience and expertise is both easier and does not need the support of power and control of resources. This question of authority is explored more fully in Chapter 19.

One of the main problems for the organisation of middle managers abandoning their technical expertise is the loss of their experience. All too often they are promoted out of work connected with the main task of the organisation at the very stage where they have sufficient experience to work confidently and be at their most effective. Our own study (Torrington and Weightman, 1982) found British organisations encouraging middle managers with proven expertise in a technical specialism to abandon this in favour of very general, and usually straightforward, managerial and administrative duties:

> We also found that middle managers often did administrative work, that is work following procedures, because they were unsure what their managerial work was. We consider the main managerial work of middle managers to be

dealing with the uncertainties associated with the difference between plans and reality and establishing networks within the system to get things done.

(Torrington and Weightman, 1988)

The conclusion is that middle managers should maintain as much contact with, and practise in, their technical specialism as they can, even though this might appear to increase their workload. This will increase the respect of their peers and subordinates and will make them less vulnerable at times of redundancy, more marketable and less dependent on organisation-specific skills.

Senior managers might consider changing the balance in the demands they make of middle managers, giving greater weight to current performance rather than an assessment of nebulous and imprecise personal qualities.

Supervisory managers

The largest number of managers are supervisors or first-line managers, with a range of titles like foreman, office manager, ward sister, sergeant, chief clerk, shift leader, superintendent, charge hand, leading seaman, head steward, floor manager, leading chef. In any organisation most employees report to a supervisor, who is responsible for assigning tasks to them, overseeing their work, making sure it is done satisfactorily and dealing with all complaints and queries. It is a job that has suffered much recently.

> For half a century or more first-line supervisors, especially those in manufacturing and clerical work, have seen their roles shrinking in status, in importance and in esteem. Where a supervisor was 'management' to the employee only half a century ago, he or she has now, by and large, become a buffer between management, union and workers. And like all buffers, the supervisor's main function is to take the blows.   (Drucker, 1977, p. 243)

The above trend is now beginning to be reversed in some organisations which have reduced the number of levels of management. This is also happening in organisations where more senior management have had to take on additional responsibilities, for example in Health Service organisations which have gone for Trust status. We see supervisors taking on management roles. For example Ward Sisters and Charge Nurses are expected to deal with staffing rotas, use of beds and other resource issues which were previously dealt with by more senior staff. In a chemical plant, which has reduced management levels, shift supervisors are now responsible for organising the work of the operators and are included in quality meetings with other members of the business team.

Most top managers have previously been senior managers and nearly all senior managers have been middle managers, but few top, senior or middle managers have ever been supervisors. The supervisory post is often the career culmination for people who start in an operative post, so that in many organisations the management hierarchy starts in the lower reaches of middle management. There are exceptions: nursing, teaching and the police service are all occupations in which the only feasible starting point for a career is at the bottom. Marks and Spencer provides one of the best-known examples of a career progression style that involves the potential manager starting at the bottom and working up from there. In most employment, however, it is rare for people to work their way up from supervisory positions. This has some interesting effects:

1. There is a clear gap between the management hierarchy or pyramid and the supervisory grades.
2. Supervisors come to rest in their supervisory position. It is the end of the road, so that their main objective soon becomes the maintenance of the status quo; they are seldom bidding for promotion.
3. Those in middle and senior positions frequently lack the ability to judge the fine detail of the actual job that the organisation exists to carry out. In the earlier section of this chapter about middle managers we saw the tendency for their technical skills to become outdated; here we are referring to the problem of their not being able to make a judgement because of never having had 'coalface' experience. This has led to such problems as production engineers specifying equipment that is technically appropriate, but inappropriate to the skills and expertise of production employees. Many industrial relations disputes and difficulties with technological innovation begin for just this reason.
4. The supervisory role has been largely neglected in the whole management development circus. Management courses seldom have relevance to supervisory, first-line duties, although there are some separate courses for supervisors.

There is a dearth of recent studies of supervisors, but some of long standing (Guest, 1956; Mahoney, 1965) show that the supervisor's life is remarkably similar to that of the senior manager in that it is likely to be busy, frequently interrupted and constantly switching between jobs, as they deal with the immediate and the urgent. Unlike the senior manager, they spend most time with subordinates, some with peers and little with superiors or outsiders.

| REVIEW TOPIC 3.2 |

If salary, conditions of employment and security were all equal, would you rather be a top manager, a senior manager, a middle manager or a supervisory manager? What are the reasons for your choice?

Table 3.3　Management assessment form

	Difficulties	Strengths
For the organisation		
For their superiors		
For their subordinates		
For themselves		

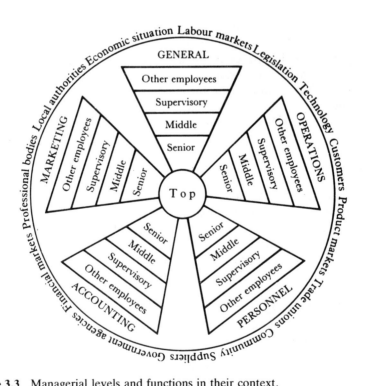

Figure 3.3　Managerial levels and functions in their context.

┤ SUMMARY PROPOSITIONS ├─────────────────────────

3.1 Management jobs are of such a variety that precise definition is impracticable.

3.2 The research of Rosemary Stewart and Henry Mintzberg has provided novel ways of classifying management jobs that enlarge our understanding of the variety that is comprehended by the term 'management'.

3.3 The most familiar methods of classifying management jobs are according to function and organisational level (see Figure 3.3).

┤ PUTTING IT INTO PRACTICE ├─────────────────────────

Consider the role of middle management – defined as anyone working with people both above and below them in the hierarchy, who have a management component to their work. Fill in Table 3.3.

References

Carlson, S., 1951, *Executive Behaviour*, Strömberg, Stockholm.

Copeman, G., Luijk, H. and Haneka, F., 1963, *How the Executive Spends His Time*, Business Publications, London.

Drucker, P. F., 1977, *Management*, Pan Books, London.

Fondas, N. and Stewart, R., 1992, Understanding differences in general management jobs, *Journal of General Management*, vol. 17, no. 4, Summer, pp. 1–12.

Guest, R., 1956, Of time and the foreman, *Personnel*, May, pp. 478–86.

Harvey-Jones, J., 1988, *Making It Happen: Reflections on Leadership*, Collins, London.

Horne, J. H. and Lupton, T., 1965, The work activities of middle managers, *Journal of Management Studies*, vol. 2, February, pp. 14–33.

Mahoney, T., 1965, The jobs of management, *Industrial Relations*, February, pp. 97–110.

Mintzberg, H., 1973, *The Nature of Managerial Work*, Harper & Row, London.

Mintzberg, H., 1975, The manager's job: folklore and fact, *Harvard Business Review*, July/August, pp. 49–61.

Parkinson, C. N., 1957, *Parkinson's Law*, John Murray, London.

Scase, R. and Goffee, R., 1989, *Reluctant Managers: Their Work and Lifestyles*, Unwin Hyman, London.

Stewart, R., 1976, *Contrasts in Management*, McGraw-Hill, Maidenhead, Berkshire.

Stewart, R., 1982, *Choices for Managers*, McGraw-Hill, Maidenhead, Berkshire.

Stewart, R., 1991, *Managing Today and Tomorrow*, Macmillan, Basingstoke, Hampshire.

Torrington, D. P. and Weightman, J. B., 1982, Technical atrophy in middle management, *Journal of General Management*, vol. 7, no. 3, Spring, pp. 5–17.

Torrington, D. P. and Weightman, J. B., 1988, Middle management work, *Journal of General Management*, vol. 13, no. 2, Winter, pp. 74–89.

Whyte, W. H., 1956, *The Organization Man*, Simon & Schuster, New York.

Part II

Goals

All managers have to set a direction, in the same way as a navigator at sea. It may be to follow whoever is in front, to keep clear of those who might get in the way, or to find the right course towards – or beyond – a distant horizon. Once set, the direction has to be constantly checked and the course of the operation corrected. In this section of the book we consider the basic direction-setting questions: Where are we now? Where do we want to be? How do we get there? How are we doing? These questions are not just for the business as a whole but for each section within the overall operation.

The main direction-setting activities are strategy, policy and planning, for which information and ideas have to be collected and analysed to produce the documentation on the course to be followed and to get all hands knowing the direction they are taking.

No matter how carefully they are prepared, plans are never the same as reality; dealing with the unexpected is an essential part of effective management.

G   R   O   U   P

Chapter 4

Strategy and policy-making

There is some confusion in the world of management about the distinction between strategy and policy, although strategy is usually related to planning and policy commonly linked to shaping everyday affairs. Strategy is what is to be achieved and policy is the framework within which the activities will be conducted. The management process is then the implementation of the strategy within the framework of the policy.

Stoner and Wankel (1986) provide contrasted definitions:

> [Strategy is] . . . the broad program for defining and achieving an organization's objectives; the organization's response to its environment over time.
>
> (p. 695)

> A policy is a general guideline for decision-making. It sets up boundaries around decisions, including those that can be made and shutting out those that cannot. In this way it channels the thinking of organization members so that it is consistent with organizational objectives. Some policies deal with very important matters, like those requiring sanitary conditions where food or drugs are produced or packaged. Others may be concerned with relatively minor issues, such as the way the employees dress. (p. 91)

An example will help illustrate the distinction. Multiparts is a company in a highly competitive segment of the computer peripherals business. To meet expansion requirements they have decided to open a new sales and service centre in Bradford and they are anxious to start trading from the new centre without alerting their competitors to the move. This bare strategy is then filled out with decisions on how many people are needed, with what skills and with what facilities. A further set of decisions determines the type of premises, the range of services within the premises and the moves needed to locate and employ the necessary people, the sequence in which they are to be engaged and the employment costs of each category.

Alongside there will be policy decisions on whether or not vacancies in the new centre will be made known to existing employees, what methods of recruitment and selection will be used, what type of remuneration package will be offered, and how legal obligations in matters such as health and safety and employment rights are to be met. Many of these matters will have been resolved beforehand, as policy is a continuing framework for a range of activities, even though each new activity tends to throw up policy considerations that have not occurred previously.

The nature of strategy

The word strategy is something of a semantic minefield as people use the term in all sorts of ways and often imply several different uses in the same statement. Mintzberg et al., (1988) is as usual delightful in trying to help us unravel this. He suggests we look at five different uses of the term: plan, ploy, pattern, position and perspective.

Usually strategy is a *plan* – that is, a consciously intended course of action. It can also be used as a *ploy* – that is, a manoeuvre to outwit competitors. Strategy can also be a *pattern* which is inferred from consistent behaviour to suggest that someone, usually a competitor, has a strategy. Depending on where you sit, different things will be strategic, so *position* is important as an expression of the environment and by definition the strategy identifies that position. Strategy is a concept or *perspective* – the important thing is that within an organisation people share that perspective.

Mintzberg argues that these five different uses are not necessarily conflicting, indeed they can be complementary, but that more careful use of the term may avoid some of the confusions which so often occur when people are talking about strategy.

We spend most of this chapter talking about strategy in the sense of planning. This is the process of deciding priorities, setting targets and agreeing what are the main purposes of the business, section, division or unit. It may include short-, medium- and long-term goals. It is likely to include some changes which may be imposed from outside but will have been tuned to local conditions. The ability to monitor multiple environments, seek out and synthesise multiple sources and types of information, and develop and implement a plan of action that anticipates trends before they are obvious, is one of the most useful skills for senior staff to have.

Thompson and Strickland (1990) describe the five tasks of strategic management (see Figure 4.1) as a continuous process.

Because of its association with decision-making and objectives, strategy is generally viewed as a 'sexy', top management activity. The grim comparison with nuclear weapons makes the point. Tactical weapons may kill thousands, but strategic weapons can kill hundreds of thousands. Strategic decisions in business are the ones that really matter. They do not, however, involve only top managers.

Kay (1993) is critical of much strategic writing with its emphasis on

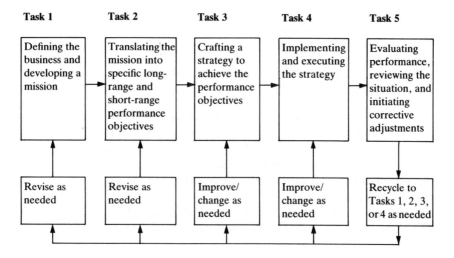

Figure 4.1 The five tasks of strategic management defined by Thompson and Strickland (1990).

military models of vision and leadership, size and share. He argues that the task of developing a strategy is identifying the firm's distinctive capabilities from among the following four ingredients and relating them to the environment.

Architecture   or the network of relational contracts within or around the firm

Reputation   which is the customers' guide to aspects of quality that they cannot monitor for themselves and is of value only in a continuing market

Innovation,   although establishing the competitive edge is often difficult

Strategic assets,   which may be monopolies or due to regulation.

Two examples of strategic planning we found when talking to and shadowing the members of a Healthcare Trust were as follows. A Care (Nurse) Manager responsible for ophthalmic surgery in a hospital was trying to work out how to respond to the Patients' Charter and the waiting lists initiative by working closely with the appropriate consultants. Another Care Manager responsible for care of the elderly was attending a lot of meetings to consider how they might implement the Community Care Act, which transfers the care of the chronically ill elderly from the Health Service to the Local Authorities' Social Services, locally, to plan, map provision and prioritise. It also meant looking at how the changes would affect directly the medical specialities within the hospital.

How are your unit's goals set?
What factors are considered?
How are individuals informed of organisation-wide goals?

In Chapter 16 we describe the organisational feature of decision-making complexes involving teams of advisers and analysts who rough-cut the decisions for managers to make. The support teams provide the expertise, the information and the analysis, while their leaders add the elements of flair, judgement, boldness and political skill to make the decision – and then make the decision work.

In his study of general managers, Mintzberg (1973a) decided that strategy-making was probably the most crucial part of his subjects' work, and wrote:

> One clear conclusion emerges from my study: the manager is substantially involved in every significant decision made by his organization. This is so because (1) as formal authority the manager is the only one allowed to commit his organization to new and important courses of action, (2) as nerve center the manager can best ensure that significant decisions reflect current knowledge and organizational values, and (3) strategic decisions can most easily be integrated by having one man control all of them.   (p. 77)

He further distinguished three modes of strategy formulation (Mintzberg, 1973b):

1. *The entrepreneurial mode* is where a single strong leader makes bold and risky decisions, relying heavily on intuition and personal experience. The organisation is able to move swiftly and decisively in pursuing its aims, always seeking new opportunities to exploit. Strategy is uncomplicated and shows no sign of modification to accommodate a variety of interests and points of view.
2. *The adaptive mode* is where managers react to situations as they develop. Instead of the bold and dramatic leaps forward of the entrepreneurial mode, there is a gradual progression of small moves, aimed mainly at defending the organisation against the competitive initiatives of others. Thus described, the adaptive mode sounds pusillanimous, unattractive and doomed to failure. In practice the lack of a single powerful leader has advantages as well as drawbacks. There may not be dramatic leaps forward, but neither are there dramatic leaps in the wrong direction. Influences on decision-making are spread widely with many people having some stake and producing an element of flexibility. It is an approach which is often called 'muddling through'; it may not be exciting but it avoids spectacular failure.

3. *The planning mode* is the most generally attractive, as it involves a systematic approach to strategy by which the top managers use their decision-making complexes and their own analysis to study the market and other aspects of the environment in which they are operating, and then use that as a framework in which they will deploy their experience, imagination and creative discussion to produce a plan for the future. Risks are calculated risks, intuition and flair are directed at matters that have first been fully explored and bounded by investigation and analysis. Bold leaps forward may be taken in the dark, but they are at least directed towards the light.

Seldom do we find only one mode of strategy formulation in an organisation. The entrepreneurial mode is usually the method adopted at the beginning of a business, when there is strong reliance on the guts and vision of a founder or founding team. Some management buy-outs make initial rapid strides forward as a result of confident, committed managers (traditionally mortgaged up to the hilt!) suddenly replacing an uninterested, muddling-through management. In very large, long-standing businesses there have been recent moves to set up new venture divisions, whereby a small team are partly insulated from the adaptive norms and encouraged to set up new ventures within the corporate fold.

Other variations in mode will be due to the nature of the functional activity. Marketing departments tend to be strong on planning, and most of the best examples of a planning approach to strategy come from marketing. Personnel departments have traditionally been adaptive, although the human resources movement seeks to replace that with planning. For research and development to bear fruit, it is usually necessary to foster an entrepreneurial mode, with individual researchers following their hunches in their own idiosyncratic ways. There are other mixtures with, for instance, some parts of purchasing being entrepreneurial while others are adaptive.

Quinn (1980) demonstrates that the fusion of the three modes, especially planning and adaptive, is often found in organisations following a practice that he calls logical incrementalism, whereby the top management has a clear plan and set of objectives for where the organisation should be moving, but is unable or unwilling to impose that plan rigidly on everyone else. Moving the organisation in the way they think it should go is then a series of nudges and shoves. If a section begins moves in a direction that is consistent with the overall strategy, then top management reinforces those developments by allocation of resources or some formalisation and extension of the corporate plan in that direction. When a section begins moves in a direction inconsistent with the overall plan, then top management may adapt, by modifying their plan or waiting, or they may take an entrepreneurial approach by trying to change the new initiative. The advances are logical, but in small, incremental steps.

| REVIEW TOPIC 4.2 |

Consider one or two organisations of which you have experience and decide which strategy formulation mode they are in. Is it the right one? What circumstances might make a change necessary?

Strategic planning

Strategic planning is about a clear sense of direction and focusing on where the business is going. Although obvious, this simple clarification and possible change in emphasis can have a profound effect, for instance, when the Canadian Pacific Railway management decided that they were not solely in the business of running a railway but in the business of transportation. From that clear sense of direction can stem specific objectives, the collation of necessary information, the anticipation of problems and the assessment of strengths, weaknesses and opportunities.

The planning process is basically concerned with the following questions:

- Where are we now?
- Where do we want to be?
- How do we get there?
- How are we doing?

Utilising this framework, strategic and business planning can be undertaken. There are of course many more sophisticated models of strategic management: see Moore (1992) for a useful summary of these. Planning can be for immediate, this year, changes. It can also be for longer-term prospects such as developing a service over five years.

Porter (1980, 1985) developed his classic model (see Figure 4.2) to describe the five forces of competition which make up the environment of an organisation. Strategic management is then mostly about trying to defend the organisation from these forces or trying to influence them. The balance between them will vary over time, place and circumstance. For example legislation on pollution may well prohibit new entrants (top box) to the business so not increasing the competition, whereas a reduction in the number of buyers (right-hand box) for foodstuffs because of large supermarket groups reduces the price that food-producing companies can charge. Both of these would affect the strategy of businesses in these markets.

A typical sequence for the planning process is:

- Establish the 'mission'
- Internal and external analysis
- Setting objectives
- Developing workable strategies
- Integration of the plan

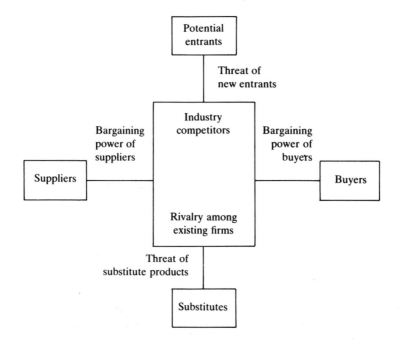

Figure 4.2 The five forces of competition defined by Porter (1980, 1985).

- Providing appropriate controls
- Evaluation measures.

There are dangers in an over-emphasis on strategic planning, which can become the purpose of the business rather than an aid to running the business. Thought is no substitute for action, plans are not an alternative to operations, and analysis can aid but never replace judgement.

The strategy development process is one in which top management decision-makers tend to surround themselves with young, sharp thinkers. The young advisers focus on the ideas and aspirations of their bosses and this can insulate the bosses from the everyday realities of the business. There is the possibility of becoming so rational in decision-making that only safe courses of action are pursued and opportunities lost or elementary errors made. In the 1960s a British company went to considerable trouble to estimate the future home demand for refrigerators. Their forecasting and strategy were accurate, with one exception: they developed production facilities to meet the total demand, allowing no scope for competing companies.

Currently the advantages probably outweigh the disadvantages for most types of business, but there are notes of caution being sounded by those who feel that entrepreneurial flair can be stifled by over-preoccupation with analysis (for example, Peters and Austin, 1985). It is also one of the well-known paradoxes of strategic management (see Quinn, 1980, or Lindblom, 1959) that large, well-managed organisations change their strategies in small ways quite different from the prescriptions found in the management literature.

The nature of strategy in managing with people

Because of the emphasis on analysis and precision there is a tendency to concentrate on economic data and overlook the way in which people and their values can influence the implementation – or failure to implement – a chosen strategy:

> Corporate strategy is . . . concerned with what people want organisations to do . . . the aspirations, expectations, attitudes and personal philosophies which people hold.
> (Johnson and Scholes, 1984, p. 116)

This can affect strategy in different ways, depending on both the aspirations and expectations of those inside the organisation and of those outside. A move for an organisation to trade on Sundays would, for instance, depend partly on the attitudes of customers to opening on Sundays and partly on the attitudes of employees. Customers might boycott or move their custom elsewhere; employees might refuse to work on Sundays unless paid double or triple time. The level of this feeling might be insignificant in relation to other benefits, or it might be sufficient to warrant the abandonment of the strategy.

Some of the constraining values are made manifest in law, while others have to be sensed by the management in interpreting a number of signals from those interested in what the organisation is doing. With the increasing number of pressure groups expressing various types of social concern, there are many issues of management strategy that come under public strategy, from the dumping of nuclear waste and the handling of radioactive emissions to the methods of selling timeshare apartments. One reaction to this public interest has been the establishment of codes of conduct for businesses in specific industrial sectors, such as the Association of British Travel Agents and the National House Builders' Registration Council.

Inside the business the values to constrain strategy are manifest most obviously in trade union organisations, but also in professional groupings (like surgeons in hospitals or pilots in an airline) and coalitions of interest which develop, particularly in response to perceived threat. This type of internal issue is dealt with in our chapter on organisational politics. The interest in organisational culture is an attempt to get a closer fit between the values of the various stakeholders in the business and the objectives of that business. Strategy is one expression of how that fit is achieved; policy is another.

Why bother with policies?

Often managers regard policies as encumbrances, curtailing their necessary freedom of action to make difficult decisions in rapidly changing circumstances. Here is a typical comment from a stock allocator in a retail chain:

> Policy is just an excuse for a jack-in-office to tell me what I cannot do and to slow down the implementation of what I have to do. My section is expanding fast and we have agreement for the recruitment of two new girls. We have the budget, we are hellishly busy, but we cannot recruit yet because of 'policy'. I have had to send explanatory memos to three different people at head office, my draft advertisements have been sent back for revision because I used the word 'her' once. I know that was a mistake, but as a woman I get really pissed off when some middle-aged male ticks me off in a sarky way for breaching the equal opportunity policy. We want to get on and do things. Policy just holds you back.

Policies are problematic for the policy-maker as well. If your policy does not work, you are incompetent; if your policy works but is unpopular, then your enemies try to undermine it; if your policy works and is accepted, you will have little chance of changing it. Why bother? Why not treat each case on its merits? Here are some reasons:

1. *Policy can introduce change.* Many aspects of organisational life are bounded by precedent, which is the *de facto* policy when there is no other guideline. In the field of industrial relations precedent, or custom and practice, has been so influential as to be regarded as a set of rules (Flanders, 1967, p. 70), carrying as much weight as collective agreements and being extremely difficult to change. In all areas of employment and management practice there is a strong tendency for things to be done the way they always have been done and any individual manager will find this dependence on precedent hard to fight. Getting agreement to a new policy is the best way of breaking out of that reliance on past practice.
2. *Policy makes a manager's position clear.* If the amount of responsibility to be carried by subordinates is to increase, there need to be clear guidelines for the delegation of that responsibility. When policy is explicit it becomes a significant element in making that delegation possible. Also managers regularly seek endorsement of their strategies from colleagues, by getting their budgets approved or their plans accepted. In making this type of bid a statement of policy on how, as well as for what, the money is to be used increases the strength of the case.
3. *Policy can make the management's position clear.* Members of organisations increasingly want to be supplied with information, especially about management intentions for the future regarding security of employment and career prospects. Policy statements on notification of vacancies, trade union recognition, consultation on redundancy and so forth partly meet those expectations.

4. *Policy can produce consistent managerial behaviour.* Policy provides a useful discipline for managers as they have to behave in a consistent way, avoiding capricious changes in direction and bewildering their colleagues. Consistent behaviour is not the same as creative action and any manager needs both. Some grumble about the need to behave consistently, feeling that it blunts their creative drive, but they soon find that a policy framework prevents them from wasting time and energy working out new solutions to problems that have already been solved, and enables them to concentrate initiative and imagination where they are really needed.

5. *Policy shapes the response to imposed change.* Frequently organisations are faced with changes being dumped on them from outside, and managers then await policy guidance so that they know what to do. When a new piece of legislation is introduced on, for example, maximum working hours, managers will receive information about what the legislation intends, but they will await an organisational initiative before taking any action. 'How are we going to respond to this change?' If there is no policy guidance, there will be no management initiative until a crisis occurs.

6. *Policy can reduce dependence on individuals.* In Chapter 14 we examine different types of organisation structure and culture. The entrepreneurial form described there is heavily dependent on the person at the centre, with all initiative stemming from the centre and the actions of individual managers bounded by their reliance on precedent and guessing what the spider at the centre of the web wants. When that ceases to be a viable way of operating, policy development is a way of making the functioning of the business less dependent on that single source of power, wisdom and judgement. At a more prosaic level organisational functioning can become over-dependent on 'treasures' and 'founts of wisdom':

> Mary is marvellous at controlling the debtors. She keeps it all in her head and we'd be lost without her. She really is a treasure.

> Frank has a system all of his own, which no-one else can understand – he makes sure of that! – so he is the fount of all wisdom on salaries.

Splendid individuals are no substitute for sound policies.

| REVIEW TOPIC 4.3 |

To what extent can sound policies be a substitute for splendid individuals?

Policy-making

Goals are put into practice through policies and procedures. One of the current approaches is through TQM (Total Quality Management) – see Chapter 7. This is a systems approach that goes as far back in the delivery chain as possible to ensure a consistent and appropriate approach. A useful exercise in trying for a quality service is to look at things from the customer's perspective rather than with the organisation's needs being paramount. For example, nurses develop 'Nursing Standards' which detail the way in which particular procedures will be done, but they also embody the policy of the particular hospital, directorate and ward towards patients.

Hugh Parker (1970) gives the following list of overall functions concerned with policy formulation:

1. To establish the longer-term objectives of the company, and the basic strategies for their attainment.
2. To define the specific policies (finance, personnel, marketing and the like) to be followed in implementing the company's strategies.
3. To decide the organizational structure of the company's management, and to appoint individuals to fill key positions in it.
4. To develop management planning, information, and control systems appropriate to the organizational structure of the company, and to use these systems effectively to ensure control by the board at all times over the results produced by the executive management.
5. To take decisions on 'such matters' as the Articles of Association may reserve to the Board (e.g. payment of dividends, disposal of corporate assets, appointments to the Board), or that the Board in its own discretion decides not to delegate (e.g. capital projects above a certain amount, diversification into a new business).

The nature of policy in managing with people

Although policies are to be found in all parts of the business, we focus here on those relating to the employment and deployment of people, which have a variety of names, such as personnel policy, human resources policy, employment policy, and industrial relations policy, although manpower policy appears to be the most widely used. The danger of slack thinking in this area is demonstrated by Sheila Rothwell:

> Too often policy is in reality a set of free-floating personnel policies, often developed in the '60s and '70s, most of which continue regardless, unconnected with each other or the business plan. For example, ruthless redundancies may take place (when a long-term gradual reduction in line with business needs might have been implemented relatively painlessly) while benefit policies encouraging long service remain in existence. (Rothwell, 1984, p. 31)

In examining policy statements from companies, one is baffled by their infinite variety and frequent meaninglessness:

> It is our policy to offer attractive terms and conditions of employment, to be a fair employer of highly-motivated people within a successful business.

This exemplifies the danger of policy statements that are so bland that they merely state the obvious. How many companies do not want highly motivated people, and how many do not want to run a successful business? For that matter, how many would publicly state their intention to offer unattractive terms and conditions? This trap is caused by two problems: first, the reluctance to be tied by specific commitments, and secondly, the need to give scope for individual managers to interpret policy for application in particular circumstances rather than having their hands tied completely.

> No action will be taken if an officer is up to five minutes late in arriving for duty. Those arriving beween six and fourteen minutes late should fill in form L2, have it countersigned by the supervisor and lodge it at the Personnel office before 12 noon. Those arriving more than fourteen minutes late should report to the supervisor, who will deliver a verbal warning.

As well as being apparently designed for a robot penitentiary, the problem with that excerpt from a policy statement is that it is not policy at all but procedure, which is the drill to implement some part of policy. We have a separate chapter on procedures and it is always helpful for the manager to distinguish clearly between these two quite different ways of making things happen.

Increasingly policy frameworks are being introduced that avoid the rigidity of collective agreements without involving the licence of unfettered managerial judgement. This can improve manpower utilisation at the same time as providing scope for individual employees to have some flexibility in their personal working arrangements.

Despite the decline in trade union assertiveness in the 1980s, very few organisations have withdrawn recognition and most have a series of formal agreements and regular dealings with union officials. This is an area where policy cannot be avoided and where it is most valuable, the alternative being reliance on custom and practice.

> Custom and practice may arise . . . from management acceptance of informal unilateral work practices developed by work groups or from an isolated management decision which employees regard as binding on future decisions in similar circumstances.   (Salaman, 1987, p. 37)

Gradually companies are developing radical employee relations policies which are designed to alter the fundamental nature of the employment relationship away from a conflict base to a cooperative base, involving strategies on employees in the management decision-making process and harmonisation of employment conditions between different categories of employee (see, for example, Roberts, 1985).

A special type of policy is on equal opportunity. Logically this type of equality is an integral part of all other policies, but legislation and the activities of pressure groups have tended to single out this area as one needing separate treatment, laying strong emphasis on policy as the way to bring about change. The strength of this emphasis can be measured by the fact that a survey of manpower and personnel policy statements from forty different organisations showed that approximately half of all the words were on this topic. In five cases the equal opportunity policy was the only one.

Whatever the policies may be, they need to be related to the corporate plan or strategy, so that the policy frames actions that are going to take place instead of actions that used to take place.

Formulating and implementing policy

Copying another organisation's policy is attractive as it has presumably proved successful in that context, so why bother reinventing the wheel? Unfortunately it may be the wrong type of wheel, even though the principles may be exactly right. Like most aspects of effective management, policy formulation requires diligence, care and time. If a policy is adopted independently of issues relevant to the organisation, and not seen by members of the organisation as relevant to those issues, then commitment is unlikely and failure is probable.

Policy is valueless without action to make it work. There will be no action without a commitment both to the policy and to the measures to implement the policy by those who can make it work. Those who can make policy work are not only managers holding key positions, however essential their commitment is. A policy decision that all vacancies will be filled only after internal advertisement will not succeed until prospective applicants know, understand and believe in the change, so that they apply for posts instead of disregarding the advertisements in the belief that it is only 'going through the motions' and that the appointee will be approached and asked to apply after the formalities have been completed.

Arthur Chisholm is the personnel controller in a mail order company with a majority of women workers. Believing that more women should progress to supervisory and management positions, he prepared a draft policy statement on equal opportunity that was discussed with shop stewards, fellow managers and the Equal Opportunities Commission. All accepted the statement and it was duly put up on noticeboards. After a year there was very little change and Arthur's attitude was of some mild irritation that he had taken a lot of trouble to no avail, and: 'Well, at least we've got it, so I'm covered if there is any criticism. Nobody can say I didn't try and we will carry on regardless.'

It is convoluted reasoning to regard a policy as satisfactory when it has had no effect. Arthur Chisholm could have advised Pontius Pilate.

We suggest the following outline procedure for formulating and implementing policy.

1. *Identify the topic.*   Events make a specific policy initiative timely. The equal value modifications to the Equal Pay Act produced a flurry of

policy moves relating to job evaluation and payment, and there are many examples of legislation stimulating policy formulation. Another type of event making the time ripe for a particular topic is management strategies, like a decision to introduce shiftworking or extend the range of the performance appraisal scheme. Other events calling for policy clarification are unexpected changes, uncertainties about the future and questions from managers asking how they should approach a particular matter. There is little prospect of a successful initiative unless there is stimulus to give it priority in people's eyes.

As well as being identified as timely, the policy topic must also be clearly defined. If appraisal interviews are being introduced, is this part of a policy on selection, or promotion, or staff development, or performance assessment?

2. *Win provisional support.* Policies need supporters. Key allies recruited early start the processes of both political commitment to the idea and practical contribution to the policy itself. Preliminary consultation and testing of reaction may cause the initiative to be abandoned or deferred, but if it is worth pursuing its value will become clear at this stage. The supporters of the policy need to confer both with those having sufficient political influence in the organisation to make eventual acceptance likely, and with those having sufficient expertise to offer constructive suggestions.

3. *Decide the key elements.* A policy will succeed or fail because of its two or three central features. In working out the arrangements for personnel travelling overseas, for instance, the class of air travel, the style of accommodation and the level of maintenance allowance will be crucial features of its success. Careful consultation at this stage ensures that the policy is developing in a way that deals with real issues rather than academic issues.

4. *Work out the details.* Policies always require interpretation, and interpretation hinges on the details. In observing the processes of international negotiations it is interesting to see how key elements and details interact. In sorting out how to reorganise the world after the Second World War, Churchill, Roosevelt and Stalin had several historic meetings, and their sessions were of two types. First were the 'three-only' meetings where the three men met alone with interpreters to decide the broad measures; then there were the full meetings of all the advisers to sort out the details. These took much longer and many matters agreed by the leaders in outline were referred back because of problems with detail. More recently negotiations on the limitation of nuclear weapons seem to have followed a similar path. Details of policy require as much care and consultation as the key elements.

5. *Win agreement.* Policy can work only with commitment. Following on the careful consultation and advice so far, there is a policy statement that

has supporters of its key elements and details. That support has now to be extended to win the agreement of most, if not all, of those affected.

6. *Implement and publicise.*   If the policy is to work it must be understood by those affected by it. Some of this will have been achieved by the stages of formulation, but now many others will have to be briefed, with their questions answered and their understanding developed. Not everyone will welcome the initiative as it will involve them in changing some aspect of what they do.

> Sometimes it seems as though a great many talented people are wasting an awful lot of time . . . they develop sensible, well-thought-out policies that would make their company one of the most progressive and highly respected of employers. And then they see their efforts continually frustrated and subverted by a management team that seems determined to ignore most of what the personnel department does.
>
> (Brewster and Richbell, 1982)

Why do they 'seem determined to ignore . . .'? That apparent determination needs to be deflected and one means towards deflection is making sure that people are briefed so that they understand as well as know about the policy.

7. *Have the procedures ready.*   Policy is implemented by procedures and drills. If a new safety policy has an element requiring the completion of an accident reporting form, the form must be ready and available at the same time as the policy is promulgated.

8. *Monitor the outcome.*   Innovations require nurture. In the early stages there will be accidental or deliberate breaches of the policy's intentions. Some people will forget what they are supposed to be doing, others will run into problems that had not been envisaged. If these problems can be picked up and resolved quickly, the policy will be strengthened, otherwise inconsistent strategies will develop from various quarters and the necessary reasonable consistency will be lost.

Soon the policy will need to be updated to suit changing circumstances and to create fresh opportunities. Having broken the mould of custom and practice it is important that another mould does not set too hard, inhibiting change and curbing initiative.

Does it have to be written down?

So far everything in this chapter has implied that the policy is written and publicised. The obvious reasons for this are to meet the main objectives of policy-making that have been set forth, but many managers hesitate to put policy in writing for fear of being trapped with a commitment to actions which later become difficult to sustain. Your reaction may be 'Well, they would, wouldn't they?' but whatever we say in the last paragraph about updating, written commitments are difficult to change and are sometimes formulated without sufficient thought for the future. Reluctance to put things in writing can produce behaviour that is devious or difficult to understand. Did President Reagan authorise the sale of armaments to Iran in 1986 or not? The widespread belief that President Nixon did authorise the Watergate break-in is based largely on an interpretation of what he did not say on the so-called Watergate tapes.

---| REVIEW TOPIC 4.4 |--

Which of the following policies do you think should be written down:

1. A policy of not using certain newspapers for recruitment advertising because of their party political allegiance.
2. A policy not to purchase goods and services from specific suppliers because of their apparent support for a particular political regime, like apartheid.
3. A policy of senior managers receiving a higher standard rate of subsistence than other managers while travelling on company business.

There is a case for some policies not to be written down, partly because the issues that will shape the policy have not become sufficiently clear so that there is no more than a tentative policy to deal with the present situation, and partly because some policies are confidential and their disclosure could disadvantage the business. A policy not to recognise a trade union, for instance, is not likely to be publicised. Brewster and Richbell (1982) make an interesting distinction between policies which are 'espoused' and those which are 'operational'. The first are officially endorsed, usually in writing; the second are the policies which managers actually follow. Sometimes there is no difference between the two; there are often slight variations and occasionally marked differences, but it is only the operational policies that are of value. Those that are espoused but not operational either are ignored or become a basis for criticising managers who are not doing what they should do.

This section of our book is about Goals and in this chapter we have concentrated on the rational approach to strategy and policy making. Of course reality is never this clear and predictable – thank goodness, otherwise we would all be robots. Like everything else in organisational life, strategy and policy-making are affected by the balance of power between various groups and individuals, the unexpected consequences of plans and the daily influences at play at work. We cover these aspects in our sections on Uncertainties and People. It is the balance between having clear ideals and goals whilst accepting that reality is different which is the art of managing.

SUMMARY PROPOSITIONS

4.1 There are no clear, generally accepted definitions of the difference between policy and strategy.

4.2 Normally strategy is linked to planning what to do, while policy forms the framework within which everyday matters are carried forward.

4.3 Modes of formulating strategy are either entrepreneurial, adaptive or planning.

4.4 Strategic planning can improve the effectiveness of a business by clarifying direction and improving the rationality of decisions, but it may impede entrepreneurial flair.

4.5 The benefits of clear policies are that they increase the likelihood of introducing change, clarify issues, engender consistent management behaviour and make the organisation less dependent on individuals.

4.6 Policies that are copied uncritically from other organisations are rarely effective, as they were designed for a different situation.

4.7 The steps in formulating and implementing policy are identifying the topic, winning provisional support, deciding the key elements, working out the details, winning agreement, publicising, having the procedures ready, and monitoring the outcome.

4.8 Policies are not always in writing, either through being only partly developed or through being confidential.

PUTTING IT INTO PRACTICE

Obtain a policy document relating to some aspect of managing with people in an organisation. This could be one published where you work, part of the company handbook of a business to which you once applied for employment, or part of the annual statement to shareholders.

1. What is the policy intended to achieve?
2. How successful is it likely to be? Why?
3. How could it be improved? If you can think of ways to improve it, why did the authors not do it that way in the first place?
4. Rewrite and develop the policy, together with the associated outline procedures, as suggested in the section on formulating and implementing policy.

References

Brewster, C. and Richbell, S., 1982, Getting managers to implement personnel policies, *Personnel Management*, December.

Flanders, A., 1967, *Collective Bargaining: A Prescription for Change*, Faber & Faber, London.

Johnson, G. and Scholes, K., 1984, *Exploring Corporate Strategy*, Prentice Hall International, Hemel Hempstead, Hertfordshire.

Kay, J., 1993, *Foundations of Corporate Success: How Business Strategies Add Value*, Oxford University Press.

Lindblom, C. G., 1959, The science of muddling through, *Public Administration Review*, American Society for Public Administration, vol. 19, Spring, pp. 79–88.

Mintzberg, H., 1973a, *The Nature of Managerial Work*, Prentice Hall, Englewood Cliffs, New Jersey.

Mintzberg, H., 1973b, Strategy-making in three modes, *California Management Review*, vol. 16, no. 2, pp. 44–53.

Mintzberg, H., Quinn, J. B. and James, R. M., 1988, *The Strategy Process – Concepts, Contexts and Cases*, Prentice Hall, Englewood Cliffs, New Jersey.

Moore, J. I., 1992, *Writers on Strategy and Strategic Management*, Penguin Books, Harmondsworth, Middlesex.

Parker, H., 1970, in *Managing the Managers: the Role of the Board in the Arts of Top Management*, ed. Mann, R., McGraw-Hill, London.

Peters, T. and Austin, N., 1985, *A Passion for Excellence: The Leadership Difference*, Random House, New York.

Porter, M. E., 1980, *Competitive Strategy: Techniques for Analyzing Industries and Competitors*, Free Press, New York.

Porter, M. E., 1985, *Competitive Advantage: Creating and Sustaining Superior Performance*, Free Press, New York.

Quinn, J. E., 1980, *Strategies for Change: Logical Incrementalism*, Irwin, Homewood, Ill.

Roberts, C. (ed.), 1985, *Harmonization: Whys and Wherefores*, Institute of Personnel Management, London.

Rothwell, S., 1984, Integrating the elements of a company employment policy, *Personnel Management*, November, pp. 30–3.

Salaman, M., 1987, *Industrial Relations: Theory and Practice*, Prentice Hall International, Hemel Hempstead, Hertfordshire.

Stoner, J. A. F. and Wankel, C., 1986, *Management*, 3rd edn, Prentice Hall, Englewood Cliffs, New Jersey.

Thompson, A. A. and Strickland, A. J., 1990, *Strategic Management: Concept and Cases*, Irwin, Homewood, Ill.

Chapter 5

Resource management

Oakhill Hospital Trust has seven operating theatres. Every surgeon was allocated various half-day sessions in the theatres through the week. Evenings, nights and weekends were for emergencies only, with one theatre kept fully staffed at all times and with another group of staff on callout if required. Mr Mehta, the chief anaesthetist, was responsible for running these. He was constantly being nagged by various people. Mr Meadows, one of the orthopaedic surgeons, was frequently frustrated on Wednesday afternoons as Mr Kent, the general surgeon in the morning, always overran his time by several hours. Ms Wynn, one of the gynaecologists, on the other hand was frustrated because she felt she was efficient in always finishing her list early but was under pressure from the director to take more patients. Mr O'Malley, the nurse manager, was worried that his staff never got their breaks or home on time. Ms Davies, the business manager, wondered who was going to pay for all the overtime the nurses, porters and theatre assistants were working. Mr Mehta had his own problems with anaesthetists not turning up for work at short notice, leaving fully staffed theatres with patients waiting without an anaesthetist.

Resource management is one approach to sorting out the various demands at Oakhill Hospital Trust. Resource management is a term widely used in public-sector organisations, particularly since the late 1980s. It represents a systematic, business orientation with an emphasis on information, planning and monitoring. In our example of hospital theatres a resource management approach would mean the following. First, it would mean setting up an information system to record exactly which operations were being done, by whom and how long they took, with what materials and which staff were required. Second, resource management would mean using this information to plan a more appropriate use of the theatres. This might mean setting normal standards for routine operations, charging against individual budgets for serious overruns, making comparisons between surgeons, using the theatres routinely at weekends or not staffing the theatres at weekends unless someone is timetabled to use them. Third, it would mean monitoring the use of theatres routinely.

In the business community resource management is frequently known as Management Information Systems (MIS). We prefer the term resource management as it emphasises why the information is being collected rather than what is being done.

This chapter deals with the information systems. The next chapter deals with the next stage of planning, and Chapter 11 deals with monitoring.

Information systems

An organisation's information systems are its nerves, without which its operating and maintenance systems would not function. Most organisations have now set computers on to the task, for information technology has increased both the capacity and flexibility of information systems. Computer networks stretch laterally as well as vertically through an organisation, so that staff can access information in relation to other parts of the organisation independently from senior management.

Terry Lucey (1987, p. 2) provides us with a useful definition of an MIS:

> A system to convert data from internal and external sources into information and to communicate that information, in an appropriate form, to managers at all levels in all functions to enable them to take timely and effective decisions for planning, directing and controlling the activities for which they are responsible.

Here are some examples we have found when visiting various organisations. The first examples come from within the Health Services:

1. Bed occupancy. Each morning the number of free beds is calculated so that incoming patients can be allocated a bed and free ones offered for emergency cases, so that lack of beds can be dealt with. The percentage of bed occupancy is also used as an indicator of comparative activity.
2. The number and type of cases seen in clinic by each doctor over a year. This was used to demonstrate that some doctors were working a great deal harder than others. Peer pressure was used to improve the performance of the worst doctors.
3. A waiting list for patients that gave information about how many and how long they had been waiting. This was used to invite particular individuals to special clinics.

Examples we have found in commercial firms are:

4. A system to alert staff when a traditional customer has not reordered. This enabled the sales team to contact the customer to find out why.
5. A system to keep track of individual expenses. This allowed the manager

to pick up on the fact that some salespeople's cars are twice as expensive as others to run.

6. A system to keep track of 'no-shows' at an hotel so they can plan for a percentage of overbooking.
7. A supermarket which gets the checkout operators to key in the length of queue every third transaction, so personnel can plan when and how many checkout assistants they should provide.

The design, implementation and operation of an MIS

Developments in information technology have opened up new opportunities for better control, reduced data-processing costs and increased speed of information handling. However, it is important that organisations are not seduced into choosing a certain type of information system on the basis of the attractiveness of the technology.

As in other areas of the organisation, there should be an information strategy, well thought out, formulated, administered and monitored. Formal communications systems in organisations can have an effect on the structure of the organisation, the style of management and the overall direction of the business. The management consultant Arthur Putnam has suggested that a successful business information system is regarded as the 'nervous and response system' of the organisation. The system must therefore be designed and developed to be the servant of the organisation's managers, who should be encouraged to voice their needs and commit themselves to obtaining the system they require. As Stewart (1991, p. 164) says,

> Information needs to be managed. It is the way that IT is used that will be important to competitive success; so management needs to be actively involved. The best information management requires technological compe-tence, an understanding of the work of the organization and its context, and an understanding of how the organization works. It also needs skill in helping people to adapt to change.

An information systems strategy is an equal partner to other organisation-al strategies such as those for finance and investment, or markets and products, or recruitment and training. It is more than just a plan for the use of computers, since it involves a greater understanding and interlinking of organisational processes, management functions, planning and decision-making processes, control principles, and the nature of communications and information flow. Bloomfield and Coombs (1992) discuss the interrela-tionship between information technology (IT), control and power and how these relationships affect the management of resources. Senker and Senker (1992) point out that many companies have failed to secure full benefits from their heavy investment in IT because they have delegated the issue to junior managers who lack the knowledge, experience and authority within the particular organisation. It is this fitting of technology to the particular nature of the organisation which is likely to be the clever trick to really delivering the potential of IT. Much of the criticism of IT has been that companies have invested heavily in IT by automating old, inefficient, functional procedures and have missed the opportunity for reorganising before they invest in IT. This process is sometimes called business re-engineering and is associated with the work of Hammer.

The importance of suitable management of IT was graphically demonstrated by the disastrous introduction of a new computer system to the London Ambulance Service in October 1992. Ambulances were sent all over the place and many people had to wait hours for one to arrive. Two management shortcomings were associated with this failure: poor industrial relations and rushing the new system through despite warnings of a lack of testing and backup.

There are three steps to the process of introducing an MIS: assessment, choice and implementation.

The assessment of MIS requirements

This stage involves gaining an understanding of the information currently existing in the organisation. A useful thing to be carried out initially is an information audit. An audit should establish two things: firstly where the gaps are, and secondly how the information already possessed is handled. Companies can seek outside help on a survey of this kind if they wish. Organisations such as the Advisory, Conciliation and Arbitration Service (ACAS) and the Industrial Society, as well as commercial management consultants, will undertake an audit of information in organisations. During this process, the objectives of the organisation should be reviewed, the strengths and weaknesses of internal resources should be identified, and the opportunities and threats of external issues should be recognised (the familiar SWOT analysis).

One way to look at how information is used is to examine the flow of certain identified pieces of information and plot their progress. This can be done by listing the various recipients of the information along the bottom axis of a graph and showing along the vertical axis the use to which that information is put: see Figure 5.1 for an example of this. Too often it may be seen that the level of usage hovers near the bottom axis, with no real use being made of the information during its passage through the organisation. Once identified, information flows such as this that do not add value can be short-circuited, redesigned or eliminated. The method has been used successfully in a variety of major industrial organisations, and is based on a technique called 'information profiling' developed by Christian Schumacher. His technique is no more than applied common sense, but gives a powerful visual representation of tortuous and inefficient information paths.

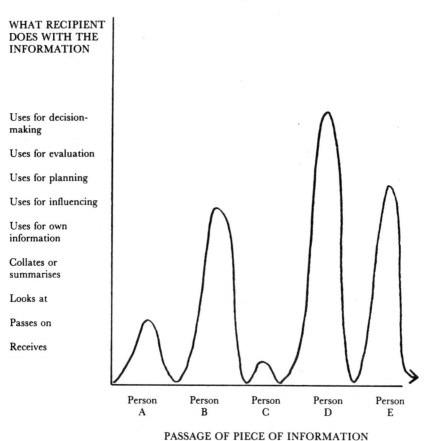

WHAT RECIPIENT
DOES WITH THE
INFORMATION

Uses for decision-
making

Uses for evaluation

Uses for planning

Uses for influencing

Uses for own
information

Collates or
summarises

Looks at

Passes on

Receives

Person | Person | Person | Person | Person
A | B | C | D | E

PASSAGE OF PIECE OF INFORMATION

Figure 5.1 The level of usage of information.

Another way to analyse the organisation's existing information system is to ask the following questions:

1. Does the information it provides satisfy the needs of individuals?
2. Does it enable people to have access when and where required?
3. What would be the effect of losing the information?
4. Is the information based upon data of sufficient accuracy and in a form that can be readily interpreted?
5. Is it easily updated?

Once the existing systems are evaluated by an information audit of this sort, the needs of the new information system are more easily identifiable.

Choosing a management information system

This next stage concerns identifying and evaluating the options available in deciding the shape and nature of the MIS. An integrated management information system, combining electronic data processing, decision support systems and logistical techniques, will probably have four or five primary sub-divisions. The following have been suggested (Putnam, 1980):

Order entry forecasting, marketing and scheduling:
Customer orders, quotations, forecast materials requirements, invoices, sales analyses, engineering specifications.

Material control and capacity planning:
Parts lists, inventories, requisitions, purchase orders, accounts payable, costs, requirements planning, distribution.

Production control:
Stocks, scheduling, workloads, costs, payroll, employee hours.

Accounting control:
Costing data, final costs, income and balance sheet information.

Personnel planning:
Recruitment targets, training plans, salary and pension costs, appraisal data.

These sub-divisions provide information for use by the various functions of the organisation. The weight given to each part of the above will depend on the nature of the organisation's business, its technology, and its corporate strategies.

The right computer system is one which will deliver the greatest improvements in productivity possible for the investment being made, and which will not become obsolete in the reasonably near future. These criteria can be satisfied if a system is chosen which accurately reflects the exact nature of the task, the size of these tasks, the quantity of information to be accessed and transferred, the degree of planning flexibility required to extend the system in the future if necessary, and the available budget in relation to costs and benefits to be gained.

Unfortunately, there is no simple checklist of features to be adopted in order to produce the perfect MIS. Good communication between management and information specialists, both with a real understanding of the principles of information systems, will make the task of developing an appropriate system much easier. As with all decisions, alternative choices have to be identified based on the information gathered during the previous stage, an evaluation has to be made, and a final path chosen. Fairbairn's (1982) Ten-point Plan for the selection of a system runs as follows:

(i) Needs are defined.
(ii) Alternatives to computer applications are examined.
(iii) Quantities in relation to file size, time scales and access requirements are defined.
(iv) Software is explored.
(v) Hardware alternatives are considered.
(vi) Software and hardware are evaluated.
(vii) Expansion capability is considered.

(viii) Suppliers are compared.
 (ix) Support and maintenance is considered.
  (x) Installation is scheduled.

The complexity of information technology in relation to the hardware, software, interrelated processes, documentation and program development, and the increasing number of suppliers and systems available, preclude us from describing specific systems in this book. There are a variety of sources of advice available. Details of many of these may be found in publications such as the Department of Trade and Industry's Technical Services for Industry.

The Government has also established Microsystems Centres in various parts of the United Kingdom in collaboration with the National Computing Centre, which offer training and consultancy as well as impartial advice and guidance, with no commercial links with the trade. The British Computer Society in London is a source of information on information systems, and there are other such professional associations. Commercial consultancy is not cheap, but compared to the cost of getting the MIS wrong, it may be worthwhile.

Implementation of an MIS

Many organisations, especially large ones, will have a management services section or information section. This consists of information, communication and computing specialists grouped in a central service division, for the specific purpose of providing an advisory and consultancy service to managers at all levels in the organisation. Such a group would have a vital role in seeking out new ideas, introducing new techniques and smoothly implementing changes to the information system within the company.

The introduction of a sophisticated communication system in an organisation may be met with scepticism or resistance. It is often the lack of top management involvement at the outset which is a key reason for the failure to develop systems which meet operating criteria. Substantial top management attention is needed at the start since the MIS network cuts across all departmental boundaries. The time and cost taken to install and convert existing equipment and programs are often underestimated: programming is a specialised technical task, installation of equipment involves satisfying space and structural requirement in offices, and there may have to be a period for the parallel running of old and new systems – a disastrous omission when the London Ambulance Service failed to do this before introducing a new integrated system in 1992. Training must be provided for personnel at all levels in the organisation, both before and after the introduction of a new information system.

Apart from commitment from top management, there are other criteria for success. A management information system must be understood by the manager – it must be simple and easy to communicate with, and inspire confidence in its output. It must also be perceived as useful – it must be complete in key areas, logical, easy to update, and controllable. Einstein once said, 'Everything should be made as simple as possible, but not simpler'.

The nature of information

To have an understanding of management information systems, it is important to have an understanding of the nature of information flow in organisations. Chapter 15, Organisational Communication, discusses the various formal and informal channels of communication in organisations. Informal information networks are flexible and ideally suited to catering for problems at a local level, so that informal and formal systems both have a contribution to make.

Formal systems start off with data. However, data is not information, and information is not necessarily communication. 'Data is an amount of numeric or quantitative notions which needs to be coded, processed or interpreted in order to become qualitative concepts and ideas forming the basis of information. Even then', says Peter Drucker (1977), 'information is logical, rigid and impersonal – almost the complete opposite of the requirements for effective communication.' Computers issue vast amounts of data, but someone must have the responsibility for checking not only that they are producing useful information, but also that there is a carefully thought out and systematic creation of communication opportunities amongst the various users. The meaning of the information depends on the perceptions, expectations and rules established for its interpretation. The following example illustrates this. The lookout on the boat signals for dangerous rocks by pointing in an appropriate direction. Depending on the perception of the person steering the boat, the lookout could be pointing either to the rock, or in the direction which the boat must be steered to avoid the rock. The signal has a meaning and is information, but there is no reliable communication unless the rules for its interpretation are clear.

We rarely communicate as effectively as we think we do. There are factors such as perceptual bias, distortion of the message, lack of clarity, lack of trust, distance and status which act as blockages. Handy (1981, p. 356) admits that, in view of all these blockages, 'it is perhaps worth admiring the fact that any sensible communication takes place at all'.

Levels of information

Bob Tricker, who has done much work on information management in organisations, also considers information to be at various levels (1982, Chapter 2):

(a) Basic data – raw data, facts and figures. These are the building blocks which contain the potential information, but which require processing.
(b) Information as message – aggregated and analysed data and reports. The needs of the potential recipient or user of the message are not identified since this level provides standard information for a multitude of users.
(c) Valuable information. The user derives meaning from the data, increases his/her knowledge, and reduces his/her uncertainty. The individual user's role and expectations are crucial to the meaning derived.

There is little use in providing far more sophisticated information systems and more reports if managers consequently feel less aware of what is going on than they did before.

REVIEW TOPIC 5.1

'What I need is information and all they give me are reports.' (Tricker, 1982, p. 20.) How do we turn data into information?

The value of information

The value of information rests upon the results of decisions and actions based on that information. Data is costly to obtain, so that there is a cost/benefit trade-off, as shown in Figure 5.2. Value is acquired only with information which is properly communicated and used. It should not be assumed that more information, in more detail and sooner, is always better. Decision-makers rarely have all the information they feel they need, but at some point the search for more information is subject to the law of diminishing returns; the real limit is the point in a given situation where you judge that the cost in time and money of obtaining more information becomes too high.

What makes information relevant

Lucey (1987, Chapter 2) provides us with a guide in the search for what constitutes useful and relevant information.

1. *Timely.* Information should arrive in time for it to be useful, and concerning periods of time which are relevant. Similarly, too frequent or too rapid information may be unnecessary and a waste of resource. For example, information regarding stock levels will probably be required at more immediate and frequent intervals than feedback on research progress.
2. *Appropriate.* Firstly, energy should be put where it matters. Only in important areas should rigorous information be produced. If labour

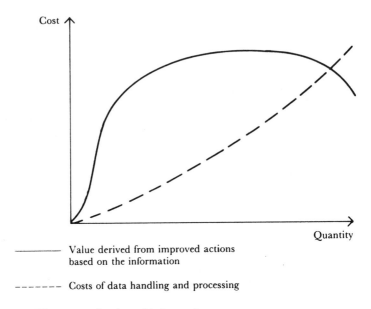

—————— Value derived from improved actions
based on the information

‒ ‒ ‒ ‒ ‒ ‒ Costs of data handling and processing

Figure 5.2   The cost and value of information.

turnover is not deemed to be as critical as, say, a continued supply of
fresh ideas into certain parts of the organisation, then information on
turnover is inappropriate. Second, information requirements will be
different at different levels in the hierarchy (see Figure 5.3) and in
different functions. Ward sisters and health workers will require different
information from the general manager or the finance director.
3. *Accuracy and detail.*   The level of accuracy must be relevant to the
decision level involved. More detail does not always provide a more
effective aid to decision-making. If accurate detail is required, it must be
reliable. Information should always relate to objectives; it must not
convey trivial facts. Information to be used for long-term planning
purposes will usually be less detailed, and it may be that absolute figures
are less important than trends up or down. Table 5.1 shows the different
characteristics of planning, control and decision-making information.
4. *Understandable.*   Over-complicated information only confuses. The style
and format presented to the user by the information designer must be
such that energy is not wasted in repeatedly trying to work it all out.
5. *Operational.*   Information should be directed towards action, and should
be passed to those with authority and responsibility to do something with
it, or to those with a legitimate interest. This should include office
workers, supervisors, team briefing groups and quality circles, as well as
senior managers.

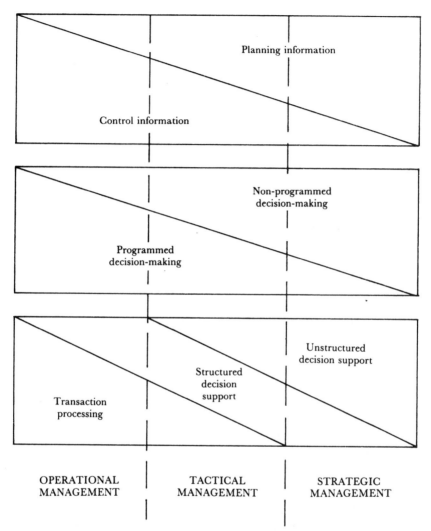

Figure 5.3 Types of information required at different levels of management.

┤ REVIEW TOPIC 5.2 ├

Tricker has suggested that organisations risk 'paralysis by analysis' (1982, p. 20). What can be done to avoid this?

Information, feedback and team briefing

Information and feedback are inextricably linked. Managers are advised to discuss plans and projects with their subordinates, report the bad news as

Table 5.1 Different types of information for planning, control and decision-making

	Level of detail	Timescale	Coverage	Focus
Planning	Patterns and trends	Long time periods	Whole organisation	Insights into future
Control	Detail and precision but also trends	Short time periods	Specific functions or managers	Relating past results to targets
Decision-making	Detailed or broad as required	As appropriate	Everything potentially affected	Future changes

(Adapted from Lucey, 1987)

well as the good, and provide information directly, honestly, and constantly. Indeed, the 1982 Employment Act places an obligation on organisations to provide employees systematically with information on matters of concern to them, and to seek a common awareness amongst staff of factors affecting the performance of the company. The Industrial Society is a strong proponent of the practice of team briefing, where employees have decisions affecting their jobs or conditions of employment explained to them face to face by their immediate boss in a systematic communication drill, rather than in a memo from the director. At the operations level, information of local relevance should comprise at least two-thirds of the information passed on the briefing session.

Briefing sessions should have an individually prepared written brief, a briefing folder should be kept, and notes should be taken, in order that the passing on of items of information is not casually left to chance. The four main groups of subjects covered in briefing sessions concern the four Ps – progress (how the section is doing), people (joiners, leavers, internal moves), policy (recruitment and training, safety, output and productivity, terms and conditions), and points for action (priorities in the coming period). See Garnett (1983) for more details of team briefing.

The passage of information is thus an essential part of the decentralisation of decision-making in organisations. An organisation can strengthen its resources by moving the decision-making down to where the information exists, rather than taking information up to the point of decision. This will invariably result in conflict, but this may be a good thing since it can result in a greater sharing of information, more contact with the problem, the voicing of preferences and the seeking of new alternatives. Good quality information can lessen uncertainty.

There is, of course, an enormous potential for the abuse and manipulation of information in organisations, since its communication is seldom either totally objective or neutral. However, the danger of the immoral use of information is lessened if that information focuses on results – on the effect of actions rather than on the effort put into them; that is, on effectiveness rather than on efficiency.

Information overload

Organisations with a high degree of uncertainty in what they do, because of either increased competition or technical change, or diversification, or the large division of labour and hence number of specialist departments, or an increase in performance standards, normally find they have to handle a vast amount of information in order to lessen that uncertainty. Computers especially have increased our capacity to generate information and there has been an information explosion. Overload can be avoided in various ways. Galbraith (1977) suggests that organisations can deliberately select one of various strategies to reduce information overload. These are as follows, and they fall into two groups.

1. Reduce the need for information processing through:
   (a) seeking to lessen demands from the environment by managing, manoeuvring or influencing relationships with the environment (e.g. ensuring access to scarce resources, making use of media to influence the environment, seeking cooperation with others in the environment, searching for new environments);
   (b) reducing performance levels and therefore the amount of information processing required;
   (c) creating self-contained tasks, with a reduced division of labour and reduction of cross-functional specialists.
2. Increase capacity to process information by:
   (a) investing in vertical information systems, for example by employing assistants, computers, etc., so that information is collected and redirected to appropriate places in the hierarchy;
   (b) creating lateral resources, decentralising decision-making by allowing direct contact between people who can share problems, or by forming short-term teams or task forces to resolve issues via interdepartmental problem-solving.

Many of these strategies have a cost. For example, with strategy (2b), greater amounts of management time have to be spent in group processes, and more integrating or liaising roles may be required. The organisation must, however, make a choice between these five strategies. Not to decide, says Galbraith, is to fall back upon reduced performance levels, option (1b), as a means of reducing information overload.

REVIEW TOPIC 5.3

Drucker (1977, p. 396) says 'An overload of information leads to information blackout. It does not enrich, but impoverishes.' How is overload avoided?

Restrictions in the knowledge market

In some organisations, there exists an almost complete absence of communication systems and structures. People are totally absorbed with mending their own fences so that their peers in other parts of the company are irrelevant. There are various reasons why information is hoarded rather than shared. Rosabeth Moss Kanter, in her study of innovating companies (1984), cites four groups likely to restrict the flow of information. Firstly, there are the 'time servers' who have virtually retired on the job and who neither receive nor seek information. Second, there are 'defensive cliques' who restrict information to prevent the threat of change. Thirdly, there are 'mutual-aid-and-comfort' groups, who are settled into a comfortable routine and resent their more ambitious colleagues. Finally, there are 'coalitions of the ambitious', who keep information in their own hands to monopolise power. The opening up of the knowledge market in organisations, where information is exchanged openly through both formal and informal channels and support is freely given, can give rise to more innovation.

There also exists the fact that most managers, understandably, prefer to get their information from people rather than machines like computers. Stewart (1986) suggests that this is largely because most managers do not know how to make the best use of computers. There is a debate about whether those who are now familiar with computers will continue to make use of them when they reach senior management, or whether computers can contribute little to top management. We would contend that Management Information Systems are of use, albeit a different kind of use, at all levels in the hierarchy (see Figure 5.3).

Key principles of management information systems

Having described in some detail the nature of information flow in organisations, it is now appropriate to have a look at some of the key principles of information systems. It is only when an understanding is gained of these issues that we can go on to examine practical steps concerning the design, implementation and operation of such systems. This section will look at the various types of information system and their purposes and we will then examine specific uses that various parts of the organisation can make of them.

Types of information system

Management Information Systems did exist before computerisation, but more often than not it has been the introduction of computers into an organisation which has prompted an examination of the way information is handled. Now, an MIS being operated without the aid of information technology, even in the smallest of organisations, is highly unlikely, even inconceivable.

There are various types of system which will be incorporated into a total MIS – and it is this combination of all the elements in a combined package which can potentially turn a random collection of functional databases into a centralised information system. They can broadly be described as follows.

1. Office support systems, such as electronic mail, word processing, microcomputers, VDUs and computer networks, which provide assistance with day-to-day office functions concerning data storage and reference, telecommunications, computing and text handling. We will not describe these in detail here but would comment that the transformation of office work by information technology is influencing the availability and type of information used by managers.

2. Data processing systems, such as accounts, payroll, production control and stock control, which record, process and report on day-to-day activities within the organisation. These types of systems were the first to make use of the power of the computer and they are the building blocks upon which an MIS is built.

3. Decision support systems, such as spreadsheets, forecasting techniques, decision models, linear programming and statistical analyses, which are intended to provide management with assistance in planning and decision-making. The user is able to interact with them and, unlike the data processing systems above, managers develop and communicate with the systems themselves via their own terminals. Such systems provide support for the manager – they do not replace his or her judgement. There is a large range of software packages available in this area, and new ones are being developed all the time.

More detail on all of these can be found in specialist texts on management information systems or information technology which date too quickly for us to suggest references sensibly.

| REVIEW TOPIC 5.4 |

A decision support system is a coordinated collection of data, systems, tools and techniques by which an organisation gathers and interprets relevant information and turns it into a basis for action. Go to your local technical bookshop and find out how many off-the-shelf software packages, for example spreadsheets or decision models, are the subject of new user guides. Are they mainly in the financial field, or the marketing field, or in other areas?

Problems and implications

Many difficulties are encountered by organisations with management information systems, no matter how sophisticated the computer equipment used. Many of the reasons for the failure of MISs to provide management with the information needed have been mentioned during this chapter. These and others are listed below for ease of reference.

1. Lack of support from top management.
2. Absence of management involvement generally with the design of the MIS.
3. Deficiency of knowledge of computers and computer applications amongst managers.
4. Mistaken application of computers and computer systems.
5. Too great an emphasis on low-level data processing applications.
6. Lack of understanding by information specialists of the requirements of management.
7. Insufficient attention to the assessment, choice and implementation stages of MIS design.
8. Absence of an information systems strategy.
9. Insufficient sharing of the philosophy behind the MIS, and little training in its nature and use.
10. Misuse of the information system in the area of control.

There is an inevitable human reaction to change brought about by a new system. People have fears about their status and job satisfaction, they are unsure about changes in organisational boundaries, they distrust systems analysts as well as computers, and they see the new system as a criticism of previous performance. Dr Schumacher states that the 'very exactitude [of computers and computerised problem-solving devices] is a sign of the absence of human freedom, responsibility and dignity' (Schumacher, 1973, p. 199). In order that these fears are allayed, it is necessary at all stages to involve personnel concerned from the beginning, encourage suggestions, contribution, communication and cooperation, make clear statements about job security and organisational changes, and demonstrate that job satisfaction will improve due to the elimination of certain routine work.

| REVIEW TOPIC 5.5 |

In the matter of decisions about the supply of eggs and bacon, the hens are involved but the pigs are committed. What factors might determine the different levels of concern and participation regarding the introduction of a management information system in an organisation?

There are potential problems, too, with the operation of the information system. These may include crises such as fire or flood, loss of power, theft, malfunctioning of equipment or systems, or difficulties such as accidental human error, deliberate misuse, sabotage or fraud. Checks and balances need to be built in to the use of equipment and programs to minimise these eventualities, both on a technical and on a human level.

The organisation also needs to guard against an information system becoming a misused power tool. There is no doubt that information is vital to the exercise of power. Disclosure has become a politically charged concept. There is power not only in what information is released, but in the ability to deprive people of information, especially where that information could be open to challenge or critical in determining the outcome of controversial issues. The 'gatekeeper' function of certain individuals or groups can lead to the control of information being used to increase spheres of influence, whilst the distortion or withholding of information is a common tactic in organisational conflict. Some of these issues are discussed in Chapter 18, Organisational Politics, and in Chapter 19, Authority, Leadership and Autonomy.

The Data Protection Act of 1984 in Britain is intended to limit the potential for misuse of personal information processed on a computer. Areas of exemption include personal data held for the purposes of tax, payrolls, accounts, criminal records, consumer credit and research. A management information system may make use of personal information for training, promotion or manpower planning purposes, and managers should be aware of their legal responsibilities and obligations in this respect.

SUMMARY PROPOSITIONS

5.1 An understanding of the flow of information in organisations is essential to the understanding of management information systems.

5.2 Data is not necessarily information, and information is not necessarily communication.

5.3 Information has a cost and a value. Information must be relevant and its value lies in subsequent results and actions, and not in the information itself.

5.4 Information, feedback and devolution of decision-making are intertwined in an organisation: they can spiral upwards or downwards.

5.5 Organisations have the ability to control the quantity of information and the way information is handled, by either reducing the need for information processing or increasing the capacity of the organisation to process information.

5.6 A management information system is a combination of data processing systems, office support systems and decision support systems. Each function in an organisation can make specific use of these various elements in its planning, decision-making and controlling activities.

5.7 An information system should serve the organisation, not take control of it. An information systems strategy should reflect and develop the corporate plan.

5.8 The three steps in the introduction of a management information system are assessment of requirements, making the choice, and implementation.

5.9 The introduction of a management information system in an organisation is rarely straightforward, but problems can be anticipated and overcome.

| PUTTING IT INTO PRACTICE |

Corporate communications – what happens?

The order in which most employees actually get information about the progress of the company and issues affecting their jobs is as follows:

1. The company newspaper
2. Local briefing meetings
3. The grapevine
4. Their immediate boss
5. The company noticeboard

The way they would prefer to get this information is as follows:

1. Their immediate boss
2. Briefing meetings
3. Department meetings
4. The company newspaper
5. The company noticeboard
6. Staff committees
7. The grapevine

There is some place for the grapevine in the informal information system of an organisation, but on the whole people would prefer to receive their information in a less random, haphazard fashion, whilst still receiving it personally. A vacuum will inevitably be filled by rumour.

Designing a short training course on MIS for managers

Imagine you work in the management services department of an organisation and have been asked to prepare a one-day course for a group of senior managers to inform them about the principles and philosophy of management information systems.

The outline structure of the day might look as follows:

1. The objectives of an MIS in relation to the planning and decision-making activities of the organisation, and the need for information to have a value.
2. How an MIS might be applied in this particular organisation, and to particular functions within it.
3. The three stages of designing, choosing and implementing a new system, and the nature of management involvement during these stages.
4. Summary of training requirements and feedback structures for management and other levels in the organisation.
5. Suggested timetable for implementation.

The contents of an information systems strategy

A written strategy statement might include the following sections:

1. An abstract summary of information systems philosophy, in the context of organisation structure and management style.
2. The nature and purpose of the strategic plan.
3. Description of the current status of information flow in the organisation, and the existing use of computer hardware and software.
4. The projected requirements, purpose and objectives of an integrated information system, as viewed from the users' perspective.
5. The means of fulfilling these requirements, with an examination of the technical and organisational implications.
6. The method and timescales for implementation, together with specific implications in the areas of finance and manpower.
7. How the effectiveness of the system will be evaluated, and how value for money will be judged.

References

Bloomfield, B. P. and Coombs, R., 1992, Information technology, control and power: the centralization and decentralization debate revisited, *Journal of Management Studies*, vol. 29, no. 4, pp. 459–84.

Drucker, P. F., 1977, *Management*, Pan Books, London.

Fairbairn, D., 1982, Chapter 10 in *Rank Xerox, Brave New World?*, MacDonald, London.

Galbraith, J. R., 1977, *Organization Design*, Addison Wesley, Reading, Mass.

Garnett, J., 1983, *Team Briefing*, The Industrial Society, London.

Handy, C. B., 1981, *Understanding Organisations*, Penguin Books, Harmondsworth, Middlesex.

Kanter, R. M., 1984, *The Change Masters*, George Allen & Unwin, London.

Lucey, T., 1987, *Management Information Systems*, 5th edn, DP Publications, Eastleigh, Hampshire.

Putnam, A. O., 1980, *Management Information Systems*, Pitman, London.

Schumacher, E. F., 1973, *Small is Beautiful*, Blond & Briggs, London.

Senker, J. and Senker, P., 1992, Gaining competitive advantage from information technology, *Journal of General Management*, vol. 17, no. 3, Spring, pp. 31–45.

Stewart, R., 1986, *The Reality of Management*, Pan Books, London.

Stewart, R., 1991, *Managing Today and Tomorrow*, Macmillan, Basingstoke, Hampshire.

Tricker, R. I., 1982, *Effective Information Management*, Beaumont Executive Press, Oxford.

Chapter 6

Business plans and budgets

Business plan is the currently preferred term for the plans drawn up before the event, year or launch. Business plans include the financial arrangements and implications of the plans. Previously these were known as budgets. We prefer the term business plans as the emphasis is on the plan and how the figures are reached rather than on just the financial arrangements. We have kept the term budget to refer specifically to amounts of money allocated for specific purposes.

Planning, control and evaluation are major aspects of the task of managing. Much of this activity concerns non-financial questions, such as the achievement of product quality, the provisions of employee welfare facilities, or the performance of sales staff. Other objectives can more easily be expressed in financial terms, and it is the process of translating the expected investment of capital and personnel into financial plans and budgets and the operation of these budgets that concerns us here. As with any control device, business plans set standards and facilitate the measurement of performance against these standards, using results and feedback. Corrective action for any deviations can then be considered. Budgets are the expression, in quantitative terms, of plans for the future, and it is with planning that the budgeting cycle begins (see Figure 6.1).

The purpose of business plans

There are three important purposes served by the business planning process. Firstly, the preparation of the business plan is a planning device; it imposes a duty upon members of departments to quantify their targets and performance levels systematically. Individual departmental plans are then supposed to interlock with each other so that they become a coordinated and comprehensive plan for the whole organisation. Without planned targets, departments' operations can lack direction and results are often meaningless. Too often, the pressures of the moment drive out the

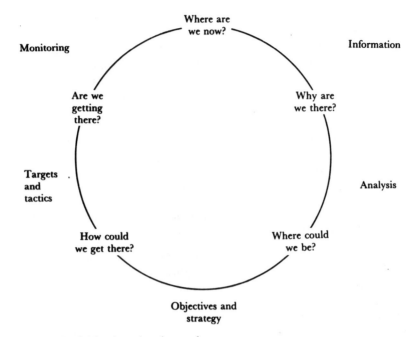

Figure 6.1 The budgeting planning cycle.

importance of looking to the future. A systematic approach, whereby organisational and departmental goals are considered, together with the means of achieving these goals, indicates that business planning is being used to try to manage the organisation for the future.

Secondly, the business plan acts as a controlling and motivating device by expressing expected performance levels which then provide criteria for the judgement of departmental performance. Progress can be compared with the targets to see whether plans are being fulfilled. If monitored expenditures are different from budgeted levels, whether below or above, the manager is alerted. The business plan acts as an early warning device as well as highlighting areas where performance is better than expected, and time and attention can thus be directed to finding out the reason for either underperformance or performance in excess of targets. It is considered that comparisons with past performance are less valid than comparisons with planned performance, since the former perpetuate the inefficiencies of the past, and ignore unrealised potential and intervening changes in technology, competition and economic environment (Horngren, 1982). Business plans, of course, are only a guide towards the achievement of planned objectives. Reality is always different with all sorts of unintended consequences and occurrences. Plans should not be regarded as a straitjacket, and like all control mechanisms should be flexibly and reasonably applied by departmental management.

Thirdly, the business planning process promotes communication and coordination. A departmental business plan highlights operational relationships both within and outside the department, and can help people to broaden their outlooks to include those of others. Equally important, it provides a framework for feedback, as well as clarifying working relationships and responsibilities. It also requires the understanding and support of top management in departmental affairs and aims.

| REVIEW TOPIC 6.1 |

Where do we draw the line between serious adherence to business plans and persevering with them indiscriminately?

The business plan of a hospital for one year sets out their objectives and describes how they propose to pursue them in the year. It incorporates:

- activity and financial plans against which performance can be measured;
- justification for planned capital expenditure;
- targets for quality improvements against which performance can be measured;
- targets for improving efficiency in the use of resources;
- plans to improve the management of the hospital's business.

The document runs to 23 pages of A4 under the following headings:

The Mission
Services
Quality
Efficiency and Effectiveness
Integration
Manpower, Training and Development
Information, IT and Resource Management
Contracts and Business Development Opportunities
The Estate
Finance.

Another business plan was drawn up to set up a small printing works. It included:

The nature of the business
The nature of the competitors
Who the potential customers are
Who the potential suppliers are
Where potential accommodation may be found
The nature of the staffing
Financial costings for all these
Monthly financial and activity targets for the next two years.

These show two contrasting styles of business plans appropriate to quite different settings. It is necessary to develop business plans for the particular business. It is beyond the scope of this book to show how to produce a business plan, but a useful text to help draw up a business plan is Johnson (1990).

| REVIEW TOPIC 6.2 |

Devise a business plan for offering a service to your colleagues. This could be frivolous or a serious proposition.

The use of resources

An organisation has various resources – time, people, space, equipment – as well as finance. Whether the organisation is labour intensive or capital intensive, it is the way in which finances are deployed that determines the effective use of the other resources. Employing expensive scientists, for example, becomes a nonsense if the research department is deprived of funds and materials for investigation and experimentation. Investing in complex, high-technology machine tools is absurd without extra money being spent on staff training. Failing to pay attention to those items which make the principal investment more effective is not only negligent, it may have a profound effect upon the future of the organisation. A positive view of the use of resources will lead to them being properly controlled and exploited, and providing a sense of ownership will lead to thoughtful use. In this way, it should not be possible to put the blame for deficiencies in the system onto lack of resources *per se* – rather it is lack of management of those resources which is at fault. Chapter 5 deals with managing information about the use of resources; this chapter deals with the financial aspects of managing resources.

Organisations also develop a resources culture. Managers handling budget forecasts should be aware that estimates may well be based on what is perceived to be likely to be granted. There are organisations which have a culture which encourages improvement and innovation, and those where there is a background of conditioning against extravagance. In addition, we may come across comments such as 'Our estimate [for stationery, man-power, extra market research, or whatever] is always cut back, so we will put in for more than we actually need'. It is the job of management to be aware of and, if necessary, to change this culture, in order to make it more positive and objective.

The way the business planning process is conducted should ensure that the organisation's finances become a reason for doing things, not a justification for not doing things. The following section details some departmental business planning methods.

The business planning process

The nature of business plans

Business plans begin with those who devise future plans and forecasts. Obtaining the commitment of all members of the organisation to departmental objectives and plans is vital. Individual members on whom the plan is imposed, and who do not have an active part in its drafting, are likely to pay it little attention or will abuse its control function. Business planning should be carried out at the working level and it is only when all the business plans have been passed up the line that they are then formed into a company-wide policy and passed back down the hierarchy, with head office issuing divisional budgets, divisions issuing departmental budgets, departments issuing sectional budgets, and so on down to a personal level.

Richard Coleman is a divisional accountant and has described to us the broad steps in his business plan procedure:

1. He and his colleagues prepare their plan and send it to headquarters.
2. Headquarters responds with guidelines such as 'We are not happy with an expected profit of £10 million in two years; try for £11 million' or 'Administration costs should be 19% not, 20%, of the budget'.
3. Richard responds by agreeing with some points and resisting others by further justification.
4. Headquarters agrees the divisional business plan.

Steps 2 and 3 may be repeated several times before step 4 is eventually reached, but Richard finally has not only a series of financial yardsticks against which divisional performance will be measured, but also a substantial degree of latitude: autonomy to exercise discretion and initiative within an agreed framework. The reason for the protracted negotiations is to ensure that the framework is acceptable to those operating within it, so that they cannot claim an unreasonable constraint as a reason for failure.

> Management control is a systematic effort to set performance standards with planning objectives, to design information feedback systems, to compare actual performance with these predetermined standards, to determine whether there are any deviations and to measure their significance, and to take any action required to assure that all corporate resources are being used in the most effective and efficient way possible in achieving corporate objectives.
>
> (Mockler, 1972, p. 2)

Tying people down precisely will always be likely to produce resistance or defensive behaviour unless the details of the controls are worked at to make them mutually acceptable as a framework. Business plans should ensure that everyone sees, understands and works towards the goals and central drives of the organisation.

Budgets

The variety of plans made by an organisation is reflected in the range of budgets that are in use. These fall into two main types, capital budgets and expense budgets.

1. *Capital budgets* are estimates of expenditure on things like new equipment or new buildings. These are regarded as assets of the organisation, rather than expenses.
2. *Expense budgets* cover the material and labour needed to achieve the forecast production and/or sales activities of the department. These are the everyday running costs of the organisation, and at a company level may include other overheads such as interest on loans. Whether the latter are regarded as departmental expenses or not will depend on the treatment of cost allocation within the company (see the later section on Profit and Cost Centres).

Some organisations set a minimum figure on items of expenditure to be included in capital estimates, but this is often a question of administrative convenience rather than logic. As capital and expense expenditure are treated differently by the Inland Revenue (the latter being a legitimate deduction from tax liability, while only the annual depreciation on capital expenditure is tax allowable), it is important that expenses should be correctly located, otherwise unnecessary costs are incurred.

In addition, alongside these there may be *cash budgets*. The organisation must have the cash resources to meet its commitments as they fall due – it has to be able to pay its suppliers, creditors, employees and shareholders. Income and expenditure are not constant over the year, and highlighting discrepancies should help to smooth out the occasions when there is either a cash surplus or a deficiency of cash. There is little point in formally estimating costs for operational activities if the organisation then runs out of cash funds for financing these activities. A cash budget emphasises that departments create the need for cash, as well as bring in cash, through their activities.

These three types of budget – capital, expense and cash – are built up on the basis of operational business plans. These are estimates of how many widgets will be made and sold or, in the case of service organisations, how many students will be taken in, hospital patients treated, legal cases handled, meals served, or guests accommodated. The more unstable supply and demand movements are, the more difficult and important accurate forecasting becomes, and the more elaborate the forecasting procedures will need to be. There are many formal trend analysis and prediction techniques in use in organisations, of both a quantitative and a qualitative nature. Sometimes, however, these may be rejected for a more entrepreneurial approach with the acceptance of the consequent risk, or alternatively for simple guesswork. If the decision is of a short-term nature and can be changed with little expense, then the use of sophisticated forecasting techniques is merely a waste of time and effort. Sometimes systems are completely discarded, and advocacy and political negotiation prevail instead. However they are drawn up, these operational business plans are the ones which are translated into the flow of finance in and out of the organisation.

Business forecasts are normally prepared along the same divisions as the functional organisation of the company, so that there will be business plans for the manufacturing section, for the marketing section, and for the administration, personnel and finance sections. Whether labour and service costs are budgeted for by the department in which they are incurred, or by the central service department, will again depend on the company's policy regarding the allocation of costs. Within these functional plans, there will be departmental plans. All these separate forecasts are then coordinated into the company's master business plan, when the system can be viewed as a whole. Alternative forecasts are considered, and restraining factors are taken into account. The period covered by the business plan is not always one year, but may be anything from, say, three months to five years. A longer-term plan will contain more uncertainties than a short-term one, of course.

Two types of budgets which may be long term or striving to cope with the uncertainty of the long-term future are as follows:

1. *Life cycle budgeting.* This is used where it is unreasonable to expect financial commitment to last a short period, for example capital projects, complex retraining programmes or research. The financial estimates are prepared over the whole life cycle of the activity, and will assume the continued success of the project.
2. *Flexible budgeting.* This requires a series of different business plans to be prepared depending on the particular scenario painted, perhaps according to different inflation rates, or changes in the availability and price of a basic feedstock, or different performance levels. This can sometimes make it easier to use the budget as a controlling and evaluating device, since it is based on what actually happens in the environment, rather than a compromised guess.

All control through business plans requires the determination of key result areas. These are aspects of the organisation that produce the performances on which everything else depends. The obvious key result areas are sales, output, stock levels and cash position, but each individual organisation will have one or two that are special to its setting or to its mode of operation. For example, in hospitals it may be occupied bed-days. In schools it might be the percentage of children passing tests compared with those passing equivalent tests when they entered the school. Research departments of universities might worry about the completion rates of postgraduate students. One organisation may have 10% of its sales volume taken up by the sales of one product which produces 50% of the gross profits. Television companies watch the viewing levels of their programmes very carefully. A car manufacturer may have one department where a strike or other form of industrial action would have repercussions elsewhere in the organisation far greater than would be assumed. Identifying these key result areas makes it possible for managers to monitor closely a selected number of performance indicators whilst allowing maximum discretion elsewhere.

The preparation of budgets

Departmental managers or functional heads will at some time find them-selves faced with decisions about how to go about formulating their budget estimates, or dealing with any special or one-off funds that may be allocated to their sections. With the latter, their aim should be to extract the maximum value from their finances. Two extreme approaches are the departmental head who makes all the allocation decisions without any sharing of the problem with his or her staff, or an open departmental finance committee which debates the issue in great detail. Brian Knight, an acknowledged authority on finance in education, describes four possible strategies (Knight, 1983, Chapter 8):

1. *Benevolent despotism.* Here staff in the department may be consulted about their individual or section requirements, but much of the money is actually allocated on a grace-and-favour basis, rather than based on real need. This method can be effective, but is open to unfair wheeler-dealing and persuasion.
2. *Open market or zero-basing.* Here estimates and justifications are submitted for each and every item making up the request. This method is quite searching, since there is no dependence on the previous year's budget. The modest and realistic estimates tend to lose out to the aggressive and artful ones here, unless the justification for each item is carefully examined.
3. *Creeping incrementalism.* This simply sorts out allocations by adding an amount for inflation equally to the previous period's allocations. This method takes no account of changing needs or new developments, and also perpetuates any previous inequities in distribution.
4. *Formula approach.* Here budget estimates and allocations are based on factors such as the number of students, number of overseas visits or number of new products, with perhaps some weightings applied to certain elements. Each 'unit' receives an amount of finance which is pre-determined and applicable across the whole section or organisation. This method can be quick, once the initial weighting and factors are agreed upon, but tends to err on the conservative and unadventurous side.

All these methods have their good and bad points, and most organisations will probably use a combination. Some are useful due to their simplicity. Others, for example strategy 3, mean that the budget is of no more value than are past results for judging performance against, and indicate that the budget is not being used as a serious planning device. Ideally, as mentioned earlier, the budget estimates should be prepared using an objective, task-orientated approach (see 'Putting it into Practice' at the end of this chapter), which considers departmental goals and the ways of achieving goals. Such 'rule of thumb' measures like strategies 1 or 3 above will generally not produce a useful budget and are certainly not business planning.

The operation of budgets

This section could perhaps be called 'good housekeeping', and concerns what goes on after the negotiating of the budget is over, and the spending starts. Value for money should always be borne in mind – if the organisation insists on certain suppliers being used, but the section head knows the supplier down the road will do it more cheaply, then this should be discussed, and agreement reached on action. It may transpire that there are reasons other than price, for example reliability or efficiency, why another supplier has been nominated, and these factors can add their own value.

Departments should also complain bitterly if their accounting function insists rigidly on allowances being completely spent by the end of the budgeting period. It risks making spending itself more important than gaining value from the budget. Some organisations we have come across not only prevent the division from keeping its underspend, but also reduce the following year's budget by a similar amount, so imposing a double penalty. Obviously, extremes of underspending will ring warning bells, but allowing departments to carry forward unspent balances prevents the frantic activity of spending on trivial items that often occurs at the end of the financial year. It also allows departments to save up for some particular but unexpected change in priority arising in a few months' time. Similarly, there should ideally be some facility for allowing occasional overspending for legitimate requirements. A large credit or debit balance at the end of the financial year should, of course, be avoided since if the business plan has been properly prepared, it indicates bad management of the budget.

Another tool of flexible budget management is virement – a term more commonly used in the public sector – which means the transfer of finances from one heading to another, within the budget as a whole. If handled with care, but not to excess, this can assist departments or individuals within it who find that their needs have changed over time. It should not be so easily granted that it prevents business planners from not taking the initial task seriously, knowing that changes can easily be made in future months.

Normally, requests for virement will have to be accompanied by a detailed justification.

The most that some members of the department will be conscious of the business plan monitoring process may be the use of the departmental key or counter to use the photocopying machine, or the need to get their section head's signature on a request for a petty cash advance, or the periodic check that all the capital items listed as being in the possession of the department are still present, or the occasional reminder that if possible long personal phone calls or sending private mail through the company system should be avoided, or the notice on the board about switching lights off and turning off taps . . . and so on. These are the signs of 'good housekeeping' in an organisation – it shows that someone, somewhere is paying some attention to the value the organisation or department is deriving from its budget. But departmental management should seek to ensure that this is not the only type of involvement with the budget which members experience. Staff need to have some sense of ownership of resources. If people have been involved in the business planning process from the beginning, they are more likely to be interested in its progress, and to share some of the responsibility for its success.

Evaluation of the business plan

When the next year's business planning cycle restarts, questions must be asked on the effectiveness of the previous period's spending. It is not enough simply to record an under- or overspend, since this tells us little about spending patterns within different sections of the plan. If the department has a large training budget, for example, the department should examine whether the money was well spent, whether some other way of spending it would have given more value (perhaps on external rather than in-house courses, or on location in Chester rather than London), and whether the pattern of spending achieved departmental training objectives. This will, of course, involve discussion between various members in the department. Similar questions can be asked for each budget heading, including hardware and equipment, consumable software and stationery, and expenses such as travel and entertainment.

Budgets, records and computers

Keeping records is part of the feedback process for the effectiveness of plans and budgets. Records are needed to measure the contribution made by departments or sections, as measured against expected performance. Without a record of how many bandage packs have been issued this month, it is not only difficult for the hospital administrator to know how many to order, it is also difficult to determine when to argue for more funds for bandages, or at what point funds should be diverted from bandages to laundry. Similarly, personnel departments need records of those off sick or working overtime, so that the correct pay calculations may be made. The computer has made a large impact on record-keeping and filing, overcoming some of the drudgery and routine. The computer can store so much information and retrieve it with such ease that there is a risk that records may be expanded unnecessarily.

There is a danger that the keeping of records becomes a burdensome administrative activity that is neither accurate nor useful, with the activity becoming an end in itself. One high-tech company we worked in had a system of wall charts on which engineers recorded the number of hours spent on each of several different parts of a project and on each project for different clients. The reason for recording this information was to provide a basis to work out costings for future projects. In practice, however, the records were made nonsensical by the fact that engineers often had to spend more time on an assignment than was anticipated. It would have been sensible to record the extra hours against the project that had been underestimated. In fact the engineers were asked by their managers to record the extra hours against a different project where there was still space on the chart, as they did not want to give the impression that they had estimated incorrectly in the first place. Nor did they want it to seem that they had lost control of the operation! This is an extreme example of how individuals make nonsensical those records that prescribe their activities too closely. There is particular suspicion of records that are maintained so that an individual manager can keep personal control of the activities of subordinates rather than the records being needed for organisational control.

To avoid these problems, we suggest three simple rules.

1. Records should be justified in terms of the stated task of the department or organisation.
2. Records should be entered on simple forms.
3. Records kept should only be those essential to running the unit.

---| REVIEW TOPIC 6.3 |---

Why was the use of wall charts (described above) made nonsensical and how could the problem have been avoided?

The impact of the computer on managing is varied, but one of the significant innovations has been the spreadsheet, which is probably the most popular piece of computer software among managers. The first of what have now become known as spreadsheets was Visicalc (1980), although that has been followed by many others both simpler and more elaborate. The financial spreadsheet is a computer program that provides a display of data relating to income and expenditure over a period of, say, twelve months. Each item of information is metaphorically in a box, with the boxes arranged in rows and columns. The row is the category of information running across each of the twelve months and the column is for the different categories of information for a single month. The computer program then enables a series of calculations to be made that link one box to another, one row to another or one column to another. In this way it is possible to enter in the figures of expected income and expenditure for the forthcoming twelve-month period and then calculate the effect of changing different variables. One can, for example, change one feature of income in month one and ask the computer to calculate the effect of that single change on all the following months, making all the necessary additions, subtractions and other calculations so that there is still a calculated figure for each row and each column with all the cumulative effects accounted for. This helps the initial business plan preparation to be more carefully worked out by considering a wide range of possible strategies. It also makes it possible to assess quickly each month what the effect of that month's performance will be over the remainder of the year. Table 6.1 shows a typical spreadsheet format.

In many organisations now, data for financial computer decision-making systems are fed in at source, which does away with some of the tedium of manual input. An example of this, which most of us will have come across, is the supermarket checkout till, where a barcoding pen or some other electronic device instantly records the fact that a particular item of stock has

Table 6.1 A typical spreadsheet format

	January	February	. . .
Sales	42,000	42,840	
Cost of sales	28,560	29,131	
Gross profit	13,440	13,709	
Less:			
Wages	7,800	7,800	
Rent	2,050	2,050	
Other	1,500	1,800	
Total expenses	11,350	11,650	
Trading profit	2,090	2,059	
Less Interest	800	850	
Net profit	1,290	1,209	

been purchased, at what time and at what price. The information generated
in this way can be used not only for stock reordering routines, but also for
sales analysis, examination of product margins, turnover levels, etc. By
connecting computerised systems with the operational and record-keeping
systems of the organisation, the potential of electronic hardware is truly
realised. (See Chapter 5, Resource Management, for more discussion on
this.)

Profit and cost centres

Organisations will vary in their allocation of accounting responsibilities to
individual departments. There are various spheres of responsibility.

- *Cost centres.* Costs are assigned to the section where the items incurring
  those costs are consumed (this may be different from where those costs
  are first incurred).
- *Profit centres.* Both revenue (income from sales or the provision of
  services) and costs are made the responsibility of departmental management. A profit centre will probably have its own profit and loss accounts
  to use in future planning activities.
- *Investment centre.* A further extension of the above where not only
  expenses and income are made the responsibility of the department, but
  also the management of the assets of the department. Such a centre would
  have its own balance sheet, showing the total resources invested in the
  department. The most important concept in all these is that the
  responsibility for all the expenses connected with running the department
  should be located at the point of consumption.

The use of profit or cost centres is a means of providing autonomy to
departments or sections of a business at the same time as providing a basis
for management control of operations that are decentralised. One method is
to set targets for a division or department in terms of profits or costs that
have to be achieved and then to measure the results obtained. It is thus a
form of management by objectives using a single criterion of success and, at
least theoretically, providing those in the cost or profit centre with greater
scope for deciding how their objectives are to be reached. It is also a
different way of using key result areas than was mentioned earlier.

| REVIEW TOPIC 6.4 |

How can the use of profit or cost centres provide both autonomy to
departments and a basis for management control of decentralised operations?

In practice individual managers seldom enjoy the complete autonomy that
the use of profit centres implies. Organisations are entities, no matter how

attractive is the idea of decentralising, so that managers in individual cost or profit centres have to work within quite tight limitations. If there is a national agreement on wages and salaries, managers in the cost centres will have to accept that constraint all the time that the agreement is accepted. Managers will also be required to use some central services, even if they do not want to, as there are economics of scale for the organisation as a whole in working this way.

Central overheads, like head office and general service departments, can be apportioned between cost centres or regarded as separate, but problems arise if a department that is a cost centre wants to reduce its overhead burden by not using a central service department such as personnel, research, purchasing, computing, public affairs or management services. A manager may review the use made by the department of management services and decide that this level of use is so low that a useful saving could be made by doing without the services altogether or using the occasional services of a consultant. Although there has long been reluctance to encourage competition for internal services, some organisations have begun turning central service departments into profit centres that have to survive by selling their services to client departments within the company and in competition with suppliers of similar services from outside the organisation. The next step can be to close the central service department altogether and depend on outside suppliers, which may include previous employees.

A necessary feature of cost or profit centres is to determine the prices at which goods and services are transferred from one department to another. One option is to use an open market price, so that the internal client pays the same price for internally supplied goods and services as they would pay for those same services supplied from outside. If, however, the internal client is free to buy externally as well as internally, then the internal supplier is at a considerable disadvantage as they do not have the same freedom to sell services. It is therefore more common for some lower value to be determined, but the precise level is problematical.

The reason why managers in senior positions use the device of profit or cost centres is to try to make the organisation as a whole more efficient, by providing control information on unit performance, and to provide job satisfaction for subordinate managers, by supplying feedback on the progress of their operations. If they are to achieve both objectives the degree of competition between cost centres has to be kept at a healthy level, without allowing it to become so strong as to be destructive.

Financial statements

Business plans are planning, decision-making and monitoring instruments. They are different from an organisation's statements of financial activity in the previous period. However, past accounting information, in the form of balance sheets, profit and loss statements, and source and use of funds statements, is necessary to help in the prediction of future events. In most organisations, these statements are produced as summaries of the organisation as a whole, rather than for individual departments, but departmental management will benefit from some understanding of their structure and purpose. In very large organisations, where the organisation is structured along profit and investment centre lines (see previous section), individual departmental or functional statements may be produced. The information contained in such statements helps to identify trends and relationships, major changes which have occurred, and strengths and weaknesses in the organisation. Such statements are snapshots of the financial structure of the business at a given time, and for this reason may not be representative of the average position of the business over a longer period. Managers should therefore exercise judgement as to how they use financial statements in the analysis of the business. The following is a brief description of the nature of the three main types of financial accounts. More detailed information can be gained by reading specialist financial texts, for example Davies (1990), Appleby (1991) and Chadwick (1991).

The balance sheet

The balance sheet discloses the property and possessions of a business together with its internal and external debts and obligations. These are known as the capital, liabilities and assets of the organisation.

Those which are tangible and measurable by cash values can be arranged on a balance sheet to show the financial situation of the organisation at a specific time. Table 6.2 shows a simplified balance sheet.

Current assets are those such as cash and marketable securities that could be turned into disposable cash at a reasonably predictable value within a relatively short time. Fixed assets show the monetary value of the company's plant, equipment, property and other items used to produce its goods or services. After liabilities have also been listed, the company's net worth is calculated by subtracting total liabilities from total assets.

Examination of the balance sheet focuses mainly on capital structure and the use of working capital, that is the excess of current assets over current liabilities. Some questions that the individual manager, rather than the accountant, might raise after studying the balance sheet might be as follows:

1. What action are we taking regarding old or obsolete equipment?
2. Do we have too much money tied up in stock?
3. Are we offering too much credit to customers?

The profit and loss statement

The profit and loss statement (sometimes called the income statement) aims to set out how much income has been generated from the capital in a given

Table 6.2 A simple balance sheet

Assets			Liabilities		
		£000			£000
Current assets:			*Ordinary share capital*		5,492
Stocks	4,784		*Reserves:*		
Debtors	4,865		Capital	706	
Marketable securities	324		Revenue	2,631	3,337
Cash	102	10,075			
			Ordinary shareholders' equity		8,829
Less Current liabilities:					
Creditors	3,133		*Long-term liabilities:*		
Bank overdraft	1,430		Debentures	2,552	
Taxation	803		Loans	1,424	3,976
Dividends	367	5,733			
					12,805
Net current assets		4,342			
Fixed assets:					
Land and buildings	3,312				
Plant and machinery	4,675	7,987			
Investments		867			
		13,196			

period of time. It helps determine the significance of different revenues and expenses in relation to profitability, and to isolate any changes in circumstances. The profit and loss statement should encourage the manager to question such things as the amount of fixed and variable costs incurred by the department, how effective spending has been (for example, on research or new technology), and how factors such as competition or labour relations may be affecting income and profitability.

The flow of funds statement

This can also be called the sources and uses of funds statement. It shows how much new wealth has been made available during the period (for example, through injections of new capital, business loans, sales of assets, and operating income), and how this new wealth has been invested in the business, whether in the purchase of new assets, repayment of loans, tax payments or operating losses. It will highlight changes in the cash position of the business. This is a particularly useful tool in budget forecasting for the estimate of future cash flows.

It is important to ensure that financial statements are objective, verifiable and consistent, and internal audit procedures are regarded as an effective tool of financial control in this respect. It must be emphasised that financial statements such as these do not in themselves provide the answers to management questions. They are a starting point towards more detailed investigation, and are a highly useful part of analysis and planning decisions. There are many systematic analytical devices concerning financial information, including the use of ratios to examine profitability, capital structure, cash flow and the use of assets.

The human side of business plans

Behavioural considerations are important in all areas of management. The effectiveness of accounting information and control systems depends on how they affect behaviour. If the original targets are too tight and highly difficult to achieve, business plans are unlikely to be a motivating force. Neither will they motivate if they are too slack to constitute any sort of challenge. Glautier and Underdown (1986) suggest that

> The budget process alone is not sufficient to maintain adequate management control. Too often, organisations tend to expect results from budgetary control and fail to recognise its behavioural implications. As a result, pressures are created leading to mistrust, hostility and actions detrimental to the long-term prospects of an organisation.

A further warning was given by Appleby (1987, p. 206):

> Human nature being what it is, individuals may be tempted to use a variety of techniques to influence the budgeting process, for example, the withholding of information until very late to highlight its importance, the overstatement of requirements, and unhelpfulness in the provision of information to the budget compiler.

There are also likely to be certain entrenched group attitudes about finance questions. Departmental staff and managers are heard to make comments like these:

1. The company budget is a bottomless pocket.
2. It's their money, not mine.
3. There is always a magic wand in the last resort.
4. I'm not paid to be an accountant.
5. Electricity costs are not my business.
6. Our section is special.

The accounting section staff may, on the other hand, have attitudes such as these:

1. We must not set a precedent.

2. You cannot use that, it is in the wrong pot.
3. They could not run a fish stall.
4. They should do it for love.
5. Beat the scroungers.
6. Keep to the rules.

(Adapted from Knight, 1983, Chapter 7).

A head of department may have to explain more than he or she thinks necessary to individual members of the department if the business plan is to be an effective motivator. Time and effort should be devoted to providing opportunities where discussion can take place and where queries, worries or feedback can be shared. This can, for example, be done by means of personal targets set in line with business goals during performance appraisal periods.

REVIEW TOPIC 6.5

Organisations are developed, not through systems, but through people.
How does human behaviour in organisations affect departmental business control?

SUMMARY PROPOSITIONS

6.1 Business plans are tools for management control of organisational performance.

6.2 The main functions of business plans are as planning, controlling, motivating, communication and coordination devices. They are guides to management, not straitjackets.

6.3 Different types of budgets are capital, expense, cash, operational and master budgets. There are also long-term budgets known as life cycle or flexible budgets.

6.4 Control is made more effective by identifying key result areas, and profit or cost centres.

6.5 Business planning procedures need to affect behaviour to be effective as control mechanisms, therefore some awareness of human behaviour and organisational culture is useful to the manager. Success is dependent on whether those operating the business planning system accept it.

PUTTING IT INTO PRACTICE

Practical problems of forecasting for operational plans

Operational business plans are the basis of capital, expense and cash budgeting activities. There are many difficulties in forecasting levels of activity for these plans, including the following:

1. The preparation of estimates of inflows and outflows of materials, products and services is time-consuming, and often imprecise in nature.

2. Assessment of demand rates, selling prices, growth rates, the life of assets, yields of plants, maintenance costs and interest rates is a difficult task, and wide margins of error occasionally have to be expected.
3. Errors in forecasting are often due not to inexperience but to unresolved uncertainties in the environment.
4. Innovations where the future market potential was initially grossly under-estimated include computers, robots, polythene and PVC. Those where success was overestimated include the airship and Concorde. Market success is a more difficult thing to estimate than likely development costs.

A task-orientated method of departmental business plan preparation

1. Forecasts covering departmental activities in physical terms are prepared by individual departments, using the planning cycle illustrated in Figure. 6.1.
2. All departmental forecasts are checked by senior management to ensure their compatibility with each other and with organisational objectives.
3. Individual forecasts are expressed in financial terms, using any organisational and economic guidelines which may be appropriate, for example inflation rates. Decisions are taken at this stage to maintain or cease certain operational activities, bearing in mind the financial costs and benefits involved.
4. These financial forecasts are again scrutinised by top management, or by the finance committee. Decisions are made regarding their acceptability in line with organisational objectives, and a master forecast is drawn up.
5. After formal approval of the master forecast by the board, each department's forecast becomes its budget and becomes an instrument of departmental control.

References

Appleby, R. C., 1991, *Modern Business Administration*, 4th edn, Pitman, London (5th edition, 1991).

Chadwick, L., 1991, *The Essence of Management Accounting*, Prentice Hall International, Hemel Hempstead, Hertfordshire.

Davies, D., 1990, *Finance and Accounting for Managers*, IPM, Wimbledon, Surrey.

Glautier, M. W. E. and Underdown, B., 1986, *Accounting Theory and Practice*, 3rd edn, Pitman, London.

Horngren, C. T., 1982, *Cost Accounting: A Managerial Emphasis*, 5th edn, Prentice Hall, Englewood Cliffs, New Jersey.

Johnson, R., 1990, *The 24 Hour Business Plan*, Hutchinson Business Books, London.

Knight, B. A., 1983, *Managing School Finance*, Heinemann, London.

Mockler, R. J., 1972, *The Management Control Process*, Prentice Hall, Englewood Cliffs, New Jersey.

Chapter 7

Quality management and problem-solving

The 'mission statement' of one Healthcare NHS Trust's first quality strategy (1992) is:

> To provide high quality services to all our patients, respecting their dignity and putting their interests first. Services will be efficient and effective, and it is our aim to ensure integration with all other agencies. We are committed to sound medical, nursing and other professional standards and wish to support our staff with excellent training and development opportunities.

Mission statements such as this are increasingly common in companies and other organisations. But what stops them from being little more than 'motherhood statements', which no one can disagree with but in practice make little difference?

Total Quality Management

Management theories come and go. But since the early 1980s one of the most enduring in the industrialised West has been the search for Total Quality. Total Quality Management (TQM) attempts to manage and coordinate the various aspects of the organisation so that it can deliver quality products and services. TQM boils down to some basic concepts. Get it right first time, every time, and make customer satisfaction the top priority. Treat everyone as a customer within and without the company or organisation. The telephone receptionist's customers are the callers on the end of the line. The factory worker's customer is the next person on the assembly belt who would have to cope with any mistake.

Total quality ideas were introduced to Japan after the Second World War by two American academics, Edwards Deming and Joseph Juran, whose theories failed to impress their compatriots – see Hodgson (1987) or Deming (1982). The ideas were shipped back to the UK from Japan in the early

Table 7.1   Common features for successful TQM

Management commitment
Prevention, not detection, philosophy
Identify and meet customer requirements
A quality system
Training
Involvement of everyone – empowerment of staff
Continuous improvement

1980s and initially adopted by manufacturing industry. Impressive results were claimed by Rover and Rank Xerox.

The first wave of quality ideas concentrated on quality control and product quality, the second on customer satisfaction. The ideas have spread to service industries, the professions and beyond, with local authorities and health departments enthusiastically affirming their commitment. There is the beginning of a third wave with an interest in reputation; see, for example, Kay (1993), which deals with those aspects of quality which customers cannot monitor for themselves.

Although many experts, for example Collard (1989), Dale and Plunkett (1990), Orvretveit (1992) and Thomas (1992), advocate differing approaches to TQM, they have certain features in common: see Table 7.1. If we look through this list we see that TQM is about *management* and the various features are covered elsewhere in this book. It is perhaps best understood as a cultural initiative rather than imposing a rigid predetermined approach from outside. Collard (1989, 1993) is probably the most widely used British text on TQM. He summarises the stages for implementing Total Quality in Figure 7.1.

All the stages in Figure 7.1 emphasise the *management* of quality and the importance of *people* in delivering quality. As an example we return to our Healthcare NHS Trust. After declaring the mission, aims and vision, the Trust then outlines the action plan for the next two years with key tasks and lead responsibilities: see Figure 7.2.

Although the basic concepts of TQM have not changed, measuring tangible results has become trickier. Financial measures in a local authority social services department are hardly appropriate. Asking the customers – the disabled, the elderly, children at risk – what they think of the service is the only real test. And new ideas are being added. The European Quality award includes a category on the impact on society, which covers involvement in the community, conservation and pollution control. So it becomes a whole management system with an emphasis on systematic auditing of the processes involved.

Kearney report (1992) a survey of 100 UK businesses where TQM is top

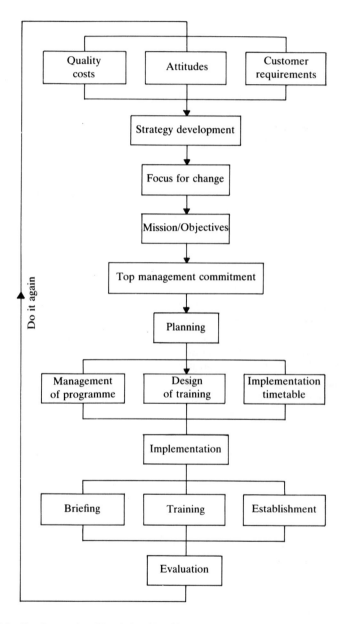

Figure 7.1 Implementing Total Quality (Collard, 1989).

Goals

Key task	Lead responsibility
Year 1	
Establish and communicate organisational objectives from Business Plan	Chief Executive
Set quality standards to comply with organisational objectives, Patients' Charter and purchasers' contract specification	Quality Monitoring Team (Q.M.T.)
Establish system for ratification, registration, monitoring and audit of standards	Q.M.T.
Develop a system for coordinating patient satisfaction survey work across trust services	Q.M.T.
Update and review all policies and procedures, to ensure compliance with relevant legislation, risk management issues and professional body policies	Personnel Department and Clinical Directorates
Establish an effective communication network and develop an audit tool to measure its effectiveness	Staff Training and Development Service
Continue Quality Organisation System (QOS) initiative on a planned basis in all service areas	T.Q.M. Coordinator
Develop internal service agreements between service heads and directorates, concentrating on quality issues	Business Manager – Community
Establish care management and joint needs assessment, concentrating on quality standards developed as part of 'Working Together' programme	Community Care implementation team
Continue to integrate key principles of resource management programme and T.Q.M. to ensure coordination of activity across all services	Information Services Manager and T.Q.M. Coordinator
Year 2	
N.B. All Year 1 tasks to be developed on ongoing basis Continue T.Q.M. training (initial and refresher) for all staff groups and levels	Staff Training and Development Service and T.Q.M. Coordinator
Progress QOS teams into all areas, with emphasis on patient and/or service user membership in all teams	T.Q.M. Coordinator
Evaluate QOS system and report back to Trust board	T.Q.M. Coordinator and Q.M.T.
Explore potential for development of joint audit tool between purchaser and provider	Q.M.T.
Continue to develop the role and function of the quality monitoring team	Q.M.T.

Figure 7.2 Key tasks and lead responsibilities: the action plan of a Healthcare NHS Trust.

Key task	Lead responsibility
Continue customer care training sessions for all staff groups	Staff Training and Development Service
Continue to implement a staff performance review and development system in all service areas	Manager of Staff Training and Development Service
Develop a link between Medical Audit and other clinical audit systems, towards the establishment of a multi-disciplinary audit process	Medical Audit Coordinator, Information Services Manager, Medical Audit Committee Chairman, Q.M.T.

Figure 7.2–*contd.*

of the agenda for 90% of chief executives. However, they also report that 80% of the programmes fail; 80% either provided no information on performance or reported no improvement. Those that practised TQM successfully emphasised:

- tangible results
- insistence on performance measures
- an integrated programme
- clear commitment from the top.

REVIEW TOPIC 7.1

What performance measures would be appropriate for the key tasks in Figure 7.2?

There can be a danger in the quality business becoming all concepts and not enough nitty gritty. The particular British enthusiasm for registration, for example to British Standard BS5750, has created extra time and cost burdens. Currently, in 1993, there are 24 accreditation bodies for quality in the UK, according to the Department of Trade and Industry. BS5750, the quality management standard, is the most common but it is in many ways inimical to the ideas of continuous development inherent in total quality. It requires organisations to write down the procedures for doing things to ensure repeatability. In other words there is an emphasis on doing things in the right way, not necessarily on doing the right things.

There may be a difference between small and large organisations in their approach to TQM. Small companies are inevitably close to their customers and so do not see quality as a separate issue, yet they often need to get BS5750 registration if they want to be suppliers to larger organisations. Many champions of the TQM movement have made something of a religion of quality, but it is not a panacea for all organisational ills. Total quality is not the whole answer and is no substitute for technology or research. It is perhaps most appropriate to describe TQM as a bag of tools needed for problem-solving. The issue is picking the appropriate tools.

There may be a better way of doing things in the department that will save money, or which will be less frustrating for the members of the department, saving wear on their nerves. There may be a better way of meeting customer requirements or enhancing the quality of the product. Perhaps the most important reason for managers being interested in quality is that it will prevent them from getting stale. Creativity engenders excitement, innovation presents a challenge. It is a risky business as effort and resources are deflected away from the main task and directed to something new and untried. There is no guarantee of success, but only some innovations pay off, others fail, and others again have quite unexpected results. Innovation is the essence of managerial work, as it is replete with decision-making and creating precedents, and it has the added attraction of being seen as the leading edge of managerial initiative in the organisation: creating the future.

Problem-solving and decision-making

There are problems, of course, which do not require subsequent action for their solution, such as crosswords or quiz games, but they are of less relevance in management. Managers good at solving these types of conundrums and brain-teasers are not necessarily those good at the action and change implied by problems requiring decision-making. The well-known 'lateral thinking' proponent Edward de Bono (1985) suggests that a more action-based problem-solving is often done by employees on their way up the hierarchy, whilst the job of senior managers is to practise the more strategic and conceptual thinking associated with larger-scale decisions. Whichever way you look at the different types of problems and decisions requiring the manager's attention, it is clear that an organisation may need different types of people to perform these different functions.

Managers need time to think, to deliberate and to conceptualise. Too often matters urgent drive out matters important. Problems are often solved by the easiest, most obvious and familiar route, when perhaps they should become opportunities for change. The manager is often concerned solely with the removal of risk rather than with increased risk and workload. In this way, a bypassed opportunity may become a problem in itself some time in the future. The product group which reacts to lower profits by immediately reducing advertising spending is solving one problem in the short term by getting the books to appear more healthy, but may be creating more problems later, by which time events may be more difficult to put right. The high-risk solution may be to increase advertising expenditure in order to tap into a different potential market and increase turnover. This is not to say that all problems are more complex than they initially appear to be. There is often a temptation to change the pressing job to be done (implementing a straightforward decision) into a less pressing one (finding a different problem to solve). Making a few long-serving staff redundant at the same time as rationalising one part of the business may be the obvious, albeit painful, solution to a changed business environment. Redoubling the number of working parties, consultations and market research in order to avoid any redundancies may achieve nothing and may be very costly. Part of the art of management is not to see problems where they do not exist, and not to dither so that something that is straightforward becomes problematical through prevarication.

It will be obvious by now that this area of a manager's work is often the least easy to describe. Problem-solving is rarely a spectacular or exciting activity, but it is one that is ignored at the organisation's peril. Success in decision-making can rarely be guaranteed, but there is scope for improving our ability to avoid failure.

| REVIEW TOPIC 7.1 |

John Adair (1985) suggests that 'thinking is the preliminary work of weighing up the pros and cons for each course of action. A decisive person is one who has the power to stop thinking and start acting.' How do you stop yourself thinking and start yourself acting?

Crises, problems and opportunities

Mintzberg, Raisingham and Theoret (1976) provide a helpful distinction between crises, problems and opportunities facing managers. A crisis is a sudden, unexpected event requiring immediate action. The canteen is burned to the ground, someone makes a bid for the company equity, the marketing director resigns, or some similar quite unexpected event requires a rapid decision or set of decisions. A problem is something of which there is warning in that it becomes apparent gradually, through clues from various sources, and is not initially clear-cut. Examples would be poor morale among the staff of the organisation, the influence of a competitor, or uncertainty about product quality. An opportunity is the chance to do something that is created by a single event and often needing swift action (opportunities are 'grasped' or 'seized' rather than 'taken', or 'missed' rather than 'ignored'). A small change in tax laws provides opportunities for the person shrewd enough to see how that can be exploited; a spell of bad weather provides an opportunity to sell umbrellas. Crises often also provide opportunities, and some languages use the same word for both. The example of the crisis caused by the resignation of the marketing director may provide an opportunity for reshaping the organisation and distribution of responsibilities.

Crisis, problem and opportunity all have in common the need for a decision to be made and all are unprogrammed decisions that are not dealt with by routine, procedure or habit. Some events that have all the hallmarks of crisis can be classified as programmed decisions in that they have been anticipated and the appropriate action prescribed. If a factory catches fire and is destroyed, the managers will have moved through a series of programmed decisions, as there will have been a procedure to be followed in the case of fire. When those procedures prove inadequate to prevent the disaster, there is a whole series of unprogrammed decisions to be taken. Most people have plans to deal with the onset of misfortune, but few have procedures to deal with the aftermath if the preventive routines fail.

Reacting to problems

We have seen that problems become apparent rather than suddenly popping up in sharp outline and this requires a manager to make a preliminary decision about how to react to the emerging problem. If it is spotted early, what should be done now? There are various choices:

1. Dealing with it. In most cases managers will deal with the problem themselves, by finding out further information, pondering it, defining the problem more clearly and deciding between alternative ways of dealing with it.
2. Passing it on. Just because a manager perceives a problem, it does not necessarily have to be dealt with. It may lie outside their competence and responsibility, so that things may be made much worse if the manager tries to deal with it. It can be passed to a superior if it is too big to be dealt with; it can be delegated to a subordinate if the subordinate will have better detailed knowledge of the situation and will thus be able to handle it more effectively (as well as being resentful if the problem is taken away); or it could be passed to a peer, elsewhere in the organisation. Deciding what to refer is a matter of nice judgement.

    A general rule of thumb appears to be that one passes down as many as possible and passes up as few as possible:

    > When confronted with an important problem requiring a decision, a manager must determine if he or she is responsible for making the decision. Here is a general rule that can be of help: the closer to the origin of a problem the decision is made, the better. This rule has two corollaries: (a) Pass as few decisions as possible to those higher up, and (b) pass as many as possible to those lower down. Usually, those who are closest to a problem are in the best position to decide what to do about it. (Stoner, 1982, p. 168)

    Referring a problem to a peer elsewhere in the organisation can be seen as avoiding proper responsibility, but failing to do it can cause ructions. An example might be dealing with the problem of an employee who is suspected of stealing. Should this be done by the immediate superior, or should it be referred to the security people or to the personnel department? If it is referred to security and the suspicion is groundless, the working relationship with the suspect has probably been destroyed. If it is not referred and the suspected employee then has time to remove confidential documents of great value to a competitor, then the manager has contributed to that loss by negligence.

3. Taking advice. A variation of the first alternative is for managers to deal with the problem themselves, but defer action until advice is taken from those with specialist knowledge or skills that help to understand the problem. This can also be preliminary to deciding to refer the problem elsewhere.

4. Working party. Remitting a problem to a working party or similar group for consideration is fraught with difficulties and dangers. The issue can be blown up out of all proportion and made more difficult to deal with rather than easier. Despite this, there are clearly situations in which a complex problem can only be approached satisfactorily by convening a group of people with varied expertise to examine the matter from different perspectives, providing that they all have the degree of commitment that will obviously be needed to solve what is such a difficult problem.

One of the critical factors in successful companies identified by Thomas Peters and Robert Waterman was a 'bias for action'. They suggest that in big companies the all-too-reasonable and rational response to complexity is to coordinate things, study them, form committees, ask for more data, etc. Over-complex systems make companies unresponsive. Successful companies do have working parties for specific problem-solving and decision-making tasks, but they are 'task forces that last five days, have a few members, and result in line operators doing something differently, rather than the 35-person task force that lasts eighteen months and produces a 500-page report' (Peters and Waterman, 1982, p. 120). Many organisations, whether commercial companies or non-profit-making units such as schools, are increasingly holding working party discussions off-site, in some other congenial location. By convening a discussion group away from the hubbub, telephones and daily crises of the working place, problems are more easily concentrated on and a creative atmosphere more readily produced. Such activities must not be arranged indiscriminately, however.

Unless some positive benefit is detected, the rest of the organisation will dismiss them merely as opportunities for a day off and a free lunch.

5. Consultants. Most managers at some time will find themselves acting as informal consultant to colleagues struggling with a problem. Increasingly,

however, companies are formally calling in external consultants to help with problem-solving within the organisation. The effectiveness of these experts is heavily dependent on how well thought out are their terms of reference. The managers calling in such outside agencies should decide beforehand whether they wish the consultants to be sounding boards, thereby helping the managers reach an understanding of the problem and reach their own conclusion. Alternatively (and there is a continuum in between these two), the consultants may be called upon to provide their own expert knowledge, so that it is the consultant who identifies options, sets criteria and makes recommendations for action. A competent consultant will probably use a mixture of techniques, depending on the balance of the remit. Sometimes probing and listening is the best thing, sometimes recommending or prescribing is appropriate.

6. Ignore it. An even more 'dangerous strategy' for a problem is to ignore it on the assumption that something will turn up to deal with the difficulty or that the passage of time will make it obsolete. This seems to most enthusiastic managers a shabby strategy and not facing up to the demands of the job. It is interesting, however, to think of what happens when you go on holiday. During your absence a number of problems will emerge and when you return you find that some of them have been dealt with by other people, but only because you were away. Other problems await your urgent attention, and others have stopped being problems at all. Managers will not survive long if they ignore all the problems that occur, but with some it is a wise strategy to leave the matter to resolve itself.

The problem-solving process

Table 7.2 illustrates a straightforward problem-solving process and is adapted from Stoner (1982). There are four stages.

Stage one. Definition and diagnosis

As problems emerge, rather than presenting themselves with sudden, sharp clarity, they first need to be defined. Is it the right problem? Is declining sales turnover a problem of pricing, or quality, or delivery times, or poor advertising, or an inappropriate product line, or something else? Getting to the correct problems among various possibilities is the first aspect of definition. The second is to question whether it is a problem at all. A taken-for-granted assumption in management circles for many years was that one should try to reduce staff turnover; if a large proportion of the employees left the organisation this was 'a bad thing'. The assumption was underpinned by calculating joining costs, leaving costs, training costs,

Table 7.2 The problem-solving process

Stage one	Stage two	Stage three	Stage four
Definition and diagnosis	Generating alternatives	Deciding between alternatives	Implementation
Define problem	Generate alternative solutions	Consider available resources	Check availability of resources
Test definition	Defer judgement	Evaluate alternatives	Check understanding of those involved
Specify appropriate solution		Select most appropriate	Implement
			Monitor

(Adapted from Stoner, 1982, p.170)

advertising costs and so on. Although these could be calculated and added up to provide a hefty sum, there was no consideration that turnover among staff employees could also avoid some people lingering on in dissatisfaction, could introduce new blood, could save on payroll costs through having some people at the bottom of pay scales instead of everyone being at the top, and could open up career opportunities for younger employees. Changes in the labour market have recently tended to produce an opposite assumption: that turnover is much needed to prevent a growing sense of frustration. The most useful approach to defining a problem correctly is to assess it in terms of what the organisation is trying to achieve and the extent to which the achievement of those objectives is being hindered by the existence of the supposed problem.

REVIEW TOPIC 7.2

Small, everyday decisions are often of the 'Yes, let's . . .' or 'No, I think not . . .' type.

How many small decisions did you make yesterday at work and at home?

How many big decisions did you take, affecting future action over the next six months?

If the problem can be satisfactorily defined, it is then necessary to determine what would be an appropriate solution. If despite the comment in the last paragraph, staff turnover is accurately defined as being too high, what would be a satisfactory solution? An example could be where a department has an establishment of fifty posts and an annual turnover of 200%, made up like this:

Total number of posts	50
Semi-permanent job holders	25
Unsettled job holders, each staying an average of only three months	100

There is an underlying stability of 50%, as 25 of the posts are held by people whose attachment to the company is settled. Without defining the problem satisfactorily the solution may be inappropriate, such as blanket attempts to persuade everyone to stay longer. These could be wasteful and might unsettle the semi-permanent job holders, who had not previously realised there was anything wrong. What is the problem here? Do we want the short-stay employees all to stay a little longer, or some of them to stay a lot longer, or is it a reasonable mix already? If short-stay employees were to stay for an average of six months instead of three, labour turnover would halve. If ten of the short-stay employees were to become semi-permanent and the remaining fifteen posts still occupied by people staying only three months, the turnover would drop to 120%. Different strategies would be involved according to how the problem was defined. It is always necessary to diagnose what has caused a problem by obtaining information, analysing it, and – probably – discussing it with others.

REVIEW TOPIC 7.3

One of G. K. Chesterton's characters remarked that 'it isn't that they can't see the solution, it is that they can't see the problem'. What techniques can be used to prevent this happening?

By now the manager knows the problem; what is wanted is to achieve a solution and know how the problem has been caused. Now on to stage two.

Stage two. Generating alternatives

The more complex the problem is, the more alternative solutions there are likely to be. The more intractable a problem has proved to be, the more alternative solutions are needed for consideration. The second stage is one of looking for alternative strategies, possibly using the brainstorming method (see end of Chapter 9), or one of the other techniques that have been devised. One system is the lateral thinking approach, described by Edward de Bono (1982), which enables people to generate new ideas and to escape from old ones by attempting radically different methods of thinking and approaches. He proffers an intriguing example:

> In a singles knock-out tennis tournament, there are 111 entrants. What is the minimum number of matches that must be played? It is easy enough to start at

the beginning and to work out how many first-round matches there must be, and how many byes. But this takes time. . . . Instead of considering the players trying to win, consider the losers after they have lost. There is one winner and 110 losers. Each loser can lose only once. So there must be 110 matches. (de Bono, 1982, p. 7)

Lateral thinking claims to do more than develop alternative solutions to problems; it can be a useful approach at this phase of the problem-solving process.

It is important to defer judgement on which solution is best until a number have been propounded. If alternatives are considered as they emerge, that act of consideration and evaluation can inhibit the generation of more alternatives. Either there is an early commitment to one that sounds attractive, and the effort of shifting one's allegiance is too great, or subsequent alternatives are conceived within the constraint of meeting only the shortcomings of what has already been proposed.

Stage three. Deciding between alternatives

When a range of options have been laid on the table for consideration, there is the stage in the process of choosing between them. There are two interrelated questions to be asked for each alternative. Can we do it? Will it work? First is the question of whether or not the strategy can be put into operation with the resources that are available. Many possibilities cannot be used because there is not the time, or manpower, or finance to mount them. Also some strategies might tackle the problem but cause others, equally or more serious. The second question of whether or not a proposal will work concerns whether or not it meets the criteria set in stage one of being an appropriate solution to the problem defined.

Sometimes there is a clearly preferred solution that is not immediately apparent, but which becomes unequivocally right through the problem-solving process. More often there are a number of inadequate solutions and the decision between alternatives is much more difficult.

Stage four. Implementation

Because problem-solving is fun, people often lose interest once the nut is cracked, just as many of the people who complete crossword puzzles cannot be bothered to send in their solution for the prize. The road to bankruptcy is paved with the gravestones of those who solved problems beautifully, but did not make the solutions work. Aspects of implementation are making sure that the necessary resources are available and that those who are to be involved in the implementation understand what they have to do and will do it. Later the managerial problem-solver has to monitor developments to see if the solution is working. Unless the solution to the problem was so obvious that the ratiocination described here was superfluous, there must be a good chance that the solution will be different from that anticipated; so the monitoring of implementation and its effects is essential.

Aids to problem-solving

A problem-solving technique which many companies, including Wedgwood, IBM and STC, have successfully used is quality circles. This is where small departmental groups of five to ten volunteers meet regularly, primarily in order to resolve quality-related problems in that department. They look, not at large-scale problems, but at those niggling local issues which are within members' scope to resolve but about which management may not be aware. Members need to be trained regularly in data collection methods, presentation and meeting skills. The group may use brainstorming techniques to generate ideas. The types of solutions this type of group might generate could include identifying some paperwork in the accounts department which was lessening its effectiveness, re-siting the riveting machine in a finishing unit to facilitate movement and flow, or rationalising quality sampling techniques in a continuous flow process whilst still ensuring top quality.

Some problems can be solved by mathematical modelling, providing that all the significant variables can be isolated and analysed in order to determine the optimum solution. One of the best known techniques of this type is the formula for determining an economic order quantity, so that material for steadily moving stock is ordered at the frequency and in the quantities that are most economical and efficient. Currently popular for this is the 'Just in Time' method which links suppliers much closer to the organisation so that stocks are delivered just in time and capital is not tied up.

Decision-making

Traditionally problem-solving and decision-making were linked together in management texts and training courses. However, many decisions that managers have to make are limited in their problematic component, and the challenge is not the intellectual question of what should be done, but other questions such as: Who should decide? What will be the reaction of the employees? How do we make it work? It is important to emphasise the aspect of decision-making that requires confidence, courage and skill in winning commitment from others. An elementary rule is that people will support that which they have helped to create, and this proposition supports the process of consultation and participation, but not all decisions are susceptible to such treatment. When action must be taken quickly, there is no time for consultation, and there is then a need for someone to say firmly 'We will do this'. When decisions are going to be unpopular, some aspects may require consultation and others may call for straight executive action.

An example might be the decision to close a factory, which has within it a series of components. There is first the business decision that the factory is to be closed because demand for the product has collapsed or because the costs are too high. There is the employment decision about what should happen about the employees generally, and there is the set of individual decisions about each employee personally. There is usually extensive consultation about the second of those three and less about the first and third.

Most decisions require the manager to come to terms with uncertainty, to cope with it, to eliminate it wherever possible, and to live with it efficiently when not possible. Good quality information can help lessen uncertainty. Any decision involves making a choice between alternatives, and is accompanied by attendant risk regarding the consequences of any action. Avoiding making a decision does not, in most cases, eliminate this risk; it merely ignores it. The decision-maker must weigh up the costs of each alternative against the benefits by selecting a solution that gives the optimum payoff. Information is thus an essential decision-making tool.

Decision-making is rarely a totally rational process. Emotion, power politics, the influence of others, individual values, the search for a satisfactory compromise, lack of time, the pressure of action – all these work against the manager following a systematic decision-making path. Logical processes can indeed help with unblocking a problem; so can creativity exercises; equally, asserts John Adair (1985), can that sixth sense, intuition. He says (p. 99):

> Encourage intuition in yourself. Become more aware of it. Be more receptive
> to its often faint whisper. Always subject it, however, to evaluation. Granted
> that safeguard, intuition can save you a great deal of time in decision-making.

Intuition is no substitute for information but can sometimes save the day in situations when information is limited, uncertainties abound, time is short, and the penalties for getting it wrong are not severe.

| REVIEW TOPIC 7.4 |

Wrong decisions are often made, not due to stupidity, carelessness or ignorance, but due to the way information is handled. Can you think of a problem you tackled in recent weeks, the solution to which you would now, with hindsight, change? Could you have had access to any information which would have improved that decision at the time? Why was it not available to you?

Planning

Another activity which involves decision-making is planning. If managers are to lead working teams, they must know where they are heading. They must constantly be thinking ahead and deciding what goals to aim for and the best means of reaching them. However, planning is not extensively used in practice. Managers tend to feel dominated by plans, especially when they are prepared by someone else. If there is too much planning, people feel hemmed in and they lack scope to deviate or express individuality. Initiative is hampered because unplanned activities are not regarded as legitimate. Planning must therefore be used as a framework, not as a straitjacket. When things do not go according to plan, the plan must be reappraised and changed if necessary. Without any sort of plan whatsoever, the organisation is reactive rather than proactive, and opportunities may be overlooked and lost.

Various elementary aids to planning include the following:

1. Gantt charts. These are visual displays of the planned order of activities over a period which allow for continuous monitoring and control. Such a chart may, for example, be used for scheduling jobs to be assigned to individual production employees.
2. Network planning. This identifies the chain of events that will determine the overall length of an activity. This 'critical path' can then receive special attention to ensure that things go according to plan.
3. Linear programming. This is a tool widely used in operations research to decide how scarce resources should be allocated to keep costs at a minimum or to maximise return, especially in areas such as production planning and transport logistics. A simple graphic method may be used to show clearly the relationship between two variables to non-numerically minded colleagues. Where the factors of a problem are more complex, solutions based on more sophisticated linear programming techniques using matrix algebra, such as the Simplex Method, have to be used. These methods are highly repetitive and highly suited to computerisation.
4. Goal planning. This is a simple device which avoids the difficulty of splendid ideas being too difficult actually to put into practice. See 'Putting it into Practice' below which shows how the method is developed.

SUMMARY PROPOSITIONS

7.1 Total Quality Management is a management approach to try to ensure that the customer's satisfaction has top priority.

7.2 Thinking is an essential part of problem-solving and decision-making, but not to excess. Many decisions for managers to make are simple, requiring speed, firmness and conviction rather than careful analysis to find the right answer.

7.3 Alternative ways of reacting to a problem are dealing with it, passing it on, taking advice, referring it to a working party, or ignoring it.

7.4 The four stages of the problem-solving process are definition and diagnosis, generating alternatives, deciding between alternatives, and implementation.

7.5 Planning should be the servant of the manager, not the master.

Who should make the decisions?

Analysing where and at what level in the organisation decisions are made can tell you something about the prevalent culture of the organisation. Are decisions in your department made by:

1. The person with the highest power and authority?
2. The person whose job description carries the responsibility?
3. The people with the most knowledge and expertise about the problem?
4. The people most personally involved and affected by the outcome? Would you do it any differently?

(Adapted from Handy, 1981)

The four steps in planning

1. Goals. What are you trying to do? What objectives are you trying to reach? What are the priorities? Without asking and answering this type of basic question there is a danger of trying to achieve too much and of uncertainty in execution. It is only if goals are brought into reasonable focus that managers can deploy resources effectively. This is particularly important where resources are scarce or time is short.

   Sally Ann Nield was a social worker having great difficulty in coping with her workload, so that there were many complaints and she was suffering considerable strain. Her section leader asked her to sort out her priorities so that she could clear some of the backlog. Sally Ann could not acknowledge that any one activity took preference over any other. She was not willing to concentrate on the preparation of social enquiry reports for a day if that meant deferring something else. As a result her affairs became even more muddled and she eventually left the career for which she had trained.

2. The present position. How far are you now from reaching the goals you have identified? What resources are available? This definition of the starting position and state of readiness begins to eliminate those features of operations that are not a problem and to direct attention to those areas where action is needed.

3. Aids and hindrances. What factors can help to achieve the goals and what might cause problems? This is scanning the future to see what is likely to change the present position for better or worse. When General Eisenhower was planning the D-Day landings in the Second World War, a crucial factor was the weather. He and his advisers had the most detailed and comprehensive weather reports they could obtain, but so did the Germans. The significance of judgement (and perhaps of luck) in the implementation of plans was shown by the fact that both sides knew the weather was expected to remain clear, but not for long. General Eisenhower decided that the landings must therefore proceed before the weather broke. His counterpart on the other side of the Channel, Field Marshal von Rundstedt, decided that the allied landings would be postponed until the weather improved.

4. The plan. The final step is to work out alternative series or programmes of action and eventually choose the one that seems most appropriate as a way of reaching the objective, taking account of the opening situation and the way in which the future is expected to develop. This activity often has contributory elements for verification, like test marketing, design prototypes, computer simulations and other ways of trying out the plan to test the likelihood of it being successful.

Goal-planning

1. Decide what particular goal you want to achieve, or change you want to make.
2. Write down the criteria you will use to judge whether the goal has been met.
3. Fill in the 'Strengths' and 'Needs' in Table 7.3. Write these as concretely as possible so you can tell you have met a need and it becomes a strength.
4. Take one of your needs that is particularly difficult to achieve. Break it down into smaller objectives on the form in Table 7.4.

Table 7.3   Strengths and needs

Goal:	
Strengths	Needs
1. Time 2. Place 3. Money 4. Materials 5. Cooperation of . . . 6. Agreement of . . . 7. Expertise 8. 9. 10.	

Table 7.4   Goal planning analysis

Need			
Objective	Method	Target date	Date done

References

Adair, J., 1985, *Effective Decision Making*, Pan Books, London.

Collard, R., 1989, *Total Quality: Success through People*, IPM, Wimbledon, Surrey (second edition, 1993).

Dale, B. G. and Plunkett, J. J. (eds), 1990, *Managing Quality*, Allan Hemel Hempstead, Hertfordshire.

de Bono, E., 1982, *Lateral Thinking for Management*, Penguin Books, Harmondsworth, Middlesex.

de Bono, E., 1985, *Tactics: The Art and Science of Success*, Fontana.

Deming, W. E., 1982, *Quality, Productivity and Competitive Position*, MIT, Cambridge, Mass.

Handy, C. B., 1981, *Understanding Organisations*, Penguin Books, Harmondsworth, Middlesex.

Hodgson, A., 1987, Deming's never ending road to quality, *Personnel Management*, July, pp. 40–4.

Kay, J., 1993, *Foundations of Corporate Success: How Business Strategies Add Value*, Oxford University Press.

Kearney, 1992, Consultant report, A T Kearney, London.

Mintzberg, H. A., Raisingham, D. and Theoret, A., 1976, The structure of 'unstructured' decision processes, *Administrative Science Quarterly*, June, pp. 246–75.

Orvretveit, J., 1992, *Health Service Quality: An Introduction to Quality Methods for Health Services*, Blackwell Science, London.

Peters, T. J. and Waterman, R. H., 1982, *In Search of Excellence*, Harper & Row, New York.

Stoner, J. A. F., 1982, *Management*, 2nd edn, Prentice Hall, Englewood Cliffs, New Jersey.

Thomas, B., 1992, *Total Quality Training: The Quality Culture and Quality Trainer*, McGraw-Hill, Maidenhead, Berkshire.

Chapter 8

Corporate governance and individual responsibility

The issues of ethics and socially responsible action by managements grow constantly more diverse and complex. From time to time there are serious accidents that can be partly attributed to human error and there is an obvious desire to avoid a repetition. Who was to blame for the Zeebrugge ferry disaster, or the Seveso atmospheric pollution, or the *Amoco Cadiz* oil slick? Are we more concerned to identify the culprits than to avoid repetitions? Do we need scapegoats while resigning ourselves to the impossibility of finding solutions? Are we conditioned to the idea that blame must be pushed as far 'up' as possible, so taking away reasonable responsibility from the rest of us?

In December 1988, three commuter trains were involved in a multiple collision at Clapham Junction, as a result of which 35 people died and nearly 500 were injured. A subsequent investigation identified the cause of the accident as being faulty rewiring in a signal box, which had been carried out by a BR technician. The Chairman of the official inquiry, however, felt that BR management were also to blame: the technician in question had not been provided with adequate training or supervision, there was confusion regarding responsibility for checking rewiring work, excessive reliance on overtime and inadequate safety systems.

Governance is a very rare word that was almost unknown outside the Book of Common Prayer and the works of Chaucer until Harold Wilson used it in the title of his memoirs after retiring as Prime Minister. It has recently been resurrected, in the term corporate governance, to encompass consideration of the way in which corporations are run in terms of being responsible for more than the immediate, legal responsibility to shareholders, just as a party elected to govern a country has a responsibility wider than to those who voted for them. A corporation has responsibilities to the community in which it is set, where it is an employer, a user of local services, perhaps a cause of traffic jams and a potential polluter. A large corporation has even wider responsibilities because of its power. During the second half of 1992 several powerful Western countries suffered serious economic problems because of speculation against their currencies and much of this was at the hands of major banks. Logging operations in South America are ravaging the rain forests, which are essential to life continuing on the planet. Error, or neglect, in the management of manufacturing processes can produce a tragedy like that of Bhopal in India, Chernobyl in the Ukraine, or the various discharges of crude oil that have occurred all over the world. Companies perhaps also have responsibilities towards the elected government and its economic objectives by, for instance, avoiding unnecessary imports or 'inflationary' pay rises.

A business also has responsibilities to those it employs. We each look for more from our employment than simply enough money to pay the bills at the end of the month. We seek opportunities for personal growth and achievement, to make a contribution that has some merit and usefulness. Furthermore we increasingly will not commit ourselves to activities that we cannot accept as being worthy.

Some people regard these as issues requiring the attention of government to introduce appropriate legislation, regulation or other types of political initiative; or requiring corporate response to public protest. Is this adequate? Is it possible? The legitimacy of corporations is based on their effectiveness in achieving economic goals, reflected in the requirements of the Companies Acts, which require companies to be successful in commercial terms in discharging their responsibility to shareholders. How can social responsibility be made consistent with corporate growth and profitability?

REVIEW TOPIC 8.1

a. Does a management discharge its full social responsibility if it obeys the law and satisfies its shareholders?
b. How can individual managers decide whether or not their individual actions and decisions are socially responsible?
c. Do individual, non-managerial employees have a responsibility for their actions apart from complying with management instructions and obeying the law? Should they obey instructions if they involve disobeying the law?

In this chapter we give a general review of some of the main parameters of corporate governance before considering specific features of management action: an organisational justice framework, employee grievances, health and safety, and privacy of information.

Current issues in social responsibility

Responsibility and the management hierarchy

Those outside management often appear to construe management action as all being determined by the person at the pinnacle of the hierarchy. This is a belief in what Milgram described as the state of agency, when someone else becomes responsible for your actions because you are both members of a hierarchy of authority:

> The most far-reaching consequence of the agentic shift is that a man feels responsible to the authority directing him but feels no responsibility for the content of the actions that the authority prescribes. Morality does not disappear, but acquires a radically different focus: the subordinate person feels shame or pride depending on how adequately he has performed the actions called for by authority. (Milgram, 1974, pp. 145–6)

This idea is convenient for politicians, journalists and campaigning groups because it focuses blame on one person or small group who are seen as powerful, privileged and therefore fair game. How nice and simple to have an easily identifiable villain, like Robert Maxwell, or an attractive miracle worker, like Richard Branson. If that person then lays the blame on an individual at a lower point in the hierarchy, they are accused of avoiding responsibility and looking for scapegoats.

In practice, this simple formula is insufficient as a way of identifying the source of initiatives to make management action socially responsible. The decisions of those at the top will always be incomplete without action and commitment from all members of the organisation – especially managers – if socially responsible initiatives are to succeed in the face of the traditional, bottom-line imperatives that managers face.

In traditional hierarchy there is a dilemma of the rational force of bureaucracy being combined with the relatively irrational processes of interpersonal interaction. The drills and procedures that are developed within any organisation to get things done in a consistent and understandable way come into conflict with the need of people at work to be individual, to do what they consider to be right, and to relate to their colleagues in a way which puts them as masters of the system rather than being its servants. Rules which are incomprehensible will be misunderstood, procedures which are unwieldy will be 'simplified' and instructions which are unattractive will be interpreted in favour of the recipient rather than the intentions of the instructor. Instructions that require people to do things which they consider unethical produce a specialised problem of the hierarchy.

In this situation individual managers have to make decisions and sometimes face uncertainty because of the ethical aspects of the actions that will follow. Jackall (1988) contends that either managers ignore the moral issues and succeed commercially or they maintain their personal integrity but are commercially unsuccessful. He argues that bureaucracy causes the loss of personal integrity in organisations. Something similar is expressed by the American philosopher Ciulla:

> I don't know how many times I have heard managers rebuke me . . . with what they consider a prudent rule of business, 'If it ain't broke, don't fix it.' This

phrase is symbolic of both competitive and moral mediocrity – the idea that we only confront problems when we are forced to. Hence we only worry about making better cars after the Japanese do, and we only worry about our accounting practices after we are convicted of fraud. . . . However, the really creative part of business ethics is discovering ways to do what is morally right and socially responsible without ruining your career and company.

(Ciulla, 1990a, p. 5)

The hierarchical imperative appears to be lessening, as organisational structures become looser and emphasis on individual managerial autonomy greater:

We are witnessing a crumbling of hierarchy, a gradual replacement of the bureaucratic emphasis on order, uniformity and repetition with an entre-preneurial emphasis on creativity and deal-making . . .

. . . managers . . . must learn to operate without the might of hierarchy behind them. The crutch of authority must be thrown away and replaced by their own personal responsibility . . .   (Kanter, 1989, pp. 355, 361)

Individual autonomy and personal responsibility

The emphasis on individual managerial autonomy brings with it a greater degree of personal choice. An interesting survey by Scase and Goffee (1989) demonstrates the increasing reluctance of managers to fulfil the debilitating bureaucratic roles in which they are cast:

They are reluctant to strive for career success if this can only be gained at the expense of personal and family relationships. Consequently, they are less prepared to subordinate their personalities to the requirements of their work and careers.   (Scase and Goffee, 1989, p. 179)

This reference to the reluctance of managers to do what they are unwilling to do, echoes the comments of Stewart (1982) who pointed out that managers have demands and constraints imposed upon them, but they also have choices they can exercise. Stewart has commented on some of her more recent findings:

[Middle managers] had new freedoms: freedom to take on new challenges; freedom to broaden their management expertise because of new responsibilities; freedom to innovate and, in some cases, risk-take; and freedom to apply relevant resources to achieving the priorities of the job.   (Dopson and Stewart, 1990, p. 14)

As managers feel a greater sense of control of their own destiny, they will feel a greater sense of personal responsibility for the social impact of the affairs of their business. It is interesting that a recent Cranfield survey of MBAs found that a large proportion of business graduates felt a need for more assistance with ethical questions in their MBA course (Holberton, 1991).

Moving towards an enhanced sense of social responsibility within the corporate setting probably goes beyond what we see at the moment in even the most socially responsible corporations, where corporate social responsibility may be seen by some employees as a fringe benefit, providing meaning because they are too passive to seek it on their own terms. Most employees, and certainly most well-educated managers, will seek more than that as a precondition for committing their enthusiasm, their creative imagination and their skills to making the corporation a success: their work must have meaning. If they are able to find greater meaning in their work, their effectiveness in all aspects is likely to be increased. Managers with meaningful roles are a prerequisite for any form of continuing organisational success, but . . .

> Meaning can not be forced on people, nor can it be found by those who have no control over the way in which their work is performed. If the corporation wants to create an environment where employees can find meaning, it has to give them the freedom and power to do so.   (Ciulla, 1990b, p. 34)

In academic analysis the question of social responsibility is profoundly affected by the disciplinary background of the researchers. The distinguished American sociologist Etzioni (1988) sees a near-universal dominance of economists' explanations for business strategy, despite economists' widespread disagreements and inaccurate predictions. He claims that the acceptance of the neoclassical economic paradigm as an explanation of human behaviour is insufficient due to its reliance on rationality. Not only does it provide guidelines for action that are too limited to succeed, it also makes it difficult to sustain a market economy. Etzioni argues that in practice most decisions are not made rationally, but on the basis of emotions and values.

Corporate governance

There is a growing awareness in company managements of the importance of social and environmental issues, indicated, among other ways, by the inclusion of community and environmental objectives in mission statements, donations to charitable causes and the secondment of senior managers to charities. At the same time some employers are making genuine efforts to improve the quality of working life for those employed in the business. This is partly influenced by government policy in creating an ideology that those in industry and commerce should collaborate with government in dealing with issues such as local unemployment.

After a flurry of interest a decade ago, comment on ethical considerations has again been appearing in professional management journals (e.g. Pocock, 1989). Codes of conduct are being developed by professional bodies in the management area. Among the extensive advocacy of identifying management competences as the basis for management development, there have been voices criticising the overemphasis on the narrow and technical at the expense of the ethical (Burgoyne, 1989; Maclagan, 1990)

Probably the biggest stimulus to social responsibility recently has been the intense interest in green issues (Elkington and Burke, 1989). In the UK as well as in the USA consumer power is being mobilised to press companies to 'green' their products and their processes (Corson *et al.*, 1989). Management response has been positive: the Institute of Directors reported that 43% of UK companies had adopted specific environmental policies and 21% had appointed managers specifically concerned with greening the company (*The Guardian*, 23 July 1990). The interesting problem comes when the customer loses interest. Supermarkets now sell fewer green products than a few years ago, but how far can a management go in developing policies which are responsible yet reduce turnover?

Responsibility, governance and culture

The extent and potential of socially responsible action by managers are considerable and their behaviour is shaped by a number of factors: legal regulation, public pressure, labour market factors, competitive threats, the personal values of individual decision-makers and considerations of company image. Most significant is the nature of the organisational culture. In 1992 British Airways apparently authorised various enquiries and activities to discredit their rival Virgin Atlantic. This was vigorously condemned by Virgin and led to expensive court proceedings. It is interesting that the activities were carried out in a covert way, although the same sort of investigations would be conducted by a national newspaper without any sense of shame or a need to keep them quiet. Values, beliefs and standards of behaviour vary between industries and between individual organisations. The Head of Organisational Effectiveness at Shell International explains how important are the Shell standards of behaviour, its norms and values, set out in 1976 and periodically reviewed:

> They are concerned with economic principles, business integrity, political activities, the environment, the community and availability of information. . . . Shell places great importance on these business principles, demonstrated by its policy to promote their adoption in any joint venture. . . . Shell has withdrawn from joint ventures and even countries where the business principles have not been honoured.   (Haddock, 1994)

A survey carried out in 1993 of 429 British companies showed that 80% already had some sort of company statement on corporate values and 89% believed that the issue of values would become more important in the next three years, but sometimes the statements are hollow:

> Six per cent of respondents admitted their corporate values were really only

slogans and more than half said they only partly made a difference. When asked what influences decision-making, three out of 10 said short-term commercial gain took priority over values and nearly four out of 10 said both were of equal value. (Mori, 1993)

The framework of organisational justice

The organisation requires a framework of justice to surround the everyday employment relationship so that everyone in the business knows what to expect of the working situation and how to deal with problems when dissatisfaction develops.

Culture and individual management style

The culture of an organisation profoundly affects the behaviour of people within it and develops norms that are hard to alter. If the norm is for everyone to arrive ten minutes late in the morning, a newly appointed manager will find that a difficult habit to change. Equally, if everyone is in the habit of arriving punctually, then a new recruit who often arrives late will come under strong social pressure to conform, without need for recourse to management action. Culture also affects the freedom and candour with which people discuss dissatisfactions with their managers without allowing them to get out of hand.

Individual managerial style reflects their beliefs about managing. The manager who sees discipline as being punishment and who regards complaints as impertinence will behave autocratically, being curt in disciplinary situations and dismissive of complaints. The manager who sees disciplinary problems as obstacles to achievement will seek out the cause of the problem. The problem may then be revealed as one requiring firm, punitive action by the manager, but it may alternatively be revealed as a matter requiring management remedy of a different kind. In either case the manager will be supported by the bulk of the employees. The manager who listens out for complaints and grievances gets to the bottom of the problems and finds that solutions will run little risk of persistent discontent from people muttering about trivial problems.

Rules

Every workplace has rules; the difficulty is to have rules that people will respect. Some rules come from statutes, like the tachograph requirement for HGV drivers, but most are tailored to meet the particular requirements of the organisation in which they apply. For example, rules about personal cleanliness are essential in a food factory but less stringent in a garage.

Rules should be clear, readily understood and sufficient to cover all obvious and usual disciplinary matters. They are the best possible topic for joint consultation and employee involvement, as that type of consultation can ensure that the rules are understood, and joint endorsement provides substantial authority. Employees must know what the rules are, and publishing the rules is not the same as ensuring that people know them.

Procedural sequence

Procedural sequence is essential to the framework of organisational justice, just as it is essential in the wider society. Procedure makes clear, for example, who does and who does not have the power to dismiss. The dissatisfied employee who is wondering whether or not to complain knows who will hear the matter and where an appeal could be lodged. This security of procedure, where step B always follows step A, is needed by managers as well as by employees, as it provides them with their authority as well as limiting the scope of their actions.

Procedures will only be a satisfactory feature of the organisational justice framework if they are seen as equitable. It is similar to the judicial process in adopting certain legal mechanisms, like the right of individuals to be represented and to hear the case against them, but some aspects of legalism, such as burdens of proof and strict adherence to precedent, may cause the application of standard remedies rather than the consideration of individual circumstances.

Notions of fairness are socially constructed and there will never be more than a degree of consensus on what constitutes fairness. Despite this, the procedural approach can exploit standards of certainty and consistency which are widely accepted as elements of justice. The extent to which a procedure can do this will depend on the suitability of its structure to local circumstances and on the commitment of those who operate it.

Managerial discipline

Finally managers must preserve general respect for the justice framework by their self-discipline in how they work within it. Some enthusiastic and hard-working senior managers maintain an 'open door' policy, with the message saying 'My door is always open . . . call in any time you feel I can help you.' This has many advantages and has become slightly easier during the times of collapsing hierarchies, but it can endanger the organisational justice framework because it encourages people to bypass middle managers. There is also the danger that employees come to see the settlement of their grievances as being dependent on the personal goodwill of an individual rather than on their human and employment rights. Openness is fine as long as it does not produce the very problem it is usually intended to overcome: middle management impotence.

In what ways may the senior manager's open door reduce the level of both responsibility and effective action by managers with less seniority? How can the problem be avoided?

Managers must also be consistent in their handling of employment issues. Whatever the rules are, they will be generally supported only as long as they deserve such support. If they are enforced inconsistently they will soon lose any moral authority and depend only on the fear of penalties. Equally, the manager who handles grievances quickly and consistently is well on the way to enjoying the support of a committed group of employees.

Handling grievances

People at work occasionally have grievances about their jobs, their working situation or their employment. It makes sense for managements to try to resolve these with the same determination as they try to resolve complaints from customers, as dissatisfaction leads to inefficiency. There is, however, a significant social responsibility to grievances as most employees are in a weaker situation than customers. People at work do not readily voice complaints about their jobs, partly because they do not wish to jeopardise their employment and partly because they are inhibited from 'taking on' their hierarchical superiors. Trade union organisation means that dissatisfactions can often be handled anonymously. In the increasing number of work situations where trade unions are not recognised, or recognised for only some employee groupings, that opportunity is missing and managers have to work harder at uncovering problems.

'Grievance' is an awkward word, closely associated with the idea of grief and generally too strong to be used by individuals about their own feelings. In our context it is a technical term that describes the possible culmination of a process of three stages:

Dissatisfaction is anything that unsettles an employee, even if it is not actually expressed.

Complaint is when that sense of dissatisfaction continues long enough or is sufficiently strong for the dissatisfied person to bring it to the attention of the manager in charge.

Grievance is when a complaint is not dealt with, or dealt with in a way that does not remove the dissatisfaction, so that the dissatisfied person takes the matter further through procedural sequence. Grievance is formally challenging the action or inaction of the manager in charge.

| REVIEW TOPIC 8.3 |

Think of an example of employee dissatisfaction causing inefficiency in the organisation that was not remedied because there was no complaint made. Why was there no complaint?

This provides us with a useful categorisation by separating out grievance as a formal, relatively drastic step, compared with commonplace grumbling. The restaurant analogy is useful. Seldom is everything entirely to the satisfaction of the customer. The bread will be stale, the plates cold, the potatoes undercooked, the service slow or the vegetables overdone, yet complaint in restaurants is rare, even when the waiter asks the potentially suicidal question, 'Did you enjoy your meal?'. Some people leave the restaurant with raging indigestion, resolved to 'write in and complain', but few do. If we generally lack the courage to complain to a waiter, or the resolution to write a letter to the management, how much less likely is it that we will complain to the manager at work who is going to carry out our annual appraisal in three weeks' time? It is even less likely that we will go the further step of formulating a grievance.

Despite these inhibitions, managers have to find some way of uncovering dissatisfaction. Although nothing is being expressed, the feeling of hurt following failure to get a pay rise or the frustration about shortage of materials can quickly influence performance.

Much dissatisfaction never turns into complaint, as something happens to make it unnecessary. Dissatisfaction evaporates with a night's sleep, after a cup of coffee with a colleague, or when the cause of the dissatisfaction is in some other way removed. The few dissatisfactions that do produce complaint may also resolve themselves. The person hearing the complaint explains things in a way that the dissatisfied employee had not previously appreciated, or takes action to get at the root of the problem.

Grievances are rare since few employees will question their superior's judgement and fewer still will risk being stigmatised as a troublemaker. Also many people do not initiate grievances because they believe that nothing will be done as a result of their attempt.

Managers sometimes conceal the complaints they are hearing, for fear of showing themselves in a poor light. Employees who feel insecure, for any reason, are not likely to risk going into procedure, yet the dissatisfaction lying beneath a repressed grievance can produce all manner of unsatisfactory work behaviours as well as leading to serious individual stress.

A further twist to the management problem of dealing with grievances is the most exasperating of all: does the complaint mean what it says? What is said (the manifest content) may not be the whole story, as there may be strong feelings behind what is being said (the latent content) that are not being expressed, and the dissatisfaction will persist until the latent content is dealt with.

Roethlisberger and Dickson (1939) concluded, for instance, that one employee who complained of his supervisor being a bully was actually saying something rather different, especially when he gave as his reason the fact that the supervisor did not say 'good morning'. Later it was revealed that the root of his dissatisfaction was in his attitude to any authority figure, not simply the supervisor about whom he had complained. Just to make life really difficult (no-one ever said management was easy), there is the conviction held by some managers that every simple complaint has a latent content that the mixed-up employee is dying for the manager to unravel. Millicent had worked as a cleaner at a hospital for ten years and decided to leave when her husband retired, because she did not like working shifts and weekends. She told George, her supervisor, and got very cross as he spent half an hour quizzing her about her relationship with her husband and with her three daughters in order to find out 'what was really bothering her'.

Grievance procedure

Grievance procedure is often resented by managers, because of the formality it introduces into the working relationship. The problem is that many people will not raise issues that could be regarded as contentious with the immediate superior. Procedure provides a framework within which individuals can air their grievances and avoids the risk of managers avoiding difficult issues. It avoids the risk of inconsistent *ad hoc* decisions and the employee knows at the outset that the matter will be heard and where it will be heard. The key features of grievance procedure are fairness, facilities for representation, procedural steps and promptness.

Fairness is needed to keep the procedure viable. If employees believe the procedure is only a sham, then other means will be found to deal with grievances. Fairness is best supported by the obvious even-handedness of the ways in which grievances are handled, but it will be strengthened by having an appeal stage either to a joint body or to independent arbitration, as the management is then relinquishing the chance to be judge of its own cause. It is rare for a joint body of management and employee representatives to be the final appeal body, but external arbitration – usually by ACAS – is more widely adopted.

Representation can help the individual employee who lacks the confidence or experience to take on the management single-handedly. A representative, such as a shop steward, has the advantage of having dealt with a range of employee problems and may be able to advise the person with the grievance whether the claim is worth pursuing.

Procedural steps should be limited to three, as there are three types of management activity involved in settling grievances.

The first step is the *preliminary*, when the grievance is lodged with the immediate superior of the person making the complaint. In the normal working week most managers will have a variety of queries from members of their departments, some of which could become grievances, depending on the manager's reaction. Mostly the manager will either satisfy the employee or the employee will decide not to pursue the matter. Sometimes a person will want to take the issue further. This is the first tangible step in procedure as the manager has the opportunity to review any decisions made causing the dissatisfaction, possibly enabling the dissatisfied employee to withdraw the grievance.

The *hearing* is when the complainant has the opportunity to state the grievance to a more senior manager, who can take a broader view of the matter and who may be able both to see the issue more dispassionately and to perceive solutions that the more limited perspective of the immediate superior obscured. It is important for the management that the hearing should finalise the matter whenever possible, so that recourse to appeal is not automatic. This is why procedural steps should be limited to three.

If there is an *appeal*, this will usually be to a designated, more senior manager and the outcome will be either a confirmation or a modification of the decision at the hearing.

Promptness is needed to avoid the frustration that can come from delay. When an employee 'goes into procedure', it is like pulling the communication cord in the train. The action is not taken lightly and it is in anticipation of a swift resolution. Furthermore, the manager whose decision is being questioned will have a difficult time until the matter is resolved. The most familiar device to speed things up is to incorporate time limits between the steps, specifying that the hearing should take place no later than, say, four working days after the preliminary notice and that the appeal should be no more than five working days after the hearing. This gives time for reflection and initiative by the manager or the complainant between the stages, but does not leave time for the matter to be forgotten.

Health and safety

Through ignorance, carelessness or neglect an employer can endanger the health of those working in the organisation, as well as customers, visitors and local residents. An aspect of corporate governance is therefore to protect both the physical and the psychological well-being of those whose lives the organisation affects. There is extensive legislation that gets ever more extensive as new technologies create fresh hazards not covered by existing laws. The basic protection for many years was a series of Factories Acts, which were directed mainly at ensuring protection against long hours and unsatisfactory space, ventilation and heating. The Control of Substances

Hazardous to Health (COSHH) regulations of 1988 comprise nineteen different regulations and at least four codes of practice.

The increase in the number of technologies and the elaboration of production processes inevitably generates an increased administrative burden on the employer in maintaining the records and carrying out the checks that are required by the monitoring systems put in place by the legislators and their administrators. There is a risk that the emphasis of management action on safety at work can be deflected away from the actual safety and well-being of people at work towards filling in the right forms.

The COSHH regulations have five main features, which contain a logical sequence for dealing with all health matters:

1. Assessing the risks and identifying what precautions are needed.
2. Introducing measures to control or prevent the risk.
3. Ensuring control measures are used, procedures followed and equipment regularly maintained.
4. Carrying out health surveillance.
5. Employee information and training.

Even the assessment in (1) can take substantial resources. Cherrie and Faulkner (1989) reported that one employer was using no fewer than 25,000 different substances, each of which had to be assessed.

---| REVIEW TOPIC 8.4 |---------------------------------------

Safety requires rules of behaviour that must be followed. Rules that appear strict and 'bureaucratic' will not be readily followed. How can we develop rules that are adequate and which will be followed?

In recent years there has been a radical change in the status of stress at work. Until the 1980s stress was popularly regarded as a feature of high-powered executive positions, and the holders of such positions wore their stress with pride, rather like battle veterans showing their scars ('if you can't stand the heat, get out of the kitchen'). Inexorably, research has demonstrated that debilitating stress is much less likely to harm only the holders of executive posts. It is experienced in all occupations, especially in manual work, with its routine, repetitiveness and lack of autonomy (Cooper and Smith, 1985). In many ways executives have the best scope for resisting stress, because of the variety in their lives and the amount of choice they are able to exercise about what they do and when they do it.

The most interesting method of dealing with stress and the personal problems of employees has been the development of access to counselling by telephone. The employer contracts with a counselling consultancy to provide a service, which employees can reach by telephone at any time. The counsellor can then either deal with the matter personally, like a member of the Samaritans, or can arrange for more specialist assistance, all on a confidential basis. In some organisations there is a counsellor on the premises, but there is still a widespread reluctance to be seen by one's colleagues 'going for help', so the telephone help line overcomes many of the problems.

Privacy

Employers hold personal information about employees and are in a position to abuse their employees' privacy in a number of ways, by the information they might provide to those not entitled to receive it, or by the misuse of such information.

Under the Data Protection Act of 1984, all organisations must register with the Data Protection Registrar if they hold in a computer memory:

> . . . data which relates to a living individual who can be identified from the information, including an expression of opinion about an individual, but not any indication of the intentions of the data user in respect of that individual.

It is then necessary to comply with eight data protection principles, requiring that personal data will be:

1. obtained and processed fairly;
2. held only for lawful purposes;
3. used or disclosed only in a manner compatible with specified purposes;
4. adequate, relevant and not excessive in relation to purpose;
5. accurate and kept up to date;
6. not kept longer than necessary for the specified purpose;
7. protected against unauthorised access and accidental loss;
8. available to the individual for inspection and, where appropriate, correction or erasure.

With the flattening of hierarchies and the rapid change in company practices as they seek elusive competitive advantage, the issue of socially responsible management action becomes more significant, especially as collective employee representation becomes less assertive and the solidarity of the workforce is reduced through varied forms of employment contract. Study of the subject is in its infancy, especially in Britain, where there is a high level of cynicism about the likelihood of social responsibility ever outgunning commercial imperatives if the decisions are to be left to managers, echoing the sentiment of George Bernard Shaw who wrote, in 1907: 'All professions are conspiracies against the laity'.

The management 'profession' has yet to establish and monitor the types of ethical codes which affect, if they do not exactly govern, the behaviour of lawyers and surgeons.

SUMMARY PROPOSITIONS

8.1 Hierarchy undermines personal responsibility for one's actions.

8.2 As organisational hierarchies either flatten or crumble, there is more scope and need for managers to exercise responsible autonomy.

8.3 Socially responsible behaviour in organisations is influenced by the organisational culture. Values, beliefs and standards of behaviour vary markedly between industries and organisations.

8.4 Responsible management action in relation to employees is aided by a framework of organisational justice and mechanisms for handling grievances.

8.5 Health and safety at work can be adversely affected by the monitoring provisions of government agencies.

8.6 Reasonable privacy of information about individuals held by organisations is maintained by statute, but only if it is held on computer.

PUTTING IT INTO PRACTICE

There are various methods that can be used to promulgate agreed ethical standards within a company.

1. Policy statement

The instrument of policy, described in Chapter 4, can be part of a process to get acceptance of ethical standards. Two aspects of policy are important when dealing with ethics that may not be present in other types of policy: a clear statement of the values on which the company's ethical standards are based, and a categorical assurance that individual action that accords with those values and any accompanying code of practice will not be penalised.

a. *Values.* The importance of the underpinning values is that they will involve ideas like duty and moral obligation which are the most powerful sources of ethical behaviour. If you believe that you *should* do what you can to ensure that people have equality of opportunity at work, that belief will influence your behaviour quite differently than simply knowing that there would be unfortunate consequences, like a tribunal hearing, if you were caught out.

b. *Assurances.* The importance of the assurance is that some people feel that ethical behaviour is a luxury that will be abandoned by their bosses if business is seriously threatened.

2. Organisational Culture

As we see in Part III, there is great management interest in developing an organisational culture that is appropriate to organisational circumstances, and culture is to do with values and beliefs. It is therefore logical to embed ethics in the corporate culture, but you must then jettison the idea of 'appropriateness'. Ethical behaviour that adapts to circumstances is not ethical behaviour.

3. Code of Practice

If there is a policy, it can be useful to have a code of practice to articulate and illustrate the policy. The code will include examples or direct guidance on action to be taken in the type of problematic situations faced by people in that particular business. Typical features could be:

a. *Confidentiality.* There are dilemmas about the handling of confidential information about the business, about clients and about employees, as we have seen in the section about data protection. The code of practice could give explicit guidance on this.

b. *Inducements.* If a sales representative takes you out to lunch in order to discuss the detailed specification of an order that you have already placed, that is not likely to be seen as an inducement. If that same sales representative takes you on an all-expenses-paid weekend in Paris before you have decided whether or not to place the order, then it presumably is an inducement to you to place the order. Business gifts, from glossy calendars to bottles of whisky, is a practice that has declined in recent years, but guidance is still useful, both on receiving and on giving inducements.

c. *Urgency.* People at work often face the pressure of a deadline, and this can generate a temptation to skimp or cut corners in order to meet a specific delivery date. In the motor trade there used to be the term 'a Friday afternoon job' to describe a car that had a number of faults, implying that it had been assembled in a hurry on Friday afternoon before everyone went home for the weekend. This is complicated by the fact that some deadlines are unnecessarily tight ('I must have it by Friday, so I will tell Sandra it is needed by Wednesday'). How does one cope with apparently incompatible demands?

d. *Priorities.* A particular version of the urgency dilemma is how to deal with conflicting priorities, especially when the conflict is generated by colleagues. On most occasions, the resolution of conflicting priorities is a business decision, but it sometimes has an ethical dimension as well, such as perhaps not mentioning a very slight potential safety hazard to a customer because of the overriding priority of getting the business.

e. *Whistle-blowing.* A code of practice could reinforce the assurance of the policy statement by setting out how potential whistle-blowers could express their concerns and how they would be protected against subsequent victimisation.

References

Burgoyne, J., 1989, Creating the managerial portfolio: building on competency approaches to management development, *Management Education and Development*, vol. 20, pp. 56–61.

Cherrie, J. and Faulkner, C., 1989, Will the COSHH regulations improve occupational health?, *Safety Practitioner*, February.

Ciulla, J. B., 1990a, Business ethics as moral imagination, in *The Teaching of Business Ethics*, ed. Freeman, R. E., Oxford University Press.

Ciulla, J. B., 1990b, Can the corporation provide meaningful work?, *New Jersey Bell Journal*, Fall.

Cooper, C. L. and Smith, J. M., 1985, *Job Stress and Blue Collar Work*, John Wiley, Chichester, West Sussex.

Corson, B. *et al.*, 1989, *Shopping for a Better World: An Easy Guide to Socially Responsible Supermarket Shopping*, Council for Economic Priorities, New York.

Dopson, S. and Stewart, R., 1990, What *is* happening to middle management?, *British Journal of Management*, vol. 1, no. 1, April.

Elkington, J. and Burke, T., 1989, *The Green Capitalists*, Victor Gollancz, London.

Etzioni, A., 1988, *The Moral Dimension: Towards a New Economics*, Free Press, New York.

Haddock, C. M., in prep., How Shell's organisation and HR practices help it to be both global and local, in *International Human Resource Management*, ed. Torrington, D. P., Prentice Hall International, to be published in 1994.

Holberton, S., 1991, MBAs at the crossroads, *Financial Times*, 9 April, p. 15.

Jackall, R., 1988, *Moral Mazes: The World of Corporate Managers*, Oxford University Press.

Kanter, R. M., 1989, *When Giants Learn to Dance*, Unwin, London.

Maclagan, P., 1990, Moral behaviour in organizations: the contribution of management education and development, *British Journal of Management*, vol. 1, pp. 17–26.

Milgram, S., 1974, *Obedience to Authority*, Tavistock, London.

Mori, 1993, reported in *Personnel Today*, April, p. 29.

Pocock, P., 1989, Is business ethics a contradiction in terms?, *Personnel Management*, vol. 12, no. 11.

Roethlisberger, F. J. and Dickson, W. J., 1939, *Management and the Worker*, Harvard University Press, Cambridge, Mass.

Scase, R. and Goffee, R., 1989, *Reluctant Managers: Their Work and Lifestyles*, Unwin Hyman, London.

Shaw, G. B., 1907, *Dramatic Opinions and Essays*.

Stewart, R., 1982, *Choices for Managers*, McGraw-Hill, Maidenhead, Berkshire.

Part III

Responsibilities

Managers have responsibilities, some of which are shared while others are individual. All have a responsibility for profitability and obeying the law, but some will have responsibilities for a function or an operation that is theirs alone.

The central responsibility for all managers is the performance of themselves, their team members and their unit. That performance will be influenced by a shrewd understanding by managers of what is going on around them and by a clear understanding of the strengths and the diversity of the individuals within the team. Managers need to develop their own effectiveness and then find ways of coordinating all activities to produce cooperative (and perhaps competitive) effort to reach the goal.

G   R   O   U   P

Chapter 9

Managing change and innovation

Change is one of the catchwords of the last ten or more years, and an ability to manage change is a prime requirement of management success. However, it is worth remembering that only two new industries emerged in the period from 1947 to 1975: computers, and systemic drugs. In contrast the period from 1856 to 1914 produced a new invention, leading to a new industry, every fourteen to eighteen months. So it may be that people in the nineteenth century in Western societies were living with even more change than we are now.

Many of the outcomes of the issues discussed in Part I of this book require the managing of change. To some people, change means excitement and the thrill of being part of the action and keeping up with trends. For others, change feels like a threatening, imposed dismantling of the stable order of things with a great deal of uncertainty which is frightening. The common saying is that change is now an everyday part of our lives. There is a useful distinction between four broad types of change experience.

First is *imposition*, where the initiative comes from someone else and we have to alter our ways of doing things to comply with this external requirement. This undermines our sense of security in being able to handle what we know, and we worry about the implications of what is now required. The initiative comes from someone else, so that we can only respond, and our response will be limited because someone else has already set the parameters. New rules, new laws, changes in working practices are all examples of this category.

Second is *adaptation*, where we have to change our behaviour or our attitudes at the behest of others. Acquiring different attitudes can be extremely difficult, as the persistence of racial prejudice demonstrates, and we are likely to feel uncertainty about our ability to become the new type of person. This is probably the main reason people retire early, as they lack the confidence to change the values and behaviours in which they have come to trust.

157

In contrast, *growth* is much more attractive. Now we are not responding to the demands of others, but to the opportunities for becoming a person of greater competence, poise and achievement.

The fourth type of change experienced is *creativity*, where we are the instigator and in control of the process, bringing into being that which we have envisaged. Most of us are probably resistant to the first, uncertain about the second, delighted with the third and excited by the fourth. Whoever is pulling the strings is most likely to overcome the difficulties of one and two by ensuring that three comes first!

Whether we are trying to get others to change, helping others to handle change, or trying to cope with change ourselves, it is worth taking some time to think it through. We need to think about what needs changing and how the change is to be implemented.

REVIEW TOPIC 9.1

The philosophers have only interpreted the world in various ways, the point is to change it.   Karl Marx, 1818–1883

Why is it difficult to move from analysis to action?

Why change?

The first indications to some that change is necessary are that things do not seem to be working quite as well as they used to. Too much time is spent patching up, filling in or dealing with crises. For example, the biscuit production line which is constantly stopping or overflowing onto the floor needs something changing. The hotel receptionist who finds rooms over-booked on several occasions clearly needs to change something. The Deputy Headteacher who is at school from 7.30 in the morning until 7.00 at night at least three days a week might want to change something to get life better balanced. These indicate changes that an individual might initiate.

Another indication of change ahead is the rumblings heard in head office, the community, parliament, at conferences or from customers. Gradually it is felt something should be done and guidelines are issued, codes of practice agreed on or laws passed. For example, laws passed on the sort of polyurethane that can be used in furniture will mean changes for manufacturers and importers. Codes of practice about late night opening before Christmas mean changes for shop workers and their managers. New common technical standards within the EC mean understanding the guidelines about the new documentation and test procedures and ensuring that everyone involved also understands them. The public services particularly have to deal with this imposed change, and decisions are taken at a political level about such matters as the content of education in schools, priorities for the health services or whether money is to be spent on nuclear

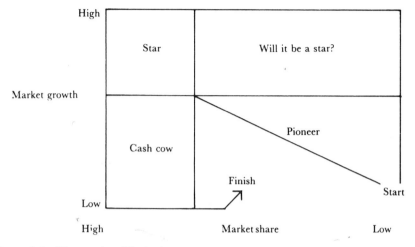

Figure 9.1 The product life cycle.

or conventional weapons for the armed forces. All of these imposed changes need careful implementation as they invariably meet resistance where people have not been involved in deciding what to change.

A third reason for expecting change is the desire to keep up to date with new products and services to offer as old ones become outdated. A much quoted model of the life of a product is that developed by the Boston Consulting Group (see, Stewart 1983, pp. 19–24), shown in Figure 9.1.

Products start off from innovation and creativity (see later) with not a lot at stake at the pioneer stage. The next stage has a question mark to indicate whether it will be a future star or not and is the risk-taking stage. The third stage is when there is rapid growth in the market and the product becomes a star. The fourth stage is when the product has an established position in the market but is no longer increasing its share of the market. The final stage is when the product makes little money and has no further prospects. Each stage requires a different sort of managing in order to anticipate a different sort of change ahead. Kay (1993) is particularly good on the complexity of gaining a competitive edge from innovation.

| REVIEW TOPIC 9.2 |

The most striking of all impressions I have formed since I left London a month ago is of the strength of this African national consciousness . . .
The wind of change is blowing through this continent.

Harold Macmillan, 9 February 1960, Cape Town

Why is acknowledging that change is inevitable so difficult for well-established people and organisations?

What needs changing?

Whatever the reason for change, deciding what has to be changed is often a difficult step. Because the *how* of change is seen as complicated, the *what* is often given less attention. For example, change may be needed in resolving the biscuit production problem because of technical difficulties with the conveyor belt, such as rollers being worn out or mismatched with the new ovens, or the operators not following the correct procedure for mixing the ingredients so that the biscuits are too brittle and, consequently, fall off more easily. Or the staff may feel aggrieved over the new shift system and not be as vigilant as previously about problems on the line.

Similarly, the hotel receptionist may need to improve the booking system, the percentage of 'no-shows' may need to be worked out again and reassessed, or the staff may need training to fill in the official booking forms, not just give over keys. The Deputy Headteacher may need to assess the work in a day and what is being done that does not need to be done, what can be done by others and what are the priorities of the job.

All these are examples of the fact that any reason for change may need several things changing. There may be technical changes required in the product, machinery or building. There may be changes in the systems of procedure, monitoring, communication or budgeting required. Changes in the organisation of the department or unit may be necessary. There may also be changes necessary in our personal beliefs, behaviour or work. We also need to decide whether we want more, different or better of whatever needs changing and whether that is possible.

McCalman and Paton (1992) have proposed a test (see Figure 9.2) known by the acronym TROPICS which allows managers, or management teams, to get a feel for the nature of the change and to establish more appropriate ways of managing the task. It allows managers to assess both the impact and the magnitude of the impending change. Where the change mostly involves factors of type A a systems approach is probably appropriate using all the 'hard' methods of planning and evaluating. Where the change mostly involves B factors an organisation development approach with its emphasis on the 'soft' management methods to involve people is more appropriate. Where there are straight As or Bs there is a clear path to a solution. More frequently the answer is a mixture of As and Bs. McCalman and Paton give the following examples (p. 21):

Case A: Time scale 'A', with all other factors 'B'. This scenario would indicate an emergency situation, a time of crisis. . . . This would be a hard-hitting dictatorial solution to overcome short-term difficulties, to be followed by a longer period of education . . .

Case B: Source 'B', with all other factors 'A'. This could represent an external technical change to a system, possibly as a result of a manufacturer's technical update. A systems approach to implement the change along with a limited education programme for operatives may be required.

TROPICS factor			Solution methodology (tendency towards)
Time scales	Clearly defined/ short to medium term A	Ill defined/ medium to long term B	A = Hard B = Soft
Resources	Clearly defined/ reasonably fixed A	Unclear and variable B	A = Hard B = Soft
Objectives	Objective and quantifiable A	Subjective and mission orientated B	A = Hard B = Soft
Perceptions	Shared by those affected A	Creates conflict of interest B	A = Hard B = Soft
Interest	Limited and well defined A	Widespread and ill defined B	A = Hard B = Soft
Control	Within the managing group A	Shared outside the managing group B	A = Hard B = Soft
Source	Originates internally A	Originates externally B	A = Hard B = Soft

Note: 'Hard' refers to a systems-based solution methodology.
'Soft' refers to an organisational development methodology.

Figure 9.2 The TROPICS Test (McCalman and Paton, 1992).

How to make changes

How to get changes effected is the concern of most managers. Sometimes it is to get imposed changes accepted. Sometimes it is to get agreement that change is necessary but the solution is still to be found. Sometimes it is persuading individuals to change their ways to comply with the norms of the organisation. Managing change can be seen from three perspectives: the individual, group dynamics, or open systems for the organisation.

As Pettigrew (1985) argues, change is not just a rational choice of events but has to be seen in its cultural and historical context. His study of ICI suggests that a sequence of episodes was involved in the dramatic changes at ICI:

1. There were rational arguments for change with a concentration on political influencing of events.
2. There was an emphasis on efficiency whose advocates became powerful.
3. There were exceptional men who were able to foresee what ICI needed and persuade people to follow them.
4. There were extreme circumstances of plants being outmoded.
5. There was the untidiness of chance events, people, materials, resources and circumstances generally.
6. There were the forces in the environment such as economic and political climate, oil prices, competitors building/closing plants, and legislation affecting pollution and health.

Pettigrew argues that change occurs because of a mixture of these; the problem is gaining legitimacy for the change proposed. He suggests (p. 434) a model for effecting change:

1. The development of concern by a subset of the organisation.
2. Acknowledgement and understanding of the problems with possible causes and alternatives by others.
3. Planning and acting to create specific change.
4. Stabilising the change including rewards, information and power to appropriate individuals to sustain the change.

| REVIEW TOPIC 9.3 |

Change is not made without inconvenience, even from worse to better.

Samuel Johnson, 1709–1784

Kanter (1989) in her very successful book *When Giants Learn to Dance* suggests three ways to make change: first, by restructuring organisations to create synergies; second, by opening the boundaries of organisations to form strategic alliances; and third, by creating new ventures from within organisations by innovation or enterprise approaches.

Detailed discussion about organisation level changes is included in our chapter on strategy and policy-making (Chapter 4), the specific arguments about technical changes are given below, and discussion about changing the behaviour of individual performers is in our chapter on staff development (Chapter 23). We also recommend our colleague Bernard Burnes's book (1992) for a review of managing change.

One commonly used device to look at how to change is force field analysis, in which the driving forces for the change are represented by arrows on the left which are contrasted with arrows on the right representing restraining forces: see Figure 9.3. A specific diagram can be drawn for any

Driving forces   Restraining forces

Personal
Interpretation
Group
Meeting
Organisation
Environment
Legislation

Figure 9.3 Force field analysis.

proposed change. It is useful for examining and evaluating the forces for and against the change. It can also be helpful in understanding the power of those looking for change and those opposed to the change, which can affect the ability to get the change into practice. The value of force field analysis is in getting people to consider the position of the other stakeholders.

Innovation and creativity

Innovation and creativity are terms used not to describe dark forces disturbing our ordered calm, but interesting activities undertaken by people at work that keep their organisations lively and up to date by exploring possible new activities and changed methods of doing things.

> Innovation and creativity have to do with development, proposal and implementation of *new* and *better* solutions. (Steiner, 1965, p. 4)

Proposals have to meet the criteria of being both new *and* better. When colleagues are reluctant to support innovations, it may be because of lethargy and lack of imagination, but it may also be because the proposed innovation is not a very good one, and not a convincing improvement on present practice. The map of underground railway stations in London is a masterpiece of design. Although it has been considerably extended to take account of new lines, the basic design has not altered for over sixty years. A recent attempt to introduce a new format was met by such a hostile reception that the original was quickly reinstated.

Other inhibitors of change are cost and acceptance. In many ways it would be more convenient if the British were to drive on the right-hand side of the road instead of the left, but the cost of the change outweighs the potential benefits. Decimal currency was initially resisted because of the cost of changing, and because of the difficulty of getting acceptance of the change. Both problems were overcome, so that now it is unusual for anyone to think of pounds and pence and then convert their sum to pounds, shillings and pence. Metrication is taking longer. An interesting example of resistance to innovation is the conventional typewriter keyboard. When

Christopher Sholes produced the first typewriter in 1874, the keys used most frequently were deliberately spaced wide apart in order to slow typists down; otherwise the keys would jam. The keyboard layout remains the same a century later, not only on manual and electric typewriters, but also on word processors and computers. It would be completely sensible to change the layout, and simplified layouts are available but are not widely marketed because of the difficulty of changing the habits of millions of typists.

Innovation is the whole process from invention to practice; creativity is the initial phase of generating the new idea, product or approach. Both of these have to be viewed in the light of finding innovations that are better as well as new, and which are thoroughly thought through to verify their practicability, cost and acceptability.

Pavitt (1979) reasons that technical innovation and industrial development are increasingly important for four main reasons. First, there is growing competition from developing countries who produce an expanding range of standard goods as their industrialisation progresses. Secondly, the taste of consumers and their expenditure level are constantly changing in the more advanced countries. Thirdly, we have to consider ways of reducing the consumption of energy and the environment: both scarce and irreplaceable resources. Finally, great possibilities are provided by the rapid technological changes in fields such as electronics and biochemistry. These may sound like matters for a few leading figures to consider and develop, but an interest in innovation is important for all members of organisations, especially managers, and it is an important approach to the regular, everyday matters as well as the exciting.

Burgelman and Sayles (1988) describe this as Internal Corporate Venturing (ICV) and illustrate the processes involved in Figure 9.4. The process begins in their view in the bottom left-hand box of the model. The process starts at the bottom where technically trained, entrepreneurially inclined managers perform two linking tasks: technical linking where new items of knowledge are combined, and need linking where the resulting solution could be shown to meet an existing market. This early definition stage then leads into product championing. Successive stages involve more senior staff who are largely reactive but control the whole process by focusing on the main business rather than agreeing to too much diversification. The model shows how the various parts of the organisation have a role to play in getting a technical innovation developed.

We can now review the main stages of innovation: invention or creativity; dissemination and development of the invention; and the consequences of the invention in practice.

□ = Key activities	Core processes		Overlying processes	
Levels	Definition	Impetus	Strategic context	Structural context
Corporate management	Monitoring	Authorising	Rationalising	Structuring
New venture division management	Coaching Stewardship	Strategic building	Delineating	Negotiating
Group leader/ Venture manager	Technical and need linking	Strategic forcing	Gatekeeping Idea generating Bootlegging	Questioning

Figure 9.4 Internal Corporate Venturing (Burgelman and Sayles, 1988).

Invention or creativity

Parker (1978) suggests that there are three theories about invention. The *transcendental model* is the theory that invention depends on individual acts of genius. In the *mechanistic model* necessity is the mother of invention in that inventions are produced to meet problems that have arisen. The *cumulative synthesis model* is one where investigation, thought, analysis and discussion are stimulated by individual acts of insight. These insights are not, however, the quantum leaps of the first theory, but a series of insights that illuminate the problem and cause progress.

A continuing academic discussion is whether the demand for a new, or revised, product is the push to innovation; or is it scientific inventions that provide the pull for innovation? The practical implications of this question for businesses are important as they centre round the issue of where one should look for innovation. Should a company concentrate its efforts on having sensitive feelers out to pick up changes in the market, like the staff in teenage fashion boutiques going to discos, or should it invest in speculative research, like a pharmaceutical company investigating pain? The academic discussion will continue for a long time, but the practical answer to the question seems to be that companies will do both, depending on the particular market and product range in which they are interested.

| REVIEW TOPIC 9.4 |

Think of examples of:

1. The demand for a new or revised product providing the push to innovation.
2. Scientific inventions providing the pull for innovation.

Whichever of Parker's models one accepts, there is always a small number of people in an organisation who produce a large proportion of the initial ideas to trigger the innovation process. Psychologists have tried to distinguish the characteristics of individuals associated with high levels of creativity. Steiner (1965, pp. 7–8) summarises these as follows:

1. *Conceptual fluency*, the ability to generate a large number of ideas rapidly.
2. *Conceptual flexibility*, the ability to discard one frame of reference for another.
3. *Originality*, the tendency to give unusual, atypical answers.
4. *Preference for complexity over simplicity*, looking for the new challenge of knotty problems.
5. *Independence of judgement*, being different from peers and seeing superiors as conventional or arbitrary.

If that listing is accurate, then creative individuals need to be nurtured, as the qualities are unlikely to be warmly welcomed by colleagues and will make it difficult for their possessor to function comfortably in an organisation. They are likely to be regarded as odd and possibly as a nuisance, so they must be identified and their potential contribution channelled effectively.

The organisational setting influences how the creative individual performs, as organisations tend to emphasise an organisational culture and norms: 'There is the right way, the wrong way, and our way'; or 'In this company we all pull together. Team spirit is our watchword.' There may be an emphasis on corporate image through aspects of dress, like the business suit. Organisations acquire a reputation for preferring certain types of skills or personality. Well-known bodies like the armed services or the BBC attract recruits with some potential but other people would never apply. The innovatory organisation needs both to attract and to sustain diverse characters in its ranks as a necessary prerequisite for innovation.

Torrance (1970) provides a classic discussion about creative children and how their inventiveness can be encouraged. Creative adults similarly need to be nurtured within the organisation and reconciled to the fact that the world about them is satisfied with its errors. Here are his suggestions of what one can provide for the highly creative:

1. Provide a refuge.

2. Become their sponsor or patron.
3. Help them understand their divergence.
4. Let them communicate their ideas.
5. See that their creative talent is recognised.
6. Help others to understand them.

Little is understood about the nature of invention, but a great deal of effort has gone in to understanding how it can be stimulated. Here are three ways in which an organization or a department can make inventiveness among its members more likely (based on Paines, 1970).

First, emphasise the importance of *keeping notes*. Workable ideas seldom leap, honed and finished, into the mind. A stray thought comes into focus for a moment but without any apparent connection with anything else, or at least without a complete connection. It beguiles because of its newness and apparent potential, but will drift away when the telephone rings, or a conversation begins. The moment has passed and the idea is lost. These moments of insight (or flashes of inspiration) have to be written down so that they are captured for future examination. Also the act of writing it down will embed it at least slightly in the mind, which may then work on it without one being aware of it. We are all familiar with the idea of deferring an idea until we have 'slept on it', often finding that a course of action that was uncertain on retiring is clear on waking. Partly this may be the diurnal rhythm of the body that tires in the evening and is rejuvenated in the morning, so that problems lessen as the sun rises; but it is also due to the fact that our unconscious unravels things for us. The philosopher scientist Arthur Koestler (1964) believed that the great acts of creativity happen in periods of rest after working hard on the problem.

Secondly, there is value in setting *deadlines and quotas* for the production of ideas. This ensures that people attempt to find solutions, rather than putting off the problem until later. Working up new ideas is hard work, and it is all too easy to distract oneself with maintenance activities instead of settling down to wrestle with thinking. One of the authors has overwatered plants and very fat cats!

Thirdly, set aside a *time and place* for generating ideas. As we saw in Chapter 2, managers rarely allow themselves this sort of time, and allow thinking to be squeezed out by the frenetic activity of responding to the demands of others before returning home in the evening having 'never stopped'. The technique of brainstorming contrives deadlines, quotas, a time and a place to ensure that idea generation happens. It is not the romantic view of genius as exemplified by Lord Byron moving sadly from one mistress to another while waiting for inspiration to purge his ennui, but it does produce results.

Fourthly, check the *housekeeping* of the organisation. Is inventiveness valued and rewarded, or is it regarded as a nuisance? Are there channels by which the inventive can advance, so that non-conformists can have a sense of career growth because of, rather than despite, their unconventionality? Are the channels of communication reasonably open, so that ideas can be expressed and discussed with a view to finding their merit instead of only finding fault? Always there is the need for balance. The organisation devoid of inventiveness and creative thought will wither through lack of nourishment, but the organisation that is taken over by the creative and where the administrators are suppressed will probably destroy itself.

---| REVIEW TOPIC 9.5 |---

The English novelist George Orwell (1903–1950) wrote in his most famous work, *Nineteen Eighty-Four*: 'Doublethink means the power of holding two contradictory beliefs in one's mind simultaneously, and accepting both of them.' How is this different from brainstorming?

Dissemination and development of the invention

The invention has to be disseminated by informing others about it and making them enthusiastic. It then has to be made feasible and put into practice. If that does not happen, the most brilliant idea will be stillborn.

Many academic researchers are criticised for not putting sufficient effort into disseminating the findings of their research to those who could put them to practical use. Ralph Waldo Emerson said that the world would beat a path through the forest to the door of a man who could write a better book, preach a better sermon, or make a better mousetrap. The world will only beat the path if they know the better mousetrap is there – and if they happen to want a better mousetrap.

In an organisational context innovators need first to influence and persuade their immediate circle that the idea is fruitful. This often happens informally in the office or is a regular part of section meetings, as the outline of the idea is tested to see the reaction. It is very difficult to get anywhere with a new proposal without the endorsement of the immediate boss and the constructive criticism of immediate colleagues, who will be the first links in the communications network that will be needed to reach implementation. If this group provides its support and commitment, then the next 'layer' of boss and colleagues have to be persuaded, see Figure 9.4.

Now all the skills of influence and political manoeuvring that are discussed in Part IV of this book become important. First the idea has to be understood as a better method than what currently operates (see Chapter 21 on how to prepare a case). Then a commitment has to be won to allocate resources needed to explore the possibilities of the idea. This often involves other departments in the organisation and can seldom be ignored. Too often new ideas are adopted by organisations on face value only and are tried out without being properly tested first, and scarcity of resources is the most common pretext. There is no budget provision for committing money to experiments, so either the proposal is implemented straight away or it is passed over.

Most readers will recall at least one instance in their working lives of an organisational change that went wrong (some may not be able to recall one that went right!). Organisational change is one of the types of innovation that is too often put into operation without being thoroughly worked out first. The broad outlines of allocating responsibility between senior managers are discussed extensively and heatedly, but the nuts and bolts and the ultimate feasibility do not receive the same, necessary, exhaustive examination. Senior managers defend such precipitate action by claiming that organisational change has to be forced in order to overcome the resistance and apathy in the lower levels of the hierarchy. To the outside observer, however, it usually seems more like simple impatience and unwillingness to work through the really difficult problems that can be encountered.

Other types of innovation are also difficult to disseminate and Parker (1978) suggests some factors that influence the success of getting an invention into practice:

1. Understanding user needs.
2. Paying attention to marketing the product.
3. Developing efficiently; not necessarily quickly.
4. Using outside technical and scientific advice.
5. Having a senior manager responsible for the innovation.

Langrish *et al.* (1972) studied all the companies that had been awarded The Queen's Award for Industry over two years, and identified the following factors that affected success:

1. The top person in the company was outstanding and had authority.
2. There was at least one other outstanding person.
3. The need to be met was clearly identified.
4. The potential usefulness of the innovation was realised.
5. Good cooperation.
6. Resources were available.
7. There was help from government.

Those two lists, and Pettigrew's mentioned earlier, have points of coincidence that are particularly relevant to the dissemination and development of any sort of innovation. The most ingenious idea will founder unless there is a user need to be met. The user may be a customer; it may be a department within the organisation, part of the administrative process linking supply and demand, or some other gap that can be filled. The need does not have to be known to the potential user, but it does have to be a potential need. There will be a potential need for a better mousetrap among people plagued by mice, but the person who invents playing cards that can be used under water is unlikely to find a queue of customers. It also seems to be an inescapable requirement for the innovator to find a patron. The sluggish processes of organisation have to be stimulated not only by the excellence of the idea and the enthusiasm of colleagues, but also by the determination of at least one person holding a significant position of power in the hierarchy.

Langrish and his colleagues also identified the factors that delayed the development of inventions:

1. Some other associated technology was not sufficiently developed.
2. No market for the idea.
3. The potential of the idea was not recognised by management.
4. Old ideas were embedded and there was resistance to new ones.
5. Resources were not available.
6. There was poor cooperation and communication.

Innovations are not automatically understood and passed smoothly into operation. Dissemination and development are harder to manage than the initial creative stage. Lewis Lehr as Chairman of the 3M company believed that all members of the organisation have to be attuned to the possibilities of a new idea being a winner.

> The attitude toward new projects or programs can be very significant. In a company where people at any given time are involved in exploring hundreds of potential developments, it is extremely important that top management do not pre-judge the activities and, for example, identify a group of questionable investment projects under the heading, 'problem programs'. Some years ago we did this. It was not until we re-named this list 'selected opportunities' that these programs received the attention necessary to eliminate them as problems and redirect them as opportunities.   (Lehr, 1982, p. 98)

Invention needs much stimulation and nurture; it is too easy to destroy.

The consequences of invention

Like all social action, there are consequences of innovation that are unintended as well as those that are intended, and we have to guard against the assumption, mentioned earlier, that change is automatically desirable. Rogers and Shoemaker (1971, p. 71) provide us with three classifications of the consequences that follow innovation.

First the consequences will be functional or dysfunctional, depending on whether the effects are desirable or undesirable. Secondly, there will be direct or indirect consequences, depending on whether it is an immediate response to innovation or a response to the result of those consequences. Thirdly, the consequences may be latent or manifest, depending on whether or not the consequences are recognised and intended or not.

Advocates of change usually expect functional, direct and manifest consequences, but invariably some latent consequences are indirect and dysfunctional. An important management activity is to anticipate as many as possible of the unintended consequences, without quashing useful innovation.

Managing innovation in the department

Some departments in organisations are set up for the sole, or prime, purpose of innovating. It is the business of the research and development department to introduce, test and develop new ideas. Display and advertising departments need to generate new methods of projection and communication, and other departments are specifically intended to seek new business opportunities and to foster new ventures.

For most departments, however, innovation is more a leavening in the continuing operations to keep excess conformity at bay. A steady stream of new ideas and methods is needed to avoid dullness and to ensure that the department is making its proper contribution within the organisation, but too many innovations may destabilise operations. In the chapter about organisational politics we see how there is a need to strike a balance between openness and political behaviour among managers. Managing innovation is a similar problem of balance. There must be a cooperative, cohesive working group maintaining an efficient operation, but a part of that cooperative effort is always to encourage and nurture individual creativity so that promising ideas are tested and developed in pushing forward the frontier of what is being achieved. Managerial innovation and creativity perhaps begin by setting up that equilibrium.

How to cope with change

In Chapter 3 we mentioned how the work of managers is a balance between those activities that give us comfort and those that give us novelty. The stimulation of novelty and change usually means we put more effort into something. However, if the stimulation becomes too great we become less able to make a useful contribution. This can be summarised graphically, as in Figure 9.5. It is at this point that stress is experienced with all the associated feelings of increased ambiguity and the possibility of failure.

Toffler as long ago as 1970 recognised that we can cope with a lot of change, pressure, complexity and confusion if at least one area of our lives is relatively stable. He suggested these stability zones were all-important. The main kinds of stability zones are as follows:

1. Ideas – moral, religious, political.
2. Places – home, town, pub, offices.

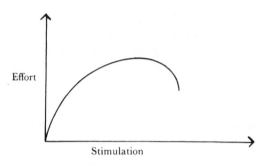

Effort

Stimulation

Figure 9.5　Effect of stimulation and effort.

3. People – spouse, parents, old college friends.
4. Organisations – Rotary, church, employer.
5. Things and habits – routines, possessions, cars.

We all need at least one of these to be secure. Working out where our stability zones are and maintaining them help us to cope with stress in other areas. For example, the salesperson who enjoys travel, new food, new ideas, new films, books and people, who is impatient with tradition and seeks novelty, often has been in the same job for years or has a group of long-lasting friends or a good, close marriage.

Ed Schein (1978) has coined the phrase 'career anchors' to suggest that there are distinct categories of stability zone at work that individuals will evaluate themselves on. Each of us will have one of these as most important in our lives. Schein's five career anchors are:

1. *Managerial competence.*　Individuals seek out and value opportunities to manage. They have a strong motivation to rise to positions of managerial responsibility.
2. *Technical/functional competence.*　People enjoy the technical activity, for example, finance, engineering, marketing, nursing.
3. *Security.*　The anchor for some who look for a stable career situation, job security, a decent income and a reasonable pension.
4. *Creativity.*　For those who want to build something entirely their own such as a new product, process, theory, company and fortune.
5. *Autonomy and independence.*　People value being free from constraints and able to pursue their own life and work style.

Various strategies for keeping one's balance during a time of rapid and unsettling change are:

1. Know what to keep stable, for example, stability zones.
2. Calm one's physiology and so control the pace at which one works. Use the pause to breathe slowly for a second or two. Meditation can help here.

3. Ask for help. It can bring new insights, new companionship, new learning. Beware of becoming an advice junkie who never gets to the action, but advice from one or two carefully chosen people can either tell you what to do or so clarify the problem that the solutions suggest themselves.

Influencing others to change

How does one persuade those we work with to change in the desired way? The research literature suggests there are several questions that need to be answered.

What is in it for them?

If the person can see that the new behaviour, procedure or technology will make their work easier, more interesting, more fun, they are likely to be enthusiastic. If they cannot see any benefit they are likely to resist it; or they will appear to change in order to test it or show loyalty, but the change disappears before long. The chapter on motivation and influence (Chapter 20) has detailed evidence about the importance of meeting a felt need for people to want to act.

Have they had a say in the change?

If people help to create a new scheme they are more likely to be committed to making it work (see Chapter 25 for details). There needs to be a genuine opportunity to participate in the introduction, design, execution, feedback and evaluation of any and all aspects of the new programme. However, retaining the option not to change is rarely included in the consultation process. An example of sham consultation was a questionnaire sent to all members of a head office whose top managers had decided to relocate. The questionnaire asked whether they would like to go to another central London, outer London, M4 corridor or north-west England location. The response showed that 70% wanted a London location domestically and 50% a London location for the business. The planning permission for the new headquarters in the North West was published on the front page of a local north-west paper the same month, suggesting that the decision had already been made. It is surprising that senior staff wondered why staff felt abused!

Is it clear what change is envisaged?

If we are trying to persuade someone to change we need to have a clear vision of what we want to achieve. This vision needs to be practical, with a clear explanation about why, what, and possibly how, it is to be done. It needs to be put in terms that are understood by the other person. Too often a rather confused picture is given because the change is not well thought out. This is perfectly sensible if the other person is to be included in deciding whether a change is necessary and, if so, what. It is quite inappropriate where the change has already been decided and we want to influence them to cooperate. Frequently we try to communicate an idea which is at the edge of our own understanding, particularly where the idea or change has been handed down from on high.

Are there guidelines for managing change?

There are lots of books and pamphlets giving guidelines on how to manage change. One we find useful is by McCalman and Paton (1992); another based on research in schools is by Loucke-Horsley and Herger (1985). They base their guidelines on seven steps:

1. Establishing the project.
2. Assessment and goal setting.
3. Identifying a solution.
4. Preparing for implementation.
5. Implementing the project.
6. Reviewing progress and problems.
7. Maintenance and institutionalisation.

They give the following wise advice:

1. Acting is better than planning. Protracted needs assessment can be worse than none at all.
2. The Head is not the key to school improvement. Although the Head is important, so are many other people.
3. Thinking you can truly create ownership at the beginning of a project is ridiculous. Like trust, ownership and commitment build and develop over time through the actual work of improving a school.
4. Help and support given to teachers after planning and initial training is much more crucial for success than the best (pre-implementation) training money can buy.
5. Coercion is not always bad. A firm push, coupled with lots of help, can launch a project on a path to success.
6. New programmes and practices imported from somewhere else may offer a viable, cost-effective, alternative to major development efforts.

SUMMARY PROPOSITIONS

9.1 Change may be imposed, to improve current performance, or to keep new products and services coming.

9.2 We may need to change the technical aspects, the systems, the organisation or our personal behaviour.

9.3 Change is not just a rational process but involves the culture of the organisation.

9.4 Change is not only something to which to respond, but also something to initiate.

9.5 Creativity is the initial phase of generating a new idea, product or approach; innovation is the whole process from invention to practice.

9.6 The main stages in innovation are invention or creativity; dissemination and development of the invention; and the consequences of the invention in practice.

9.7 Inventiveness among organisation members is made more likely by the use of notes; deadlines and quotas for the production of new ideas; setting aside a time and a place for generating ideas; and checking the housekeeping of the organisation.

9.8 To cope with change ourselves we need to keep something stable.

9.9 To influence others to change we need to think what is in it for them.

PUTTING IT INTO PRACTICE

Drill for brainstorming

Brainstorming is frequently used within organisations to generate new ideas. This can be new products, services or ways of working. For example, one plastics business team used the following procedure one morning to generate ideas on how to develop partnerships with their customers.

Brainstorming is a specialised technique for developing a range of new ideas for examination. You need a flipchart, blackboard or overhead projector and someone who can write quickly and legibly.

Before the session

1. Decide the purpose of the session. Is it:
   (a) To find uses for a new idea?
   (b) To find a better way of doing something? or
   (c) To find a solution to a problem?
2. Make a note of any ideas you have about the subject.

Conducting the session

3. Appoint a note-taker.
4. Ask group members to call out any idea that comes into their heads.
5. Write ideas on blackboard, flipchart or overhead projector, so that all group members can see them.
6. Encourage group members to develop the ideas of others, as well as 'sparking' in different directions.
7. Eschew judgement by anyone in the group. All ideas are valid, however bizarre, and even if they seem to be repeating what has been said already.
8. Generate momentum, so that the group keeps going.
9. Reach a target number – say 75 – ideas in 15–30 minutes.

After the session

10. Classify the ideas generated into five or six groups, possibly adding others that are suggested by the classification.
11. Ask the group to rank the ideas in each classification against questions such as
    (a) How new?
    (b) How relevant?
    (c) How feasible?
12. Decide on action, if any, to be taken to develop preferred ideas.

References

Burgelman, R. A. and Sayles, L. R., 1988, *Inside Corporate Innovation – Strategy, Structure and Managerial Skills*, Free Press, New York.

Burnes, B., 1992, *Managing Change*, Pitman, London.

Kanter, R. M., 1989, *When Giants Learn to Dance*, Unwin, London.

Kay, J., 1993, *Foundations of Corporate Success: How Business Strategies Add Value*, Oxford University Press.

Koestler, A., 1964, *The Act of Creation*, Hutchinson, London.

Langrish, J. R., Gibbons, M., Evans, W. G. and Jevons, T. R., 1972, *Wealth from Knowledge*, Macmillan, London.

Lehr, L. W., 1982, Entrepreneurs, innovation and change, quoted in *How to Manage*, ed. Wild, R., Heinemann, London.

Loucke-Horsley, S. and Herger, L. F., 1985, *An Action Guide to School Improvement*, Association for Supervision and Curriculum Development, Andover, Mass.

McCalman, J. and Paton, R. A., 1992, *Change Management: a Guide to Effective Implementation*, Paul Chapman, London.

Paines, S. J., 1970, Education and creativity, in *Creativity*, ed. Vernon, P. E., Penguin Books, Harmondsworth, Middlesex.

Parker, J. E. S., 1978, *The Economics of Innovation*, Longman, London.

Pavitt, K., 1979, Innovation and industrial development, *Futures*, p. 458.

Pettigrew, A. M., 1985, *The Awakening Giant: Continuity and Change in ICI*, Blackwell, Oxford.

Rogers, E. M. and Shoemaker, F. F., 1971, *Communication of Innovation*, 2nd edn, Free Press, New York.

Schein, E. H., 1978, *Career Dynamics: Matching Individual and Organizational Needs*, Addison Wesley, Reading, Mass.

Steiner, G. A., 1965, *The Creative Organization*, University of Chicago Press.

Stewart, V., 1983, *Change: the Challenge for Management*, McGraw-Hill, London.

Toffler, A., 1970, *Future Shock*, Pan Books, London.

Torrance, E. P., 1970, Causes for concern, in *Creativity*, ed. Vernon, P. E., Penguin Books, Harmondsworth, Middlesex.

Chapter 10

Management in an international organisation

Working internationally has a much wider meaning now than ten years ago. Then the phrase conjured up visions of expatriates acting as technological or managerial missionaries in developing countries, overseas sales representatives doing deals in cosmopolitan hotels, or the foreign predator buying up your business cheaply and making everyone redundant. Although each of those images is still apt, they do not constitute the whole. The patterns of international management are diverse and few companies work in the same way. There is a great deal more collaboration and working together across national boundaries between organisations with common interests (see, for example, Caulkin, 1993), and international working is no longer the preoccupation of a small elite group of managers.

> Successful international managers, whether mobile or non-mobile, must be able to act locally, but to plan and think strategically and globally.
>
> (Barham and Rassam, 1989, p. 149)

There is a great management challenge at the close of the millennium for managers to place their local actions in a framework of global thought and strategy. This is particularly demanding because of the persisting variations in practice, despite international initiatives like that of the European Community:

> Systems which in most countries have evolved incrementally over the course of many decades – even centuries – have each acquired a distinctive coloration, adapted to the idiosyncrasies of national socio-economic structure, national political regimes, and perhaps also national temperaments.
>
> (Ferner and Hyman, 1992, p. xvii)

At the same time there is the ever-increasing significance of the multinational company as the means whereby individual economies are integrated into a global economy, with a small number of very large companies accounting for a disproportionately large number of people in employment.

Management implications of international activities

International business involves both *decentralisation* and *expansion of management*. As an organisation increases its international activities, it steps up the degree of decentralisation, but it would be an oversimplification to suggest that internationalisation is simply a form of decentralisation. It is the most complex form of decentralising operations and involves types of difference – language, culture, economic and political systems, legislative frameworks, management styles and conventions – that are not found in organisational growth and diversification that stays within national boundaries.

In a detailed analysis of what they see as necessary for companies to survive in the global marketplace, Bartlett and Ghoshal (1989) argue that international businesses need both to fragment and integrate. The fragmentation is the decentralisation that is needed to empower the subsidiaries, so that they become autonomous units within a corporate family instead of being overseas subsidiaries of a parent company. Some features, like recruitment and industrial relations negotiations, are almost entirely fragmented, so that there is little need for a coordinated, centrally driven policy.

| REVIEW TOPIC 10.1 |

Think of other examples of how an international business fragments its business by decentralising management decision and action. What scope is there for further fragmentation?

Integration is the expansion and intensification of management activities in increased coordination to ensure that the business remains whole. New features are added, like advanced schemes of remuneration for cosmopolitan employees, and new forms of communication to ensure the necessary 'corporate glue'. Although nearly all recruitment and selection is decentralised, a new activity is developing in the recruitment, selection and training for an elite corps of international managers.

Effective international management is also concerned with *managing cultural diversity*. It is not simply transferring complete operational practices from one country with its set of cultural assumptions to another where the cultural assumptions are different – no matter how slight the difference may be. Technically, operationally and financially that may be appropriate, but not in that subtle essence of management – the organisation of the people – that makes the difference between failure and success. There is some discussion of cultural differences in Chapter 14, but at this point it is appropriate to mention the work of Hofstede (1980, 1991), who has identified clear differences for country groupings.

Hofstede identified four key factors to explain differences in national cultures, two of which were power distance and uncertainty avoidance.

Power distance is the extent to which less powerful members of the society accept the unequal distribution of power. Uncertainty avoidance refers to the extent to which societies socialise their members to accept the uncertainty of the future and to take risks. He argues (1991, pp. 140–6) that countries emphasising large power distance and strong uncertainty avoidance in their cultures were likely to produce forms of organisation that relied heavily on hierarchy and clear orders from superiors: *a pyramid of people*.

In countries where there is small power distance and strong uncertainty avoidance there would be an implicit form of organisation that relied on rules, procedures and clear structure: *a well-oiled machine*.

The implicit model of organisation in countries with small power distance and weak uncertainty avoidance was a reliance on *ad hoc* solutions to problems as they arose, as many of the problems could be boiled down to human relations difficulties: *a village market*.

The picture is completed by the fourth group of countries where there is large power distance and weak uncertainty avoidance, where problems are resolved by constantly referring to the boss who is like a father to an extended family, so there is concentration of authority without structuring of activities. The implicit model of organisation here is *the family*. Table 10.1 shows which countries are in the different segments.

So now we have a classification of cultural diversity that tells us that the implicit form of organisation for Britain is a village market, for France it is a pyramid of people, for Germany it is a well-oiled machine and for Hong Kong it is a family. If we can understand the organisational realities in those four countries, then we have clues about how to cope in Denmark, Ecuador, Austria or Indonesia, because they each share the implicit organisational form of one of the original four.

It is not quite as easy as that, because the clusters show only relative similarities, but the four-way classification is useful, if not completely reliable, although all the research material was gathered in the 1970s: there may have been radical changes since then.

In Hofstede's second book he produces a refinement of the uncertainty avoidance dimension: 'Confucian dynamism', or long-term versus short-term orientation. Management researchers are typically from Western Europe or the United States, with all the cultural bias that such an orientation involves. Working with the Canadian Michael Bond, Hofstede used a Chinese value survey technique in a fresh study and uncovered a cultural variable that none of the original – Western – questions had reached. This was long-term orientation, and the highest scoring countries on this dimension were China, Hong Kong, Taiwan, Japan and South Korea. Singapore was placed ninth. Leaving out the special case of China, we see that the other five countries are those known as the 'Five Dragons' because of their dramatic rate of economic growth. As Hofstede says:

The correlation between certain Confucian values and economic growth is a surprising, even a sensational, finding.   (Hofstede, 1991, p. 167)

He argues that countries in the West have derived their culture largely from the three religions of Judaism, Christianity or Islam, all of which are centred on assertion of truth that is accessible to true believers, whereas none of the religions of the east is based on the assertion that there is a truth that a human community can embrace.

They offer various ways in which a person can improve him/herself, however these do not consist in believing but in ritual, meditation, or ways of living. . . . What one does is important.   (*ibid.*, p. 171)

The 'Confucian' values found attached to this long-term orientation included perseverance, clearly maintained status differentials, thrift, and

Table 10.1 Types of organisation implicit in different countries

Pyramid of people	Well-oiled machine	Village market	Family
Arab-speaking	Austria	Australia	East Africa
Argentina	Costa Rica	Britain	Hong Kong
Belgium	Finland	Canada	India
Brazil	Germany	Denmark	Indonesia
Chile	Israel	Ireland	Jamaica
Colombia	Switzerland	Netherlands	Malaysia
Ecuador		New Zealand	Philippines
France		Norway	Singapore
Greece		South Africa	West Africa
Guatemala		Sweden	
Iran		United States	
Italy			
Japan			
Korea			
Mexico			
Pakistan			
Panama			
Peru			
Portugal			
Salvador			
Spain			
Taiwan			
Thailand			
Turkey			
Uruguay			
Venezuela			
Yugoslavia			

having a sense of shame. In many ways these values are valuable for business growth, as they put social value on entrepreneurial initiative, support the entrepreneur by the willing compliance of others seeking a place in the system, encourage saving and investment, and put pressure on those who do not meet obligations.

Management methods do not necessarily transfer from one culture to another, but international management is not a process of all managers learning the cultures of every country in which they have to deal and suitably modifying their behaviour when dealing with those nationals. This is simply too difficult. Cultures are robust and subtle and we have great difficulty in achieving more than a modest level of behaviour adaptation. International management requires the understanding and managing of cultural diversity. It is not a process of becoming polycultural.

In many ways international management is simply national management on a larger scale; the strategic considerations are more complex and the operational units more varied, needing coordination across more barriers. It is possible, however, to identify some activities that are different in nature when a business is international and we review three of these in this chapter.

People working internationally

International management involves the employment of people who spend part of their time in another country. There are four broad categories of such employees and we consider the different management implications of their working.

The cosmopolitan

A very small number can be described as cosmopolitans. Constantly on the move and having their main working arena away from their home base, these managers develop their own culture and ways of working together, acquiring the ability to work and negotiate with each other in a separate cultural world, inhabiting identical international hotels.

Cosmopolitans will be mobile and experienced in a number of overseas locations. George van Houten describes the Philips job rotation approach:

> The job rotation practice leads to a rich exchange of perspectives. When you send a Norwegian to Brazil, a Pakistani to Singapore, or an American to the Netherlands, the cultural influences that are traded are bound to result in an international point of view in the company as a whole.
>
> (van Houten, 1989, p. 110)

Managing the cosmopolitan requires careful selection, so that those who move into these demanding roles are emotionally and physically equipped for the challenges involved. It requires extensive and specialised preparation

– probably through a well-chosen MBA – to acquire international competence and expertise. It requires people with language proficiency and the intercultural self confidence that such proficiency develops. This is, however, a small group in any business:

> The number of executives falling into this category is extremely small, with each firm counting them in tens rather than hundreds, and even in the largest firm in our study, this group was said to number about 200. It is therefore as numerically insignificant as it is qualitatively vital.   (Atkinson, 1992, p. 74)

The expatriate

Cosmopolitans touch down in foreign countries; expatriates go and live in them, probably taking a family and staying for two or three years. This requires thorough management of the process, before they go, while they are away and – crucially – when they come back:

> UK multinationals are becoming increasingly conscious of the importance of a successful repatriation process . . . preparing for expatriation and developing an adequate support system for expatriates while overseas . . . are now well established and are generally well done. Attention must increasingly turn to repatriation as the third element in the process.   (Johnston, 1991, p. 108)

Although many Western countries have long experience of expatriates, this has been mainly in the colonial mode, with companies assigning young managers to manage local workforces. Expatriation is no longer one-way; there are fewer people who spend their whole career overseas and more who include one or two overseas assignments in acquiring the necessary breadth of experience and vision to operate at senior level in an international organisation.

The effect of expatriation on the expatriate and on the expatriate's family is likely to be considerable. The great majority of expatriates are married men, whose wives are nearly always placed in a position of total or partial dependency by corporate expatriation: one career is subordinated to another. For the increasing proportion of expatriate wives with a professional career in suspension, this can require considerable ingenuity to adapt.

The question of expatriation or not is the major question in selection, but the particular location is the next most important determinant in matching the person to the job. Among the most important issues are:

Culture.   How different from home is the culture of the country – religion, the social position of women, the degree of political stability/instability, personal security and petty crime, local press and television, cable television, availability of foreign newspapers, health hazards.

Economic development.   How well developed is the economy of the country – standard/cost of living, availability of familiar foods and domestic equipment, transport, post and telephone, local poverty, health and education facilities, availability of international schools.

Geographical location. How far away is it and where is it – climate, in a cosmopolitan city or more remote, the importance/unimportance of language proficiency, the size of the local expatriate community, employment prospects of spouse.

The job. What has to be done and what is the situation – nature of the organisation, proportion of expatriates, technical, commercial and managerial demands of the job, staffing and support, the extent of role in managing local nationals. Many expatriates are simply moving to exercise their company expertise in a different location, but the situation will always be different, no matter how similar the conventions and procedures, especially when managing local nationals.

Coming back from an overseas assignment seldom receives the attention it needs. Why should there be problems about coming home?

There is first the issue of what the overseas experience was like. If it has been thoroughly satisfactory for all members of the family, there may not be much enthusiasm for returning. On the other hand the overseas experience may have been difficult, so that the prospect of returning home produces a great build-up of anticipation, that leads to some let-down on actually getting back.

Secondly is the career situation of the returning expatriate. Johnston (1991, p. 103) found that virtually all repatriated personnel had problems in reintegrating on return to a UK organisation, loss of status, loss of autonomy, lack of career direction and lack of recognition of the value of overseas experience.

> . . . little appears to be done at a personal level for the returning managers who are expected in the main to work things out for themselves. No companies within the Chemicals, Manufacturing and Services sectors sample had a formal company reorientation for repatriates to aid their social and professional integration into what will inevitably be a substantially different organisation from that which they left. (Johnston, 1991, p. 106)

REVIEW TOPIC 10.2

Can a manager be an effective cosmopolitan without first being an expatriate?

The engineer

The term 'engineer' is used here broadly to cover all those technical specialists who spend spells of a few weeks or months at a time in an overseas location to carry out a particular job, such as commissioning new plant or training local personnel in its use. The overseas spell is not as long and the role more specific than that of the expatriate. It is similar to seafarers, airline crew, travel couriers and the increasing number of Western academics who spend a few weeks or months abroad. They are not living abroad: simply away from home for a spell.

The engineer needs complete technical expertise and the personal resourcefulness to cope with unforeseen technical problems and a wide variety of social situations. Compared with cosmopolitans and expatriates, engineers are more likely to be assigned to remote locations, even though they are usually accommodated in an international hotel. It can be a monotonous life, with little scope for social activity apart from the hotel bar and pool. Regular health checks are essential and efficient administrative arrangements for travel, accommodation and contact with base during assignment. Some engineers find it very difficult to settle back into the more routine tasks that often await them when the days of travelling are over.

The occasional parachutist

Occasional parachutists are those people who 'drop in' occasionally for a few days to deal with some very specific question that has cropped up, like a problem with the computer system, or an input to a training course, or technical assistance with a round of commercial negotiations. Like the engineer, they are representatives of the company and can form invaluable network connections for formal and informal communication. Many employees move between countries only in this mode and the exchanges can be vital in developing mutual understanding between nationalities and compatibility of the systems and procedures in different parts of the business. They can also do harm. Someone visiting for only a few days has little incentive to learn about the country and the people, and may therefore carry stereotyped assumptions that could be damaging to relationships within the company. It can be helpful if novices travel together with an experienced person and talk before travelling with an expatriate or someone else familiar with the culture.

Coordination in international companies

> To operate as an effective strategic whole, the transnational must be able to reconcile the diversity of perspectives and interests it deliberately fosters, integrate the widespread assets and resources it deliberately disperses, and coordinate the roles and responsibilities it deliberately differentiates.
>
> (Bartlett and Ghoshal, 1989, p. 166)

We saw at the beginning of this chapter that international companies have to pursue both fragmentation and integration simultaneously. The above quotation shows how managers give themselves major problems of coordination by adopting the measures that they see as necessary for business success. Approaches to coordination must increasingly move to a more intercultural style, as the dominance of the parent company nationality declines in favour of the multinationality of the global business. Coordination is the way to synergy, so that the global business does more and better together than it could possibly achieve as a number of independent units. There are four suggestions of how the fragments can be coordinated.

Evangelisation

The word evangelisation is used here to describe the process of winning the acceptance throughout the business of a common mission and a shared purpose. This is a familar idea in management thinking, but it is particularly challenging in international management because of the number of barriers to be surmounted in coordination, especially the barriers of language, culture, national boundaries and parochial self-interest. Evangelisation is used to describe this process because evangelists confront the same barriers as those dealing in the world of global business.

One of the most successful great international companies has been Matsushita, the founder of which established in 1932 a development plan that was set out to cover a 250-year period! All employees undertake a programme of cultural and spiritual training and all worldwide units of the company have a daily assembly ritual. This sounds bizarre to most managers, but Matsushita have enjoyed over 60 years of business success. By the 1990s the example of the American electronics giant IBM was less convincing, but throughout its years of market leadership, the company had some evangelistic features, including the IBM hymn, which caused one team of French analysts to describe it as *la nouvelle église* (Pages *et al.*, 1979).

Evangelisation works through *shared belief*, relatively simple doctrines to which members of the organisation subscribe and through which they are energised. In the 1970s a British company, Vitafoam, was established by a man who required his senior executives to copy out his annual policy statement by hand, three times, before handing it back to him. It is now commonplace for companies to have mission statements, which come close to being unifying articles of faith.

> At the top is the mission statement, a broad goal based on the organization's planning premises, basic assumptions about the organization's purpose, its values, its distinctive competencies, and its place in the world. A mission statement is a relatively permanent part of an organization's identity and can do much to unify and motivate its members. (Stoner and Freeman, 1992, p. 188)

They can also be seen as wish lists, with all the associated difficulties of unrealised aspirations.

Evangelisation also works through *parables*. Ed Schein (1985, pp. 237–42) identified 'stories and legends' as one of the key mechanisms for articulating and reinforcing the organisation's culture. The company house magazine can help to circulate the good news about heroic deeds in all parts of the company network. Word-of-mouth exchanges and accounts of personal experience are better. Those who visit another country have stories to tell to all members of the company when they return, not just to the senior managers conducting the debriefing.

REVIEW TOPIC 10.3

Think of examples where you have felt a greater degree of understanding about what your organisation is doing, and what its activities mean through listening to parables about it.

Evangelisation can work through *apostles*, ambassadors sent out to preach the faith. These are the cosmopolitans described above. Because of their frequent movement they know the worldwide organisation well and can describe one component to another, explaining company policy, justifying particular decisions and countering parochial thinking. They can also move ideas around ('In Seoul they are wondering about . . . what do you think?') and help in the development of individual networks ('Try getting in touch with Oscar Jennings in Pittsburgh . . . he had similar problems a few weeks ago.')

Apostles are likely to be especially busy at times of crisis, strengthening resolve and cooling anxiety. It may be important that they come from headquarters and have personally met, and can tell stories about, the founder. Anita Roddick's Body Shop grew rapidly by working in a way that was markedly different from the conventions of the cosmetics industry that it was challenging. People in all parts of the business identified closely with the vision and personality of the founder:

> The inductresses' eyes seem to light up whenever Anita's name is mentioned. We are told, in semi-joyous terms, the great tale concerning that first humble little shop in Brighton. And . . . one of our inductresses uses the phrase, 'And Anita saw what she had done, and it was good'.   (Keily, 1991, p. 3)

Standards and norms

Coordination can be improved by the development and promulgation of shared standards and norms, and they do not necessarily have to be developed at the centre. Decentralised standard formulation can enable different parts of the global business to take a lead as a preliminary to universal adoption of the standard they have formulated: an excellent method of integration.

Few businesses will be able to develop universally applicable standards in all aspects of management. Many manufacturing developments in Asia have been for the explicit reason of being able to enjoy the benefits of low labour costs. It is most unlikely that the American/European/Japanese parent company would develop a company-wide standard on the level of pay rates in manufacturing. In contrast a company-wide standard set of terms and conditions for expatriate assignment would be much more feasible. The Institute of Personnel Management Library in London has just such a document from IBM in the form of a sample letter of 24 pages!

Systems and procedures

Many global businesses are dominated by a single system, which reaches every part of the business. An airline has a ticketing and booking system which links thousands of computer terminals. At a booking desk in Moscow you can book a seat on an aircraft travelling from Hong Kong to Manchester. Hotel chains have central reservation systems to book rooms throughout the world. These systems are useful only if they provide the global link, and providing the systems link constantly reinforces with all personnel the interrelationship of the company's activities. All businesses have systems and they provide a useful management opportunity for integration. In one country, for example, a team might develop a spare part retrieval system that is quickly adopted for use throughout the business, while in another country they concentrate on an aspect of accounting procedures or systematic advice on training opportunities. In this way there is coordination through interdependence, as well as avoidance of duplication.

Capability

Another possibility is the concentration of *capability* by encouraging the development of particular expertise in different locations, but for group-wide application. Bartlett and Ghoshal (1989, pp. 106–7) describe how Teletext was developed by Philips. Because of an interest from the BBC, the British Philips subsidiary began work on the possibility of transmitting text and simple diagrams through a domestic television set. Within Philips generally it was regarded as 'a typical British toy – quite fancy but not very useful'. The British persisted and ten years later there were three million Teletext receivers in use in Britain. Philips had established a world lead in a product for which there was initially only a British market.

Philips have pioneered this type of development, settling activities in places where the culture suits the activity.

> . . . their centre for long-range technology development was recently moved from the United States to the Far East, where the time orientation was seen as more conducive to innovation than the 'quick fix' mentality of North America.

Some major research departments are located in Italy, which is seen by other firms as an impossible country for important facilities. Yet their Italian research laboratories are highly successful, as are the important R & D facilities of IBM and DEC in the same region. All of them run in a uniquely Italian way, and are left to do so since this appears to lead to their success. Manufacturing plants are likely to be located elsewhere – Germany, for example. (Evans *et al.*, 1989, p. 116)

REVIEW TOPIC 10.4

Are there activities in your business that would be better located in a different part of the world because the culture of that country would be more suitable for the activity?

International communication

The dissemination of information throughout the organisation helps managers to think globally before taking local action, so that members of the different units in the business understand why a company has been acquired in South America, even though it seems to threaten the livelihood of some parts of the parent organisation. Foulds and Mallet (1989, p. 78) suggest the following as purposes of international communication:

- to reinforce group culture so as to improve the speed and effectiveness of decision taking;
- to encourage information exchange in internationally related activities and prevent the 'reinvention of the wheel';
- to form the background to the succession planning activity – certain cultures demand certain types of people;
- to establish in people's minds what is expected of them by the parent company;
- to facilitate change in a way acceptable to the parent company;
- to undermine the 'not invented here' attitude and thereby encourage changes;
- to improve the attractiveness of the company in the recruitment field – particularly where the subsidiary is small and far from base;
- to encourage small activities, which may be tomorrow's 'cream', and give such activities a perspective within the international activities.

There is an assumption in that list that the company is a parent with subsidiaries, and this is not always true, but it remains a useful summary. There is a need for constant communication throughout the organisation to disseminate information and to sustain changing values. The organisation must operate holistically. It is not the sum of its parts: the whole exists in every part. Customers have a holistic view of the organisation. If your motor car breaks down you are dissatisfied with the manufacturer or the supplier and you are not mollified to be told that the problem was caused by a component manufactured in the Korean subsidiary. Managers cannot work effectively in their part of the business without understanding its simultaneous relationship to the whole. Businesses function holistically and holism is a function of constant, efficient communication, like the bloodstream and the central nervous system.

Communication in any organisation mainly follows the work flow, as members communicate with each other in connection with their work, first within a particular work group, then between one work group and another which is adjacent in the work flow, and then between departments. When a company is operating internationally the work flow pattern may provide the logical main channel for communication. If a washing machine is produced by manufacturing electronic components in California, sub-assemblies and wiring harnesses in Korea and final assembly in Scotland, there is an easy sequence to follow. Among the most effective international communicators are airlines, as their entire business is moving not only customers but also staff constantly across national boundaries to different organisational outposts of the business: the business activity creates the communications.

When the company is operating not serially but in parallel, organisational communication becomes much more difficult. Using the analogy of a hotel chain, the hotel in Manila is a complete operation in just the same way as the hotel in Copenhagen that is part of the same group: guests are not bedded in one and passed on to another to be fed. The work flow communications link is missing. All international businesses require centralised, coordinated communications to create common purpose and to share ideas and benefits, but those that do not have a natural work flow link across national boundaries will have this need more highly developed.

SUMMARY PROPOSITIONS

10.1 Managing an international organisation requires management to fragment by spreading some responsibility to be carried as near as possible to the local action, and to integrate by having some features of organisation that are closely followed throughout the component units.

10.2 Employees who work internationally can be classified as either cosmopolitans, expatriates, engineers or occasional parachutists.

10.3 Expatriates need thorough preparation for both expatriation and repatriation; the problems of repatriation are frequently overlooked.

10.4 Among the means of coordination in a fragmented international business are evangelisation, sharing standards and norms, systems and procedures, and distributing activity according to local cultural capability.

10.5 Communication in an international business confirms the holistic nature of the enterprise.

| PUTTING IT INTO PRACTICE |

How do you deal with the salary and expenses of someone who is to be relocated to an overseas posting for a limited expatriate contract? The following example is based on a method developed by the consultancy Employment Conditions Abroad, and is used with their permission. The figures relate to a hypothetical person earning £45,000, married with two children, moving from the United Kingdom to Canada.

There is a country index to represent the relative cost and standard of living in different countries, and the main calculation is to work out what the expatriate needs in the new country to maintain the standard of living at home, at the same time as maintaining status in the housing market, national insurance and so forth for the return.

Index for Canada:	UK = 100, Canada = 110.8
Exchange rate (March 1992):	UK £1.00 = C$ 2.0617

UK salary	£45,000
Net income	£32,295
Spendable income	£20,918
Housing and savings	£11,377

Local spending component = UK spendable income × Index/100
× exchange rate
= 20,918 × 1.108 × 2.0617

Total = C$ 47,784

Home component

Housing and savings	£11,377
Expatriate incentive	£6,750
Location allowance	£0
Class One contributions	£1,336
(for first year)	
Total	**£19,463 (C$ 40,127)**

Local spending component + Home component	C$ 87,911
Additional amount to cover Canadian income tax	C$ 89,929
Total gross salary	**C$177,840**
(Not including benefits in kind)	

Additional costs to the company

Company car	C$ 6,078
Utilities	C$ 2,508
Local education (one child)	C$ 8,700
Home education (one child)	C$16,298
Club	C$ 1,404
Medical insurance	C$ 2,480
Furniture storage	C$ 1,100
Air fares	C$ 6,065
Accommodation	C$29,000
Total	**C$73,631**

Notes:
  1. The expatriate allowance is 15% of notional UK salary.
  2. The location allowance is specific to each country depending on an assessment of the inconvenience of the new location. The range is from 0% to 30%. For Canada it is 0%.
  3. The UK National Insurance contributions are assumed to be Class 1, contracted out. UK social security is payable for the first 52 weeks of employment in Canada, in addition to Canadian contributions.
  4. It is assumed that free accommodation will be provided separately by the employer and that the posting is to Montreal.

References

Atkinson, J., 1992, Corporate employment policies, women and 1992, in *Women's Employment: Britain in the Single European Market*, ed. Lindley, R. M., HMSO, London.

Barham, K. and Rassam, C., 1989, *Shaping the Corporate Future*, Unwin Hyman, London.

Bartlett, C. A. and Ghoshal, S., 1989, *Managing Across Borders*, Random House, London.

Caulkin, S., 1993, British firms resurrected by courtesy of Japan, *The Guardian*, 8 May, p. 38.

Evans, P., Lank, E. and Farquhar, E., 1989, Managing human resources in the international firm: lessons from practice, in *Human Resource Management in International Firms*, ed. Evans, P., Doz, Y. and Laurent, A., Macmillan, London.

Ferner, A. and Hyman, R. (eds), 1992, *Industrial Relations in the New Europe*, Basil Blackwell, Oxford.

Foulds, J. and Mallet, L., 1989, The European and international dimension, in *The Communications Challenge*, ed. Wilkinson, T., Institute of Personnel Management, London.

Hofstede, G., 1980, *Culture's Consequences: International Differences in Work-Related Values*, Sage Publications, Beverly Hills, California.

Hofstede, G., 1991, *Cultures and Organizations: Software of the Mind*, McGraw-Hill, London.

Johnston, J., 1991, An empirical study of the repatriation of managers in UK multinationals, *Human Resource Management Journal*, vol. 4, no. 1. Summer, pp. 102–9.

Keily, D., 1991, Body Shop Blues, *The Sunday Times*, 8 December, p. 3.

Pages, M., Bonnetti, M., de Gaulejac, V. and Descendre, D., 1979, *L'Emprise de l'Organisation*, Presses Universitaires de France.

Schein, E. H., 1985, *Organizational Culture and Leadership*, Jossey-Bass, San Francisco.

Stoner, J. A. F. and Freeman, R. E., 1992, *Management*, 5th edn, Prentice Hall, Englewood Cliffs, New Jersey.

van Houten, G., 1989, The implications of globalism: new management realities at Philips, in *Human Resource Management in International Firms*, eds. Evans, P., Doz, Y. and Laurent, A., Macmillan, London.

Chapter 11

Managing performance

We now have great attention paid to the idea of performance management, which marks the introduction into business life of regular progress checks of the sort most of us have not had since we left school. Children have their performance monitored and reported upon. Week by week marks out of ten are written in the margins of exercise books, already sprinkled with ticks and crosses. Comments are made about the exercise which has been completed, pointing out any errors and emphasising what has been done well. At the end of each term or school year the general judgement of the teacher on the progress of the child is compressed into a few sentences on the school report. These regularly reported judgements are regarded as essential by the recipients as they give clues to the perennial question: 'How am I getting on?'.

When children start work, the reporting stops. It may continue in a different form during apprenticeship or similar initial training, but once the rudiments of the job are learned, feedback on the quality of performance is usually occasional, accidental and ill-considered, especially where there is not an obvious unit of production to be completed. Also there are not the same milestones through the year; life just goes on.

Although we are usually glad to leave school and school reports behind, we still hanker after feedback on our performance in order to feel secure, to have a sense of progress and to enjoy praise. It is only the fear of bad news that makes us uncertain.

In some jobs the 'report' is easily available. The barrister wins or loses a case; the salesman gets a repeat order or sees new business moving to competitors; waiters and waitresses experience the direct response of their customers, possibly reinforced by a tip. Others have a clear quota of work to do, and its completion indicates success. The coach driver finishes the journey, the chambermaid completes the designated number of bedrooms that have to be prepared, a magazine editor completes an edition. But satisfactory completion of the assignment does not answer such questions as

'Could I do better?', 'How?', 'Can I look for promotion?', 'What do I have to do to achieve it?'. Also most of those in managerial, administrative and clerical jobs do not even have the satisfaction of regularly completing a quota of work. Many people in such positions provide substitute goals for themselves, so that when the goal is reached they can enjoy the satisfaction of achievement that the continuous nature of their duties denies them. An example is clearing the in-tray. This may provide satisfaction, but is it an appropriate yardstick of effectiveness?

From appraisal to performance management

Performance appraisal is intended to overcome the lack of all that is involved in the progress checking system of school examinations and reports: it is intended to provide milestones, feedback, guidance and monitoring. A further development which aims to ensure that the best and most effective use is made of the appraisal process is by tying it into a larger and more complete system of performance management. These systems, which are being increasingly used (see, for example, Fowler, 1988) highlight appraisal as a central activity in the good management of staff. The difference from traditional appraisal is that the assessment process tends to be more rigorous and objective, and is clearly linked into precise job definitions and organisational objective setting, individual development plans and the pay system. The normal stages of performance management are:

1. Written and agreed job description, reviewed regularly. Objectives for the work group which have been cascaded down from the organisation's strategic objectives.
2. Individual objectives derived from the above, which are jointly devised by appraiser and appraisee. These objectives are results rather than task oriented, are tightly defined and include measures to be assessed. The objectives are designed to stretch the individual, and offer potential development as well as meeting business needs.
3. Development plan devised by manager and individual detailing development goals and activities designed to enable the individual to meet their objectives. The emphasis here is on managerial support and coaching.
4. Assessment of objectives. Ongoing formal reviews on a regular basis designed to motivate the appraisee and concentrate on developmental issues. Also an annual asssessment which affects pay received depending on performance in achievement of objectives.

One of the major advantages of performance management is that managers are forced to give emphasis to formal and planned employee development, and indeed a similar system described by Harper (1988) is referred to as Performance Review and Development. Another advantage is that it also enforces a clear role description and set of objectives agreed by managers and individuals. On the down side there is potential conflict between the aim of improving job performance, which requires openness and a developmental approach, and the link with pay. This conflict is usually dealt with by separating, in time, the performance development and the performance pay reviews.

How do we know what performance has been achieved?

Deciding what performance is desired and how this is communicated to the employee is covered in Chapters 15 (Organisational Communication), 16 (The Organisation of Jobs and Departments), and 23 (Staff Development). It is important that the task is clear and understood by the task holder. Information about the actual performance can be collected in several ways.

First, there are records such as personal files, time sheets, sickness and absence records, work and record cards and the reject book.

Second, there are other people who come into contact with the individual such as colleagues, customers, and staff in other departments, who may be a source of information about the person.

The third way is by making a comparison with other people who do similar work, such as the amount of unfinished work, wastage or complaints.

Fourth are measures of personal attributes. Traditionally traits such as drive, application and enthusiasm have been rated by managers for appraisal purposes. This has the difficulty of different interpretations and focusing on the person rather than the job done.

The final means of collecting information is through management by objectives. Here a set of objectives is set for the following year, or other suitable period, and at the end of this period the extent to which these have been met is measured. Depending on whether these objectives are organisation objectives or more local, some negotiation may be possible. The difficulty is that the objectives may or may not have been achieved because of factors outside the individual's control.

Focusing on performance inevitably means that dealing with the poor performer is more likely to occur, although having a problem with one person is not an appropriate reason for introducing performance management, as this will be resented by the others. Often it is better to concentrate one's management systems on the good and average performers. Managing the individual who is performing badly over a long time is amongst the most difficult management tasks. There are no easy solutions. It is worth trying to fathom out why it is they are performing badly as this will suggest solutions. To say 'they are poorly motivated' or 'there is a personality clash' is only the starting point for analysing the reason. Why are they poorly motivated or clashing personalities? Once some reason or reasons become clear it is worth sitting down and talking to the individual concerned. They may also have been worrying about their performance. It is also worth seeking help from personnel or one's boss to talk about strategies for managing the problem.

Paying for performance

Performance-Related Pay (PRP) is a widespread phenomenon that has had great emphasis during the 1980s and 1990s. To quote Kanter (1989, p. 223),

> Can anyone be against the idea that people's pay should reflect their performance? Isn't that how the system is supposed to work?

But it has also caused considerable problems, and satisfaction with its effectiveness is by no means guaranteed.

An example of a systematic approach to performance management is a computer company we visited. This organisation has PRP in place and they report general satisfaction with its operation. Their method of assessing performance is to use the following sequence:

1. They first derive a grade for the job by using a job evaluation questionnaire and database to evaluate the job as described in the job description.
2. A development plan is devised for each individual, including agreed measures and objectives for both training and career development.
3. The performance of the individual is then evaluated, using the following headings:
   Team working
   Decision making
   Initiative
   Creativity
   Safety
   Planning
4. Then a ranking is given to each individual out of the following: unacceptable/acceptable/good/very good/excellent/exceptional. This is not on a weighting basis but a matter of judgement.

   There is a ranking meeting annually to compare peers in the same or similar jobs, for example grade 5 secretaries or grade 6 administration or production workers. The aim is for a normal distribution of appraisals, but they don't force the fit. Ranking criteria are based on performance evaluation. Rank drives pay. Then they use the matrix given in Table 11.1.

Each grade has a development curve, e.g. grade 1 takes two years to full development – in reality, however, it can be shorter. Developers get an increase every six months which changes to every nine months towards the

Table 11.1 Rank matrix for PRP

rank

	UA	A	G	VG	E	E
max						
mid						
min	*					

* = % increase expected to give for this rank at this current place in matrix, e.g.
  exceptional at min salary is 14–20% whereas
  exceptional at max salary is 0–9%,
  or excellent at min salary is 12–17% whereas
  excellent at max salary is   0–8%, etc.

end of two years and later every twelve months, on average. The total amount of money available is checked and monitored by personnel.

The experience of PRP

Kinnie and Lowe (1990) chart the spread of PRP, given in Figure 11.1, from its 'white-collar heartland' to the shop floor and survey the benefits and problems it can bring.

Wyatt (1990) discusses the success, or otherwise, of appraisal schemes and the link between pay and performance. This survey studied the effectiveness of performance management in 598 companies and measured how well current schemes work and plans to change the schemes in the future. The important results are as follows.

a. Only 20% of personnel managers consider their appraisal systems effective.
b. Only 11% suggest it effectively links pay to performance.
c. On the impediments to an effective system:
   37% mentioned that targets were hard to establish
   32% mentioned the lack of an objective measurement system
   32% mentioned lack of support from the organisational culture.
d. On the problems of the rating system:
   60% mentioned inconsistency
   56% mentioned subjectivity
   34% mentioned there were too many average ratings.

Despite these results 93% regarded pay for performance as a major or emerging priority. Considerable time and effort are being devoted to reviewing and updating performance-related pay systems. This involves

This study investigated the experience of eight companies who introduced PRP for manual workers.

Benefits of PRP

(a) Improvements in commitment of staff.
(b) Easier identification of training and development needs.
(c) Improved job satisfaction. 'Once people find they are actually listened to they respond very positively and contribute with enthusiasm.'
(d) Provides opportunity to harmonise conditions and to encourage flexible working where this is included as one of the performance criteria.
(e) Provides a way of being seen to be focusing attention on the individual employee. 'PRP could therefore be used as a key component in a wide-ranging attempt to change the managerial style, or even the whole culture of the organisation.'
(f) Improves communication in the organisation by improving dialogue between supervisors and their subordinates. Employee idea generation on methods of working was seen to be an important by-product.

Problems of PRP

(a) Carrying out the appraisals. This involved the difficulty in setting meaningful individual objectives, the ability of the appraisers both to assess the subordinate and to adapt to the new task required of them.
(b) Translating appraisals into pay. This may be a reflection of the inadequacy of the appraisal interview, but just as important is the opportunity for bias and favouritism, undermining the credibility of the scheme.
(c) Trade Union attitudes. The unions feel that the essential problem with PRP is the threat associated with it in, for example, the apparent lack of an objective appraisal system.

Figure 11.1   'Performance-related Pay on the Shopfloor' (Kinnie and Lowe, 1990).

building on the factors regarded as essential to a successful scheme – employees and supervisors developing standards together (49%), a form of self-appraisal (53%), and a good communication system to explain how the appraisal system works.

It seems the overall conclusion to the study is that suggested by Derek Hall, the Manager of Personnel, London and Manchester Insurance Company, when talking about the implementation of their scheme: 'Do not even start unless you are prepared to make a huge commitment'.

PRP is different from the type of incentive schemes that have run in manufacturing industry for very many years, and which still continue; about one manual worker in three has an incentive element in the pay packet. The difference is that incentive schemes are collective and impersonal. The idea of performance pay is usually to make it individual and personal, so that some do better than others – or some do worse than others. Therein lies the problem. If the performance pay arrangement is to be effective it must have an apparent impact on individual performance, but selective individual reward can be divisive and lead to overall ineffectiveness unless everyone perceives the rules to be fair. Overall they have their greatest impact when there is scope for expansion of both business and earnings:

> Individualised pay seems tailor-made for a period of competitive expansion. . . . By all accounts this has had a considerable initial effect on company performance. But at the same time it produced a tremendous inflationary spiral. The systems introduced have generally been highly geared, with a high pay threshold as a carrot to attract employees and secure acceptance of the new arrangements. Awards for below-standard performance have often been higher than the general run of increases in other industries.
>
> (Incomes Data Services, 1988, p. 5)

When schemes are individualised, there is raised expectation all round and it is difficult to limit pay rises only to high performers. If a business is struggling, it cannot afford performance pay as performance pay is always inflationary.

We concluded at the end of a report on PRP for the North West Regional Health Authority (Weightman *et al.*, 1991) that:

1. PRP is widely used in the organisations we visited and read about. It is essentially a *cultural* initiative rather than a *pay* initiative, to emphasise individual initiative and responsibility. The effect of the initial cultural 'shove' may be considerable.
2. Apart from the attempt to change culture, the advantages of PRP are found to be in staff commitment and job satisfaction; identification of training and development needs; the opportunity to harmonise conditions and to encourage flexible working; improving dialogue between supervisors and their subordinates.
3. Despite its popularity, there are obvious difficulties in administering PRP, such as the difficulty of appraisal, the difficulty of formulating objectives, the risk of bias or perceived bias, the inevitable inflationary tendency, high costs of administration, paper work and monitoring.
4. We were unable to find any real evaluation of the effectiveness of PRP, despite many people being committed to the principle. We suspect the demotivating effects of PRP on a large percentage of employees who receive 'average' may be underestimated.

Marsden and Richardson (1992) conducted a survey on behalf of the Inland Revenue Staff Federation, following the introduction of PRP. They surveyed 2,500 Inland Revenue staff in 1991 and found that the principle of PRP was generally accepted, although a significant minority were hostile. They then asked respondents to assess their personal responses to it.

Performance pay has led you to:	YES %	NO %
Show more initiative	27	61
Give sustained high performance	27	63

Performance pay has led you to:	YES	NO
	%	%
Improve your priorities	22	64
Work beyond the job requirements	21	70
Improve your sensitivity towards colleagues	14	63
Increase the quantity of work	14	78
Express yourself with greater clarity	13	67
Improve the quality of your work	12	80
Be more effective with the public	9	63
Work harder	9	71

They then asked a question only of those who had to carry out the appraisals – the reporting officers – about the impact of PRP on their staff.

Performance pay has:	YES	NO
	%	%
Led to an increase in the quantity of work of many staff	22	71
Caused many staff to work beyond the requirements of their job	15	79
Led many staff to give sustained high performance at work	14	77
Made many staff more committed to their work	12	79
Helped to increase the quality of the work of many staff	10	82

So we have here a picture of some impact. After all, if a scheme has the effect of making 12–14% of people in a category work harder and 27% to show more initiative, that is not bad. It may not be the wave of the magic wand that changes the world, though considering the glacial speed with which human behaviour and attitudes change, it is not bad at all; but we do not know what is hidden by the noes. Is it the status quo or a deterioration?

There was some evidence on this as 55% of respondents believed that the scheme had helped to undermine staff morale and 62% (not surprisingly) believed it had caused jealousies, but remember that they generally agreed with the principle of PRP and merely found fault with the particular scheme that they had. The difficulty, of course, is that the fault they find is that not a large enough proportion of people get big rises. Presumably most people would support a method of payment that gave them above-average increases. These respondents appear to support the principle of discriminatory increases rather than the going rate. They appear to support the idea that people should be rewarded on the basis of an assessment of their individual performance. Furthermore these are the responses from civil servants in the Inland Revenue staff association, not people selling IT systems, or producing rock music or indulging in arbitrage, where one might believe that the individual had more scope.

Two approaches to appraisal

There are two broad approaches to appraisal: the control approach and the personal approach. The first is the most common, but the second is gaining popularity. Increasingly appraisal schemes have elements of both approaches, but describing them as polar opposites helps to illustrate the key elements.

The control approach starts with an expression of opinion by someone representing the view of controlling, responsible authority in saying something like this:

> We must stimulate effective performance and develop potential, set targets to be achieved, reward above-average achievement and ensure that promotion is based on sound criteria.

It seems like an inoffensive objective, yet the reaction of those to be appraised will be apprehensive as anxious eyes scan the job ads. This is because people construe the message in a way that is seldom intended: something like this.

> They will put pressure on poor performers so that they improve or leave. They will also make sure that people do what they're told and we will all be vulnerable to individual managerial whim and prejudice, losing a bit more control over our individual destiny.

This approach works best when there are clear and specific targets for people to reach, within an organisational culture that emphasises competition. There are considerable problems, like who sets the standards and who makes the judgements? How are the judgements, by different appraisers of different appraisees, made consistent? But it is still potentially useful as a system of keeping records and providing a framework for career development that is an improvement on references and panel interviews. It works best in bureaucratic organisations and the emphasis is on filling in forms.

The personal approach starts with a question in the mind of the individual job holder:

> I am not sure whether I am doing a good job or not. I would like to find ways of doing the job better, if I can, and I would like to clarify and improve my career prospects.

This question is addressed by the job holder to the job holder. It is not asking to be judged, but seeking to find someone with whom to talk through plans, progress, hopes and fears. Who can help me come to terms with my limitations and understand my mistakes? Where can I find someone with the experience and wisdom to discuss my performance with me so that I can shape it, building on my strengths to improve the fit between what I can contribute and what the organisation needs from me?

This approach works best with people who are professionally competent and self-assured, so that they can generate constructive criticism in discussion with a peer, or in protégé/mentor situations, where there is high mutual respect.

There is a view read between the lines of that by those in authority, which is something like this.

> This leads to people doing what they want to do rather than what they should be doing. There is no coordination, no comparison and no satisfactory management control.

This approach tends to confront issues and produces searching analysis as well as impacting directly and constructively on performance. It requires high trust, engenders loyalty (which can become dependence) and stimulates initiative. The emphasis is on the face-to-face discussion rather than on form-filling. The benefits of this view can be enormous but there are two problems: first, the lack of systematic reporting, and secondly, where are the paragons in whom you can trust?

The two essential elements of appraisal are *judgement* and *reporting*. The performance is not simply being measured, as in the completion of a work quota; it is being judged. This obviously involves discretion, worry about bias and the possibility of being quite wrong. This judgement is not, however, made in isolation. It has to be not only made, but also passed on to one or more other people in such a way that the other(s) understand what is intended and take action on it. Those devising performance appraisal schemes devote most of their energies to finding ways of making the judgements as systematic as possible and the reporting as consistent as possible between different appraisers.

Our working definition of performance appraisal is therefore 'The process of judging a person's performance and reporting that judgement'.

Purposes and problems in appraising performance

Why do managers seek to appraise the performance of organisation members?

1. *Social control.* It is first a method of shoring up the hierarchy, confirming the authority of those supervising the activities of others, and sustaining the dependence of subordinates within the cohesive structure of the organisation. 'Big Brother is watching you.'
2. *Human resource considerations.* The second consideration is that of maximising the use of human resources. The abilities and energies of employees are an input to the organisational processes, and there is a logical argument for monitoring the performance to see whether the resources are being effectively deployed.
3. *Training.* If employees are to develop their skills and their contribution,

they will require periodic training. Appraisal can identify the training that individuals need.

4. *Promotion.* Organisations need regularly to move employees up the hierarchy or across it, and occasionally down. Appraisal can aid the decision-making involved in determining who goes where, as it can keep up to date knowledge that is held about employee's skills, experience and aspirations. In some large organisations, like the armed services and a number of multinational corporations, career movements are frequent and involve a regular use of annual appraisals.

5. *Planning.* Associated with promotion considerations are those of pre-paring for future manpower requirements. Theoretically the regular appraisal process can feed into a manpower inventory, making it possible to pinpoint future skill shortages and to prepare succession plans.

| REVIEW TOPIC 11.1 |

Consider the five purposes of performance appraisal cited here: social control, human resource considerations, training, promotion and planning. Are there alternative methods of achieving any of these that would be better than performance appraisal?

Problems

The problems encountered in running schemes of appraisal are formidable, despite constant attempts to build bigger and better schemes that cannot possibly fail.

1. *Paperwork.* Systems always involve a lot of paperwork and documenta-tion which is disliked by the managers who have to carry out the appraisals. There is no escape from the documentation, as an essential feature of appraisal is reporting and schemes invariably include attempts to make both the judgements and the reporting consistent between different appraisers. This involves forms and detailed instructions.

2. *Formality.* The forms and the general paraphernalia introduce an inhibiting feature into the everyday working relationships between managers and their subordinates, who dislike the idea of formal evaluation and prefer a more relaxed, easy-going basis to their working relationship. Performance appraisal thus becomes a burdensome extra to the manager. Managers usually argue that they provide regular, informal performance feedback and evaluation hour-by-hour in the superior/ subordinate relationship, so that form-filling is irrelevant. This conve-niently ignores the benefit of thinking out a considered view of the whole working performance rather than pointing out errors when they occur. It also does not take account of providing the counselling and training

aspects of feedback to the person appraised, which are only likely to register when there is a serious discussion about performance.

3. *Outcomes are ignored.* Managers will not stick with their judgements, so if it is agreed that Ms A should have six months' training elsewhere, the manager may still not find time to send her. Promotion decisions often are inconsistent with the results of the most recent appraisal, in that the most appropriate person, according to the appraisal forms, is not the one chosen for promotion. This may be due to the promotion decision being irrational, or a need to maintain a necessary political balance by advancing someone's protégé, or experience and judgement overriding the dictates of the system.

4. *Performance is measured by proxy.* Performance appraisal is used in situations where performance cannot be readily measured, so proxies for performance are often measured instead.

> It may be difficult for me to determine if you are effective at your job; however, I can tell if you are at work on time, if you look busy, if you are pleasant and agreeable, or if you respect authority. While these characteristics may or may not have a relationship to performance, they are frequently easier to measure than performance *per se*. So, what we often find in organizations is the use of one or more proxies for performance rather than actual measures of performance. The use of proxies by managers, especially inadequate ones, can produce considerable dysfunctional behavior among employees. However, this does not stop managers from using them.
>
> (Robbins, 1978, p. 209)

5. *The just-above-average syndrome.* The appraisal carries either an explicit or an implicit statement about the general ability and acceptability of the person appraised. Designers of appraisal systems go to great lengths to force appraisers to provide a range of judgements, but there is great reluctance to tell anyone that they are not doing well enough, or to put 'black marks' on paper. There is also a reluctance to tell people that they are outstanding, as this raises expectations that may not be satisfied. There is thus a tendency for most people appraised to be judged as comfortably above average. There is then no demand for remedial action by poor performers and no problem about high-flyers asking for more money. The best that this achieves is to prevent the scheme causing too much trouble: the high-flyers are frustrated through lack of recognition and the under-achievers leap enthusiastically to the conclusion that they are doing just the right thing.

The unwillingness of managers to face up to unpopular judgements is not because they lack moral fibre or powers of judgement. They are concerned that it will destroy the working relationship between them and the subordinate hearing the bad news, and this is compounded by the preference for informality. A formal structure enables you to be critical. Without that structure adverse criticism is likely to develop into recriminations and vituperation, especially when it is judgement that is being deployed rather than measurement.

6. *Incomplete coverage.*   For appraisal schemes to be fair they have to be applied to all employees in a particular cadre, and for schemes to be effective they have to be seen as fair. In operation most schemes fail to achieve complete coverage. In schemes we have looked at, the completion rate has been between 50 and 75% in many cases. This can produce strange side-effects and reinforces some of the other problems mentioned so that the scheme is regarded as an administrative burden, dreamed up by the personnel people to give themselves something to do.

Ron Barnes is twenty-five, employed at the British headquarters of a multinational company based in New York. He has been with the company two years and is a marketing specialist. His main career objective in the short term is to get 'off reports'; that is, he will no longer have an annual appraisal. This is an indication that one has risen above the everyday ranks of managers and administrative staff and been 'noted' for the future. This is a completely unofficial move, but has become established as one of the ways in which senior managers assert their authority and control by undermining aspects of the system that keeps them in power.

Jean Whitehorn is a member of the same company and feels that she is not making progress, but cannot figure out why that should be. Last year all her immediate colleagues had appraisals completed, but she was left out. She asked her immediate manager who explained that 'he had not got round to it' but would do it as soon as he could. He was then suddenly transferred to Rome, so Jean enquired of the management development officer who told her that her erstwhile manager had declined to complete an appraisal on her because 'she wasn't going anywhere'.

Another aspect of complete coverage being lost is in the decay of schemes. Enthusiasts with their careers at stake may succeed in bullying all colleagues to complete appraisals once or even twice, only to be succeeded by someone seeking to try appraisal in a different way and gaining the approval of colleagues by leaving the existing scheme in abeyance for the time being. However, schemes begin to pay off only when they become an established part of the way the organisation functions. Altering them can be as damaging as digging up a plant to see if it is growing.

7. *Ill-informed appraisers and context problems.*   A prerequisite for sound appraisal is knowledge by the appraiser of the performance that is being appraised. Without safeguards, managers may be asked, because of their rank, to appraise members of the organisation whose work they do not know. Alternatively they may be unduly influenced by recent events which are clear in their minds. A trainee health visitor was doing very

well until she dropped a baby. The baby was not unduly concerned and passed the matter off with a cynical cough and a weary shake of the head, but all the members of the general public and the nursing profession in the vicinity had a topic of discussion that kept them going for days. 'Did you hear about the trainee who dropped the baby . . .?'. Her end-of-training performance review took place just over one week later and she was asked to repeat the final phase of her training.

The problem of context is how one disentangles individual perform-ance from its context, especially if the scheme is one based on setting objectives.

| REVIEW TOPIC 11.2 |

1. For an organisation that you know, write notes of a management argument against performance appraisal.
2. For the same organisation write notes of a union or employee bent against performance appraisal.
3. Write notes that seek to satisfy both sets of reservations.
4. Repeat the exercise, but place it in a quite different organisational context.

Appraisal interviewing

This form of interview is not easy to conduct. Randell *et al.* (1984) conducted a survey in a large pharmaceuticals company and found that managers had difficulty in interpreting the factors contributing to a person's overall performance, such as intelligence and life goals; they were not able to pursue these in interview and did not agree firm recommendations and actions towards improvement. Long (1986, p. 38) describes a widespread reluctance:

> Although most managers acquire a good deal of experience in interviewing techniques during the course of the everyday activities, the performance review discussion still tends to be approached with as much circumspection by the reviewer as by the reviewed.

Norman Maier (1976) describes three alternative approaches that are used for this type of interview:

1. *Tell and sell.* The role of the interviewer is that of judge, using the interview to tell the appraisee the outcome of the appraisal and the need to improve. This method is seldom used in appraisals of managers but can be appropriate for appraisees who have high respect for the appraiser and are insufficiently experienced to have developed self-confidence and the capacity to analyse their own performance.
2. *Tell and listen.* This is a modification of tell and sell. The appraiser is still in the role of judge and is passing on the outcome of an appraisal

that has already been completed, but they then elicit the appraisee's reactions, including resentment and disappointment, and this may lead to a change in the evaluation as well as enabling the two to have a reasonably frank exchange.

3. *Problem-solving.*   This is a quite different mode of interview. The focus is not the judgement of the appraiser but the growth and development of the person appraised, with the appraiser acting as helper rather than judge. The assumption is that discussing job problems leads to improved performance in that job, and the more skilful the appraiser, the greater the change and improvement that will take place. There is still the need for follow-up and there are problems if the appraisee lacks ideas or has ideas that do not fit in with what the appraiser regards as appropriate. It is important not to be over-optimistic about problem-solving, which sounds ideal. The appraiser will normally be in a hierarchically superior position to the appraisee and this could inhibit the type of candid exchanges that this style of interviewing requires. Also it requires the appraisee to be reasonably confident, secure and knowledgeable about possibilities. If all circumstances are favourable, it is the most appropriate for the appraisal of managers and an outline is given later in this chapter.

The contingency approach to appraisal

A number of articles suggest how a contingency approach may be applied to the appraisal process. Much of what has been written concentrates on the personal interaction that is part of the appraisal process. George (1986) suggests that an effective appraisal scheme is dependent on the style and content of appraisal not conflicting with the culture of the organisation. He suggests (p. 32) that the degree of openness that is required in the appraisal process is:

> . . . unlikely to materialise without an atmosphere of mutual trust and respect
> – something which is conspicuously lacking in many employing organisations.

The appraisal, therefore, needs to reflect wider values of the organisation in order for it to be properly integrated into the organisation and survive in an effective form. The appraisal system can in fact be used to display and support the culture and style of the organisation. George suggests that it can be used to help integrate people into an explicit and purposeful culture. The appraisal process can also be used to help change the culture in an organisation, but this would need to be done in conjunction with other supportive activities and be seen to be led from the top.

Other aspects of the contingency approach to appraisal include the appraiser's style in relation to their normal management style and in relation to the needs and personality of the appraisee. Pryor (1985) argues that appraisers should aim to achieve consistency between their normal day-today management style and the style that they adopt in appraisal interviews. George (1986) talks of the few really open relationships that individuals have at work and how in the appraisal situation we may be expecting interactions of a nature and quality which are not evident in most relationships. Pryor's ideas led to a reappraisal of the three interviewing styles defined by Maier (see earlier). In particular he re-evaluates the usefulness of the tell-and-sell and tell-and-listen styles, and suggests that they can effectively be adapted to the needs of appraisees with little experience who require less participation in the appraisal interview. One other important factor to be taken into account would be the appraisee's personality, which is somewhat more difficult to measure.

The contingency approach therefore takes into account the organisational culture and the characteristics of the appraiser and appraisee when an appraisal scheme is being formulated. The contingency approach should not, however, be used to bolster up the status quo when the status quo is clearly unsatisfactory.

SUMMARY PROPOSITIONS

11.1 Describing what performance is desired can be done both formally and informally.

11.2 Knowing what performance has taken place can mean using a variety of sources of information.

11.3 Performance-related pay is popular but has difficulties.

11.4 Performance appraisal is used in working situations where the achievement of satisfactory performance is not obvious from the nature of the task, and it is the process of judging a person's performance and reporting that judgement.

11.5 Schemes of organisation-wide performance appraisal frequently break down in practice because appraisers dislike the discipline and the amount of work involved, and because appraisees may be apprehensive about the outcome.

11.6 Interviewing is a central feature of appraisal and the problem-solving approach is the most effective, providing that both appraiser and appraisee have the skill and ability to handle this mode.

PUTTING IT INTO PRACTICE

Interaction guide for the appraisal interview

1. *Before the interview*
   - Brief appraisee on purpose and form of interview, possibly asking them to complete a self-analysis questionnaire in readiness.
   - Review reports, records or other sources of memory-jogging regarding appraisee performance in the period under review.
   - Check previous appraisal and outcomes.

2. *During the interview*
   Begin with rapport, to calm down the appraisee (and the appraiser) who may be nervous due to the significance of the interview. Explain how interview is to be run, reiterating points made in pre-interview briefing.

   - Review main facts about performance, without expressing opinion about the facts, but merely summarising as mutual reminder.
   - Encourage aspects of performance that are clearly satisfactory, mention them and comment favourably.
   - Ask for statement from appraisee about queries or problems, and a statement from appraisee about any dissatisfactions. (Talk these out fully with appraisee, adding the appraiser's perspective and opinion on those points. Some will be talked out as baseless, some will be seen as less drastic than they first seemed, and some will be confirmed as problems needing attention.) Offer comments from appraiser about aspects of performance that they do not regard as satisfactory, but which have not already been mentioned.
   - Agree action to be taken – by appraiser and appraisee – to improve future performance and satisfaction.

3. *After the interview*
   - Record problems and agreed action.
   - Take action on points requiring appraiser action.
   - File interview notes for later review.

Drill for management by objectives

Table 11.2 gives an example of a pro-forma worksheet for setting and reviewing objectives.

Table 11.2   A pro-forma worksheet for objectives

Prepared by (appraiser)......................and ....(appraisee)......................

Date of objective-setting...................Date of review...............................

Job objectives	Per cent of work time	Measure of results	Target	Date	Results	Date

References

Fowler, A., 1988, New directions in performance pay, *Personnel Management*, pp. 30–4.

George, J., 1986, Appraisal in the public sector: dispensing with the big stick, *Personnel Management*, May.

Harper, S. C., 1988, A developmental approach to performance appraisal, *Business Horizons*, Sept/Oct, pp. 158–74.

Incomes Data Services, 1988, *Performance Pay*, IDS Focus 49, Incomes Data Services, London.

Kanter, R. M., 1989, *When Giants Learn to Dance*, Unwin, London.

Kinnie, N. and Lowe, D., 1990, Performance related pay on the shopfloor, *Personnel Management*, November.

Long, P., 1986, *Performance Appraisal Revisited*, Institute of Personnel Management, London.

Maier, N. R. F., 1976, *The Appraisal Interview: Three Basic Approaches*, University Associates, La Jolla, California.

Marsden, D. and Richardson, R., 1992, *Motivation and Performance Related Pay in the Public Sector: a Case Study of the Inland Revenue*, Centre for Economic Performance, discussion paper no. 75, London School of Economics, May.

Pryor, R., 1985, A fresh approach to performance appraisal, *Personnel Management*, June.

Randell, G. A., Packard, P. M. A., Shaw, R. L. and Slater, A. J., 1984, *Staff Appraisal*, Institute of Personnel Management, London.

Robbins, S. P., 1978, *Personnel: The Management of Human Resources*, Prentice Hall, Englewood Cliffs, New Jersey.

Weightman, J., Blandamer, W. and Torrington, D., 1991, *Pay Structures and Negotiating Arrangements*, Research Report for the North Western Regional Health Authority.

The Wyatt Company and Personnel Today, 1990, Do you play the rating game?, from 'Performance Management 1990', The Wyatt Company, in *Personnel Today*, 23 October.

Chapter 12

Personal effectiveness

Most advice to managers, like the other chapters in this book, is about how to understand the organisational context one is in, or how to organise other people and materials. At the centre are the managers: how well organised are they personally? Understanding the context and organising subordinates, or the decision-making processes, or the performance appraisal procedures is of little avail if the person taking initiatives is not sufficiently well organised to push those initiatives through to successful completion and to exploit successfully whatever responses are received.

Poorly organised managers are a major impediment to organisational efficiency, slowing things down, producing errors and generating dissatisfaction. Among the clues are the comment 'I just have not had time'. The workload for any manager inevitably varies, from day to day, from week to week and – for many people – from season to season. The manager who 'has not had time' usually is not able to deal with that fluctuation. It may also be that arrears of work are accumulated as a justification for concentrating on those things that are of interest and passing over those that are unwelcome.

The manager knows that some of the less interesting things will be dealt with by someone else or overtaken by events. Arthur Brown was a sales manager who enjoyed a deserved reputation as a brilliant salesman and a very nice man. He was also known as not being keen on office work and he had three filing trays on his desk: 'In', 'Out' and 'Too Hard', with the third being used for all those matters that could not be dealt with straight away. A mischievous colleague altered 'Too Hard' to 'Too Dull', and that is all too true for many prevaricating managers.

Another clue is the phrase 'Let's play it by ear'. Here we see lack of preparation, lack of initiative and a mode of operating that is doomed to be responsive to the initiatives of others rather than creating initiatives of one's own. A somewhat similar clue is 'I'm still waiting for . . . (the boss)'. Although some periods of waiting are inescapable, there are occasions when managers await instructions because they are unsure of what to do, or because they believe that having passed a matter to the person next up, or along in the hierarchy, they then forget about it until it returns, because theirs is a dependent role.

Finally there is the clue 'Really? I don't remember that at all'. Managers have to organise their memory and recall to cover a wide range of matters, moving between those matters quickly and effectively. Not for them the purposeful single-mindedness of, say, the sculptor or the research physicist who can concentrate on one task for weeks and in whom absent-mindedness is either a beguiling eccentricity or an indication of absolute, unswerving dedication. In the next few pages we consider how managers can achieve the type of personal organisation that will protect them from giving these damning clues to perceptive observers, and which can greatly enhance their job performance and job satisfaction. As with other features in the book, we are not advocating the only ways in which things can be done, as one person's organisation can be another's straitjacket, but all of us can find help in considering alternative ways in which things can be done better.

REVIEW TOPIC 12.1

If you were able to organise yourself better,

1. Do you think your overall management performance would improve?
2. Do you think you would enjoy life more or less?
3. Do you think you would be a more or less stimulating and helpful person to work with?
4. Do you think other (less well-organised) people would become more reliant on you?
5. If you say 'yes' to the last question, in what ways would this enhance, and in what ways weaken, your managerial and administrative effectiveness?

Organising one's time

One method of organising one's time is to analyse how it is spent by using a temporary diary method to note down what is being done and how long it takes. With such an analysis it is possible to review the proportion of time spent over several days on various activities and to decide whether or not this is how the time should be spent. Another strategy would be to use Rosemary Stewart's (1982) categories of the demands, constraints and choices of the job to analyse how time is spent. Stewart recommends trying to increase one's choice by rethinking the demands and constraints.

The next step is to decide where changes need to be made, if at all. Are there things being done that could be cut out, or reduced, done differently or delegated? We have found, for instance, several instances of managers keeping careful notes handwritten in a black book – of figures that are available at the touch of a button on the keyboard of their own computer terminal or workstation. Alternatively there may be some things which should be done and which at the moment are not being done.

The more normal use of the diary is to plan the working day. This is partly an assertion of the individual manager's autonomy, but it is primarily an organising device to fit in various types of meeting. If the weekly marketing meeting takes place at 2 o'clock on Wednesdays and usually lasts all afternoon, that half-day is blocked out for other activities. There are normally between one and a dozen such events in a manager's weekly diary: meetings involving a number of people, at a fixed time, mainly at the behest of someone else (no matter how important you are) and those are the immovable blocks in the week, around which other things have to be fitted within the general framework of the working week/day. Although the immovables block out large chunks of available time, they can be used to make good use of what remains. If you need to talk to a colleague who you know to be verbose and indecisive, it may be worth getting the diary out and asking if the meeting could possibly be fitted in at 1.30 on Wednesday . . . 'It's only half an hour before the marketing meeting, so I'll have to be off promptly about five to . . . but God knows when the next opportunity would be'.

One factory manager of our acquaintance discovered that the works convener suffered from acute acid indigestion that worsened as meal times approached and was alleviated by eating. Gradually more and more meetings could only be fitted into the diary towards the end of the morning. Although those are two slightly silly examples, an even sillier one was of the manager so dominated by his diary that he burst into a colleague's office in a state of great agitation saying, 'We shall have to have a crisis meeting. Can you manage three weeks on Wednesday?' They all demonstrate how the manager needs to calculate the time needed for different types of meeting and structure the times in the diary according to those estimates. We have already seen that managers spend most of their time talking to other people and these encounters – whether one-to-one or on a larger scale – tend to expand or contract to fill the time available for their completion. If one allows too little time, the meeting is abortive as it has not been possible to deal with the business, and if one allows too much time, then opportunities to do other things are wasted.

A refinement of diary usage is to allocate blocks of time to particular activities, just as doctors' surgeries are always at the beginning of the day and in the early evening. Examples of this are doing all the dictation at the beginning of the day, making telephone calls early afternoon (when they are cheaper), reading reports on the train, or touring the plant just before lunch. This reinforcement of a habit can make for greater personal efficiency and for more efficient working relationships with colleagues, who can organise some of their activities to suit. 'We'll ask Charlie. He usually comes by about this time.'

Managing the boss

The idea of managing one's boss may sound like a contradiction or a usurping of proper authority, but it is most inappropriate to regard the relationship with the organisational superior as one in which they cope with you and you respond with deference or what the Americans call 'apple-polishing'. It is also insufficient to regard the relationship as one in which the subordinate seeks to comply precisely with what the superior asks for and then awaits further instructions, so that the job is satisfactorily discharged when the wishes of the boss have been met. Virtually all the jobs that people in organisations hold are those in which there are a range of responsibilities, accountabilities and obligations, both formal and informal. Also all jobs require some skill and some initiative, and the more autonomous a job is the less precise is the nature and degree of the supervision provided by the superior.

Very little has been written on this subject, although there is a helpful article by Gabarro and Kotter (1980) which points out that the relationship with the boss is not only crucial but has to be managed. Such management is not political manoeuvring or apple-polishing, but consciously working with the boss to obtain better results. Alistair Mant (1983) makes the distinction between binary-thinking managers and ternary-thinking managers. The first are those who see the relationship as that of master and servant, while the second are those who see the relationship as being of two servants, relating to each other via a third point in a triangular affiliation. The third point is the task on which they are both engaged, the customers they seek to serve or the employees they seek to satisfy. Binary thinkers will find it difficult to see how one can manage one's boss; ternary thinkers will be doing it already.

The process is mainly one of mutual accommodation and adjustment, as the two parties find the most effective way of sharing duties between them. They start from the position that the boss has, for instance, more formal power and access to more extensive information, while the subordinate may have better grapevine information and a more flexible programme of work.

To this will then be added the advantages that each has in terms of personal qualities, qualifications and experience. By discussion and getting used to each other, both boss and subordinate can improve their joint and individual results, but it needs initiative from both of them; not just from the boss.

From the point of view of the subordinate alone, it has to be remembered that the boss can influence the promotion and career development prospects of the subordinate, and this can inhibit the degree of candour in everyday exchanges. It also illuminates the need for the subordinate to work within the consent, even if only the tacit consent, of the boss in taking initiatives. In this way there will be support in times of difficulty and a greater likelihood that decisions on action are well judged.

Sometimes the boss has to be used to get things changed. It may be anything from an administrative procedure that is not working or policies about particular clients that need changing to tasks traditionally associated with one's job that no longer seem appropriate. Boursine and Guerrier (1983) make the point that subordinates often assume that bosses know when in fact they do not know what the subordinate's job involves and what is happening within its framework. A useful tactic is to keep the boss advised of what is irritating or frustrating. In doing this, however, it is well to remember the transactional analysis idea. The subordinate is more likely to be successful if the transactions with the boss are adult/adult transactions rather than those of the intemperate child whining to the uninterested parent.

There are also the range of tactics that are involved in organisational politics: reciprocal support for a patron.

Organising what has to be done

Management jobs inevitably have a delicate balance of long-term and short-term future objectives. Long-term considerations are dealt with in our chapter on policy-making and strategy, but there are ways in which managers prepare for short-term eventualities that lie somewhere between the projections of planning and the day-by-day control of diary keeping. In talking with managers during the preparation of this book we have been struck by the difficulty managers have in keeping a number of different issues all in play together. Furthermore this seems to be a growing rather than diminishing problem and was discussed by Kotter (1982) in his study of general managers.

| REVIEW TOPIC 12.2 |
---

1. List five ways in which you manage the relationship with your boss.
2. Think of three more ways that you have not yet tried.
3. Who benefits from the way you have managed your boss so far?

For those who do not currently have a boss in the conventional sense, use the example of a parent, a teacher, a sports team captain, leisure activity organiser, etc.

One method many managers use is to develop the use of the diary until it almost becomes a timetable. We call this event anticipation as people mark in their diary not only the events that are to happen, but also the jobs they have to do in anticipation of those events. A technical manager noted the dates of meetings in his diary and then noted three days before the meeting that he had to look through the agenda in order to chase up information or queries. A fashion manager used her diary first to mark the definite dates of fashion shows and similar promotions, and then fixed back in her diary earlier dates for such items as 'contact press office', 'order invitations'.

Although this may seem elementary, attendance at any committee meeting shows how few people arrive at the meeting prepared for the proceedings. There are now wallcharts and personal planners commercially available to aid this simple process. For managerial jobs with a strong administrative component and where there is a cycle of seasonal or annual events, the year can be partially mapped out in advance; we looked at the work of one very busy university administrator who had done this several times during the year when the workload was especially heavy. By careful examination she was able to identify a number of jobs that could be done either completely or partly at different times of the year in order to smooth the flow and to improve the quality of jobs done at the peak times.

Similar is the bring-out system, long used by private secretaries, in which notes or correspondence about a matter are stored against a date when they will be 'brought out' for review. This avoids the pile of papers on the desk generally awaiting attention or the bulging briefcase which is all too often a sign of a manager who reacts to situations instead of being proactive. A familiar comment by a manager asked about the progress of a particular issue is that 'it is getting near the top of the pile'. This refers to the real or metaphorical pile of papers on the desk and implies that they are being dealt with in strict chronological sequence. Usually they are dealt with only as a result of a query or complaint, which is sometimes described as the 'decibel' planning system: the louder the complaints, the more likely they are to be dealt with. With that arrangement everything becomes urgent and other people are always dissatisfied. Jeff Moores is a plant engineer who operated in this way: he dealt with things according to how loudly and often people grumbled at him. It was getting him down, so one week he agreed that he would abandon his standard, defensive, 'I'll get to it as soon as I have time. It's getting nearer the top of the pile.' Instead he said to each enquirer that he would deal with their query at a specified time, often weeks ahead. All the enquirers were satisfied and he suddenly found the breathing space in which he could begin to control his activities and move into a more satisfying and rewarding way of working. The bring-out system can also be used to prevent other people overlooking things which they regard as too hard or unattractive, like the old Jeff Moores before he took hold of his life.

Many managers keep lists of jobs to be done. These are typically kept on odd scraps of paper and reviewed morning and night. This is mainly to keep a check on what has to be done, so that things can be brought to mind in the relative calm of the train journey to the office and later reference to the list can prevent them being overlooked in the rush and bustle of the working day. There is a secondary benefit in running through the list at the end of the day, as it makes one realise that something has been achieved, despite the feeling of frustration and lost opportunity. We make no comment about those people who remember something to be done that is not on the list, do it, and then write it on the list in order to cross it off! This is essentially a personal, informal activity, and it changes its nature when it becomes an administrative system. A building society manager had a semi-permanent list of all the routine tasks that had to be done in his branch, and either he or his assistant initialled each item when it was done. It included such items as checking each cashier's till randomly each month, sending returns to regional office, and staff training.

Those especially conscious of the problem of getting things to the top of the pile try different ways of assigning priority. On the list of jobs, described in the previous paragraph, one or two would have an asterisk beside them and some might even have two asterisks to indicate that these were things that should be done first, or that should be done even if some of the others were deferred. Some people use a system of 'must do', 'important' and 'would like to do'. Less effective is to colour-code internal memoranda. One local authority manager had an extremely elaborate system of different-coloured paper for different types of message:

White – advisory
Pink   – information
Blue   – interest
Yellow – critical for implementation
Orange– needs reply

The idea was that memoranda would be sent on paper of a colour to indicate the attention it should receive, with the urgent matters being dealt with immediately and other matters being dealt with later. This seems to be an extreme of administrative precision that does not quite fit in with the vagaries of human nature. Will white, pink and blue be read at all? What actually is the difference between advisory, information and interest? Is the coding not reinforcing the idea among managers that they are too busy to read all their paper, when the majority of them can probably cope with it easily? Also, if there is this sort of ascending scale of importance, the lower scales are soon abandoned. In the Foreign Office telegrams are marked 'Most Immediate', 'Immediate', 'Priority' and 'Routine' and much self-discipline is required to ensure that not everything gets the top two markings.

The chief executive of a medium-sized company was anxious that the memoranda that he sent should be acted on quickly and he also wanted to spot easily the memoranda that came in to him from his main colleagues, so a system was introduced whereby all the memoranda from his office were on green paper, all those from directors were on blue, and everyone else had memoranda typed on yellow paper. Quite apart from the explicit declaration of differential status, that caused a lot of difficulty, there soon came the problem that important matters typed on yellow paper were sometimes overlooked. To deal with this the colour-coding was modified so that non-directors could have their memoranda typed on pink paper if they were urgent. These were soon christened 'pink frighteners' and people quickly realised that the way to get a response was to write on a pink frightener. Various people were grumbled at for not treating the system properly, but within a fortnight pink frighteners outnumbered the yellow memoranda being typed and the whole initiative failed.

These last two ideas were used by busy people trying to organise their own work, but the methods they chose depended on others organising their work in a reactive, dependent way. Personal reminders, like the list on the back of an envelope, seem much more effective.

Organising personal recall: making notes

As managers have to keep in touch with a range of different matters simultaneously, they benefit from being able to recall quickly and accurately information that they have received. Some they retrieve from files, some they remember, but a preliminary to the first and an aid to the second is the ability to take notes. In meetings, while reading journal articles, while telephoning, while talking with colleagues are all occasions when the manager may need to make jottings of material to be used later.

One method is to use shorthand, which enables the writer to record verbatim what someone is saying. Another is to make a tape-recording, but both of these methods are of dubious value as preliminaries to data storage or as aids to recall. The effort of the writer is in getting the record accurate and the effort of the person using the tape recorder is simply to switch on the machine. The understanding and the internalising, or taking in, of the material comes later as an extra job to be done. It is interesting to consider the experience of researchers and students, who are dedicated listeners. The researcher who is interviewing people at some length, and who uses a tape recorder to make sure that nothing is overlooked, will spend approximately four hours in writing up a one-hour interview. That is not transcribing it, word-for-word, but writing a summary of what was said, with nuances, illustrations and some interpretation. Nearly all those who use a recorder for this purpose take notes as well, so that the writing-up is based on the notes and the personal recall of the interviewer, with the recording being used only to check details. Students often make tape recordings in lectures in order not to miss anything, but seldom do they persist with the practice after a few weeks because the recorder takes away from them the need to be actively listening during the lecture, and the lecture becomes even more boring as a result, with the added tedium of having to listen to it all over again.

The purpose of taking notes is to record what the listener has understood

Table 12.1   Abbreviations used for note-taking

= is equal to	+ add or and	& and
≠ is not equal to	∴ therefore	∵ because
> greater than	< less than	n many
♂ male	♀ female	
acs accounts	ca (circa) about	cf compare with
do (ditto) the same	e.g. (exempli gratia) for example	etc. (et cetera) and the other things
et seq. (et sequentia) and the following	ibid. (ibidem) in the same place	i.e. (id est) that is
no. (numero) number	non seq. (non sequitur) it does not follow	NB (nota bene) note well
op. cit. (opere citato) in the work cited	pro tem. (pro tempore) for the time being	sic. so written
stet let it stand	v. (versus) against	vv. vice versa

and wants to be able to recall, as well as specific details that enlighten that understanding. It is always selective and always interpretive.

In taking notes the manager is summarising as much as possible in as few words as possible. An example is the way in which some people make a note at the back of their diaries of funny stories they have heard so that they can recount them on later occasions. The note is seldom more than a phrase or even a single word, even though the story may take five or ten minutes to relate. The funny story has a pattern, so that a few words are sufficient to recall the entirety. In listening to anything that we are being told, we look for a pattern or interconnection of ideas that we will be able to recall. Each of those patterns then produces a note in the form of a trigger, either a word or phrase that will be sufficient to summon up the complete grouping of ideas and data we are recording. In this way the listener is working while listening, structuring understanding and deciding on the triggers.

When it is necessary to record verbatim, there is value in mastering a set of abbreviations. Table 12.1 gives a list that is commonly used, but each individual will have a personal set, linked to the context of their own work. In preparing this book, for instance, we have used the following:

Mgt   – Management
MM   – Middle management
Gps   – Groups
F-to-F   – Face-to-Face
Orgs   – Organisations

These have been helpful to us, but would be useless to others. There are various ways of adding emphasis in notes. Some words are underlined, or have asterisks put beside them, as in the personal lists we have already described, but another method is to outline items that are to have a special degree of emphasis.

Organising personal recall: memory

All of us can improve our ability to recall information from our memory as the potential of the human brain is greatly under-utilised and some individuals who are otherwise perfectly normal are able to recall much more than others. Actors need to memorise their lines and thus develop an ability to recall that is much greater and better organised than that of most other people; some indeed have been able to recall a major Shakespearean role after little more than a single reading. In the 1950s the music-hall performer Leslie Welch was known as 'The Memory Man' and his fifteen-minute act consisted of answering questions from the audience on sporting events and records.

One widely accepted theory of human memory is that memorising is a two-stage process: a short-term memory and a long-term memory.

> The difference between them is like the difference between recalling a telephone number you just looked up in the directory and your own telephone number. Your own is stored in LTM along with memories of such items as your name, the words and grammar of the language, addition and multiplication tables, and important events in your life. Except for occasional mental blocking on a word or the name of an acquaintance, these memories are relatively permanent. In contrast, the telephone number you have just looked up, the definition the instructor has given you in class, and the name of the stranger to whom you have just been introduced remain in STM only momentarily. Unless you make a conscious effort to focus your attention on the information, that is, to transfer it to LTM, it is quickly lost.
>
> (Hilgard *et al.*, 1975, p. 236)

Recall is summoning things up from long-term memory and the effectiveness of the recall will be influenced by the way in which items were stored in that memory bank in the first place. Buzan (1977, pp. 33–5) provides an excellent summary of this process and the possibility of improvement, but we will here mention only one method of data storage for effective recall, known as the method of loci. In this a series of items to be learned for recall are identified in the mind of the learner with familiar, connected locations, the most familiar example being of the shopping list, which is memorised by identifying each item on the list with a room in the house. They are not, however, simply identified with the room, but visualised in it, so that there is a picture of a dozen eggs on the hall floor, a loaf of bread on the dining room table, breakfast cereals on an armchair in the sitting room, and so forth. On entering the shop, the items are easily recalled by summoning up the series of images.

Organising personal recall: filing

As the amount of information circulating in organisations increases, there is a growing problem of what to do with it after it arrives. Much can be thrown away, either because it did not need to come in the first place or because it will not be needed in the future, but how do you store correspondence, reports and other items in such a way that they can be found when required? The average filing cabinet contains material that will never be looked at again except when you are looking for something else, so that one effective means of filing is to file as little as possible. This can be achieved either by throwing away more, more often and more purposefully, or by relying on other people's files to a greater extent. We realise that some readers will find it difficult to follow this advice. In visiting different organisations it is striking to notice the different number of filing cabinets deployed in operational situations which seem in all other ways to be similar. Some managers are surrounded by filing cabinets while others seem to manage with only one, so filing practice is governed as much by the personality and individual methods of managers as by any objective notion of what is appropriate. One manager we know who is an inveterate hoarder always goes to work between Christmas and New Year when he clears out his filing system.

How do you classify what you decide to keep? Most people operate in a way similar to the short-term memory. Earlier in this chapter we mentioned managers who refer to matters 'nearing the top of the pile'; nearly all the managers we have spoken to have a 'pile'. It may be literally a pile of papers on the desk, it may be a bulging briefcase or a dog-eared folder, but it will still have the same characteristics: it contains material that is current and not organised in any particular way. When it ceases to be current, it may be thrown away or filed – transferred to the long-term memory. Once in the filing system, the material is valueless unless first you can remember that it is there, and secondly you can find it. Both influence how the filing should be arranged.

The most common system of classification is by subject and source. Some files contain material about a topic, while others contain material received from Mr X or Company A. Other common files are for committees, with all the minutes and papers relating to the Staffing Committee going into a single file. The difficulty of finding material is demonstrated by the way in which many experienced secretaries have a secret 'spare copies' file. It contains copies of all the significant letters and memoranda they have typed in the previous six months. When they are not able to locate an item, they flip hurriedly through their spare copies to find the item or a clue to its whereabouts.

The filing system needs a key. The simplest is a typed list of the files that are kept, so that you remember you have a file on a particular subject; otherwise many of the files are forgotten. If you look in your filing cabinet now you will find that 15% of the files contain 75% of the filed material, and 25% of the files are probably empty or contain only forgotten material. The filing system has to match the needs and mental processes of the user, or it is of little value:

> If possible files should be conceptually organised to fit in with the way the users of the files work. Thus project, case and company file names are likely to satisfy the needs of those concerned with research work, litigation and suppliers respectively. If simplicity and comprehensibility are maintained in this way, staff are more likely to use and rely on the filing system.
>
> (Lock and Farrow, 1983, p. 827)

Self-development

In this chapter we have reviewed the main ways in which individual managers can improve the quality of their personal organisation. A more detailed approach to this is to be found in a remarkable book by Pedler, Burgoyne and Boydell (1986) who provide a practical means of self-development. A slightly different approach is by Michael Armstrong (1988).

A final consideration is the way in which the managers manage their own careers, so that not only is the here-and-now competence increased, but also the working life meets the ambitions for variety, challenge and reward.

To do this the manager should first realise that 'up' is not the only way to move. In the early stages of a career it may be more judicious to move sideways, so as to broaden experiences and prepare for a move upwards in a different field. Secondly, the attempt to move upwards is one that few can satisfactorily achieve; most people stop going upwards earlier than they would wish. That is the time when so many managers become bored, frustrated or disillusioned, yet the manager who has developed the substance of the current role, rather than always looking beyond it, has the opportunity of deriving satisfaction from doing a difficult job well. Life holds few deeper satisfactions than that.

SUMMARY PROPOSITIONS

12.1 Poorly organised managers are a major impediment to organisational efficiency.

12.2 Time can be managed better by using diary sheets to analyse how time is spent, keeping a future diary to plan the working day and the working week, and allocating blocks of time daily or weekly to specified activities.

12.3 The working relationship between boss and subordinate is crucial to the effective working of both parties to that relationship, and both of them have to work at managing the relationship.

12.4 Methods of organising the work that has to be done include event anticipation, a bring-out system, keeping lists, and assigning priority.

12.5 The quality of personal recall can be organised in making notes, memorising and filing.

References

Armstrong, M., 1988, *How to Be an Even Better Manager*, 2nd edn, Kogan Page, London.

Boursine, M. and Guerrier, Y., 1983, *Surviving as a Middle Manager*, Croom Helm, London.

Buzan, T., 1977, *How to Make the Most of Your Mind*, Colt Books, London.

Gabarro, J. and Kotter, J., 1980, Managing your boss, *Harvard Business Review*, Jan/Feb, pp. 92–100.

Hilgard, E. R., Atkinson, R. C. and Atkinson, R. L., 1975, *Introduction to Psychology*, 6th edn, Harcourt Brace Jovanovich, New York.

Kotter, J., 1982, *The General Managers*, Free Press, New York.

Lock, D. and Farrow, N., 1983, *The Gower Handbook of Management*, Gower, Aldershot, Hampshire.

Mant, A., 1983, *Leaders We Deserve*, Martin Robertson, London.

Pedler, M., Burgoyne, J. and Boydell, T., 1986, *A Manager's Guide to Self-Development*, 2nd edn, McGraw-Hill, Maidenhead, Berkshire.

Stewart, R., 1982, *Choices for Managers*, McGraw-Hill, Maidenhead, Berkshire.

Chapter 13

Equal opportunities and the management of diversity

The issue of equality of opportunity has received great attention throughout the last century, especially in the last thirty years, as those groups who see themselves as disadvantaged in the workplace seek a fairer deal. More recently the phrase 'managing diversity' concentrates slightly more on the practical questions that are involved and slightly less on the argument. This is not to suggest that equality of opportunity is now an established fact, but that the focus of attention has moved away from whether the case is justified towards considering the management processes that will gradually increase the range of opportunities to those who are currently disadvantaged.

> Successful organizations will react to diversity as the important business issue it is by implementing proactive, strategic human resource planning. Short-term strategies designed to circumvent the situation will keep an organization from effectively positioning itself in tomorrow's world of cultural, gender and lifestyle diversity. (Foster, 1988, p. 59)

By far the most attention, in terms of public interest and legislation, has been paid to the position of women and those from ethnic minorities. There is, however, some legislation relating to disabled people, and in the United States there is also legislation affecting the employment of people aged over forty.

The types of preconception that affect the employment of these four groups are:

1. Ideas that women do not want too much responsibility at work because of their home commitments, and that you can't move a woman to the other end of the country if her husband works at this end.
2. Ideas that Moslems are difficult to employ because of problems with religious holidays and practices, that Indians overstate their qualifications, that qualifications gained abroad are not as good as those gained in this country, and that Jews are greedy.
3. Ideas that a person in a wheelchair will be an embarrassment to fellow

workers, that someone who has suffered from mental illness will inevitably crack under the slightest of pressure, and that employees would not be willing to work with someone suffering from epilepsy in case they had a fit at work.

4. Ideas that older people are less adaptable, that they cannot cope with new technology, and that they work much more slowly than younger people.

| REVIEW TOPIC 13.1 |

We have suggested four groups who represent the diversity of the workforce to be managed. What other groups would you add to that list?

Even the most liberal and enlightened reader will acknowledge that not all of these are outrageous. It is only a minority of people who are explicitly racist, sexist, ageist or hostile to people with disabilities. Most of us are convinced of our reasonableness, but this tends to become a position of principle, like believing in the United Nations, while practical action is inhibited by a combination of hearsay ('They have to keep Indians and Pakistanis in different departments at . . .'), convention ('Well, these jobs have always been done by women before . . .'), particular incidents ('After three days he gave up because of his heart; they should never have given a job like that to a man of his age') and occasional, vivid personal experiences ('My uncle had an artificial leg and it made him very bad tempered. One day I was with him when it got trapped in some lift doors: it was terrible.').

The problem of managing diversity is twofold. First we have to overcome the uneasiness – felt by ourselves and our colleagues – about the practical aspects of avoiding unfair discrimination against members of a particular social group simply because of their group membership. Secondly all our management approaches and actions have to accept and cater for the range of diversity in our employees, our colleagues, our suppliers and our customers. People are not all of a type and if our organisational practices are based on the assumption that they are, then the effectiveness of that organisation is almost certainly impaired and the practices need to change.

Most of the discussion in the last thirty years has been directed towards the removal of discrimination, and this chapter largely deals with that issue, as it relates to particular groups. The most compelling argument against discrimination is one of rights and obligation. Those who see themselves at a disadvantage are likely to assert their rights and point out that the discrimination from which they suffer is unjust and probably unlawful. Most of those who do not personally experience discrimination against them will still support that argument, claiming that the more fortunate have an obligation to level up opportunities.

Less effective is the human capital argument, which says there is a need for managers to make sure they do not waste talent, as it is in such short supply. First of all that line of reasoning does not help much in times of labour surplus, and secondly it can actually encourage discrimination by putting an over-emphasis on level of qualifications. One example of that is the building society where women were concentrated in junior management positions 'because that is what they are so good at'. Another is the construction company where recruitment sought qualifications of six GCSEs for basic manual work 'because the situation in the labour market now means that we can ask for that and get it'.

The employing organisation is always a part of its surrounding community, not only as a source of prospective employees, but also in the sense that those employees import attitudes and experience into their employment from the world outside. A company that is seen to discriminate unfairly against members of its community will be contributing to a situation in which social stability is put at risk and economic growth may be held back.

It is principally through our employment that we make progress. If employers open up employment opportunities for women, then women will acquire the confidence gradually to broaden their social role. If employers open up employment opportunities for black people, then they too will grow in confidence and achieve social integration. Managing diversity constructively reduces discrimination and makes sound business and social sense. Mahon (1989) demonstrates how equal opportunities at Wellcome have shifted from good employment practice to sound business sense, and from personnel policies to business issues.

Women

Women form a large and increasing proportion of the working population. In some parts of the United Kingdom a higher proportion of women are now in employment than men. This is a dramatic change, although the practice of women working outside the home is not new. After the advent of the factory system women worked long hours away from the home in factories, and played a major role in outside employment during the world wars of the twentieth century. The difference now is that women continue to increase their participation rate in employment, despite high male unemployment. In earlier times periods of high male unemployment have eased women away from employment outside the home, but women are now seen as being equally entitled to a career outside the home on the same terms as men, and male unemployment is no longer a widespread inhibitor of women's opportunities, although some working women whose husbands are unable to find employment feel it is easier for domestic harmony if they relinquish work as well.

Though women have mainly overcome the resistance to the idea that they should be employed, they have been less successful in making progress to the higher levels of pay, status and responsibility within organisations. The term 'glass ceiling' is used to describe a situation where the opportunities are explicit and clear, but there remains an invisible barrier to progress. There is an interesting example in the question of women professors in British universities. There are very, very few and in long-established universities there are even fewer. Many people in positions of power in those universities bewail the shortage of women candidates and the failure of women candidates to be appointed. The university system is, however, one of hallowed traditions geared to male behaviour, so there is a barrier to the appointment of women that has nothing to do with individual prejudice against women, either as individual candidates or as 'a monstrous regiment', although it would be foolish to deny that such prejudice exists.

The legislative framework

Equal pay between men and women has been promoted by the *Equal Pay Act*, which was passed in 1970 and implemented, with amendments, progressively between 1975 and 1984. The Act specifies circumstances where the pay of a woman should be equal to that of a man:

- where the woman is doing the same work as the man;
- where she is doing different work, but the work is rated as equivalent by job evaluation or a similar procedure;
- where the work can be shown to be of equal value to that of a specific male comparator.

The description here is of a woman seeking pay equal to that of a man because that is the most common situation. A man is similarly entitled to seek pay equal to that of a woman.

The *Sex Discrimination Act* 1975 is more wide-ranging in trying to promote equal opportunities between men and women and to eliminate discrimination on the grounds of sex or marriage by making it unlawful. The Act covers direct discrimination, such as advertising for male applicants only, and indirect discrimination, which applies unreasonable conditions which have the effect of making applicants from one sex unappointable. Immediately after the Act became law there were several silly examples of indirect discrimination, like the advertisement for people to dig ditches, who were required to have a minimum 38″ chest measurement and to work stripped to the waist in the summer. Gradually, however, forms of indirect discrimination that were not immediately apparent have been uncovered and tested by the judicial process. Minimum height requirements inevitably favour male applicants for the obvious reason that the average height of adult males is greater than that of adult females and minimum length of uninterrupted service can be unfair to women who take maternity leave.

There are a number of exceptions to the Act's provisions, such as employment in private households, where you could specify that you wish to employ a woman as housekeeper, for example, and the armed forces, where it is possible to recruit only men to serve in the infantry. There are also a number of specified instances where sex is acknowledged as a genuine occupational qualification, as in the modelling of women's clothes, for example.

The Act set up the *Equal Opportunities Commission* to monitor progress and to promote equality between the sexes. One of the Commission's main proposals has been that employers should have declared policies on equality of opportunity, and that the effectiveness of those policies should be regularly monitored.

What progress have women made?

What has been the effect of the legislation, the campaigns and the educational initiatives as far as the employment opportunities and achievements are concerned?

There has undoubtedly been much removal of overt discrimination, particularly in recruitment advertising, following on quickly from the Acts, but there is much less evidence of change in indirect discrimination, especially in training and promotion practices (Snell *et al.*, 1981). O'Sullivan (1989) reports that only 8% of the executive workforce are women. Dickens and Colling (1990) explain how continued job segregation in respect of both role and hours/arrangements is one of the factors which results in discriminatory agreements between employers and unions. They also point to the problem of job evaluation schemes which perpetuate old values and hence encourage rather than discourage inequality of pay.

Women have equal access to pensions schemes, since the Sex Discrimination Act, and certain continuing inequalities were outlawed by the Social Security Act (1989), but the major inequality of retirement age and entitlement to pension remains, despite repeated rumours that it is to be ended. McGoldrick (1984) notes that pensions schemes are still normally organised on the basis of the traditional male employment pattern, rewarding long and continuous service and based on full-time rather than part-time employment.

Legislation can only go so far in promoting equality of opportunity and a number of commentators have pointed to the need to understand the general differences between men and women, apart from the obvious biological differences, and to question the universal assumption that the world of management is dominated by the traditional male qualities of rationality, logic, competition and independence, rather than the traditional female values of emotional expression, intuition, caring and interdependence (Marshall, 1985). Masreliez-Steen (1989) explains how men and women have different perceptions, interpretations of reality, languages and ways of solving problems. If this diversity is recognised and properly managed, there is great benefit to the organisation as well as to the heterogeneous people who make it up. She described women as having a collectivist culture, forming groups, avoiding the spotlight, seeing rank as unimportant and having few but close contacts. On the other hand men are described as having an individualistic culture, keen on forming teams, developing a profile, enjoying competition, and having many superficial contacts. This diversity means that men and women behave differently and often fail to understand each other. The great advantage of this difference is that it concerns only methods of doing things; not what is to be achieved. In explaining some of the physical bases of sex difference, Moir and Jessell (1989, p. 169) pointed out:

> Women are now doing remarkably well in firms they have set up themselves. Here they don't have to play the male game according to male rules. They are free to make up their own rules, make relationships rather than play games, run their businesses more on a basis of trust than of fear, cooperation rather than rivalry.

REVIEW TOPIC 13.2

Is the place where you work dominated by male characteristics? What signs are there of female values? What specific examples can you identify? What would be the effect on the business of female values spreading further?

Women need different forms of organisational support particularly in terms of flexibility, to enable them to combine a career with parenthood. Such forms of support include career breaks, flexible working hours, annual hours, job sharing and part-time work, childcare facilities and support. Liff (1989) also suggests that non-linear career paths and the restructuring of jobs are important. This type of facility is reluctantly offered in male cultures. Consider the response by two headteachers to an almost identical request from a young woman teacher, who was asking for a very small modification to her working hours to help with her two small children. The Headmaster was extremely sympathetic and understanding, but explained that he really could not make an exception, otherwise it would be unfair to all the other staff and a difficult precedent would be set. The Headmistress, who had four children of her own, immediately agreed to the modification of hours, saying that she knew from experience that any small help she could give to individual members of staff would be repaid several times over in other ways.

Racial minorities

Before the change in British immigration arrangements, there had been substantial immigration of black and Asian workers from the New Commonwealth countries in the 1950s and early 1970s. There had been waves of immigration before, but these were mainly Europeans and there was no widespread disadvantage experienced by them because of their racial origins, apart from some anti-Semitism. The New Commonwealth immigrants were different, because of the colour of their skin, their religious practices and their lifestyle. Furthermore they mainly came to take poorly paid and low-status jobs, which tended to confirm a traditional, prejudiced view that they were not only different but 'lower': an underclass. It was a recognition that this group of people was disadvantaged in employment and other areas that prompted anti-discrimination legislation. The legislation, however, is designed to protect members of any ethnic minority group.

In the 1990s prejudice against ethnic minorities is less, but still persists. Change in attitudes probably has more to do with popular sporting heroes, like Viv Richards, Linford Christie and John Barnes, than legislation. Much popular music is the province of black people and the notion that 'black is beautiful' has been personified by a few highly paid and extremely elegant black fashion models. Marriage between people of different skin colour is now much more common than the occasion in 1948 when Peggy Cripps, the daughter of the British Chancellor of the Exchequer, caused widespread amazement by marrying a black Ghanaian politician.

The legislative framework

There has been legislation since 1968 making it unlawful for employers to discriminate directly on the grounds of race, colour, nationality, or ethnic origin. The *Race Relations Act* 1976 replaces the 1968 Act, and extends it by, for example, making indirect discrimination illegal. It also set up the Commission for Racial Equality. The Race Relations Act identifies ways in which racial minority groups may be discriminated against, and makes both direct and indirect discrimination unlawful. The concept is very similar to that of discrimination on the grounds of sex and there is again a list of genuine occupational qualifications, so that you can, for example, specify Chinese waiters as being necessary to serve in a Chinese restaurant. A rather different provision is to permit the recruitment of people from specified ethnic groups to act as community social workers, if they are providing services to members of a particular racial group.

What progress have members of ethnic minorities made?

Some of the early discrimination against members of ethnic minorities could almost be justified. There were often difficulties with language and culture (especially the role of women in society) among those who had recently arrived in the country that made it genuinely difficult to employ them and to open up opportunities for them. Although there are still difficulties with culture and although some Asian women are still occupying a social role that Western women find an affront to human dignity, the remotely justifiable grounds for discriminating on the grounds of ethnic origin steadily grow less. With an increasing proportion of the ethnic minorities having been born and educated in this country, the language problem has almost disappeared and the repatriation argument, that was seriously discussed in the 1970s, is now limited to the lunatic extremes.

Unemployment, however, remains higher among ethnic groups, promotion prospects seem poor and motivation towards education and training is often lower. This may be a cultural variable, but it is much more likely to be a reaction to perceived lack of realistic employment prospects when the training is complete.

| REVIEW TOPIC 13.3 |

If you received two application forms for the same job and they were virtually identical, except that one had a name that sounded African or Asian, while the other had a simple English-sounding name, what would your reaction to each application be? Would it vary according to the job to be filled? If so, how and why?

As with discrimination on the grounds of sex, employers frequently feel that they should wait until public opinion has changed before they make changes in employment conditions, but with racial discrimination in particular one can argue that it is the place where public opinion is formed. Over twenty years ago Tom Connelly, the first Chief Executive of the Commission on Racial Equality, put it this way:

> What happens in employment is crucial for the whole issue. A person's job and employment prospects obviously determine his current and material welfare, the well-being of his family and his status in the community . . . An indispensable condition for fuller acceptance is the breakdown of the association between colour and inferiority. If coloured workers are seen mainly in low status jobs and in poor housing, the association will be sustained and strengthened. The more they are seen in higher status jobs, particularly those which involve the exercise of authority, the weaker the association with inferiority will become. The experience of coloured workers in industry will therefore influence crucially the attitudes and behaviour of the host society.
>
> (Connelly, 1972, pp. 194–5)

In attempts to stimulate progress two administrative devices have been authoritatively advocated by the CRE (1978), as they have by the EOC. One is the development of equal opportunity policies in companies and the other is monitoring. Research has not succeeded in showing the introduction of policy 'from the top' as being effective except in situations where the employment of minority employees has produced major problems that needed to be resolved (Torrington *et al.*, 1982).

The idea of monitoring is that records should be kept of those in racial and ethnic minorities who are employed in the organisation. This produces the immediate reaction that it is a discriminatory act in itself. However, the potential dangers are offset by the need to take positive steps to check what the penetration into the more attractive areas of the organisation actually is.

People with disabilities

There are nearly half a million people on the disabled register, but the accurate figure must be higher than this, as many people resist registration because they do not want to be classified in that way. Walker (1986) charts the generally difficult employment situation for those who are disabled: higher levels of unemployment, longer periods of unemployment and limited choice of jobs.

Employers have a more specific basis for diffidence about employing disabled people than they do with reluctance to employ women and members of ethnic minorities. These include worries about general standards of attendance and health, safety at work, eligibility for pension schemes and possible requirements for alterations to premises and equipment.

The legal framework

The impetus behind the present legal framework for the disabled was the political and moral pressure to make provision for those disabled during the Second World War, together with a practical need to reduce labour shortages. There remained strong feelings about the situation encountered by wounded men returning from the First World War to 'a country fit for heroes to live in' only to find poor employment prospects. A committee chaired by George Tomlinson produced the ideas of rehabilitation and resettlement on which the 1944 Disabled Persons (Employment) Act was based. A further act with the same name was passed into law in 1958. Some additional regulations came into force in 1980.

The legislation provides first for the *assessment* of people who have suffered disability, usually by occupational psychologists at employment rehabilitation centres. This is followed by a period of *rehabilitation* at the centre for a period of approximately six weeks. There is a *register* for people with disabilities, who then have certain minimal rights in the labour market through the establishment of the *quota* system and the designation of *reserved occupations*. At Job Centres there are *DROs* (Disabled Resettlement Officers), whose role is both to assist people with disabilities in their search for training and employment and to advise employers about the possibilities of employing disabled people.

The quota scheme is a method of positive discrimination where every employer of more than twenty people has to employ sufficient disabled people to make up 3% of their total workforce. If firms are under their quota they should not employ another non-disabled person until they are up to quota unless they have obtained a special permit, on the grounds that the work is unsuitable or no suitable disabled person is available.

What progress have disabled people made?

The quota system has not proved to be very effective. More and more employers are requesting and receiving special permits and the percentage of employers not fulfilling their quota increased from around 40% in 1961 to over 60% in 1978 (Manpower Services Commission, 1980). Walker (1986) reports that since the scheme began only ten firms have been prosecuted and Disablement Resettlement Officers have attempted to persuade employers to take on disabled people rather than invoking the law. An MSC working group considering ways of improving the quota scheme, made a number of recommendations including changes in the issue of permits and methods of increasing employers' awareness of the quota scheme (MSC, 1985). Thus far measures of this type do not seem to be a substitute for the establishment of clear rights to employment protection, as practised in some other European countries (Walker, 1986, p. 45).

Certain jobs are reserved or designated to be filled only by registered disabled people. So far these jobs are car park and lift attendants. There has probably been a demand for an increasing number of car park attendants, which will gradually decline as electronic pay systems are installed, but how many times in the last year have you seen a lift attendant? Disabled people employed in reserved occupations cannot, however, be counted towards the 3% quota, which is another reason why the quota system is not very effective.

| REVIEW TOPIC 13.4 |

What other jobs do you think could be added to the list of reserved occupations, and why do you think the list has not been increased?

As a result of the Companies (Directors' Report, Employment of Disabled Persons) Regulations of 1980, all employers with 250 or more staff are obliged to include, in the Directors' Report, a statement of their policy on the employment, training and career development of disabled people. The Code of Good Practice (MSC, 1984) recommends that this policy should include items about communication and consultation in the drawing up of the policy; objectives of the policy; the role of managers, employees and their representatives; the advice and help that are planned to be used; good practices and the areas where these are particularly important; and how it is planned to monitor and assess the policy.

Older people

The main protection for older employees is against redundancy, for which they may well be financially compensated, but there is no protection in seeking fresh employment, training or promotion. The continuing high levels of unemployment in the 1990s have worked against the employment prospects of those who are older, because the working population appears to be too large for our total employment requirements. People have been under pressure to retire early in many circumstances, although companies have become less willing to make these arrangements because of the high cost. It is also very difficult to continue working after normal retirement age.

In the United States legislation has been introduced to prevent discrimination in employment on the grounds of age. There are few signs of this spreading to the United Kingdom, although there is less explicit age discrimination than there was until quite recently, with more recruitment advertisements omitting any reference to age ranges, and others blurring the edges slightly with phrases like 'applicants will probably be between 35 and 45'.

It is not only a question of whether citizens' rights are being impaired because of the lack of such legislation, but also (as with managing other types of diversity) whether the effectiveness of organisations is being impaired by it being suggested, or implied, to older employees that they are becoming less effective and that they may be standing in the way of the legitimate career aspirations of others. Taking specific initiatives to overcome the problem makes it worse:

> To ask a manager to devise measures for the over forties may often simply serve to make him more negatively disposed towards a group which suddenly become a 'problem'. Even if measures and policies specially directed to the over forties are eventually instituted it may well be problematic as to whether the value from these comes quickly or strongly enough to outweigh the harm done, through possible reinforcement of myths and stereotypes, to the most effective use of the over forties . . .   (Kenny, 1981, p. 37)

Everyone requires self-confidence to succeed and a culture which implicitly devalues people who are of a particular sex, of a particular race, or in a particular age range, will undermine the effectiveness of that category of employee.

Megginson (1972, pp. 235–6) put some of the reasons to favour people over forty years of age:

> . . . greater experience and better judgement in decision making; more objectivity about personal goals and abilities, as the older men have already satisfied many of their needs for salary and status and are able to concentrate more on job responsibilities; increased social intelligence and the ability to understand and influence others; decreased risk, as the older person's potentialities can be more easily determined from their performance record; reduced training time, as their previous experience is easily transferable, especially into management positions; and proven value as the older workers have proven their abilities . . .

At the time of the great concern about reduced number of school leavers entering the labour market and the resulting 'demographic time bomb', a number of companies developed recruitment schemes targeted at people over the age of 55. They had little difficulty in filling posts and have not abandoned the policy, even though the demographic time bomb has failed to go off.

REVIEW TOPIC 13.5

For what types of post would you positively discriminate in favour of people over 55 and for which would you positively discriminate in favour of those under 18?

Managing diversity

Much discrimination is not intentional and stems from our unconscious learning experiences as individuals and as a society. We are conditioned by our experiences that, for example, women make better nurses and surgeons are men. Furthermore we reinforce these in our everyday lives, by the need we have to deal with other people. If, in emergency, you need help with lifting a heavy load, you would probably ask a man. If, in a different emergency, you had to leave your small child in the care of a stranger, you would almost certainly choose a woman. Every one of us can immediately think of exceptions, but time after time we have to make decisions about what to do in relation to other people: who is best for what? In the supermarket you will ask anyone wearing the appropriate uniform. In the shopping precinct, when trying to find the supermarket, you have to ask a stranger and you have not the time to ask for references and a comprehensive CV, so you make a snap judgement on the basis of your stereotyped assumptions about other members of the human race.

REVIEW TOPIC 13.6

In each of the following situations you have to choose between two types of person. Which would you choose, and why?

a. Stopping your car to ask directions from a passer-by. Under 20 or over 50?
b. Asking for help in reading something in English that you cannot quite understand. Black or white?
c. Asking for advice on what colour wallpaper to use in your sitting room. Male or female?

These form a framework within which we operate and react to new experiences or the possibility of change. We make inferences from this framework, for example that women make the best nurses and men make the best surgeons. Frameworks determine our attitudes. Gradually, as more new experiences of a particular type arise, we change our framework to accommodate these. This is not a speedy process and may take many generations. For a long time many people will react defensively to new experiences and will reject or deny them.

Discrimination therefore reflects frameworks that have not yet adapted to a new societal view or to changing circumstances. This may be because of very high defences to change or due to a lack of direct experiences to assimilate. Attitudes and frameworks may be changed by a variety of means. Literature can be aimed directly or indirectly at changing attitudes. For example, literature available from Job Centres is aimed directly at changing attitudes about the employability of disabled people. Books published by the Women's Press have a role in indirectly changing women's perceptions of themselves. Research into the opportunities for disadvantaged groups focuses attention and highlights areas of disadvantage and the mechanisms that support this. Much research has been funded or initiated by the Equal Opportunities Commission and the Commission for Racial Equality. Both these bodies also produce large amounts of pamphlets, codes and guidelines, and the existence of the bodies itself acts to highlight equality of opportunity for women and racial minorities.

However, it is direct experience that has the most powerful impact on the mental frameworks within which people operate, and this is where the law has its most important, but least recognised, impact. The law attempts to force employers and others to provide opportunities on an equal basis for all groups. Other developments flow from the symbol that the law provides, as well as from the behaviour of opinion formers.

When a woman is appointed as prime minister, or editor of a national newspaper, or managing director of a business dealing in soft pornography, the idea of a woman holding a post 'always' occupied by a man is no longer outrageous or laughable, and it gradually becomes acceptable and normal.

When black athletes win Olympic medals and are then shown to be personable, articulate and shrewd as well as being superb physically, then the idea of those from ethnic minority groups being in some way second-rate becomes even more ludicrous. When film idols, like Sean Connery, Clint Eastwood, Joan Collins and Elizabeth Taylor, are able to arouse worldwide sexual desire at 'advanced' ages, then the idea that someone is too old at 45 for the rather less hormone-dependent activity of management is difficult to sustain. When Evelyn Glennie can become the country's leading exponent of percussion instruments, despite being deaf, then the concept of disability has to be reinterpreted.

The workforce and the potential workforce is diverse and managers have a social obligation to maintain full opportunity for all groups in employment, training and promotion. Of equal importance, managers have to make the most of those they employ. They will only do this if they appreciate and then manage the rich diversity of experience, perspective and potential that any workforce presents.

SUMMARY PROPOSITIONS

13.1 The essence of much management is to discriminate between individuals. The essence of equal opportunity is to avoid unfair discrimination.

13.2 Equalising employment opportunity is not only meeting legal and social responsibilities; it is also ensuring organisational effectiveness through managing workforce diversity.

13.3 Unfair discrimination often results from people being treated on the basis of limited and prejudiced understanding of the groups to which they belong rather than on the basis of an assessment of them as individuals.

13.4 Although employers can usually find ways of avoiding the effects of legislation relating to discrimination, this is short-sighted.

13.5 Changes in practice relating to equalising opportunity at work are happening, but largely as a result in attitude changes taking place in surrounding society.

PUTTING IT INTO PRACTICE

Write job advertisements for the jobs below without stating or implying features that are unlawfully or unnecessarily discriminatory:

1. A cook for school meals
2. A head chef for an international hotel
3. A care assistant in a nursing home
4. A hospital porter
5. A bricklayer
6. An apprentice electrician

References

Commission for Racial Equality, 1978, *Equal Opportunities in Employment and Monitoring an Equal Opportunities Policy*. CRE, London.

Connelly, T. J., 1972, Racial integration in employment, in *A Handbook of Industrial Relations*, ed. Torrington, D. P., Gower, Aldershot, Hampshire, pp. 194–5.

Dickens, L. and Colling, T., 1990, Why equality won't appear on the bargaining agenda, *Personnel Management*, April, pp. 48–53.

Foster, B. P., 1988, Workforce diversity and business, *Training and Development Journal*, April.

Kenny, T. P., 1981, Getting the best out of the over forties, in Cooper, C. L. and Torrington, D. P. (eds) *After Forty: The TIme for Achievement*, John Wiley, Chichester.

Liff, S., 1989, Assessing equal opportunities policies, *Personnel Review*, vol. 18, no. 1, pp. 27–34.

Mahon, T., 1989, When line managers welcome equal opportunities, *Personnel Management*, October, pp. 76–9.

Manpower Services Commission, 1980, *The Quota System for the Employment of Disabled People*, MSC, Sheffield.

Manpower Services Commission, 1984, *Code of Good Practice Employment of Disabled People*, MSC, Sheffield.

Manpower Services Commission, 1985, *Suggestions for Improving the Quota Scheme's Effectiveness*, MSC, Sheffield.

Marshall, J., 1985, Paths of professional development for women managers, *Management Education and Development*, vol. 16, pp. 169–79.

Masreliez-Steen, G., 1989, *Male and Female Management*, Kontura Group, Sweden.

McGoldrick, A., 1984, *Equal Treatment in Occupational Pension Schemes*, Equal Opportunites Commission, London.

Megginson, L. C., 1972, *Personnel: A Behavioural Approach to Administration*, Irwin, Homewood, Ill., pp. 235–6.

Moir, A. and Jessell, D., 1989, *Brain Sex*, Michael Joseph, London.

O'Sullivan, A., 1989, Women in senior management, *MBA Review*, vol. 1, part 2, pp. 5–7.

Snell, M. W., Glucklich, P. and Povall, M., 1981, *Equal Pay and Opportunities*, research paper no. 2, Department of Employment, London.

Torrington, D. P., Hitner, T. J. and Knights, D., 1982, *Management and the Multiracial Workforce*, Gower, Aldershot, Hampshire.

Walker, A., 1986, Disabled workers and technology: quota fails to quote, *Manpower Policy and Practice*, Spring.

Part IV

Organisations

Effective management depends on effective organisation, and effective organisation requires a knowledge of both organisations and the people who make them up. The way in which Formula I racing cars are handled during pit stops is a marvel of precise 'human engineering', with a smooth, constantly practised routine that coordinates the activities of people with different specialist jobs to do, but not all work is well done with that type of tightly-structured, closely-specified tasks.

Managers work in an organisation within which they and their unit have to fit, and they may be able to bring about some changes in the surrounding organisation to make the unit fit in better. Managers also create and constantly adapt the organisation of their own units so that the work is well done by people who are satisfied with what they have to do, so that they remain responsible and able to adapt well to the constantly changing circumstances of contemporary working life.

G　　　R　　　O　　　U　　　P

Chapter 14

Organisation structure and culture

The term 'organisation structure' conjures up a model of integrated precision in human action:

> What you may expect to see – but don't – is an animated organisation chart – a pyramid of little boxes, each sitting astride seven others, and seven more under each of those seven, and seven more, and so on. Perhaps too, you expect to see each of the top boxes occupied by a faceless figure in a gray flannel uniform and the lower boxes occupied by figures, also faceless, in overalls. Each figure is busily pushing levers to make other figures turn and jump in unison until the whistle blows, when they all stop together.
>
> (Leavitt *et al.*, 1973, p. 3)

For some of those outside the little boxes this is a vision of perfection, taking the comfortable Victorian view of class structure – a place for everyone and everyone in their place – and adding to it the feature of specialised, interlocking tasks, so that the organisation will work like a well-oiled machine: efficient, predictable and effective.

There are difficulties about this view. First, it is not true; no organisation operates with that degree of mechanical precision. Secondly, attempts to achieve that type of precision always fail because employees are not sufficiently uniform in their abilities and experience to fit neatly into boxes and they are seldom willing to be constrained to that degree. Thirdly, the rigidity of the arrangement inhibits change and makes the organisation inappropriate for new challenges from the environment and the opportunities provided by technological change.

In the 1970s distaste for the formal structure became so great that there was a tendency to throw the baby out with the bathwater as enthusiasm for anti-structure developed. Face-to-face relationships were to replace formal reporting as the norm and the purpose of the organisation was no more than to service the freewheeling activities of its members. That vogue has altered but the feasibility of the rigid structure has been shown as dubious. A more

241

common view now is that structure is necessary, but it should be sufficiently flexible as a system to enable bits of the structure to be altered or removed so that the remaining bits can adapt to change, rather than having the entire edifice collapse. There is much more emphasis on communication between people and groups in the structure, and an acknowledgement that it is the people in the structure, individually and collectively, who achieve results: procedures can do no more than enable people to achieve.

One feature of this change in emphasis has been to increase interest in organisational culture, the characteristic spirit and beliefs in an organisation, demonstrated, for instance, by the values held in common by all members on how people should treat each other, the nature of working relationships that should be developed and views of change. It is appreciated that features of the working environment like these have a more profound effect on people's behaviour than the formal structure of reporting relationships.

Managers pick up this idea of culture and apply it in two ways. First there is the approach epitomised by Handy (1985, 1989), which advocates understanding what the culture is so that you work with it rather than against it, using the strengths of the organisation to enable you. A second approach is to attempt to change an unproductive culture and make it more appropriate to the prevailing situation. Peters and Waterman (1982) and Schein (1985) have been used by managers in efforts to break out of a situation in which all action seemed to be bound by precedent, or inward-looking, or with strong feelings of them-and-us, alienation and lack of commitment. The new type of culture to be developed is likely to have 'requisite' values such as service to the customer, ready acceptance of innovation, high consensus and cooperation. The other features of culture that will deliver these requisites vary considerably, although openness, informality and social skill training are often common elements. The changes are likely to be brought about by an emphasis on leadership, although leadership is also being reconstructed, as we shall see in Chapter 20. Trade union organisation is likely to be marginalised and life becomes uncomfortable for those who have lost – or never found – enthusiasm for the job.

The elements of organisation structure

Organising requires a combination of differentiation and integration. First, the arrangements for individuals' jobs have to be set up so as to differentiate what the job holder has to do from what everyone else is doing. Secondly, integration is achieved by coordinating the activities of individuals so that the total task of the business is undertaken satisfactorily.

Methods of differentiation and integration vary according to the predictability of what has to be done. Waiters in a restaurant have their activities integrated by a tightly specified system for taking orders from customers, passing those orders to the kitchen in strict sequence, taking completed orders to the table and then clearing the table. Their activities are differentiated by two definitions of territory. The kitchen is the territory of the chef, not the waiter, and each waiter has a set of tables to service. Their activities are further differentiated in their dealings with the customer, where they have considerable latitude to use personal, idiosyncratic social skills to persuade the customer to spend money, not complain, be quick, and come again. The only uncertainty is the behaviour and reaction of the customer. In contrast, jobs in social work or marketing, for instance, have greater unpredictability and a constant flow of new problems. This type of situation produces frequent redefinition of job boundaries, great individual autonomy and a tendency to flexible networks of working relationships rather than rigid hierarchies. The four essential building blocks for organisations are job descriptions, the structure of working relationships, decision-making complexes, and operating procedures, all of which can be used to ensure the attainment of objectives.

Job descriptions are not popular among managers, especially when they are contained in lengthy typewritten documents lost in filing cabinets, and all too often the job description is the epitome of stifling, irrelevant bureaucracy. However, each member of an organisation has a job to do and some understanding is needed, by themselves and their colleagues, of the content and boundaries of that job. Much is achieved by the job title. Titles like managing director, electrician, chief telephonist, newsreader and window cleaner all describe what the job holder does in a way that will meet most organisational requirements. Other titles are less readily understood as descriptions of job content – despatcher, clerical assistant, key account director, head of investor relations, information strategist or owners' executive, for instance. Also all jobs need some clarification at the boundary. What are the limits of responsibility held by this person? Do areas of influence overlap?

The job description is a problem for managers. It is a basic, essential requirement for allocating people to jobs and work to people in a way that can be understood and be used to avoid gaps and duplication, but there is always the risk that it becomes a restriction that people fight against or a defence behind which they hide when there is a need for change or when the unpredicted is encountered.

| REVIEW TOPIC 14.1 |

Why is the job description a problem for managers and how can the problem be overcome?

An excellent use of job descriptions is for a group of managers with interrelated jobs to write out their own, according to an agreed format, and then exchange copies with each other before meeting to discuss gaps and overlaps. This requires each one of them to work through the various parameters of their jobs and then explain aspects on which others ask for clarification. The draft documents will probably be thrown away after the discussion, but the process of which they have been the central part will have been invaluable in producing a mode of working that is more effective than any that could be achieved by other means.

The structure of working relationships is most commonly expressed in the organisation chart or 'family tree', which sets out the membership of the various working groups or departments and how they interconnect. This describes the hierarchy and the system, expressed by that hierarchy, for distributing power through the organisation. As a tool of old-fashioned 'classical' organisation theory it has been criticised as limiting the scope of individuals, emphasising subordination and rank and producing conformist, narrow thinking. It remains necessary to provide general guidance on where to find expertise and information, to legitimise the formal aspects of authority and to provide one of the means of resolving disagreements: the crossover point in the hierarchy. When two or more people cannot agree on a course of action, such as the interpretation of policy on an issue, one of the ways of resolving it is to 'go upstairs'. If the head of mathematics and the head of English in a school meet a point of fundamental disagreement about the distribution of timetable hours between their respective subjects, they may well resolve that by seeking a judgement from the head teacher. It is not the only way of resolving such problems, but is one of the possibilities.

The hierarchical emphasis in organisation charts can be modified by the presentation device of drawing them laterally rather than vertically. They still describe the grouping of activities and the distribution of power.

Some decisions in organisations are made by individuals, others are made by groups. The scope of decisions to be made by an individual will be contained either in the job description or in the position on the organisation chart. Decisions to be made collectively are allocated to decision-making complexes. The obvious example is the board of directors who make certain decisions by majority vote, and those decisions cannot be made in any other way. Other decisions are reserved for particular committees or councils, sometimes as specified in collective agreements with employee representatives. We call these decision-making complexes rather than decision-making groups because the process of reaching decisions goes beyond the face-to-face discussion to include the collection and presentation of data. This decision-making formulation is a significant feature of jobs done by people outside the central decision-making group and sometimes is the sole activity of committee secretariats. The ways in which decisions are formulated prior to being made are described in Hickson (1986) and Mintzberg *et al.* (1976).

Just as the organisation chart is the main expression of power distribution, the composition and operation of the decision-making complexes can be another basis on which organisation members channel their interests in obtaining access to power.

Operating procedures are ways in which decisions are implemented and the standardised means whereby the everyday activities of organisation life are conducted. The sundry administrative routines range from the drill that is followed in determining who has time off with pay to attend funerals, to the elaborate routine of consultation that is required in authorising a purchase order for a new piece of equipment. John Child (1984, p. 8) includes in this grouping two further aspects, first the specification of working routines for how tasks are to be performed and secondly the determination of performance standards, such as level of output or quality of performance, when the methods of doing the job cannot be precisely tied down.

The entrepreneurial structure

Most organisations start life as an entrepreneurial structure (see Figure 14.1) in that they are brought into existence to extend the capability and capacity of an individual, who has discovered a way of meeting potential customer or client need, but cannot achieve results without assistance. The two essential components of any dictionary definition of the word 'entrepreneur' are risk and initiative. The fact of having had the initiative and taken the risk gives the entrepreneur such dominance in the evolving organisation that every-thing depends on that individual and most activities of other members are either replicating or mirroring what the entrepreneur is doing. The initiative shown usually includes a powerful ingredient of expertise or specialised knowledge that nobody else can supply, and which is the secret of success.

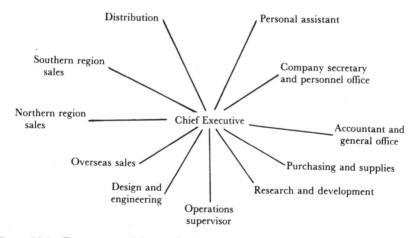

Figure 14.1   Entrepreneurial organisation structure.

Erle Stanley Gardner was a writer of crime novels that were so successful that he was able to employ a team of writers who wrote large parts of later novels according to his outline or formula, while Mr Gardner provided the vital ingredients of the formula, the characters and his own name. The popular singer has a small entourage of acolytes (interestingly they are usually called managers) whose duties are to enable the performer to do well: they have no function or purpose apart from that. Eddie Land invented the Polaroid lens and later the Polaroid camera, so that all the members of his organisation centred their activities on his inventive genius.

The questions about entrepreneurial structures are to decide where such structures are appropriate and how practicable it is to maintain that form with increasing organisational size. Most people are employed in organisations that do not depend absolutely on the continuing, irreplaceable contribution of a single entrepreneur. The large oil companies, most public-sector undertakings like the National Health Service or the Civil Service, high street banks, schools, colleges, airline companies, insurance companies have a quite different type of drive to their activities. Other types of organisation, however, appear to need the strong centralisation of the entrepreneurial form to be effective. Where there is the need to move fast and take major decisions requiring flair and skilled judgement rather than a measured weighing of alternatives, then the entrepreneurial form is maintained.

There are many examples of entrepreneurial structure at the micro-level in larger organisations. The passenger aircraft in flight has a pattern of routine organisation that is decentralised: all members of the crew are trained and self-confident in discharging their specialised tasks, but at any hint of danger the crew members look to the captain for precise instructions which they will obey without discussion or argument. The routine of the hospital operating theatre is similar. There is not time for all those involved to confer about the most appropriate course of action while the patient bleeds to death. There is common consent to the need for someone to make decisions quickly, even if they turn out to be wrong. Larger-scale activities that have this same need are the printing of daily newspapers, running a fashion house, much of merchant banking and some marketing operations. It is interesting that some other types of operation that are in many ways similar to journalism actually operate on a different, highly consultative basis. Advertising campaigns and magazine editing have been complex activities drawing upon and merging the expertise and insights of a team rather than imposing the ideas of a single person. These situations require strong leadership to avoid the pitfalls of 'groupthink' that can come from trying to satisfy all participants, but the lack of immediacy provides the opportunity to work at getting the best possible formula.

The entrepreneurial form is attractive to many managers because of its emphasis on individual power and risky competition. There are few rules and procedures, little bureaucracy. Control is exercised by the centre, largely through the selection of key individuals, by occasional forays from the centre or summonses to the centre. It is a political organisation in that decisions are taken very largely on the outcome of a balance of influence rather than on procedural or purely logical grounds (Handy, 1989, p. 89).

The bureaucratic structure

Bureaucracy is the most common form of organisation and has been used, as we saw in the opening chapter, in various forms for most of human history. It is only recently that the word has taken on the unattractive overtones that turn 'bureaucrat' into a term of abuse.

The principle of bureaucratic organisation is that jobs are grouped according to some common feature and then ranked in a conventional hierarchy of responsibility to distribute power between organisation members. The most common grouping is function, with a marketing hierarchy, an operations hierarchy and so on (see Figure 14.2). An alternative is the geographical grouping, where there is a factory hierarchy and another for the London office and a third for the warehousing and distribution centre. In bureaucracy employees focus on their roles in the organisation rather than on the relative power of individuals.

Bureaucratic structures are characterised by an advanced degree of specialisation between jobs and departments, by a reliance on formal procedures and paperwork, and by extended managerial hierarchies with

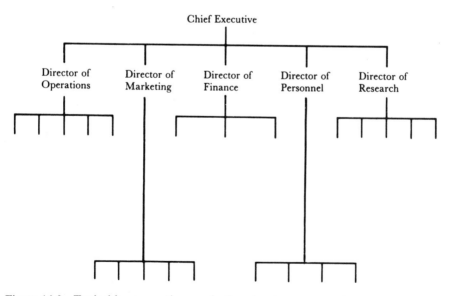

Figure 14.2 Typical bureaucratic organisation structure.

clearly marked status distinctions. There tends to be a strictly delimited system of delegation down these hierarchies whereby employees are expected to use their discretion only within what the rules allow (Child, 1984, p. 7).

In its extreme form bureaucracy gives rise to the sort of picture mentioned at the opening of this chapter, but is more usually a necessary and agreeable environment for people to work in, providing that the nature of the organisation's task is appropriate to this organisational form. The working routine is predictable and understood, jobs are defined so that individuals know what they are to do and how to do it, and efficiency derives from rational allocation of work and responsibility rather than individual flair and judgement. Standardised performances are required and it is a form of organisation that is reasonably equitable and proof against corruption.

A useful example is retail banking or the work of building societies. Here the operations have to be standardised, not only in all branches of the same bank but also between competing banks, so that customers find the system easy to deal with. The work of bank clerks and, in a different way, bank managers requires knowledge, skill and accuracy, but it must be carried out strictly in accordance with the rules and there is little scope for individuality apart from one's manner in talking with customers and manual dexterity in counting banknotes. Bureaucracy provides scope for economies of scale and extensive specialisation at the expense of flexibility and product innovation. Their predictability provides a secure environment for the employee and a clear line of safe career progression.

Bureaucracy has recently acquired a bad name for a variety of reasons. It has been pointed out that it is not always efficient, especially in times of rapid change and with increasing complexity of organisational tasks. It is also criticised as pushing people to clone-like uniformity instead of developing individual ability and potential. The inflexible and immutable procedures of bureaucracy can become means of avoiding rather than discharging responsibility. If the secure, predictable environment changes, especially if it changes suddenly, the bureaucratic system is likely to collapse and the bureaucrats find their skills in running that system to be obsolete, while their capacity to acquire new skills for a new situation has not been developed.

The matrix structure

As the entrepreneurial and bureaucratic structures have such obvious drawbacks, a third general mode has been evolved and used in some situations: the matrix. The method is simply to overlay a second set of hierarchical connections over a first, but at right-angles to it (see Figure 14.3). This was first developed in the American aerospace industry because

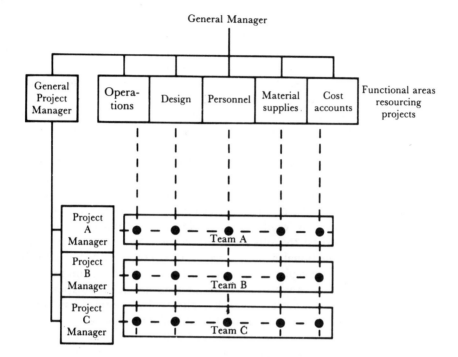

Figure 14.3 Typical matrix organisation structure.

of government demands for a single project manager who would be responsible for the progress of each government contract and to whom government officials could channel all their queries and instructions. Companies soon found big advantages in this arrangement and expanded it so that the project manager was not only a communications link but also a direct superior of employees in different functional groups, although these employees would also still report to their functional superiors. This was directly flouting Fayol's dictum about unity of command that we saw in the opening chapter, to say nothing of the New Testament observation that a man cannot serve two masters. Despite this, the form proved popular because it provided a measure of individual autonomy and formalised the necessary, informal lateral lines of communication that are developed by people coping with interrelated problems.

An example could be the making of a television programme, which will require a range of specialist skills, such as set-building, make-up, special effects, design and engineering. The necessary specialists are a part of their functional area and have a place in that hierarchy, but they will mainly work on attachment to a particular programme. The attachment may be for a few weeks, like preparing for a major state occasion; a few months like a cricket season; or several years on a magazine programme. Whilst attached they are part of that programme team and thus have a dual link. For technical expertise they refer to their functional grouping, but for regular direction and control they are responsible to the producer of the programme. In this way individuals have full scope to use their expertise and judgement and to organise their contributions, the project team leaders have 'their own people' as full-time members, and yet there is the backup of the functional organisation if additional resources are required and as somewhere for the team members to return to and identify with.

For the matrix to succeed there has to be depth of skilled personnel, so that a person can be allocated full-time to a project, and the operating context of the organisation has to be appropriate to the mode of working. There are still likely to be problems in dealing with resource allocation, as the project manager may want more people than the functional manager deems necessary and all too often the project manager wants a particular person whom the functional manager wants to deploy elsewhere. A further difficulty is with the specialist personnel themselves who have the benefit of independence but lack opportunities to develop specialised expertise, as they have to work on a variety of tasks. They will develop flexibility and experience but may not deepen their specialist skills. This can also lead to uncertainty about career progression and occupational identity. Do you stay with the functional career path or do you try to become a project manager? The administrative costs can be high due to a multiplication of hierarchies that tends to increase overheads as more and more people establish the inescapable need for private secretaries, personal assistants, larger offices, more telephones and computer facilities. The level of conflict requires managerial time for its resolution and an increased amount of political behaviour can lead to excessive paperwork as people make out their case in seventeen copies. The matrix organisation does, therefore, need time and care in its creation, balancing the power of the two axes and working out a basis of trust and understanding among the key participants. It is not something to work out on the back of an envelope during a train journey; it requires extensive consultation and discussion, progressive implementation over several months and monitoring for several years as it settles down and moves towards effectiveness. Davis and Lawrence (1979) suggest three stages of matrix evolution. First temporary overlay, during which project teams are created only for special and immediate needs; secondly permanent overlay in which project teams are established as a continuing form of organisation working across the functional hierarchy; and thirdly the mature matrix, at which point the project lines of authority and influence are brought into balance with the functional lines. It is doubtful how many matrix organisations nowadays ever achieve maturity, as acquisition and merger, development and decline mean that radical organisational change occurs so often.

Useful guidance on matrix management is in Hellriegel and Slocum (1989) and in Galbraith (1977).

Mintzberg (1979, Chapter 21) uses the term adhocracy to describe a variant of the matrix organisation, where the work is complex and innovative, such as theatre companies and some computing specialists. Such an organisation is one in which there are many highly trained specialists with an organic structure that always remains flexible, and which tends to be very big in the middle. Organisations of this type have problems in balancing workloads between individuals and groups and in managing the conflict that such a diverse group of people generates.

Combining different structures

It should not be assumed from the foregoing that an entire organisation must follow the same organisational pattern. The structure of organisation follows the requirements of the environment and the needs of organisation members rather than the whim of highly placed individuals seeking control, so that appropriate structures will vary from one part of the undertaking to another. The marketing manager will be properly concerned about satisfying customers' demands today, while the R & D manager will be more interested in the development of products for the future. It is unlikely that the same form of organisation structure would suit both situations. A hospital will have within it an operating theatre in which surgeons conduct their high dramas in a way that has to be centralised and autocratic to cope with the crises on the operating table, but the same hospital will have a psychiatric unit requiring a different approach.

The pattern of the organisation could, therefore, have a tight-knit entrepreneurial structure at the centre and bureaucratised functions or a matrix elsewhere. Bureaucracies can have within them small entrepreneurial organisations, as some large companies have set up such small groups to develop new business ventures. What is crucial in organisation differentiation is that the different structures are independent of each other in their operations. The entrepreneurs must be relatively free of set procedures and the bureaucrats must be able to escape the power-play needed by the entrepreneurs.

The seminal work on this aspect of organisation is by Paul Lawrence and Jay Lorsch (1967) working in the United States. They demonstrated that companies operating in an unstable, unpredictable environment had the greatest variations in organisational structure and style and those in the predictable environments had little differentiation. They also established that the high-performing companies in both situations had a higher degree of integration than low-performers. Whilst it is essential for subunits of an organisation to be independent in their operations if their styles are different, it is also essential that their operations are integrated.

Culture

Through the 1980s in particular, there was great interest in organisational culture as the key to improved organisational effectiveness. This was largely directed to comparisons within national boundaries (for example, Deal and Kennedy, 1982; Handy, 1985) and has complemented the earlier preoccupation with organisational structure. Organisation charts may be useful in clarifying reporting relations and subtleties of seniority, but the culture or ethos of the business is believed to be an equally important determinant of effectiveness.

Organisations do take on distinctive identities. Olins (1989) cites the example of the world's great chemical companies, which produce virtually identical products selling at the same price by the same means in the same markets. Yet they each have strong identities and in culture are as different as individual human beings. Managers need to understand the nature of the culture in which they are working, so that they can work out how to operate most effectively within it. They will also want to work out how to influence the prevailing culture as it evolves, and to understand the influence that the culture may have on their personal style and success. This can be very difficult when moving to a new organisation. Accustomed to doing things 'your' way, you do not always realise how much your previous success depended on reflecting accurately the values that obtained in the previous organisation. We like to think that the success was ours: we resist the idea that our effectiveness is a function of the setting in which we work.

Much of the recent discussion on culture has been based narrowly on how to change it, largely because so much of all management thinking has been taken up with innovation and change. Managers therefore need to understand to what extent and by what methods culture can be changed and how the changes can be made. They may also need to appreciate that the changes may be much harder to make and slower than most managers believe and most circumstances allow.

Managers who deliberately or unwittingly work counter-culturally will constantly be frustrated by failing to get a response from colleagues, by being misunderstood or by being bypassed. Managers who try to work out the nature of the culture in which they are operating can at least begin the process of their own personal adaptation to the situation and can influence the direction of the cultural evolution, because culture has qualities that structure can never enjoy. It is dynamic and human in the sense that it is the creation of all those who participate, both past and present. It will strengthen and support the efforts of those who adapt to it, as surely as it will frustrate the efforts of those who ignore or contradict it.

The most penetrating analysis of organisational culture is by Schein (1985), who distinguishes between the need for an organisation to develop a culture which enables it to adapt to its changing environment (pp. 52–65) and, at the same time, to build and maintain itself through processes of internal integration (pp. 65–83). He suggests that there are primary and secondary mechanisms for the culture change process. Schein's primary mechanisms (pp. 224–37) are as follows:

1. What leaders pay most attention to.
2. How leaders react to crises and critical incidents.
3. Role modelling, teaching and coaching by leaders.
4. Criteria for allocating rewards and determining status.
5. Criteria for selection, promotion and termination.

The difficulty with emphasising leadership is the implication that an organisation can only succeed when led by a great person, on whom everything depends and to whom everyone else responds. Some of the most productive organisational cultures avoid that extreme interpretation of leadership by tolerating a plurality of views and styles that make for a lively community, and handling through discussion and meetings the conflict that invariably ensues. Organisational culture is the concern of all organisational members and developing that culture is most effective when a majority of members agree on and own the changes that they all want to bring about. That degree of consensus is rare, but it remains a necessary, practical objective to aim for.

Schein's secondary mechanisms (pp. 237–52) for the articulation and reinforcement of culture are as follows:

1. The organisational structure.
2. Systems and procedures.
3. Space, buildings and façades.
4. Stories and legends about important events and people.
5. Formal statements of philosophy and policy.

This introduces a greater variety of possible strategies, and it is interesting that formal statements are placed last. All too often the attempt to develop some aspect of culture actually begins with a formal statement of policy, and sometimes cultural inertia is attributed to the lack of such a statement. In fact, such statements are useful only in summarising and expressing what is achieved by other means.

Without a shared sense of mission all organisations lose their essential integrity and become no more than a collection of people who would rather be somewhere else, because they lack effectiveness and conviction in what they are doing. The effective organisation has a few central values about which there is a high degree of consensus. Those are supported and put into operation by simple rules and clear procedures, which are subordinate to the values. The organisation that depends principally on rules for its cohesion is in the process of decay.

There are a number of examples of organisations taking resolute action to modify and develop a part of their culture. Allied Dunbar used an approach based on three key beliefs ('commitment to service', 'demanding and caring' and 'positive management') to deal with a period of rapid growth (Carby and Stemp, 1985), and Schein's methods were used by the Sheffield City Works Department to produce a major shift in culture (Kilcourse, 1985).

The international dimension of culture

No organisation is isolated and insulated from its surroundings, so attempts to develop its culture must take account not only of the intentions of those in charge and the expectations of those employed, but also of developments in the surrounding society, both nationally and internationally.

Managers in organisations with an international dimension have a job that is forcing them to be more internationally minded almost daily, yet seldom are they aware of the impacts of different national cultures on management practices. In this chapter we include some comments on the distinctive quality of British management culture.

British culture remains obstinately anti-business and somewhat xenophobic. Managers do not enjoy the professional status accorded to their American counterparts and their relatively high earnings are often resented by those in other walks of life.

> As a rule, leaders of commerce and industry in England over the last century have accommodated themselves to an elite culture blended of preindustrial aristocratic and religious values, and more recent professional and bureaucratic values that inhibited their quest for expansion, productivity and profits.
>
> (Wiener, 1985, p. 127)

Foreigners are typically seen as people who are 'foreign' in every sense of the word, who seldom treat the British with the respect they deserve. This is a hangover from an imperial past and is intensified by one of the great advantages of that past and from the position of the United States since the Second World War: the worldwide use of English as the contemporary lingua franca. 350 million people have English as a mother tongue, but the population of countries in which it is an official language is 1,400 million.

> English is used as an official language in over 60 countries and has a prominent place in another 20. It is the main language of books, newspapers, airports and air-traffic control, international business and academic conferences, science, technology, medicine, diplomacy, sports, international competitions, pop music, and advertising. Over two-thirds of the world's scientists write in English. Three-quarters of the world's mail is written in English. Of all the information stored in the world's electronic retrieval systems, 80% is stored in English.
>
> (Crystal, 1987, p. 358)

This is a problem as well as an advantage to native English speakers. There is insufficient incentive to learn other languages and it is difficult to appreciate that someone who speaks your language with apparent ease may not necessarily share the same cultural assumptions that you do.

British management education exhibits the same characteristics. Although there has long been an element of international business teaching in management schools, it is only recently that this has moved beyond an interest in international trade towards an interest in how business is done and how businesses are managed in different cultures.

A distinctively British aspect of business management is what some European commentators (for example, d'Iribarne, 1985) describe as consensualism. Open conflict is avoided at all costs and British managers seek to convince everyone that they are pleasant, sociable and wishing to please everybody. Individual convictions tend to adjust themselves and to converge:

> Although each individual remains responsible for his own decisions, he has to consult everybody before making the decision. Listening to the others, explaining, convincing, good faith and good reasons become crucial to such a society. Acceptance must be created by arguing: facts, data are prevalent to create a pragmatic agreement. (Lalanne, 1990)

Lalanne offers the intriguing explanation of British economic decline as being caused by the convention of the 'shared secret', combined with a lack of action attributed to a lack of expression. Whereas a standard sociological explanation of secrecy is as a means to gain and reinforce power (Crozier and Friedberg, 1977), in British organisations it is used as a means of group cohesion. The secret is shared by insiders but not outsiders, creating a complicity between members of a group. In organisational terms this leads to complacency, as a common secret among members of a management team is that all is well, despite the worrying signs. In the end the managers convince themselves that it is actually the case – simply because it is the shared secret. Allied to this is the traditional British reserve and a distaste for expressing anything other than carefully considered opinions.

A different version of this in the 1990s has been an increase in mutual appraisal and evaluation in management circles. Considerable management time has been devoted to the management process itself with objective-setting, negotiation of targets, assessment of progress, review of achievement, auditing of effectiveness, appraisal of performance, evaluation of programmes and similar activities until there is a danger that management becomes a self-sufficient, mutual admiration society, forgetting the customer and the non-managerial member of the organisation altogether – to say nothing of the product or service that the organisation supplies to its customers.

─┤ SUMMARY PROPOSITIONS ├────────────────────────

14.1 The four elements of organisation are job descriptions, the structure of working relationships, decision-making complexes and operating procedures.

14.2 The most common forms of organisation structure are entrepreneurial, bureaucratic and matrix.

14.3 Although undertakings may adopt more than one form of organisational structure, integration will be an element of their operations that will influence the success of their business.

14.4 The behaviour of people in an organisation, and the effectiveness of their combined activities, is crucially determined by the culture of the organisation.

14.5 Organisational culture must be understood by managers, and can be changed.

─┤ PUTTING IT INTO PRACTICE ├────────────────────────

Drill for tackling problems of organisation

Table 14.1 gives a preliminary drill for deciding how to approach problems of organisation and similar issues, with the advantages and disadvantages of each.

Identifying problems of organisation

To identify problems of organisation one must have some criteria against which to judge the various features of the organisation being studied. There is a dearth of absolute standards in this field, but the following is a list of statements that are generally valid on the basis of the extensive research about organisations that has been carried out. They are useful as broad criteria, but should not be taken to have any more reliability than that.

1. Size of organisation unit
   (a) As organisations grow they tend to become more bureaucratic, with a taller hierarchy.
   (b) Large units tend to have problems of morale among members low in the hierarchy or remote from the centre.
   (c) Increasing organisational size provides career progression moves (mainly for middle and senior managers) and the facilities of specialist departments.
   (d) Small working units tend to have high morale among members.
2. Age of organisation unit
   (a) As a unit grows older it will become more stable (otherwise it would not have survived) and the conventions of custom and practice will become strong.
   (b) As units grow older their structures become less flexible but their goals more flexible.
3. Setting of organisation unit
   (a) A unit cannot operate independently of its setting and many of the norms, procedures and practices will be dictated by the setting.

Table 14.1 Drill for tackling the problems of organisation

Approach	Advantage	Disadvantage
1. Use one's own judgement	Reinforces one's role as the person in charge	No testing for the accuracy of diagnosis
2. Ask for guidance from one's hierarchical superior	Tests own judgement against that of person with wider view, who shares responsibility	Might make superior's view of own judgement questionable; advice from superior difficult to ignore
3. Consult with key subordinates	Several views expressed and those consulted become partly committed to eventual solution	Spreads uncertainty about existing arrangements, which *have* to be changed
4. Survey attitudes of all subordinates	Comprehensive expression of opinion from all those most directly concerned, with anonymity of survey method ensuring reasonable frankness of views	Some subordinates will feel that they are being asked to solve problems that are the proper domain of the manager, who is showing incompetence by asking subordinates
5. Consult peers	Coordinating views with those from other units and perspectives in the organisation	Some peers may regard consultation as sign of weakness and indecision. May influence competition for resources
6. Seek external advice	Tests own judgement against that of person with experience in a variety of organisation settings, who is detached from one's own	Advice could be expensive and adviser does not carry responsibility to temper advice

   (b) The unit will be able to make its strategic objectives more ambitious if
       the setting is buoyant or competitive or both.
   (c) The unit will tend to be innovative, and its members creative, if the
       setting is changing and being challenged.
4. Job descriptions
   (a) All organisation members need some definition of their role and tasks,
       especially where their activities interlock with, or overlap, those of
       other organisation members.
   (b) Job descriptions written for them by others can cause members to
       ignore the descriptions or to use them as a means of limiting their
       contribution.

(c) Job descriptions written by members themselves can stimulate creative thinking about the members' roles and working relationships.

5. Structure of working relationships
   (a) Different forms of organisation structure are most appropriate for different settings.
   (b) Entrepreneurial structure is most appropriate in situations of rapid change or constant crisis, or where the unit is not performing well in comparison with competing units.
   (c) Bureaucratic structure is most appropriate in situations of relative stability with readily measurable performance standards and/or public accountability.
   (d) Matrix structure is most appropriate when responsibility for action has to be devolved to individual specialists so that they can work on their own account with peers having different qualifications of a comparable standard.
   (e) Differentiation of structure is most appropriate when an organisation has diversity of objectives and methods of operating in its subunits, which can operate with reasonable independence of each other providing that there are coordinating mechanisms.
   (f) Diversified organisations need coordination. This can be achieved by using various forms of face-to-face meeting to develop trust and understanding; by using the crossover point in the hierarchy when a 'ruling' is needed; and by using coordinators to assist in finding solutions to major disagreements.

6. Pitfalls of organisational change
   (a) It is not possible to predict precisely the outcome of any particular organisational change: there are always unintended consequences.
   (b) Individual organisation members sometimes seek changes which would satisfy their personal needs but which would not necessarily satisfy the needs of the organisation.
   (c) The presenting symptoms may not necessarily be due to problems of organisational structure.

More detailed suggestions about identifying problems of organisation can be found in Khandwalla (1977).

References

Carby, K. and Stemp, P., 1985, How Hambro changed its name and much more besides, *Personnel Management*, October.

Child, J., 1984, *Organization: a Guide to Problems and Practice*, 2nd edn, Harper & Row, London.

Crozier, M. and Friedberg, E., 1977, *L'Acteur et le Système*, Editions du Seuil.

Crystal, D., 1987, *The Cambridge Encyclopaedia of Language*, Cambridge University Press.

Davis, S. M. and Lawrence, P. R., 1979, *Matrix*, Addison-Wesley, Reading, Mass.

Deal, T. E. and Kennedy, A. A., 1982, *Corporate Cultures: the Rites and Rituals of Corporate Life*, Addison-Wesley, Reading, Mass d'Iribarne, P., 1985, La gestion française, *Revue Française de Gestion*, Janvier–Fevrier, pp. 5–13.

Galbraith, J. R., 1977, *Organization Design*, Addison-Wesley, Reading, Mass.

Handy, C., 1989, *The Age of Unreason*, Business Books, London.

Handy, C. B., 1985, *Understanding Organisations*, 2nd edn, Penguin Books, Harmondsworth, Middlesex.

Hellriegel, D. and Slocum, J. W., 1989, *Management*, 5th edn, Addison-Wesley, Reading, Mass.

Hickson, D. J., 1986, *Top Decisions: Strategic Decision-making in Organisations*, Basil Blackwell, Oxford.

Khandwalla, P. N., 1977, *Design of Organizations*, Harcourt Brace Jovanovich, New York.

Kilcourse, T., 1985, How culture can be the key to management development, *Personnel Management*, December.

Lalanne, H., 1990, The roles of accounting and management information systems in different management styles and different national contexts, paper presented to the European Accounting Association Congress, Budapest, April.

Lawrence, P. R. and Lorsch, J. W., 1967, *Organization and Environment*, Harvard University Press, Cambridge, Mass.

Leavitt, H. J., Dill, W. R. and Eyring, H. B., 1973, *The Organizational World*, Harcourt Brace Jovanovich, New York.

Mintzberg, H., 1979, *The Structuring of Organizations*, Prentice Hall, Englewood Cliffs, New Jersey.

Mintzberg, H. A., Raisingham, D. and Theoret, A., 1976, The structure of 'unstructured' decision processes, *Administrative Science Quarterly*, vol. 21, June, pp. 246–75.

Olins, W., 1989, *Corporate Identity*, Thames & Hudson, London.

Peters, T. J. and Waterman, R. H., 1982, *In Search of Excellence*, Harper & Row, London.

Schein, E. H., 1985, *Organizational Culture and Leadership*, Jossey-Bass, San Francisco.

Wiener, M., 1985, *English Culture and the Decline of the Industrial Spirit*, Cambridge University Press, Cambridge.

Chapter 15

Organisational communication

The evangelist Billy Graham was due to address a meeting in an American city, but was prevented by a dense bank of fog that lay between his circling aircraft and the airport near to the stadium in which his audience had assembled. The thousands who had gathered to listen to his message could hear the noise of the aircraft engines and Billy Graham lacked nothing in conviction or material for the message he wished to convey, but the bank of fog prevented the message from being conveyed and the response elicited. Those working in contemporary employing organisations often feel a sense of frustration similar to that experienced by the evangelist and his expectant audience.

Most people feel reassured by contact with those making decisions about their destiny. Airline passengers convinced that the aircraft is about to disintegrate and drop them 40,000 feet into the sea will pay close attention to the message relayed over the public address system prefaced by the words 'this is your captain speaking . . .'. Being in touch with those who decide gives one a sense of control over one's affairs, no matter how slight this may be. One of the effects of organisation is to distance people from the centre of actions which affect their lives. The rank-and-file employee, concerned about whether or not the factory is to close, will see that the yes/no decision is to be taken by, say, the Board of Directors, who are separated by a 'fog' of people and lines of communication that emphasise both the employees' detachment from the decision and their helplessness to influence it.

The irony of the present situation is that the 'fog' has been made dense by brave attempts to penetrate it and to compensate for it: more committees, handbooks, procedures and representatives. For the people waiting in the stadium to hear Billy Graham's message, books, pamphlets, tapes and addresses by close associates of the evangelist were not a satisfactory alternative to hearing the message in person. They were merely an incentive to hearing the words direct.

In organisational life there is often no satisfactory alternative to face-to-

260

face conversation, and the substitutes may simply dissatisfy both the senders and the receivers. Managers can feel that dealing with employee representatives makes it harder rather than easier for them to get their messages through to employees, while employees often regard the carefully minuted proceedings of the works committee as a poor substitute for getting an engineer with a kit of tools to come into the workshop and mend the leaking radiator about which they have been complaining for months.

A further contradiction of the present is that we have problems of communication while having a surfeit of information, which turns the fog into smog! Drucker (1977, p. 390), as usual, has a trenchant comment:

> The communications gap within institutions and between groups in society has been widening steadily – to the point where it threatens to become an unbridgeable gulf of total misunderstanding.
>
> In the meantime there is an information explosion . . . the abundance of information changes the communication problem and makes it both more urgent and more difficult.

| REVIEW TOPIC 15.1 |

How do you understand the comment of Peter Drucker quoted above?

How do you find out what's going on?

Often the reply to this question is something like: 'Oh, I generally ask Bill, or Ben; they usually seem to know what is going on'. Here we have the growth of an informal network of 'ears and mouthpieces' of management, or *the Bill and Ben system*.

In another case the answer is something like: 'Oh, my head of department sometimes tells me if he thinks it's something I need to know. Isn't that the way it is supposed to work?' Indeed it is, but it does not work very reliably. With these bureaucratic 'cascade' systems, much depends on the people controlling the 'taps' at each level. All too often the staff on the ground floor are without water, or else it arrives over-filtered or even polluted. We might call this *the noisy plumbing system*.

One method of finding out what is going on is through the minutes of meetings, *the just a minute system*. Traditionally, minutes are issued only to those who attended the meeting or sent their apologies for absence. But another view is to regard the minutes as a method of communication as well as a record. Several organisations are experimenting with supplying copies of minutes to wide groups of staff. Those who are interested will read them; others will throw them away.

Increasing the amount of information can impair rather than improve communication, as information becomes communication only where there is exchange, with the receiver signalling understanding of the correct meaning by feedback to the sender. Information output that is not attuned to the needs of the receiver will obscure rather than clarify the receiver's understanding. People in organisations show a general preference for word-of-mouth communication. Mintzberg (1975, p. 52) found that chief executives spent 78% of their time in verbal communication. It might be assumed that this was a feature of a very specialised job in the hierarchy, but another study was made among research chemists and engineers, a group of people who, one would assume, spend less time talking to others than chief executives. The findings were that they spent, on average, 61% of their day interchanging facts, information, ideas, attitudes and opinions.

If there is preference for communicating by direct conversation rather than in other ways, it is at least debatable whether it is productive to push information into other channels, such as memoranda or announcements on the noticeboard, unless these are supplementary to the preferred mode of face to face and not a substitute. Equally there are some communications for which a channel such as a formal letter is preferred to word of mouth, like the offer of employment or notice of terms for early retirement.

Organisational communication programmes

Barbara Townley (1989) gives some useful lists of the sort of communication used in organisations to communicate with employees.

How the communication is done can be any of the following:

Written:
    House journals
    Noticeboards
    Direct to individuals
    Employee reports
    Shareholders' reports
    Notices in pay packets
    Notices at home

Oral:
    Briefing groups
    General meetings of employees
    Conferences and seminars
    Immediate boss
    Senior management
    Shop steward
    Trade Union official
    Works/staff council
    Loudspeaker
    CCTV/video
    Audiovisual

Other:
Grapevine
Newspaper/radio/TV

What is communicated includes the following:

Pay and conditions
Manpower/personnel data
Performance/production issues
Future plans
Financial information

Why things are communicated are:

Participation and involvement
Production benefits
Educative purposes
Industrial Relations purposes
External pressures from legislation and interest groups
Broader political considerations.

Organisational communication and media

Several chapters in this book deal with specific aspects of communication. Discussion here is therefore limited to one major form, organisational communication, which is best defined by distinguishing it from interpersonal communication:

> Interpersonal communication is face-to-face. It is person-to-person exchange of information that conveys meaning. Organizational communication is the deliberate establishment and use of a system to transmit information conveying meaning to large numbers of people both within and outside the organization.
>
> (Carlisle, 1982, p. 421)

Organisational communication is not, therefore, all the communicating that takes place in the organisation, but simply that which is a product of deliberate attempts by managers to communicate or enable specific communications within the organisational structure and to the outside environment. In a study to which we refer again shortly, Greenbaum (1974) has suggested that there are four main objectives that managers have for organisational communication:

1. *Regulation* Seeking conformity of employee behaviour with organisational objectives.
2. *Innovation* Seeking to change aspects of organisational functioning in specific directions.
3. *Integration* Maintaining the morale of the workforce and developing a feeling of identity with the organisation and its members.

4. *Information* Passing out the mainly factual information that people need in their everyday duties: what has to be done, quality standards, customers' requests, and so on.

The value of this distinction is, of course, that the method of communication will vary according to its objective.

Organisational communication takes place in a variety of ways, using different media, and there are some messages that are conveyed unintentionally.

The formal organisational structure

The organisation chart or formal arrangement of working relationships is itself a communication as it tells organisation members important things about their 'place': how distant they are from the centre and what their official status is. The structure is also a prime communications medium, as there is an assumption that information will travel up and down it, enshrined in doctrines of responsibility, accountability and reporting, to say nothing of grievance and disciplinary procedures, which invariably nominate stages in the procedure by identifying them with office holders in the structure. Katz and Kahn (1978, pp. 440–8) list the main types of up and down communication:

Down	*Up*
Job instructions	Information about selves
Job rationale	Performance and problems
Procedures and practices	Organisational practice and policy
Feedback on performance	What needs to be done
Indoctrination about goals	What should not be done

The formal structure also has lateral as well as vertical connections, which are used to provide communication relating to coordination, mutual support and advice.

The informal organisational structure

Behind and between the formal lines is the informal structure or grapevine, through which information passes that has not been officially sanctioned. Although this is not deliberately created, no organisational communication is complete without it.

The grapevine has the advantage of being a spontaneous form of expression, providing the satisfaction of talking face to face, and it can often be both more rapid and more informative than official communications. Its operation does not follow the same pattern as the spread of rumours, where the amount of rumoured information increases as the amount of official communication decreases. Davis (1953) and Hage (1974) both found a

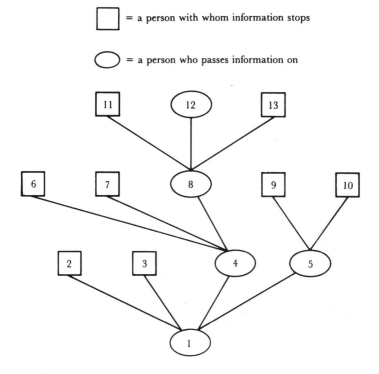

Figure 15.1 The cluster chain in the informal organisation structure.

positive correlation between official and unofficial communication. As the level of official communication goes up there is a fuelling of informal discussion and interpretation of it. Only in extreme cases of information suppression is there a sufficient stimulus to speculation for rumour to grow in order to fill the gaps that the official processes leave.

Davis was also able to identify aspects of how the grapevine works, so that the most common was what he called a cluster chain, which is shown in Figure 15.1. The person with the information (1) tells several others (2, 3, 4 and 5). Only some of them (4 and 5) pass on the information, so that the flow of information gradually peters out. Of any group who hear information, there will be only a proportion willing to pass it on. Some will feel constrained, some will forget and others will not bother. Davis found that 81% of the executives in his study had been told the information he was tracking, but only 11% communicated it to others. A later study by Knippen (1974) found that although managers accounted for only a small proportion of the 1970 employees in a grocery store, they were the source of half the grapevine information and told an average of eight people each; other employees told only four people each.

Word of mouth

Most of the messages passing through the formal and informal organisation structure will be by word of mouth, and we have already seen the preference for this mode of communication demonstrated by research. It is not, of course, only one speaking with one other. It includes interchange face to face, in small groups and committees, as well as the rarer address to a large meeting.

Written messages

Written material sometimes stands on its own as a message, so that the monthly statement of pay and statutory deductions is seldom a basis for discussion, unless it is incorrect. Other written material is an adjunct to discussion: the agenda for a meeting, the notice of a claim prior to negotiations, the draft report, the letter confirming an order of material from a supplier '. . . as discussed with your representative'.

It is a form of communication which is used often not to convey information for the first and final time, but as a preliminary to, or confirmation of, some action being discussed. The form can vary from letter to memorandum, from a notice on the noticeboard to the house journal, from job specification to sales order to instruction manual and many more. It is important that it should be used in circumstances for which it is appropriate. Changes in behaviour are seldom likely to follow from written instructions or particulars only. Pirani and Reynolds (1976) studied aspects of safety training in a Merseyside factory and demonstrated, *inter alia*, the relative ineffectiveness of posters and warning notices in persuading employees to adopt safer working practices.

REVIEW TOPIC 15.2

Envisage an important decision that you have to make in your organisation that needs to be extensively communicated. What aspects would you communicate formally in writing, what formally by word of mouth, and what would you use informal methods for?

Electronic means

A rapidly developing means of communication is that provided by the advances in microtechnology. In some ways these merely expand the amount of written material, as photocopiers and word processors make it possible to generate an almost infinite number of copies of items. This adds considerably to the volume of information in circulation without necessarily improving communication, and with the possibility of making it worse by overload. This is a problem we consider later in this chapter.

The computer terminal and visual display unit introduce a fundamentally new method of communicating in organisations, with a variety of exciting potentials like the paperless office with the visual display unit replacing the memorandum, but it is difficult to see that the amount of word-of-mouth communication will decline.

Meetings

Meetings have become the focus of adult interactions and communication within organisations. Although the overt reasons for the meeting may be to make decisions and recommendations, and to analyse and report and deal with information, the covert reasons are often as important for organisational communication. For example:

Cohesion Physically bringing people together allows them to chat before or after, catch each other's eye, joke, feel part of the whole.

Catharis Allows people to get anger out even where nothing can be done about it.

Manipulation Often senior staff are accused of manipulation. Indeed they frequently have discussed things beforehand, so decisions have essentially been made prior to the meeting.

Involvement The symbolic importance attached to participation is an obvious covert reason for holding meetings.

Learning about both content and process, takes place in meetings, but also learning about the culture of the organisation or section.

Structures for dissent Disagreement, conflict and dissent are an inevitable part of organisational life. Meetings can deal with this in different ways – by allowing heated discussion, by suggesting that people report back next time, or by ignoring the dissent.

Running meetings

The Production Director of a large chemical plant has on his wall a framed certificate, beautifully executed in copperplate script with elaborately illuminated capital letters at the beginning of the words in the title, 'The Chartered Institution of Meetings Engineers'. He explains that the Manager of the Design Office retired recently and spent the first few weeks of his retirement inscribing one of these certificates to present to each of the company directors, in commemoration of the thousands of hours of managerial time spent sitting round a table taking a long time getting nowhere.

Meetings are an essential part of the managerial job, yet every manager has tales to tell of frustration with the process. Why are they so necessary when they are so exasperating for those who participate? Is there any way of making them better? Elsewhere in this book we have material on communication and on team-building; the following sections deal with the mechanics of running meetings.

What sort of meetings?

It helps to review the types of meetings that are most common in organisations where people are employed.

Large meetings

A large meeting will be of several dozen or more people and is usually to present information with some opportunity to field questions. They are rare and usually only a matter of great significance can justify taking so many people away from their jobs at the same time. Meetings of this type are likely to take one of three forms.

Bad news meetings are to let everyone know at the same time some particularly disconcerting information, so that the message is not likely to change by being conveyed through a chain of reinterpretation by intermediaries, and so as to try to develop some concerted response. Hostile bids for the company's equity, the loss of an anxiously awaited order to a competitor, a need to shed staff or the announcement of a new venture by a competitor that will threaten the business are the type of topics of such meetings. They are extremely difficult to run and require careful preparation, as well as personal authority and skill from the person in charge.

Good news meetings are the direct opposite, but still are directed towards achieving a concerted response. The hostile bid has been defeated, an important order has been won, expansion is on the way, or a company has been acquired that will strengthen an otherwise weak situation. Running them is easy.

Change of course meetings are usually approached by the people in charge with campaigning enthusiasm, and they get fairly cross when the audience seems less than exuberant. It will probably be the introduction of a new cultural initiative through which more people will be empowered and challenged to ensure the future viability of the operation. Most members of the audience will react by saying to themselves, 'I'll get enthusiastic, when I feel that my future will be reasonably secure, that I can handle what they want me to do, and that they actually know what they're doing'. Their overt reaction will be to ask a series of cautious questions which seem to those in charge to miss the point of all the excitement and opportunity.

Vertical slice meetings

Vertical slice meetings are where a group meets to deal with matters which affect people at different levels in the hierarchy, but narrowly rather than broadly. An example could be a meeting of representatives from various sections of a laboratory to discuss aspects of operational safety. It would be unrealistic and unwieldy to have all members of the laboratory staff present, but it is not a matter that cannot satisfactorily be resolved without input from all staff categories. It is the specialist activities and technical skills of the participants that form the core agenda for any vertical slice meeting.

Horizontal slice meetings

Horizontal slice meetings are of people with similar levels of responsibility across an organisation, so that the selection is on the basis of rank or to represent the interests of a particular section in discussion with others. People meet to find common ground and coordinate with each other to resolve issues that affect all, or a number, of the organisation's departments.

Expertise or interest meetings

There are an increasing number of working parties or task forces running, where a group sets out to tackle a particular topic that potentially involves staff across a number of different sections and where working out of ideas is needed before progress can be made. Membership of the groups is likely to be on the basis of particular staff expertise, or on the basis of picking those interested in the topic. Thus the group membership does not necessarily coincide with the established groupings in the business, so the effectiveness of their deliberations can be hampered by that indeterminate status, unless there is a clear and feasible brief.

Interface meetings

Sometimes meetings provide an interface at the boundary with those from a different undertaking, like case conferences in the health and social services or meetings with members of the local college to discuss progress on a scheme to provide NVQs. These are not difficult to run. Partly this is due to the technical nature of the work that is being undertaken, but also the involvement of outsiders tends to draw organisation members together.

REVIEW TOPIC 15.3

How would you expect the approach to running these meetings to differ?

Running different types of meetings

People taking part in *large meetings* generally find them unsatisfactory. This is partly due to the significance of the event. There is either the expectation of bad news or uneasiness about the implications of other developments, however enthusiastically they are presented. There are also problems caused by the number of people present and consequent unwieldiness as a means of discussion or questioning for clarification. Managers running such meetings find the occasions difficult to handle and some regard them as destructive of their authority. Difficulties can be reduced by preparation.

First the room should be as suitable as possible. Few companies have places suitable for large meetings, but unsuitability can be reduced by considering matters such as background noise, potential audibility and visibility of the speaker and the organisation of the space in which the listeners will sit or stand. Also remember that the audience has eyes as well as ears. An inappropriate background can be distracting, especially if it conflicts with what is being said. A slogan proclaiming a bright, independent future is not a good background when you are announcing that a Japanese conglomerate has purchased a majority holding in the company and you have been given three hours to clear the premises.

What is to be said needs preparation so that it suits expectation. June Hollingsworth took over the running of her small family business when her father died, and all was well for several years, but then the company got into difficulties and she had to file for bankruptcy. In an emotional address to the employees she withheld the crucial information – that the company was to close – while making a tribute to her father. She failed to realise how anxious the listeners would be to have rumours of closure either confirmed or denied, and was mortified when a voice called out, 'Get on with it, for God's sake'. Definite news – good or bad – is best given first and put into context later. Change of course needs full preparation and explanation first. It may well be that those attending large meetings receive explanatory material or information before the meeting takes place.

Vertical slice meetings pose fewer problems because there is a tangible and objective matter for discussion, with hopes and fears issues relatively absent. Where meetings are informal and frequent, there is the great advantage that all participants share a common language and set of assumptions that makes communication relatively easy and helps the process of group solidarity. A further advantage is that these meetings often have to resolve issues that do not involve individual status, career prospects or deeply held conviction. An interesting example was from a series of meetings by the English staff in a large school. One of the teachers said: 'Deciding whether to use "Zigger-Zagger" or "The Merchant of Venice" is infinitely easier than resolving whether or not children should wear school uniform.'

Horizontal slice meetings are often seen as a major power centre and thus have all the problems attached to any political process. There is jockeying for relative advantage and considerable interest in the proceedings by those excluded from it. This type of meeting is often chaired by different members of the group on a rotational basis. There is less intensity about horizontal slice meetings which are designed to share information rather than to make decisions. They tend to be more mutual support sessions and discussion to facilitate coordination, usually chaired by an experienced and comfortable rather than dynamic figure.

Meetings centred on *expertise or interest* are not difficult to run, but can be immensely difficult to follow up, especially if they have been created merely to buy time in a difficult situation. When there is no apparent solution to a knotty problem, setting up a working party defuses the situation and gives hope for a satisfactory outcome eventually. The main difficulties are that group members may be a mismatch, chosen more to neutralise their potential for disagreement than for their ability to contribute, and that they are not clear on their terms of reference. Skilled and experienced members of staff will find their way round those problems, but their prospects are improved if they receive a reasonably clear brief on how far they can go and what they are expected to achieve.

Our observations of working parties over many years have found some to be well run with enthusiastic participation generating useful output, but many showed signs of considerable frustration among participants, and some were clearly causing mistrust and harm to the ethos of the organisation. Difficulties often stem from the ill-considered way in which the working party was set up. Among the cynical aphorisms from management folklore are: 'When in doubt set up a working party . . .', and 'Decision-making too easily degenerates into a call for further analysis'. The meetings need to have a clear brief so that the enthusiasm of members does not turn sour.

The relative ease of *interface meetings* is because latent interpersonal rivalries or antagonisms are suppressed in the interests of a common approach. Their suppression has the effect of helping participants to look favourably and collaboratively upon one another – sometimes for the very first time!

REVIEW TOPIC 15.4

Have you personal experience of a meeting that was of the wrong type to achieve its objectives? How could the problem have been overcome?

How to get the right types of meeting

Allow 30 minutes, ask group members to draw up a personal, or collective, action plan for their own situation around the following suggestions:

(a) Only convene a meeting or set up a working party if it is necessary; not as a solution to some other problem.
(b) Review the regular meetings that are held now. Are they all correctly constituted for the purposes they serve? Are there whole staff meetings dealing with matters better handled by vertical or horizontal slice groupings? Are horizontal slice meetings dealing with matters that should be handled in vertical slice groupings or vice versa? Can any meetings be amalgamated? Should any meetings be wound up with their work being taken on by an individual? Are there matters being dealt with by individuals that should be remitted to meetings?
(c) Review the working parties currently operating. How many are operating effectively? Do the others have a clear brief? Are the matters being investigated suitable for working party study? How and when do they report their findings? When was the last ineffective working party? Why did it not succeed? Will that problem recur?

Chairing a meeting

The main art of chairing a meeting is in maintaining a balance between the stimulus of competition and a reasonably secure, agreeable atmosphere for discussion. Competition between members must not reach a point where it destroys the possibility of cooperation and making progress.

Guidance notes for meeting chair

Before the meeting:

1. What is the meeting for – decision-making, briefing, generating ideas, or something else?
2. Review papers for the meeting to consider timing and pacing.
3. Review meeting arrangements with secretary.

During the meeting:

4. Introduce new members.
5. Call for apologies and minutes of last meeting.
6. Introduce agenda items.
7. Call on members to speak, seeking a balance of views, style and authority.
8. Focus discussion on disagreements that must be resolved.
9. Periodically summarise discussion and point a new direction.
10. Ask for clarification from a member whose comments others find puzzling or unacceptable.
11. Pick a workable hypothesis from the discussion and choose the right time to put it to the meeting for acceptance.
12. Finish on time.

After the meeting:

13. Check with secretary that the notes or minutes of the meeting are drafted, agreed with you, and circulated.
14. Ensure that those who have to take action know what to do, and do it.
15. Review your role as chair; what will you do differently next time?

Being an effective member of a meeting

The best meeting members are essential to the purpose and not people who might be useful. They should be interested in its purpose, with some stake in its success, and should have relevant knowledge and experience. They should have enough time to attend and prepare for meetings.

Guidance notes for meeting member

Before the meeting:

1. What is the meeting for?
2. What is your role – sage, brake, synthesiser, diplomat, delegate, adviser, stimulus, or something else?
3. Review papers for meeting and notes you plan to use.
4. Check that you have taken the action agreed for you at last meeting.

During the meeting:

5. Use social skills to persuade others.
6. Be objective in seeking solutions that will be acceptable to others.
7. Avoid personal attacks on others that would isolate you from other members.
8. Support and develop contributions by others that you regard as constructive and potentially acceptable after modification.
9. Constantly monitor the mood of the meeting to judge when best to make your contributions – facts, opinions, suggestions or hypotheses.
10. Always 'work through the chair', recognising the authority that the group always invests in that role.

After the meeting:

11. Consult with those you represent to advise them of meeting decisions and required action.
12. Study the minutes, when circulated, noting corrections needed and consider suggestions for future agenda items.
13. Take action on those items requiring your action.
14. Review your participation; what will you do differently next time?

Systems and management objectives

Greenbaum (1974) provides a technique for looking at the variety of systems, or structures, necessary to meet managers' objectives. If, for example, one considers the number of people one wishes to reach and the appropriate media, one can summarise it as in Table 15.1. By considering how people in organisations communicate about regulation, innovation, integration and information to individuals, groups and the whole, one learns a lot about how people in that organisation handle central issues. For example, the quantity and quality of communications on regulations will show something about control/autonomy issues. What is communicated about integration will show the nature of the culture, coordination, cohesiveness and valuing within the organisation. Similarly the kind of communication about innovation can tell us something about participation and change and we can ask whether information about resources is exchanged. So this communication grid can help examine an organisation's approach to the wider issues of management and organisation. Conversely, this grid forms a helpful planning device, prompting us to think about each of the squares and whether some appropriate method is used or should be initiated.

Overcoming problems of organisational communication

Very often people will complain about the communication in their organisation. Managers constantly seek better methods of communicating and yet still one can hear the following typical snatches:

'Nobody tells me anything . . .!'
'The Press always seem to know before us . . .'
'Oh no, not more bumph in my pigeonhole . . .'
'. . . I'm sorry I didn't know about it . . .'

It seems impossible to satisfy everyone all the time and no matter how well designed the system of communication there will always be breakdowns. This is partly because problems of communications can in reality be a wide variety of different problems. In view of the variety of means whereby information can be passed around, it is of limited use to speak of designing a system of communications, but it is helpful to identify some of the problems and review methods of alleviating them.

Formal structure

The flow of information and the effectiveness of communication are affected by the type of formal structure that exists. The first problem is one of size. In an organisation with a strong central focus, like the entrepreneurial form

Table 15.1 Media for communication

		Regulation	Innovation	Integration	Information
Face to face (2)	*Oral*	Directions and requests	Superior/ subordinate ideas meet	Selection interview	Induction of new recruits
	Written	Job description and performance standards	Reports on visits, courses	Letter of welcome to new recruit	Memoranda
	Non-verbal	Gesture		Gesture	Demonstration of task to be performed
Small groups (3–10)	*Oral*	Departmental meetings	Problem-solving meetings	Coffee break	Training groups
	Written	Agenda	Suggestions after meeting	Invitation to lunch	Works handbook
	Non-verbal	Pauses, silences	Seating arrangements	Meeting area conditions	Demonstration
Organ-isation-wide	*Oral*	Meetings of department heads		Address to members of organisation	Mass meeting
	Written	Organisation chart	Suggestion scheme	House journals	Notice board
	Non-verbal	Style of office for organisation member		House style in stationery, etc.	

mentioned in Chapter 14, satisfaction with communication is likely to decrease as numbers of organisation members increase. Structural alteration to split the overall organisation into a number of relatively autonomous units will be more successful than trying to generate more information for dissemination through a monolithic structure.

The problem of hierarchical levels has been discussed earlier in this book.

In the last quarter of a century numerous experiments have demonstrated the validity of the simple hypothesis advanced by Robert Dubin in 1959, that the smaller the number of communication links in a system, the greater the efficiency of the members of the system in task performance. Every communicator is selective in what they pass on, even if it is only selective in emphasis or inference. One method that reduces this problem is to operate briefing groups, whereby a superior briefs not one but a group of subordinates simultaneously. Through question, answer and discussion the message understood by each subordinate will take on greater similarity and reinforcement than if they had been briefed separately. In turn they brief their own subordinates, and so on. This improves the accuracy of the conveyed message, but eliminating a level in the hierarchy is much more effective.

Many difficulties surround the official lines of authority and communication in the organisation. First there is the problem of uncertainty amongst employees about means of access to information or decision. This difficulty was so widespread that legislation was introduced whereby the individual contract of employment now has to specify a person to whom an employee can apply to seek redress of any grievance relating to their employment, but there remain many other matters on which organisation members remain unsure of where to obtain information. A second problem arises when a point of access becomes congested. In the 1960s it could take twelve months for a matter to proceed through the engineering industry disputes procedure, with the result that the procedure was eventually abandoned. Similarly management action may be reserved to too few people, so that decisions are held up because of the non-availability of a key manager to agree or disagree.

Michael Winston was the production manager of a furniture-making plant who had to adjourn a meeting with shop stewards for fifteen minutes in order to sign a handful of release notes for material from stores. A production line of 32 people had been idle for an hour and a half because the storekeeper was not allowed to release the material (which was of particular interest to DIY enthusiasts) without Winston's authority. Eventually the foreman persuaded Winston's secretary that the matter was sufficiently important to justify interrupting the meeting with stewards. At home that same evening Winston received a telephone call from his production superintendent, who had been trying to see him for four days about two design draughtsmen who had been offered employment by a competitor but who would stay if there were small adjustments to their pay, which only Winston could authorise.

These problems become less severe when those with centralised authority in their own hands are able and willing to let some of it go, remembering that delegation does not mean giving people jobs to do. It means giving people authority and responsibility. The problem is, however, just as likely

to be one of horizontal rather than vertical lines, emphasising the importance of the integrating devices described in Chapter 14.

Social distance

Social distance is the problem that people may limit communication when
dealing with someone holding greater prestige or on a higher hierarchical
level in the organisation. To some extent the opposite applies also, with
those in senior positions feeling inhibited about being candid with those
holding more humble posts. Mainly this applies to adverse comments about
company affairs. Two salespeople may readily discuss with each other the
incompetence of the sales manager and the ineptitude of the marketing
policy being followed by the company, but both will feel inhibited about
expressing those same views to the sales manager. They feel dependent on
the manager's goodwill, which would be jeopardised if they disagreed. The
much-cherished concept of tenure in British universities has evolved for
precisely the purpose of providing lecturers with sufficient security for them
to be able to disagree with their professors.

The anxiety to propitiate the person with more power than you have also
extends to bad news for which the messenger cannot be held responsible.
Cleopatra and her contemporaries were hampered in their military campaigns by their practice of tossing bags of gold to the bringers of good
tidings and beheading the bearers of bad, so that the reliability of their
intelligence reports was low. Hitler is described as making serious strategic
blunders because none of his close advisers dared to tell him bad news for
fear of his rage. These are extreme examples, but in every organisation
subordinates seek the favour of superiors and are thus inclined to tell them
what they like to hear.

Superiors can be restrained from candour with subordinates for fear that
the subordinate will lose confidence in the superior. A senior manager will
not readily say to a subordinate 'I have no idea how to deal with this
situation' because of a feeling that the subordinate will regard this as a sign
of weakness or incompetence.

In our interviews with managers we have frequently heard them comment
on how to handle situations where they don't know something. To appear
fallible is obviously a minor nightmare for many people. Arthur Tweedle is
the manager of a city centre building society branch and has to know how
far to go when lending money. One client may ask for much more than is
actually needed, while others may underestimate their requirements. In
uncertainty about the right course of action he prevaricates and steps away
from the decision itself, by saying: 'Well, *we* will obviously have to think
about that and let you know', not 'Yes, *I* will be glad to arrange that for
you'. In uncertainty it becomes something that *we* will have to think about.

Social distance is desired by superiors and subordinates for certain reasons (authority, for instance) but at the extreme it can seriously impair communication. So some moves to its reduction are needed. One method is to tinker with status symbols, so that they become less inhibiting to those who have not got them. Segregated dining facilities, for instance, not only provide more agreeable and opulent catering for senior members of the organisation, but also cut off those people socially from everyone else by setting them apart at times of relaxation and communion. Another aspect of social distance is territory. People will often communicate more openly if they are in familiar surroundings. One of the authors was interested to observe this aspect of behaviour in a large food-processing plant. The foremen and superintendents all wore white overalls and white straw hats, while the plant manager also wore a white overall but not a hat. The manager used to monitor affairs in the plant by calling each foreman and superintendent in turn into his office to talk in a very informal way about what was going on. He also made frequent tours of inspection of the plant. When entering the manager's office the foremen took off their hats and sat upright in a chair, often on the edge, and said very little that was not called for by the questions that were put to them. The manager changed his routine by incorporating the informal chats with his tours of inspection, so that he called in on the offices of the foremen and superintendents while going around the plant. The foremen did not now take off their hats and were much more relaxed and informative. They were on their own territory.

Intergroup hostility

The contrasted aims and norms of groups in organisations often generate hostility, between both groups and individuals, which can seriously impair the quality of trust and communication between them. It is almost a commonplace that those involved with production are not always in sympathy with those concerned with sales and marketing; and technical personnel typically blame administrators for every misfortune that befalls them. This is a basic problem of organisation and some of the remedies have been examined in Chapter 14. It is necessary to accept the differences and to attempt coordination and integration by devices such as committees, coordinating departments, business teams or individuals. In many cases the difference grows worse through being suppressed. Those in Department A have a minor criticism about those in Department B, whom they talk about among themselves but not to those in Department B, to whom they become slightly cool. Those in Department B discuss among themselves the odd behaviour of Department A. Uncertainty and suspicion harden into hostility, even though the substantive cause may be trivial and, if talked about, the suspicion would collapse like a burst balloon. It may therefore be helpful to bring about a confrontation between the two parties to discuss what causes the hostility between them.

Physical setting

Increasing organisational complexity can increase the number of contacts that organisation members need to have with each other, while an increasing number of people in the organisation can make that contact less likely. When a department is set up, it is an elementary move to group those people near to each other, on the assumption that the interaction of their duties and responsibilities make such a juxtaposition necessary, but is it more important than some alternative juxtaposition? Should quality assurance personnel be located in some central corral from which they are sent out into the factory to assure the quality of production, or should they be based in production departments and only occasionally called together with other quality assurers to ensure appropriate standards and incorruptibility? Should typists and word processor operators work together for the benefits of flexibility and variety, or should they be located in the same place as those who generate the words they process?

Often the answer is whichever alternative some individual person regards as preferable, but another method is to prepare a relationship chart, plotting the frequency of communications between individuals.

A similar question is whether people should be segregated in single or double offices, or whether they should share large open-plan offices. Where there is frequent communication there is a good case for opening offices up, but office planners and organisation and methods experts have to remember that the social requirements of personnel will triumph over office landscaping plans, if the two conflict.

John Charles was a gifted chief designer of underground locomotives and worked in a small office adjoining a large drawing office containing twelve draughtsmen. When he wanted something from the drawing office Charles would throw a paper clip against the frosted glass window separating him from the drawing office and his assistant Charlie Johnson would come bustling in saying, 'Yes, Chief'. If Charlie did not hear or see the paper clip signal one of the draughtsmen would say, 'Chop chop Charlie, big chief Charles throw clip'. Inevitably a newly appointed organisation and methods officer heard of the practice and arranged for a small hatch to be placed in the frosted glass so that John Charles could speak to Charlie Johnson direct to attract his attention. In everyday use the hatch would never quite work; it may have been poorly fitted or covered with too much paint, or it may have been that the draughtsmen and Charlie Johnson and John Charles preferred time-honoured methods. Two years later Charlie was still responding to paper clips.

In open-plan offices it is amazing how carefully placed filing cabinets are gradually shifted, rubber plants appear, desks move to a different angle and hatstands are mobilised to provide a series of mini-offices in an open-plan layout.

Overload

A common reason for managers not communicating with others is that they lack the time. Although this may be partly due to indolence or a failure to acknowledge the importance of communication, the amount of information to be handled is certainly increasing, as has been mentioned earlier. One way of dealing with the problem is to develop specialised scanning skills in reading, and another is to develop delegation, as has already been described as a means of dealing with problems about lines of authority. Few managers, however, can avoid having large amounts of paperwork to deal with, so they have to work out ways of coping with it, such as setting aside a particular period each day – usually at the beginning or the end – for reading, writing and dictating. General Douglas MacArthur never left his office in the evening until all the day's paperwork had been cleared.

Organisational communication is only as good as interpersonal communication

Whatever initiatives are taken by managers in organisations to manipulate and 'improve' organisational communications, they will only be as good as the quality of the interpersonal communication that is taking place.

The line-and-box drawings we call organisation charts are not the structure of the organisation they describe. Structure is the development of relatively consistent patterns of interaction among the members of an organisation.

> These patterns begin to develop when a group of individuals, in response to certain characteristics and needs of the environment, create a system of patterned activities for the accomplishment of a specific task. The process by which these relationships are formed and maintained is interpersonal com-
> munication.   (Baskin and Aronoff, 1980, p. 97)

It is not practicable for employees to develop confidence in a series of procedures or routines. They can only acquire confidence in what those systems produce and in those other members of the organisation with whom they interact. That confidence is built by the substance of what people say and do, but it is also built by a climate in which people feel encouraged to express ideas, make suggestions and question the validity of decisions. Communication and behaviour are so closely connected and interwoven that everything which influences behaviour also influences communication. It is closely related to the particular culture of the organisation.

SUMMARY PROPOSITIONS

15.1 Communication is the most time-consuming activity in which managers engage. Improving management usually requires an improvement in communication.

15.2 The fewer the number of communication links in a system, the greater the efficiency of members of the organisation in task performance.

15.3 Managers generally prefer word-of-mouth communication to other methods.

15.4 The growth of electronic methods of handling information will affect the amount of written communication in organisations, but will have little influence on the amount of word-of-mouth communicating.

15.5 Only in extreme cases of censorship is the grapevine a substitute for the formal system of communication: normally formal and informal systems complement each other.

15.6 Problems of organisational communication which can be at least partially overcome include those of the formal structure, social distance, inter-group hostility, the physical setting and overload on individual communicators.

15.7 Organisational communication is only as good as the interpersonal communication taking place in the organisation.

PUTTING IT INTO PRACTICE

Drill to study patterns of contact with other organisation members

Stage one

Draw a personal organisation chart, with yourself at the centre, using a square to indicate job positions and showing the names of those currently holding those posts. The chart should include formal relations you have inside and outside the organisation. The circle represents the organisation boundary and your drawing might look something like Figure 15.2.

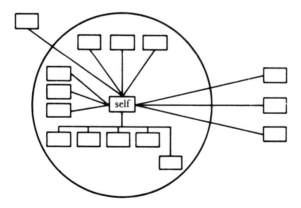

Figure 15.2 A personal organisation chart.

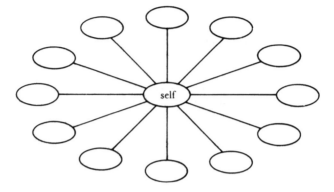

Figure 15.3   An informal network drawing.

Table 15.2   Network action plan

Rank	Contact	−3 −2 −1 0 1 2 3	Improvement by . . .
1			
2			
3			
4			
5			
6			
7			
8			
9			

Stage two

On a second chart list all the individuals or groups who can affect how effective you are in your job, but with whom you do not have a formal working relationship included in the first chart. Give both names and positions. The drawing, which may look something like Figure 15.3, will describe your informal network.

Stage three

(a) Using Table 15.2 rank-order the contacts, formal and informal, in their importance to you in getting your job done effectively.

(b) Rate each contact on a scale between −3 and +3, according to how helpful the person is to you.

(c) What can be done to improve communication with those you have rated between −1 and −3?

Stage four

Is there anyone who should be in your network but is not yet?

References

Baskin, O. W. and Aronoff, C. E., 1980, *Interpersonal Communication in Organizations*, Goodyear, Santa Monica, California.

Carlisle, N. M., 1982, *Management: Concepts, Methods and Applications*, 2nd edn, Science Research Associates, Chicago.

Davis, K., 1953, Management communication and the grapevine, *Harvard Business Review*, Sept/Oct, pp. 43–9.

Drucker, P. F., 1977, *Management*, Pan Books, London.

Greenbaum, H. W., 1974, The audit of organizational communications, *Academy of Management Journal*, pp. 739–54.

Hage, J., 1974, *Communication and Organizational Control*, John Wiley, New York.

Katz, D. and Kahn, R. L., 1978, *The Social Psychology of Organizations*, 2nd edn, John Wiley, New York.

Knippen, J., 1974, Grapevine communication: management employees, *Journal of Business Research*, January, pp. 47–58.

Mintzberg, H., 1975, The manager's job: folklore and fact, *Harvard Business Review*, July/August, pp. 49–61.

Pirani, M. and Reynolds, J., 1976, Gearing up for safety, *Personnel Management*, February.

Townley, B., 1989, Employee communication programmes, in *Personnel Management in Britain*, ed. Sisson, K., Blackwell, Oxford.

Chapter 16

The organisation of jobs and departments

The two activities in the title of this chapter are fundamental to the process of management, yet they are not often undertaken deliberately. It is more common for jobs to develop or to be brought into being as a response to some aspect of organisational change, than it is for jobs to be thought out. It is more common for people to be grouped together in a rough-and-ready form of departmental structure than it is for departmental organisation to be thought out to find the best method.

Departments in companies usually come into existence as a result of company expansion. An example could be that at one stage there will be one or two safety officers in a company, each attached to a factory and reporting to the production manager. When there are eight or nine safety officers, they are likely to be grouped together with a safety manager in charge. The method of working in this new alignment will evolve gradually, so that initiatives in organising the members of the department will come in stages rather than being worked out in detail before operations begin.

This chapter contains material on both the design of jobs and the design of departmental organisation, but our opening comment is that most managers will find few opportunities for approaching either task from scratch. Redesign is a much more common activity than design.

The nature of job design

Most people reading this book will remember the disaster at Chernobyl and will have heard of the continuing plans to deal with the hazard of this nuclear reactor that was inadequately designed. Fewer will remember the near-disaster of the nuclear reactor at Three Mile Island, near Harrisburg, the capital of Pennsylvania. In 1979 that reactor came very close to meltdown and the probable death of thousands of people. Charles Perrow investigated the accident at Three Mile Island and concluded that its cause had nothing to do with the design of the reactor, but was due to the unsatisfactory features of the way individual jobs of the operators were organised (Perrow, 1985). That is an extreme illustration of the importance of job design, which is too often dismissed as being no more important than a vague 'feelgood' factor.

Job design is the process of putting together a range of tasks, duties and responsibilities to create a composite for individuals to undertake in their work and regard as their own. It may make people feel better about the work they are doing, but the purpose is to get the job done efficiently, economically, reliably – and safely. Some of the job dimensions begin with the reasons for people to be employed in a particular organisation. This can be illustrated by using the example of employees in a department store.

Shop assistants are employed for product market reasons. The customer expects some type of sales service, ranging from detailed advice and technical explanation to simple cash-and-wrap operations. This is why shop assistants have to be on view, standing, identifiable and willing to respond to customers' requirements. The technology of the product requires cosmetics saleswomen to wear what they sell and those selling recorded popular music to be able to tolerate sustained high-volume noise. Others are employed for administrative reasons and the administrative structure will be the main influence on their jobs, so that wages clerks spend most of their time sitting and doing solo manipulations with figures, while buyers spend most of their time not buying at all but filling in forms to get the right balance between materials bought and materials sold.

Others are employed for social system reasons and a particular aspect of the social system determines the main dimensions of their jobs. The fire officer wears a special uniform so that people will respond in times of emergency. Catering staff have to fit in with the grossly inefficient timescale of their operations: intense activity around teabreaks and lunchtime.

Part of the management process is to mediate operational constraints and requirements like these in dividing work up between members of the organisation, so that there are a number of composites – or jobs – that employees will be motivated to undertake and that are combined in such a way as to produce satisfactory working performance in the coordinated effort of the department and the organisation.

Much of the interest in job design has centred round attempts to improve employee satisfaction with the working situation. It is inappropriate, however, to regard this type of initiative as only suitable for mass production jobs. Administrative and managerial jobs, especially in large organisations, can be crying out for job design initiatives. Creating opportunities for senior managers can all too often involve limiting the scope of middle and junior managers to such an extent that the initiatives of their seniors are jeopardised. An American study was carried out among forty large organisations that were chosen because they made particular efforts to use their managers effectively, yet:

Management in the typical organization was characterized by having rather narrow jobs and very tightly written job descriptions that almost seemed designed to take the newness, conflict and challenge out of the job.

(Campbell *et al.*, 1970)

REVIEW TOPIC 16.1

1. Reproduce the elementary matrix shown in Table 16.1 on a piece of paper.
2. Write in a job dimension in each column against each of the printed jobs and then add in three or four more jobs with which you are familiar, with the dimensions.
3. Are there any of those job dimensions that could be altered to make the job more efficient and more satisfying?

Job design sets the individual to work and organisation design sets that work in a departmental, coordinated setting.

Factors in job design

John Child (1984) points to three key aspects of the ways in which jobs can be shaped: specialisation, definition and discretion.

Specialisation

The extent to which a job is clearly identified and different from others, so that there is a clear justification for a person doing it, due to skill,

Table 16.1   An elementary job design matrix

	Product market reasons	Technology reasons	Administrative reasons	Social system reasons
Job				
Film actor				
Fire officer				
Nurse				
Teacher				
....				
....				

experience or some other distinguishing factor. The reason for this is obviously that it enables the greatest degree of expertise to be developed. The teacher who concentrates on teaching French, rather than on teaching French, Physics and Woodwork, is likely to become more skilled at teaching French because of the specialised development that is then possible. But how specialised should a role be? If the French teacher were also to teach German or Latin, would that enable the development of complementary skills and understanding to produce a generally higher quality of work?

Specialisation develops expertise and expertise produces authority and autonomy, so that the right degree of specialisation enables the job holder to 'own' skills and knowledge in a satisfying way, but if jobs are made too narrow there is the risk of the problem identified by Campbell and his colleagues that we have just seen. Specialisation is not always based on skill; sometimes it is a simple administrative division of duties.

Child illustrates this most effectively by contrasting the practice in two companies:

> In one organization . . . 'Peter Jones from Quality or one of his team, and a chap from Engineering – quite often Phil Bond or Jim Dankworth – usually get together on that one. They will sort it out, and call in anyone else, as they think best'. In another organization, you might be referred to page 23 of the procedures manual where it states that 'customer complaints are the responsibility of the Assistant Quality Control Manager – Warrant and Complaints'. This man, you are told, 'has a job description which lays down quite specifically the way he should deal with a complaint, including the maximum amount of expenditure he can incur. Should he wish to spend more, or involve anyone from another Department, he must first refer to the Quality Control Manager'.
>
> (Child, 1984, p. 25)

The first of those two organisations emphasises skill rather than position and responsibility, with the specialisation not being too precise. It appears more civilised and constructive as a way of running a business, as long as one is looking at it from inside, where individuals can be deployed and appreciated as individuals. Once the interface with the outside world becomes important, then the emphasis on role becomes more logical. The customer telephoning from Land's End to John o'Groats with an urgent complaint would probably begin to foam at the mouth when told about Peter Jones and Phil Bond or Jim Dankworth.

Definition

The degree to which job boundaries are clearly marked is the area of job descriptions, procedures and drills. There will always be a degree of such definition; the managerial problem is again to decide how much. The process of definition has the great merit that the manager has to work out exactly what is required, how it can be done and what the contribution of each team member can be. Ambiguity is lessened and the mission of the individual becomes clearer. Organisational practices can be made identical so that swapping people about is easier.

The overwhelming danger of precise definition is its lack of flexibility and the risk that job holders regard the definitions as challenges to be defied rather than as guidelines for effectiveness. However precise or imprecise the definition, the objective should be to define jobs in a way that makes them 'whole', so that the scope is sufficient for job holders to see assignments through to completion. They can seldom do all that they would like, but the work needs to have both variety and integration for it to be a coherent, satisfactory whole. This was the direction of many of the job enlargement initiatives that became popular in the early 1970s. The satisfaction of seeing something through is not limited to the job holder; there is a greater satisfaction for the client, whether inside the organisation or outside. Most people have experienced the frustration of being a client in a large, bureaucratic system, like a hospital or an insurance company, where the client feels helpless as the organisational machine grinds through its cycle. Individuals to whom they speak can always answer only some questions and deal with only some requirements before they are passed on to someone else.

In considering job boundaries, the manager needs to think in terms of whole jobs, with a logic and coherence that meets the needs of clients as well as the needs of job holders. The manager must also think in terms of what has to be done in the longer term, as this will give a sense of purpose and responsibility that is more complete than that of dealing only with the immediate, and it describes the duties of the job holder in a way that produces a clear contribution to organisational affairs.

Discretion

Discretion is the degree of autonomy that the job holder enjoys. Effective leadership requires the autonomy of the led, but again the vexing question is to decide how much discretion job holders should have.

Discretion leads to responsibility and thoroughness, as the blame for mistakes cannot easily be transferred elsewhere. The job enrichment initiatives that have been widely documented (e.g. Wild, 1975) have the deepening of discretion at the heart of the strategy for 'enriching' manual jobs. More recently the idea of giving greater discretion has been at the heart of ideas on 'empowerment' and performance management:

> Performance management consists of a systematic approach to the management of people, using performance, goals, measurement, feedback and recognition as a means of motivating them to their maximum potential. It

embraces all formal or informal methods adopted by an organization and its managers to increase commitment and individual and corporate effectiveness.

(Armstrong and Murlis, 1991, p. 195)

Although specialisation, definition and discretion are the main issues in job design, there are one or two commonsense points to add. Where people are employed at the same status in an organisation, doing jobs that are interdependent, it is sensible for them to be of roughly equal complexity, with critical matters also distributed between all posts. It is always useful to look for a combination of duties that fits the logic of the situation rather than a random collection. Some combinations are obvious, like one person doing all that is involved in servicing a motor car, but others are less clear. Consider your experience in eating out at a restaurant. Taking your order, serving your meal and taking your payment are three separate activities; you will have visited restaurants where they are all done by one person and others where they are divided between two, three or more people. It is difficult to say which is the most effective.

The span of control

One idea that has fascinated management analysts for decades is the span of control – what is the optimum number of subordinates for a manager? The idea of an optimum number has been so ridiculed in recent years that interest in it has waned, but we resurrect it here because it includes some of the detailed decisions that have to be taken by managers about how work should be organised and how bits of the organisation fit into the overall structure. Decisions about job descriptions and working relationships, for example, will affect the number of subordinates and will determine the number of posts in the organisation and the relative steepness of the hierarchy, with all the implications of cost, communication problems, potential overmanning and inefficiency.

No executive should attempt to supervise directly the work of more than five, or at the most six, direct subordinates whose work interlocks.

(Urwick, 1974)

At first sight that is an amazingly uncompromising statement, but the word 'interlock' is significant. To Urwick the feature of the work interlocking was important, as that required the executive to resolve problems more often. Such a pattern of 1:5 or 1:6 may be appropriate when looking at the question from the point of view of how the individual performs, and it is the pattern found in most hierarchies, but another aspect of the question is the amount of management and managers that such a norm builds into an organisation and the degree to which it introduces the inefficiencies of over-management. Table 16.2 compares two actual organisations, one manufacturing and one retailing, but both part of large conglomerates. At

Table 16.2   A comparison of management structures

Rank and grade		Manufacturing	Retailing
Senior management	1	4	4
	2	9	—
Middle management	3	16	8
	4	40	—
Supervisory management	5	55	12
Total managers		114	24
Total other employees		1500	600

first glance the disparity is enormous, even though both have ratios of managers to others that exceed the 1:5 or 1:6 suggested by Urwick, but there are a number of factors to explain the differences.

The manufacturing operation is technically sophisticated, requiring a range of technical expertise, it is physically more widely distributed and shifts are worked over 24 hours for five and a half days a week. The retailing unit does not have to buy or advertise and has a relatively simple operation, even though it is carried out with great skill. However necessary the larger number and proportion of managers in the manufacturing organisation, there is both extra cost and administrative burden caused by the number of managers and levels: more secretaries, more memoranda, more necessary communication, more problems with role definition and boundary, less scope for subordinates to exercise responsibility, and a larger salary bill. There is obviously a potential benefit in increasing the average span of managerial control if this has the knock-on effect of reducing the number of levels in the hierarchy, which Child (1984, p. 59) claims to be typically four in the organisation employing up to 100 people, rising to six when, 1,000 people are employed and seven or eight in the organisation with 10,000 people. The significance of the span of control is summarised by Stoner and Freeman, using their preferred term 'span of management':

> Too wide a span may mean that managers are overextended and subordinates are receiving too little guidance or control. When this happens, managers may be pressured to ignore or condone serious errors. In contrast, too narrow a span may mean that managers are underutilized.
>
> (Stoner and Freeman, 1992, p. 314)

The 1980s were a time when everyone spoke of flattening hierarchies and reducing the number of management grades to make the organisation leaner and fitter. This has also increased the span of control. Among the factors that can be examined to enable a widening of control spans to flatten the hierarchy are the following:

1. Standardising the work to be done. If the work to be done by the managed can be standardised, then the need for supervision will decline as individual employees are working to a standard, clearly understood procedure for which they will require little instruction and guidance. There is a narrow line separating the constraining standardisation of the many mindless tasks that are to be found in mass production and the liberating standardisation that can be found in skilled jobs, like that of the craftsman or travel agency booking clerk, where the standard is set for the output rather than the details of method.

2. Autonomy. Closely related to the methods of standardisation are the methods of providing autonomy, whereby supervision is virtually removed from the work of those sufficiently skilled and experienced to be able to do their own management. One version of this is the converse of Urwick's point about work that interlocks. Where there is close interaction between the work of people or departments, that interaction needs careful management to keep the varied activities in balance. Whether that is done by managers or by the people themselves, it is still a time-consuming activity. If the interlocks can be removed, then the management requirement can reduce.

3. Specialist advisers. Theoretically the use of specialist advisers or departments eases the management burden in the line, by taking over responsibilities for activities such as safety, personnel or quality control. The introduction of these services should allow spans of control in the middle of the hierarchy to widen, although it means more departments for senior managers to coordinate. Such specialists can also develop standard procedures to simplify general administration. Specialists are, however, a dangerous drug as they are always likely to increase rather than reduce the managerial burden: the tail wags the dog. Information is called for, forms are required to be filled in and the specialist becomes aloof and didactic rather than genuinely easing managerial loads in the line. This is often because the detachment of the specialists enables them to be uninterested in everyday problems, but also it can be because the position of the specialist adviser is always precarious and they feel a need to make themselves necessary by becoming a part of the administrative system of the undertaking and thus being 'indispensable'.

Quite apart from the possibility of increasing the span of control and the number of levels in the hierarchy, managers have to guard against the strongest pressure of all in the organisation towards increasing the number of levels, namely the managers themselves. When a hierarchy is established the members of the hierarchy want to go up it, so they are always looking for openings higher up and can often make out the most convincing case for a new opening that does not already exist. In a medium-sized chemical plant there was a plant manager, four production superintendents reporting to him and 22 supervisors: a clear three-level hierarchy. Safety was the responsibility of the personnel manager, but the plant manager was anxious to be in charge of his own safety arrangements and eventually won a battle with the personnel manager to appoint his 'own' safety officer. This involved not only a flurry of administrative activity in redefining the limits of responsibility between the personnel manager and the plant manager, it also required redefinition in the three-level hierarchy of the plant. The safety officer reported to the plant manager, so the four superintendents wanted to know whether he ranked above or below them (which was partly a coded question meaning 'Does he get paid more than we do?'). It was confirmed that he 'ranked' below superintendent but above supervisor, which produced a problem in the personnel department, where the safety officer was on a supervisory scale. It also introduced a new level and within two years six of the supervisors had been promoted to the new position of senior supervisor, ranking equal with the safety officer.

This same tendency has been seen as groups of people have sought 'improved career prospects'. Nurses in the National Health Service used to have vague career prospects beyond the clear and well-understood posts of ward sister or charge nurse. After that there was deputy matron and matron. When the case for career advancement was made, those two vaguely defined and amorphous levels became four: nursing officer, senior nursing officer, principal nursing officer and divisional nursing officer. Concern about the span of control led the Lockheed Corporation to devise a means of evaluating managerial posts in order to decide the number of subordinates for whom the job holder could be held responsible. This was used in 1961 to reduce the number of management levels in several sections of the undertaking. It has not proved to be a popular method in other organisations and is thus little more than a footnote to the development of management ideas, but some readers might be interested in the account of the method provided by Barkdull (1963). Child (1973) accounts for the growth of specialists' numbers in organisations as being related to the size, dispersion, technical complexity and number of divisions in the organisation. Howells (1981) made a comparative study of the Marks and Spencer chain store and the Civil Service. He found distinctive styles of decision-making with Marks and Spencer putting very little on paper and emphasising decision-making by individuals, whereas the Civil Service put a lot on paper and used committees to make decisions. Howells considers that the Civil Service operates in this apparently laborious way because of the complex decisions that have to be made with less clear criteria and operating with external accountability. This demonstrates how both environment and product influence formal organisation structures.

REVIEW TOPIC 16.2

How useful is the idea that there is an optimum span of control for an individual manager?

The nature of departmental organisation

Company-wide organisation structures and processes, of the sort we considered in Chapter 14, provide an overall framework and philosophy for the integration of all the jobs in the undertaking. Between that and the ways in which individuals and small groups perform their everyday tasks lies the process of departmental organisation.

'Department' designates a distinct area, division, or branch of an enterprise over which a manager has authority for the performance of specified activities (Koontz *et al.*, 1980, p. 334).

This is an aspect of organisational practice that has received little attention recently. Company-wide organisation has been much studied and has been the focus of debates about industrial democracy, employee participation and rationalisation in the face of recession. In industrial relations the interest is always in getting to the top, speaking to 'the decision-makers'. In the analysis of company performance, profitability, merger and acquisition there is similarly a focus of interest in overall performance, with the assumption that a Rupert Murdoch, a Richard Branson or a Donald Trump will produce a miraculous change single-handedly through the overall strategy that is pursued.

There is a different sort of close interest in the individual: the profession-al, the apprentice, the trainee, the executive. We have received a plethora of advice on how such people should be recruited, selected, trained, paid, developed, appraised, counselled and given enlarged or enriched jobs.

The importance of both these areas is obvious, but sometimes departmental organisation can be more important, even though it is a concept that fails to fire the imagination. It lacks the fascination of the power play of the boardroom and the attraction of the individual's humble hopes and fears, yet the individual person at work often finds the greatest frustration in minor aspects of departmental affairs, and grand new company strategies can founder through inadequate coordination of individual activities, usually euphemised as 'communication problems' or 'the human factor'.

The lack of interest in departmental organisation was demonstrated in an extensive review of research and organisational design by Kilman and his colleagues in 1976, when they found that the process of organising activities in a department was usually intuitive rather than analytical, and was likely to express the personality and whims of the 'designer'. They also found that when the pattern of organisation had been designed it was put into operation in a relatively rigid way, allowing little flexibility in practice.

The basis for grouping or clustering activities can be one of several. Most common is function, like the safety officers mentioned earlier, who were grouped together because of that specialised interest and identity. Grouping on a basis of territory is logical when activities are dispersed, so that a fire station is a unit within the fire service and a ship is a unit of organisation in a shipping company. We also see departments based on common interest in a product and others, like night shifts, based on a time period.

| REVIEW TOPIC 16.3 |

Think of some departments you know and categorise them as having their basis in function, territory, product or time period.

Although most departmental organisation may be intuitive rather than analytical, it is easy to establish a logical sequence, shown in Figure 16.1. First, a purpose for a department is decided and tested against such questions as: 'Is it really necessary?', 'Is there a better way of achieving the same objectives?', 'What will be the knock-on effects of this elsewhere in the undertaking?'. Secondly, the activities necessary to achieve the purpose are identified. Thirdly, the activities are grouped together (job design) in ways that make up jobs that can and will be done. Fourthly, the necessary formal authority for individual job holders is attached to them, and, finally, the jobs are connected through information systems and lines of reporting.

This assumes the ideal situation of organising a department from scratch, but the sequence is still useful when trying to identify problems of organisation in a long-standing department.

The nuts and bolts of departmental organisation

We now consider in more detail four of the steps described in Fig. 16.1 (the third step – job design – has already been dealt with at the beginning of the chapter).

Purpose

The purpose of creating a department may be a basic organisational objective, such as production, or sales, or maintenance, or it may be a purpose of hoping to make things run more smoothly. Much organisational tinkering is of the second rather than the first type: the creation of a new department for organisational rather than business objectives. The regrouping of safety officers, mentioned earlier, is such an example. Another very common creation has been the establishment of a systems department to intercede between the people in the organisation and the electronic

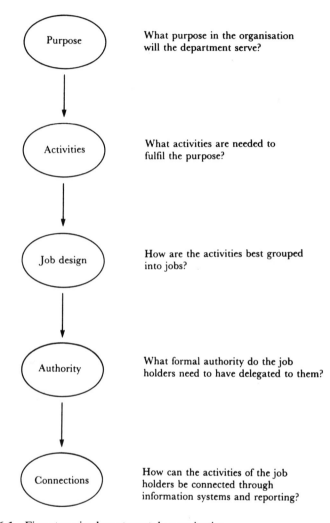

Figure 16.1 Five steps in departmental organisation.

monsters that process data. Those who understand the electronic gadgetry are grouped together because of a skill they have in common.

The search for a basis of classifying activities that leads to the association of those which are similar eventually brings organisers to the skills of people. At first, they may be persuaded that the important element is the object to which labour is applied. But that which results from labour depends on the skills applied to it. After determining what needs to be done and what skills are required, the organiser can then group them under such heads as typing, chemical analysis, process engineering and accounting. In this way, people who perform similar activities can be grouped in one department, and the advantages of occupational specialization can be realised.

(Koontz *et al.*, 1980, pp. 387–8)

There is always a countervailing argument against the grouping of skills together and in favour of their dispersion. Matrix patterns of organisation go part-way towards this dispersion. Once a skill-based department is established there are the risks of separation, aloofness and problems of communication. All the while that the personnel department has one or two of its members who are interested in computing and who spend part of their time introducing computer-based systems for the personnel function, they are personnel people working with computers. Once such specialists are taken into a systems department and merged with other systems specialists, they become systems people, the personnel department is bereft of that type of expertise and there is the risk that the developing systems will fall into disuse or that new methods developed by the systems department will be not quite what is required.

Setting up a new department to deal with something that senior managers do not understand (like computers or new pensions legislation) or something they find unattractive (like dealing with trade union negotiations) may give them an easier time in the short term, but there will be headaches in the long term if there is not a well thought-out organisational purpose.

An alternative to organisation on the basis of skills in common is to group people in departments on the basis of frequent contact. The obvious example is the grouping of secretaries and word-processing operators. If they are all together in a secretarial services department there are the benefits of flexibility, shared facilities – from dictionaries to laser printers – specialised supervision and general economies of scale. On the other hand, if they are located individually with the people for whom they work, there are the advantages of easy access for receiving what has to be typed, a wider range of duties, etc.

Creating a new department always brings problems as other departments either resent losing some part of their role or eagerly offload chores they have been trying to get rid of for years. There are also problems of more communication, more memoranda, more meetings and so on, so any such decision must answer the questions about whether there is a better way and what the knock-on effects will be.

Identification

Identifying the activities to meet the purpose is largely straightforward when the purpose is to bring together those who have a skill in common, although there will follow arguments about how many typists, errand boys and tea ladies are required.

Organising on the basis of frequent contact can be more difficult as the criteria are less precise, members of staff to be drafted into the new department may wonder whether such a move is in their best interests or whether it represents a veiled demotion, and other managers will be resistant to losing their star team members and over-cooperative in offering the services of people they do not like.

Simon Petch was the son of the chairman of a small printing company that was expanding quickly. He had just joined the company after university and a period of working experience in a larger organisation. He was put in charge of a newly created marketing department to deal with marketing, sales promotion and advertising, although his father would continue to handle sales through agents and two company representatives. Those joining the new department had mixed feelings. Some welcomed the opportunity to be part of a new departure with fresh ideas and working with the man 'who would be chairman one day', while others felt that they were being moved sideways and that their careers and livelihoods were being jeopardised by being used as a training ground for a tyro. The chairman was about to see those who were uncertain and tell them that they would have to do as they were told, but Simon dissuaded him and offered to take a much smaller initial role, dealing only with marketing and leaving sales promotion and advertising to his father. Also he would start by having only two members of staff both of whom were particularly interested in marketing and keen to work with him. He was very successful and his success brought him onto a number of informal communications networks that had previously been closed to him. Progressively he assumed control of advertising, sales promotion and then all sales, so that within two years he had a 'department' of people readily working with him and smoothly coordinated.

Authority

Allocating authority in departmental organisation is the process of enabling employees to trigger other processes in the organisation by delegating authority to them, so that others recognise them as being authorised to act. One familiar method is the job description and its definition of boundaries, but other methods can be simpler and more effective in some circumstances. Being authorised to sign documents is one way of giving power to subordinates. If material cannot be issued from stores until Mr Jones has initialled the docket, then Mr Jones is clearly and effectively given that authority. Knowledge of computer codes, or possession of keys to the safe, are similar allocations of authority and not to be confused with status symbols, like having a key to the executive washroom.

Communication

The departmental organisation is finally made to work by the means of communication between the members. Standard methods are multiple copies of memoranda, meetings and departmental drills specifying the routing of paperwork or other material undergoing transformation. Less obvious is office landscaping, considering how closely people should work together and who should be next to whom.

Those who are constantly swapping items between them, who share a skill and need regular interaction should probably sit together. A set of records to which four different people regularly refer should logically be equally accessible to each of them. There are many ways in which the layout of the working positions of people can aid the communication between them, but this is always limited by the social needs and expectations of employees. Very few people indeed really need an office to themselves and the private office is an impediment to communication, yet the interest in privacy and status is such that many people regard it as a basic requirement.

We conclude this chapter with an example of the informal integration that is so vital in any department. The pensions department of a large multinational business at one time had to send out 3,500 letters and the particulars on each letter had to be checked. It was not only a very boring job, but also one that took a lot of time. Often such work is 'delegated' to the most humble member of the department, who takes too long to do it, makes mistakes, produces complaints and everybody gets cross. In this company all members of the department did it, working in the last half-hour of the working day. It was completed in a week, so that the task was completed quickly. It was also done thoroughly and the members of the department were integrated not only socially through sharing a single task but also all of them thoroughly understood the letter and its implications, so that they were all able to deal with queries that came from recipients of the letter.

| REVIEW TOPIC 16.4 |

To what extent is the design of departments, jobs and procedures all part of the organisational design? Can individual managers design their own, or do they all have to comply with overall designs?

| SUMMARY PROPOSITIONS |

16.1 There is more scope for redesigning jobs than for designing them; and more scope for modifying the organisation of departments than for setting up a complete department from scratch.

16.2 The three key aspects of job design are specialisation to ensure scope for expertise, definition to make clear the boundaries between jobs, and discretion to give job holders autonomy.

16.3 The most common bases for clustering activities to create departments are according to a functional role that job holders share, a territory where people are grouped, a common interest in a product, or the fact that a set of people come together to work at a particular time of day – like a shift.

16.4 Tendencies in organisations to being over-managed can be partly mitigated by increasing the managerial span of control and reducing the number of managerial levels.

16.5 The five steps in departmental organisation are deciding the purpose of the department, identifying the activities to achieve the purpose, grouping the activities into jobs to be done, attaching necessary authority to job holders, and connecting jobs together through lines of reporting and communication.

PUTTING IT INTO PRACTICE

Checklist for reviewing the organisation of your department or section

Step 1. The *purpose* of the department or section
(a) Does it meet a basic business need, like sales or production, or is it intended to make things run more smoothly, like personnel? Is it necessary?
(b) Is it set up on the basis of output, like business objectives to be achieved, or on the basis of inputs, like people and problems? Are the outputs already being produced elsewhere?
(c) Does the department exist to deal with matters which other managers find uninteresting or unattractive? If 'yes' are the reasons good enough?

Step 2. The *activities* to meet the purpose
(a) Does the section bring together those who share a particular skill or those with a particular responsibility?
(b) What activities have to be carried out to meet the purpose?
(c) How many people with what experience and qualifications are needed for those activities?
(d) How many ancillary employees are needed? How can that number be reduced? How can that number be reduced further?
(e) Are all the identified activities needed? Is there any duplication with other sections and departments? Is there a better way?

Step 3. *Grouping* the activities
(a) How much specialisation is needed? How will this specialisation affect job satisfaction, commitment and efficiency?
(b) Are boundaries between jobs clearly defined and in the right place?
(c) Will job holders have the amount of discretion needed to be effective?

Step 4. The *authority* of job holders
(a) Do job titles and other 'labels' indicate satisfactorily what authority the job holder has?
(b) Do all job holders have the necessary equipment – like keys, computer codes and information – for their duties?
(c) Do all job holders have the required authorisations – like authorisation to sign documents – that are needed?
(d) Is the authority of any job holder unreasonably restricted?

Step 5. *Connecting* the activities of job holders
(a) Do job holders know what they need to know about the activities of their colleagues?
(b) Are there enough meetings of staff, too few or too many?
(c) Are there enough copies of memoranda circulated for information, too few or too many?
(d) Are job holders physically located in relation to each other in a way that will assist communication between those who need frequently to exchange information?

References

Armstrong, M. and Murlis, H., 1991, *Reward Management*, Kogan Page, London.

Barkdull, C. W., 1963, Span of control: a method of evaluation, *Michigan Business Review*, vol. 15, pp. 25–32.

Campbell, J. P., Dunnette, M. D., Lawler, E. E. and Weick, K. E., 1970, *Managerial Behaviour, Performance and Effectiveness*, McGraw-Hill, New York.

Child, J., 1973, Parkinson's progress: Accounting for the number of specialists in organisations, *Administrative Science Quarterly*, September, pp. 328–48.

Child, J., 1984, *Organisation: A Guide to Problems and Practice*, 2nd edn, Harper & Row, London.

Howells, D., 1981, Marks & Spencer and the Civil Service: a comparison of culture and methods, *Public Administration*, Autumn, pp. 337–52.

Kilman, R. H., Pondy, L. R. and Slevin, D. P. (eds), 1976, *The Management of Organization Development*, North Holland, New York.

Koontz, H., O'Donnell, C. and Weihrich, H., 1980, *Management*, 7th edn, McGraw-Hill, Kogakusha, Tokyo.

Perrow, C., 1985, *Normal Accidents*, Free Press, New York.

Stoner, J. A. F. and Freeman, R. E., 1992, *Management*, 5th edn, Prentice Hall, Englewood Cliffs, New Jersey.

Urwick, L. F., 1974, V. A. Graicunas and the span of control, *Academy of Management Journal*, June, pp. 34–54.

Wild, R., 1975, *Work Organization*, John Wiley, London.

Part V

Uncertainties

If it was possible to hold everything steady and just get on with the job, management would be quite straightforward. What makes it problematic is the continuing uncertainty that surrounds every management job. Will we get the contract? What will happen now that we have merged with . . .? What will be the effect of this design fault? How will we be affected by the unexpected change in exchange rates? This section of the book deals with those processes of management work where no-one can quite predict and control outcomes.

Some of the greatest uncertainties concern features of power and authority. Who has the authority to make things happen? The answer is not simply a question of who holds office, but also whether the office holder is highly regarded by colleagues. The leader columns of daily newspapers detail the ebb and flow in the effective authority of political leaders dealing with their colleagues. Managers also have fluctuating influence according to the processes of organisational politics.

Another source of uncertainty surrounds the question of how to get things done by other people. There is no single sure-fire answer to this question. The managerial approach that inspires some will infuriate others and the motivational framework that has developed to work well in one situation will be inoperable in another.

The manager who copes well with uncertainty in organisational affairs will succeed as a manager and remain healthy as an individual.

G　　　R　　　O　　　U　　　P

Chapter 17

Procedures for administrative action

Procedures are the life blood of any organisation, yet are scarcely ever discussed. Many books on general management extend over more than 500 pages but the term 'procedure' does not appear in the index. The reason they are ignored is that they are dull. The reason they are important is that organisations get things done through their effective use of well-designed procedures. Exciting decisions may be taken, creative ideas may be developed, new products may be conceived, but all of them depend on organisational procedures for things to get done.

In some organisations one major procedure is the key determinant of success or failure, like the procedure for booking seats in an airline, or order processing and despatch in a mail order company, but in all organisations procedures are essential to success; they get things done. Three universal examples are post, pay and minutes. When post is delivered to a company, a procedure is operated. There are two stages of sorting, as some letters and packages will be addressed to individuals, but others will be addressed simply to the company, or to the general manager, and will require opening so that a decision can be made about where they should be routed. Sometimes records are kept of the arrival of particular categories of mail and many companies stamp the date and time of arrival on the envelope so that any subsequent queries can be dealt with. After sorting there is distribution to the various departments and offices within the organisation where the mail is to be dealt with. Then there is a reverse procedure whereby outgoing mail can be collected, franked and taken to the post office.

When new employees join an organisation there is a procedure for getting them on the payroll: the right rate of pay, the right arrangements for routing the pay, the correct deductions and so forth. After meetings there is a procedure for disseminating the minutes and preparing for the next meeting.

Managers' lives are dominated by procedures and much of their creative energy is spent in trying to circumvent them or expedite processes through them. A popular managerial self-image is of the person who can 'beat the system' or 'get things done without waiting for procedures which always take such a hell of a long time'. The idea of procedures is such anathema to most managers that many readers will have passed over this chapter entirely! There are obviously many occasions when procedure is not appropriate – like the apocryphal story of the man in the burning building who could not find the right requisition form for a fire extinguisher – but the impersonal, dead hand of administrative routine is the best way to put into practice the majority of the decisions taken within organisational structures. Managers need, therefore, to consider and design procedures with consummate care, so as to save money, so as to save time, and so as to run a successful operation.

| REVIEW TOPIC 17.1 |

What types of decisions in organisations are best implemented by the impersonal, dead hand of administrative routine?

The purpose of procedures

Procedures . . . establish a customary method of handling future activities. They are truly guides to action, rather than to thinking, and they detail the exact manner in which a certain activity must be accomplished. Their essence is chronological sequence of required actions.   (Koontz, *et al.*, 1980, p. 166)

The relationship between procedure and policy is one needing careful understanding. A policy is a general statement of intention about how things will be done, for example:

1. Wherever possible we will purchase component parts from British rather than foreign suppliers.
2. We are going to switch our advertising from television to national dailies.
3. We are going to discontinue manufacture of . . .
4. We are an equal opportunity employer.

Each of those statements requires to be 'sold' to members of the organisation before it can become effective, not only for them to be advised, but also for them to be convinced that the policy is appropriate, so that they will put it into practice with enthusiasm and thoroughness. The policy statements also, however, need procedures to make them work. If British rather than foreign suppliers are to be used, there will need to be a modification of the administrative routines operating in research and design, development engineering, production engineering, purchasing and production scheduling.

Procedure is the link between policy and practice, and policies that fail may be poor decisions or good decisions that people elsewhere in the organisation never understood, but most often they are good decisions that foundered because there was no procedural follow-through.

The reasons for using procedures are first to reduce the need for future decisions. This is like the cookery recipe. A chef does not say 'How should I bake a cake?' and then work it out by trial and error or even from first principles: a recipe is used, a routine that has worked before and will work again. The personnel manager needing to fill a vacancy for a clerical assistant will similarly use a 'recipe' or standard operating procedure. This not only has the advantage of speed in implementation because the decision-making has been done before, it also provides the opportunities of efficiency through practice and a modest amount of de-skilling. The smooth procedure can be operated by those with less skill than the decision-maker and procedure inventor, just as a million cooks can use one of Mrs Beeton's recipes.

The second value of procedure is consistency. Most operations that are to be repeated benefit from being repeated in the same way, particularly when they involve other people who have to respond to the operation. Customers gradually become familiar with an organisation's procedures and practices, so that they waste less of the organisation's time if all organisation members treat them consistently. Organisation members become accustomed to a routine of departmental practice and are able to develop smooth interaction and swift handling if the method remains the same. Herein lies one of the great problems, as well as an advantage, of procedures: they are very difficult to alter and those who use them will abandon them only under duress. This is well illustrated in the field of industrial relations, where not adhering to procedure is the most heinous of crimes.

Thirdly, procedures should provide autonomy for members of the business. Without procedure as a guideline, people have to await decisions from others. They have to be told how to do things as well as what to do, so that they remain dependent with little scope for individual action. Procedure authorises and informs. Individual members of the organisation know what to do and how to do it. In uncertainty they may ask a colleague, but they can also 'look it up'. Good procedure always provides scope for individual decision and action to interpret the rules in particular situations. The importance of close management attention to devising procedures is shown by the frequent problems that occur when they are poorly conceived or inappropriate. Poor procedures can be worse than no procedures at all as it is only the experts who can cope with them – usually through custom and practice – so that the relatively inexperienced are not authorised and informed, but made dependent on the experts.

A final main advantage is that procedure is a means towards management control of operations. The delegation that was implicit in providing the autonomy mentioned above means that managers can turn their attention to other things, confident in the system that will keep things moving in the right general direction. There will be fewer requests for information and guidance, fewer complaints and errors, fewer worries about the minutiae of organisational life. At the same time as providing freedom from control for individual members of the organisation, procedure provides effective control of operations to the management generally.

Types of procedure

There are four types of procedures generally found in contemporary organisations: task performance, planning and expenditure authorisation, information and coordination, and mutual control.

Task performance procedures

These are among the most common.

> How does the part get fabricated? How are the books kept? How are the products priced? In terms of quantity of words, probably most of any given recorded standard operating procedure consists of specifications of methods for accomplishing whatever task is assigned to an individual member or subgroup of the organization. (Cyert and March, 1963, p. 103)

The ability of the engineering craftsman to work to drawings is an ability to work to procedures. Other examples are the job description, which describes a job partly in order to explain to job holders what to do and how to do it; the training manual, which is used by the new recruit to acquire a knowledge of the routine which the job involves; the list of operations that are run through in closing down a plant; and the fire drill for evacuating the premises in cases of emergency.

Some task performance procedures are brought to the organisation by trained, newly-recruited personnel. The typist arrives knowing the procedures involved in producing a page of accurate typescript, the electrician arrives knowing how to wire a plug. Many of the tasks to be done in the organisation depend on task performance drills that are learned elsewhere, but there is a further set – for all personnel – that is specific to the organisation in which they are carried out. The typist knows how to type, but does not know where to obtain supplies of paper and envelopes, where to put outgoing mail for despatch, nor a whole series of procedures relating to house-style, number and destination of copies and so on. The accountant charged with pricing a product to ensure a proper return needs to know not only good practice in the accountancy profession and a technique for making the calculation, but also the organisational practice on credit in order to establish the appropriate criteria for the calculation.

An important subset of task performance drills are those concerned with changing the rules and coping with new situations. An example is the introduction of legislation that presents new problems. Legislation on electronic data protection was a simple idea that spawned innumerable one-day seminars, training packages and computer programs to explain it to managers. However, what was being 'explained' was not the law, but devices for changing organisational procedures in task performance so that organisational members did their routine operations in a different way. It was the daunting nature of *that* task that caused the managerial anxiety.

Planning and expenditure authorisation procedures

These are mostly the responsibility of senior managers, but minor authorisations are replicated at all levels of the organisation. Although long-range, corporate planning is not as comprehensive an activity as the writers of management books would have us believe, there is always some amount of planning which seeks to set goals and targets for achievement. The plan specifies not only the ultimate destination but also the intermediate steps to be reached on the way. A marketing plan would, for instance, specify not only a target market share of x by a stated date, but also steps of 25% of x to be achieved by an earlier date, 50% of x to be achieved six months later and 75% to be reached six months after that.

Any such plan is based on untested assumptions and is therefore theoretical, so it is not as tight and specific as the task performance procedure, but it provides a more general operating framework that is susceptible to change and updating as circumstances evolve. The way in which the plan is given influence over the behaviour of organisation members is by allocating resources and authorising expenditure. The retailing organisation that has a plan to double its number of outlets in three years will not see any action until resources are allocated and expenditure agreed, but once the personnel director is authorised to recruit 700 more staff in each of the next three years and the marketing director is allocated £x million in each of the years to acquire and convert premises, then the plan becomes more than a possibility: it becomes a requirement for those two executives to implement the proposals.

> The budget in a modern, large-scale corporation plays two basic roles. On the one hand it is used as a management control device to implement policies on which executives have decided and to check achievement against established criteria. On the other hand, a budget is a device to determine feasible programs. In either it tends to define – in advance – a set of fixed commitments and (perhaps more important) fixed expectations. Although budgets can be flexible, they can not help but result in the specification of a framework within which the firm will operate, evaluate its success, and alter its program.
>
> (Cyert and March, 1963, p. 111)

We are concerned here with the procedures of planning and expenditure authorisation, rather than with planning methods, and the procedures of planning are unusual in the participative nature of their generation. Agreeing on the budget and setting operating plans are nearly always collaborative acts in which a range of interests are reconciled to obtain consensus support for the programme. Key aspects of procedures are thus the meetings at which plans are agreed and any possible power of veto which an individual, or another committee, might deploy; the timing of such meetings; and the source of initiatives for consideration. Procedures for expenditure authorisation are of two kinds. Setting the overall budgets is aligned with the planning agreements and probably follows the same procedures precisely, but authorising items of expenditure against budget is an activity delegated to officers who have task performance rules for this procedure. Spending the company's money is not just being allowed to do it because your proposal has been accepted by the senior management team, but following the drills which check that the expenditure is in accordance with another set of rules on proper organisational behaviour.

Information and coordination procedures

These have a less precise objective in that an organisation can limp along without them, but performance is generally improved if people know what is going on and feel that they are kept in touch. Typically information flows in from the outside of the business to the apex of the organisation pyramid or to other well-identified places in the hierarchy. The method of passing information on to other members of the organisation will lie in procedure, so that there is some semi-automatic means whereby dissemination takes place, rather than dependence on the individual recipient to take thought and decide on dissemination.

| REVIEW TOPIC 17.2 |

The procedure for sales representatives claiming expenses in a large chemical company was elaborate. Four authorising signatures were needed plus two separate clerical checks. The time from claim to settlement was usually between 16 and 20 working days. An internal consultant devised a different procedure that needed only one signature and one clerical check. The time from claim to settlement would drop to 5–8 days. There were no objections to this new arrangement, but four months later it had not been implemented. Why do you think this was?

Among the procedures found for information and coordination are the use of minutes of meetings, which are often circulated to a wider group than just those who attended the meeting at which the minutes were taken. A common refinement is to include a note about who is expected to take action on the decisions made at the meeting. Another procedure is the checklist of recipients of memoranda, so that a manager will have two or three standard routine lists for passing information onwards. Noticeboards are a potentially useful means of distributing information, but a procedure is needed to make it an effective means: who is responsible for putting items on the board and removing them? What items are appropriate, bearing in mind that all have to be read and understood in a very brief timespan? How long should items be displayed? A procedure which deals with these questions can make good use of a noticeboard system.

Mutual control procedures

These enable the employing organisation and the individual employee to exercise a degree of control over each other. Grievance and discipline procedures are the main example, as the parties to the contract of employment have a series of procedural steps available to them so that they can limit the action of the other.

> Joint regulation seeks to reconcile the interests of viewpoints of management and employees by a process of negotiation but it begins with the recognition that there are such differences of interest and viewpoint and that there is sufficient strength behind them to make the quest for agreement necessary and desirable. Agreed procedures establish a *modus vivendi* reflecting the interests and strength of the parties. (Singleton, 1975, p. 5)

These industrial relations creations should not only be seen as ways in which action is prevented or made more difficult, they also authorise certain actions by managers and others. Discipline procedures, for instance, specify who has the authority to make relevant decisions, the circumstances which would justify those decisions and the means whereby a decision would be implemented.

Problems and solutions

Procedures present problems as well as opportunities, the most difficult of which is their dullness.

> Managers often fail to obtain the interest and support of top managers in the tedious and unromantic planning and control of procedures.
> (Koontz *et al.*, 1980, p. 769)

That is difficult to resolve, but has to be recognised. Another problem is that they inhibit change. When they eventually become operational and everyone is used to them, they provide a comfortable, secure routine, an aspect of organisational maintenance where people can feel at home with the familiar. This is much like the way in which managers move from management to administrative activity, when the management work gets too hectic. There is always the risk that procedure becomes custom and practice and as immutable as the laws of the Medes and the Persians.

Overlapping and duplication cause problems when each section of the organisation has its own procedures that do not quite coincide with those of other sections. Purchasing has procedures that are not quite the same as Accounts and both are quite different from those in Engineering. The varying emphasis is necessary, as accountants have different responsibilities from buyers. The problems come when the overlapping or duplication becomes too great.

A less obvious problem is when procedures are used to try and solve problems that require a policy solution. Just as procedures are needed to put policy into practice, policies are needed for procedures to be effective. The personnel manager in a small textile company was anxious to eradicate racial discrimination from personnel practice within the organisation and made a number of procedural adjustments to this end. Standardised forms of words to be used in job advertisements were devised, instructions were given to telephonists about handling telephone enquiries, short-listing arrangements in the personnel office were altered and various other methods of preventing unfair discrimination were introduced. He failed, however, to explain these moves to anyone outside the department and was accused of high-handedness and deviousness by his colleagues. He also found that the procedural devices did not work: checks on advertisement wording were overlooked, departmental managers disagreed with short lists and there was a formal complaint to the Commission for Racial Equality. All of this was due to a lack of policy decision and commitment. The policy decision was made only in the personnel manager's mind, being neither discussed with, nor communicated to, anyone else. The telephonists and personnel staff did not fully understand the reasons for the changes they had been asked to make and other managers did not understand what was being done. Once the policy was clear, sold and accepted, the procedure worked well. Procedure can only deal with organisational problems for which a procedural solution is appropriate.

Procedure has all the inherent risks of rigidity. In producing a standard way of doing things, there is the danger that it is regarded by some as the only way of doing things. Grievance procedures nearly always specify that aggrieved employees should raise their dissatisfaction first with their immediate organisational superiors. This is for a number of very good reasons, such as to prevent the immediate superior being bypassed and to ensure that the matter will be resolved as quickly as possible and by the people most closely involved. Carried to an extreme, that could be interpreted as prohibiting an employee talking to a more senior manager about anything. When organisational change is needed, the rigidity of procedures can prove too much for the enthusiasm with which the change is sought.

A common problem is the complexity of procedures. This is where the procedural steps are intended to eliminate any discretion at all. Such procedures are difficult for people to remember and to understand, so that they may be used only by literally following the book. They are also a challenge to the ingenuity of people who resist the lack of scope for personal judgement and interpretation. An example is in safe working procedures, which are regularly ignored by skilled and experienced operators who have sufficient skill and knowledge to do safely what would be highly dangerous for others.

To overcome these difficulties those designing procedures should always aim for simplicity, so that they can be readily understood by those who operate them and those who are affected by them, allowing scope for interpretation to suit particular circumstances. Procedures should always be as few as possible, so that there is less to remember and so that the degree of overlapping and duplication is limited. Also a new procedure should not be introduced unless it is deemed as really necessary. To be necessary a series of future incidents has to be likely so as to require some thought-out decisions in advance. Producing a procedure to deal with a situation that occurs seldom but with similar results is useful. Producing a procedure to deal with a situation which occurs seldom and with very varied results is pointless. A sombre example of the first is a procedure for dealing with attendance at funerals of those who die while in the employment of the organisation – who attends the funeral, how much time off with or without pay, in company cars or not, etc. An unbelievable example of the second is 'Procedure for the Golden Jubilee of the Monarch', found to be still available in the head office of an insurance company.

Procedures should be tested to see if they meet their objectives. A hospital was receiving a number of complaints from patients' relatives, so a complaints procedure was set up. This had the unfortunate effect of lengthening the time taken to deal with complaints and increasing their number. We have to make sure that procedures not only have an internal logic, but also do what they are set up to do.

Procedures must have the before and after stages of policy and communication. There must be a policy for the procedure to implement, even if it is only the implicit policy of established practice, and all affected must know what the procedure is. 'Knowing' is not the same as 'being told about'.

Monitoring can prevent procedures becoming obsolete and inefficient. Not only must they be communicated, they must also be monitored in operation to make sure that they are being worked properly and that there are no unintended effects that should be smoothed out before too much damage is done.

Procedural method

There are four methods of producing procedures: task logic, modelling, checklist and flowcharting.

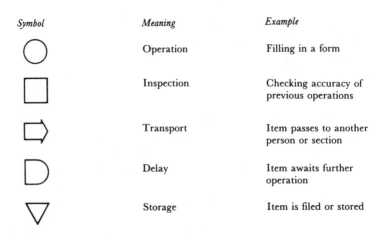

Symbol	Meaning	Example
◯	Operation	Filling in a form
▢	Inspection	Checking accuracy of previous operations
▷	Transport	Item passes to another person or section
◻	Delay	Item awaits further operation
▽	Storage	Item is filed or stored

Figure 17.1   Symbols used in flowcharting.

Task Logic   This is the method of work study and associated techniques, whereby the logic of the task to be accomplished dictates a sequence of actions or activities to be carried out in task performance. This method is not dealt with in this book, but a standard reference is Larkin, 1969.

Checklist   The checklist method is to set up a series of check questions as a basis of formulating the drill. Such a list could be derived from the sections of this chapter.

Modelling   A method much used with industrial relations procedures. A typical procedural system is devised as a model that could be used, with modification, for a wide variety of similar situations. At the end of this chapter there is a model of a grievance procedure.

Flowcharting   The most sophisticated method is flowcharting, which is a simplified form of systems analysis. This is appropriate for those administrative drills that consist of a lengthy system of interrelated activities, possibly involving several different departments and certainly involving a number of different people. It can sometimes be elaborated from its basic linear form into a network analysis. Figure 17.1 shows the symbols used in flowcharting and Figure 17.2 gives an example of a flowchart.

There is a danger in regarding procedures as dull and not requiring managerial time and attention. The organisation without satisfactory procedures can rarely operate effectively unless it is in an unusually favourable

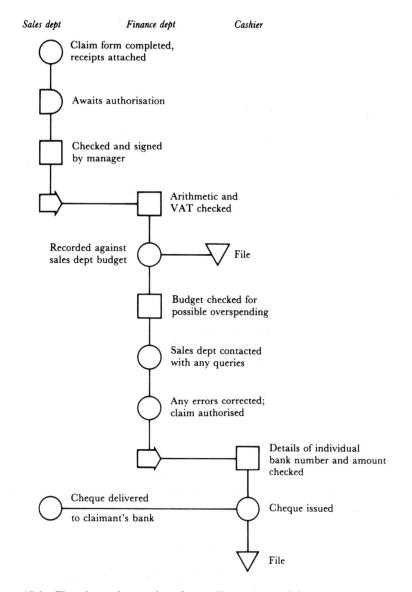

Figure 17.2 Flowchart of procedure for settling expense claims.

business situation. Any organisation can be hamstrung if its procedures get out of control. The need for swift action and consistent decision-making has to be balanced against the need for managerial initiative and employee creativity.

SUMMARY PROPOSITIONS

17.1 Procedures are the link between policy ('what we would like to happen') and practice ('what is happening').

17.2 Reasons for using procedures are to reduce the need for decision-making in the future, to ensure consistency, to provide autonomy for members of the organisation and management control of operations.

17.3 Types of procedure are task performance, planning and expenditure authorisation, information and coordination, and mutual control.

17.4 Problems with procedures are that they can inhibit change; overlapping and duplication; providing the wrong solution to a problem requiring a policy solution; rigidity and complexity.

17.5 Problems can be overcome by having few, simple procedures; meeting objectives with before-and-after phases and monitoring.

17.6 Methods of procedure are task logic, checklist, modelling and flowcharting.

PUTTING IT INTO PRACTICE

Outline model for grievance procedure

Statement of purpose

The purpose of this procedure is to enable intent individual employees of . . . employed in . . . to obtain satisfaction of grievances which they have about their employment. It provides a framework for the employees to voice their dissatisfaction and seek improvement. It is separate from the disputes procedure for resolving matters relating to employees collectively in their relationships with the management.

Step 1

The dissatisfied employee discusses the complaint (Preliminary) with the immediate superior and serves notice that he/she would like the case heard at the next stage if a satisfactory reply has not been received within . . . days.

Step 2

The dissatisfied employee duly presents the case (Hearing) to a more senior manager (position to be specified). The reason for this being that this manager will be able to take a more dispassionate view of the matter than the immediate superior and will have the benefit of a broader range of responsibility to judge potential problems in meeting the employee's requirements.

Step 3

If still not satisfied the employee may take the (Appeal) case to appeal within . . . days of the hearing. This will be with a more senior manager or committee (position to be specified) or external arbiter, invoking greater authority to examine the first two decisions.

If the employee is still not satisfied there is no further recourse within this procedure.

References

Cyert, R. M. and March, J. G., 1963, *A Behavioural Theory of the Firm*, Prentice Hall, Englewood Cliffs, New Jersey.

Koontz, H., O'Donnell, C., and Weihrich, H., 1980, *Management*, 7th edn, McGraw-Hill, Kogakusha, Tokyo.

Larkin, J. A., 1969, *Work Study, Theory and Practice*, McGraw-Hill, London.

Singleton, N., 1975, *Industrial Relations Procedures*, HMSO, London.

Chapter 18

Organisational politics

The idea of behaving politically is one that managers do not readily accept for themselves. This is partly because of the immediate association of the word 'political' with national and local government, but also because the word carries connotations of insincerity and deviousness, and managers disparage these qualities in their colleagues (not themselves being guilty of such behaviour) and deplore the extent to which they detract from the main tasks of the organisation in which they are employed.

When Shepherd Mead wrote his book *How to Succeed in Business Without Really Trying*, he described the activities of his central character who achieved power and influence through appearing to do the right things whilst actually doing very little: image without reality. This idea was so unthinkable in the context of American business that it could only be expressed by making the whole thing a joke. It is a very funny book, but it became a best-seller because it also had the qualities of the good horror story, near enough to reality for the readers to thank their lucky stars that they were not such unprincipled people, at the same time as working out how close each of their colleagues came to the model.

Much of management development activity in recent years and the underlying emphasis of organisation behaviour punditry is that openness in one's behaviour brings results, as relationships with colleagues become more candid and constructive through stripping away the veneer of posturing and guile that otherwise masks integrity. The attractiveness of candour and integrity are so obvious that it may seem strange to bring discussion of politics into a book about management. Why should managers understand politics?

Power in organisations

The formal structure of the organisation, as described in Chapter 14, is a map of working relationships that are official and is the main device for distributing power among organisation members. The formal distribution is not the only determinant of the power held by individuals: it is the main factor in providing people with resource power, but not power from other sources. Dalton (1959) conducted a detailed study of the power structure in a large American manufacturing plant and included a grading of the relative influence wielded by different members of the management. In many instances this did not correspond with their position in the hierarchy. An example was the relative influence of a plant manager, Stevens, and his assistant, Hardy:

> In executive meetings Stevens was clearly less forceful than Hardy. Appearing nervous and worried, Stevens usually opened meetings with a few remarks and then silently gave way to Hardy, who dominated thereafter. During the meeting most questions were directed to Hardy. While courteous, Hardy's statements usually were made without request for confirmation from Stevens. Hardy and Stevens and other high officers daily lunched together. There, too, Hardy dominated the conversations and was usually the target for questions. This was not just an indication that he carried the greater burden of minor duties often assigned to assistants . . . for he had a hand in most issues, including major ones. (Dalton, 1959, p. 23)

Hardy apparently was more strongly motivated than Stevens towards acquiring power and probably had more skill.

The amount of power can also vary according to the problems that are paramount for an organisation at a particular time, so that power accrues to those organisation members or sections who are coping with critical organisation problems.

Harry Denton was an order clerk in a company that supplied portable, battery-operated equipment for use in coal mines. Harry's job was to deal with all the orders that came in for the batteries, ensuring that the goods were despatched and invoiced. He was so quietly efficient that he got on with his job year by year and was left alone. Then there was a nationwide selective strike by a union that sought to bring industrial action to support its case by calling out on strike its members in some companies where the interruption of supply could be particularly effective. Harry's company was one of those where strike action was called because of the importance of the batteries that Harry despatched. Suddenly Harry was a man of great influence in his company, taking part in meetings with directors and senior managers much concerned about how many batteries were in stock, how many were in depots, how many in transit, how many orders pending: all questions to which Harry, and only Harry, knew the answers. He was an unassuming man, not seeking promotion or other personal advantage, but he had been trying for years to get a small change made in the warehouse administrative routines, and had been asking for months if he could have a direct telephone connection to the vehicle loading bay. Both requests were now agreed and dealt with in a few hours. Harry Denton had suddenly acquired power because of the critical organisation problem with which he was dealing.

Another factor governing the political activity of managers is the degree of their dependency on others. A management development officer, for instance, is more dependent on colleagues than the chief accountant, as an important part of the job is convincing others of the value of management development activities and persuading them to participate in training activities and to cooperate in identifying training needs. Managers in dependent positions have to spend more time in building relationships with their colleagues and worrying about breakdowns in communication and understanding.

Kotter (1978) examined the situation of two managers. X was a plant manager whose main dealings were with only four groups: the company president, plant employees, customers and suppliers. He had high dependency on the president and the customers, but only medium dependency on employees and suppliers. Y was a hospital administrator with six high dependencies and seven medium dependencies. Kotter (p. 30) found that Y spent 80% of her day in activities relating to power and influence over others, but X spent only 30% of his time on that sort of activity. This matches some of Rosemary Stewart's conclusions, reported in Chapter 2, about the different types of management job, one of which is peer dependent.

Having reviewed these aspects of the importance of organisational politics, it is useful to take note of the following definitions of Pfeffer (1981, p. 7):

> Organizational politics involves those activities undertaken within an organization to acquire, develop, and use power and other resources to obtain one's preferred outcomes in a situation in which there is uncertainty or dissensus about choices.

Power is a property that exists in any organisation or system; politics is the way in which that power is put into action.

The place of politics in management

Dahl is one of the political theorists who helps us to an understanding of organisational politics, as he points out that political behaviour stems from conflicting aims:

> If everyone were perfectly agreed on ends and means, no-one would ever need to change the way of another. Hence no relations of influence or power would arise. Hence no political system would exist. Let one person frustrate another in the pursuit of his goals and you already have the germ of a political system; conflict and politics are born inseparable twins.   (Dahl, 1970, p. 59)

Any organisation has within it limited resources for its members.

Organisation members compete with each other for promotion in developing their careers. On an everyday basis they will be competing for resources in material terms: a bigger departmental budget, more space, newer equipment, more staff and greater influence over the direction of the general organisational policy. This competition causes the nature of political activity to vary according to the state of growth or decline that the organisation is in. With growth there is the opportunity for all members to 'win' the above sort of competitions. If the organisation is stagnant, then the person who gets a bigger amount of resources can only do this at the expense of someone else, so the arguments may be more bitter. If the organisation is declining, the political activity will often be less sparkling because of the demoralising effect of decline and possibly the greater anxiety to stick together in adversity. In the stable situation politics cause some to win while others lose, but the dynamics of that situation and the range of external considerations should cause the winners to be those who have a stronger substantive case. Only in growth is there likely to be a situation in which all are winners.

It may be that political behaviour often involves being devious and cunning, but the substance of political activity is the manipulation of power. Those who understand the subtleties of power in relationships are better able to get things done than those who ignore them:

> The graveyards of history are strewn with the corpses of reformers who failed utterly to reform anything, of revolutionaries who failed to win power . . . of anti-revolutionaries who failed to prevent a revolution – men and women who failed not only because of the forces arrayed against them but because the pictures in their minds about power and influence were simplistic and inaccurate.
> (Dahl, 1970, p. 15)

Organisations have power as one of their crucial dimensions, and only by understanding how power is distributed and deployed can members of organisations get things done. The innovative idea or the accurate diagnosis is insufficient without the means for their implementation. This is considered further in Chapter 9.

Importance of organisational politics

Here are some of the ways in which organisational politics are important.

1. *Competition.* Members of organisations compete with each other. They compete for more attractive posts further up the hierarchy and for opportunities to develop their careers and express their individual interests. The most important aspect of competition is for resources, which are always scarce in relation to the needs of organisation members and where one person gets the extra resources only at the expense of someone else who does not.

nance measurement. There are few objective means of measuring
mance of those holding managerial and administrative posts
ᴜᴄᴄᴀ se of the interdependence of their activities. An author writes
books, the sales of which are a measure of their worth; a batsman scores
a certain number of runs; a tennis player wins or loses a match; a
research scientist can discover a new cure for a crippling disease; but the
manager embedded in the complex web of relationships of a contemporary organisation is bereft of such objective criteria for determining
personal success and failure. They therefore have to win friends and
influence people by impressing their superiors with their personal
qualities and loyalty, by building an empire of subordinates or by making
alliances with colleagues.

3. *Job mobility.* Political behaviour is encouraged by job mobility. In
many large organisations job mobility is a requirement for all those with
career aspirations, who are moved from post to post and often from
location to location for most of their working lives. Geographical
mobility has become less attractive with the tightening of the labour
market and the development of career expectations among women, who
may be very reluctant to abandon a satisfying and well-paid job in
Birmingham to follow a husband to Aberdeen, where they may find their
employment prospects to be poor and their husbands to be even more
preoccupied than before with their own careers. Although less attractive,
geographical mobility still features strongly in the organisational life of
many high-flying young managers, and movement within the organisation
structure is very common. This means that it is even more difficult for
mobile managers to show depth of accomplishment in any one position,
and they feel they need to impress and manipulate the perceptions of
those around them. After moving from Birmingham to Aberdeen the
spouse will be left even more to their own devices because the manager
has to spend so much time winning friends and influencing people in the
strange, new business context, to make sure that eventually they are
promoted away from Aberdeen.

4. *Style of leadership.* There has been a gradual change in leadership style
in recent years which has changed the nature of politics in many
organisations. The entrepreneurial form which was described in Chapter
14 is an overtly political situation as there is high concentration of power
in the centre. Modern management thinking in bureaucratic and matrix
structures has become more democratic than autocratic, and much of this
book is devoted to winning consent rather than simply telling people
what to do. Going along with this has been the increasing impracticality
of an individual manager being able to get approval for a programme of
action simply by selling the idea to the boss: there is more dependence on
committees, task groups and alliances. Not only does this require the
deployment of what could be called the skills of diplomacy (tact, skill and

cunning in dealing with people to win their support for your aims) it also tends to produce underhand, Watergate-type behaviour among managers who are uneasy with a democratic style.

5. *Political context.* All organisations operate in political contexts. They are concerned with national political movements, with international events that could close an export market or jeopardise the supply of a raw material, and with the volatility of the stock market. The salesperson trying to land an order has to establish where in the customer's organisation the authority to purchase lies. Is this the right person? Some companies depend on changes in government policy for an improvement in their business, and those in public sector organisations are closely concerned with national political thinking.

6. *Partnerships.* With an increase in partnerships between stakeholders both within and between organisations there is a need to understand power and the shifts of power taking place. Kanter (1989, p. 143) found:

> *The labor–management partnership* shifted the action away from events favoring professionals in the union and toward the events favoring local presidents; away from processes favoring the national union and toward processes favoring local decision-making; . . . *The supplier–customer partnership* shifted the attention of staffs from routine administration of strategic considerations, empowered the purchasing department, and necessitated a more collaborative web of interfunctional relationships across departments inside the company. *The joint venture* shifted the locus of power from the traditional management hierarchy to those who could effectively influence the partners and represent the home organization's strategic agenda.

Kanter also points out later (pp. 162–3) the difficulties for partnerships where there is an imbalance of resources, information or benefits; in other words, power.

REVIEW TOPIC 18.1

The English philosopher and essayist Francis Bacon (1561–1626) made the comment 'It is a strange desire to seek power and to lose liberty'. Are the two necessarily connected in organisational life?

Sources of power

There are four main sources of power for the individual or group to garner in order to exercise political influence: resources, skill, motivation and obligations. The most obvious is the control of resources. Those who control what others need are in the position of relative power. We have seen this in the early historical developments, where it was the granaries of the pharaoh that gave him the power to weld together the nation state of Egypt. The power of a contemporary government resides largely in the system of taxation and state spending, and the power of the British crown lies largely in the accolades of social esteem which only the monarch can bestow, whether it be an earldom or a telegram for your diamond wedding. The resources which managers control are similar. They may not be able to ennoble their subjects, but they do offer or withhold promotions. This is why most public sector employment has rules and procedures to ensure that at least the appearance of the process whereby people are appointed to posts is 'democratic', so as to prevent any individual wielding too much power. Equally managers influence the level of earnings which people can receive, and employees have worked hard in their collective organisations to reduce managerial power over the pay-packet. Incremental pay scales are a further device for prising power away from managers, and unions invariably resist 'merit' payments for individuals with as much resolution as managers display in trying to introduce them.

Most of the comments in the previous paragraph relate only to the power of superiors over subordinates, but another battle over resources takes place between peers, and that is the share of the budget, the staff, the time of the committees that make decisions, and all those other ways in which the relative power of functions or departments is mediated and altered. It would be quite inadequate to regard power through control of resources as being solely the exercise of power over subordinates. It is also power vis-à-vis peers and power against superiors.

Whatever resources you have, you still need skill to deploy them. The best-loved aspects of patriotic folklore are those in which one's countrymen won battles against the odds. The Battle of Britain retains pride of place in the annals of the Second World War, partly because of the turning point it marked, but mainly because it seemed as if skill and courage outwitted an enemy with more planes and pilots. Control of resources is not sufficient to be powerful, because the political system is only brought into being as a result of competitive bids for power.

Neustadt (1960) has compared the effective use of power by three consecutive American presidents, Roosevelt, Truman and Eisenhower. All held the same office with the same resource control, yet achieved different degrees of success because of the varying skill with which they exercised their control.

This can also explain why one manager has more power than another, even though they both possess the same resources and skills. Some seek power much more enthusiastically than others and use their resources to try and get it; others use their resources and skills for different purposes. This can be due either to varying degrees of personal need for power or to the feeling that only by obtaining power can the manager's function be effective. Personnel managers have long tended to be politically active (whilst often deploring 'political behaviour' in others) because of the belief that they could only be effective by achieving influence over their colleagues through having power to deploy. Accountants seldom have this worry.

Another reason for individuals having varying amounts of power is the obligations owed by 'dependents'. The dependent may be a subordinate hoping for a favourable report at the next annual performance appraisal; it may be someone on an equal footing who is under an obligation to the manager for past favours; or it may be a superior who requires the particular skill of the manager with no satisfactory alternatives being available. The more of these debts managers have to call in, the more powerful they are.

Winning consent

Winning consent without having formal authority is becoming more important to managers for several reasons. First, the complexity of organisations increases the number of contacts managers make in which they have no authority. In the 1976 study by Rosemary Stewart (described in Chapter 3), 7% of the managers interviewed were in solo jobs, spending a low proportion of time in contact with other people. In our own research we have found an increasing number of people in this type of lone, specialist role. Such a person not only has to be constantly persuading and influencing to get things done, but has continually to justify this position. Secondly, managers find their formal authority curbed. It is a long time since any but a few managers had the straightforward, unchallenged right to dismiss people, but legislation has gradually reduced that type of authority further, so that the power to dismiss is seldom held by an individual manager in an organisation.

As technology advances and companies diversify, managers find they have limited expertise in technical matters and therefore have to depend increasingly on the autonomous competence of others, whether in a subordinate position or not. The Nobel Prize winner, H. A. Simon distinguished between authority and other types of influence:

> The characteristic which distinguishes authority from other kinds of influence is . . . that the subordinate holds in abeyance his own critical faculties for choosing between alternatives and uses the formal criterion of the receipt of a command or signal as his basis for choice. (Simon, 1974, p. 330)

Winning consent without having authority is a process that assumes the other person will not hold their own critical faculties in abeyance and will use their own judgement, accepting responsibility for the outcome.

There are at least three common barriers to this type of interpersonal influence. One is the differences between individuals. The person you want to influence may not like you or trust you. Secondly, the climate of the organisation may be inappropriate. If intensive competition between individuals is encouraged or unavoidable, then political means are more likely to achieve compliance than the more personal methods discussed in the next two chapters. The third reason is the number of mechanical barriers that can exist. It is difficult to influence the person you never meet and it can be suspect when you try to influence someone where there is a formal organisational barrier between you and that person.

Leavitt (1978, p. 127) suggests that we need to consider three factors if we wish to influence another: ourself, the other person and the interaction that is to take place. It is worth adding to those a need to consider the environment in which the attempts to influence take place.

We need to understand ourself so that we can consider the reaction of others and their expectations of us individually in our role. In considering the other person we take account of their experience, personality and position. Then we can think of how to approach the interaction between self and other. The environmental points vary. Seating arrangements, for instance, can affect the outcome of conversations. In counselling, career advice and similar discussions it is helpful to have relatively informal seating arrangements without a direct, head-on orientation between self and other. In arguments where there is a direct conflict of opinion, it can help to face each other across a table.

Another aspect of the environment is the degree to which influence is achieved in group situations. Most people find it easier to participate in the discussion of a small group (say ten people or fewer) than a large group. It is easier to have a turn to speak and it is easier to win round half-a-dozen people with different views and expectations than it is to cope with twice that number of varied positions. Large committees struggling with a difficult issue may delegate it to a subcommittee or working party to make suggestions. Unless opinions are strongly polarised on the committee, the small working party should be able to produce recommendations with which all members agree, so that the consequent meeting of the full committee will be faced with a caucus of its members who are committed to the working party proposals, and that degree of commitment will be hard to counter.

Empowering

Many of these issues are now summarised by the term 'empowerment'. The word is often used instead of the older word 'motivation'. It means feeling that one has the power to carry out one's responsibilities. The term came to prominence through the women's movement but is now widely used (Block, 1987, is the classic text; see also Kanter, 1989) within organisations to describe the process which enables individuals to show initiative and take responsibility. One hotel chain used it as the basis of advertising with suggestions that the hotel receptionist was empowered to drive customers to the airport when they failed to raise a taxi. It can also feel from the junior staff's perspective that senior staff are getting them to do more for less.

Techniques used to obtain power

There are further aspects of power and authority to be discussed in Chapters 19 and 20; so we conclude this chapter by reviewing some of the methods that can be used by individuals seeking to achieve power in organisations.

1. *Alliances.* Individuals collaborate in their power search with those who have interests sufficiently similar for an alliance to be mutually beneficial. The managers of manufacturing and personnel may form an alliance to block moves by a marketing manager to scale down production and buy in more ready-made materials, for instance. The benefits of an alliance are the obvious ones of having someone else on your side, together with their resources, skills and motivation; the drawbacks are the degree of commitment which you have to contribute. Also alliances cannot be readily discarded; in discarding an ally you probably make an enemy.

2. *Lobbying.* Falling short of the alliance is the process of drumming up support on a particular issue – 'I hope I can rely on your support for this . . .'. This is much used in getting one's way with committees, as is described in Chapter 15, but is also appropriate for all the minor dealings that take place throughout the working day.

3. *Doing favours.* There are various ways in which people with some power use that to provide services for others and therefore extend their power with the person they have helped. This is a time-honoured way of ensuring the loyalty of subordinates, who feel grateful to the superior who has been benevolent and whose benevolence may be used again. It is also a method to be used with peers and superiors, who are put in the debt of the person providing the favour. There is a need to be cautious when using one's own power to elevate another, as the person elevated may then be wary of the erstwhile helper.

> Whoever is responsible for another's becoming powerful ruins himself, because this power is brought into being either by ingenuity or by force, and both of these are suspect to the one who has become powerful.
>
> (Machiavelli, 1981, p. 44)

4. *Being present.* It is the powerful person who can afford to be away. At one extreme, post holders may find that they do not have a job to come back to; it is so much easier to dispossess someone who is absent. More common than that is the need to be present when significant decisions are made. Such decisions usually involve the balancing of conflicting interests in competing for resources or advantage. Each interest will have its spokesperson and the interest that is absent will not be heard, so that the decision will seldom be favourable to that interest, unless there is some other aspect of power – like a veto – which can be exercised afterwards to nullify the decision that has been reached.

5. *Cornering resources.* Empire builders reason that their importance to

the organisation is in direct proportion to the number of subordinates in their sections. That conclusion may be very dubious, but at least the number of subordinates can be measured, whereas contributions to organisational objectives cannot be.

6. *Being indispensable.* A variant on cornering resources is to make oneself indispensable. This is done either by being a lone, but essential, expert or by being an essential part of administrative, decision-making procedures. Safety officers often have influence as a result of their familiarity with health and safety legislation, which no-one else except shop stewards finds very interesting, but the expertise is essential to the organisation. Personnel officers trying to establish a personnel function usually aim to break in on well-established procedures. A typical initiative is to get a ruling that in future recruitment advertisements will have to be placed by the personnel officer, and not by anyone else, or that all management dealings with full-time union officials will be made only by the personnel officer.

7. *Reciprocal support for a patron.* Peter (1969) pointed out that it is much better to be pulled up in an organisation than to push yourself up. Political power can be enhanced by having a powerful patron. Those appointed to newly-created posts nearly always define their influence by confirming to whom they report: 'I am directly accountable to the Chief Executive' or 'I am part of the Manufacturing Division but have direct access to the M.D.'. Some people have difficulty in finding such a patron and Jennings (1967) has coined the odd word 'visiposure' to describe the need first to be in a position to see enough potential patrons to pick one, but secondly to be in a position where a potential patron can see you. The first is visibility, the second is exposure; visiposure is both. Once the patron is found, support will only be given to the acolyte if the acolyte helps the patron to achieve objectives. Patrons enhance one's power but also exact fealty.

The remorseless logic of Machiavelli described the nature of the relationship between the patron and the patronised:

> To keep his minister up to the mark the prince, on his side, must be considerate towards him, must pay him honour, enrich him, put him in his debt, share with him both honours and responsibilities. Thus the minister will see how dependent he is on the prince; and then having riches and honours to the point of surfeit he will desire no more; holding so many offices, he cannot but fear changes.   (Machiavelli, 1981, p. 125)

8. *Being able to cope with uncertainty.* The customary routines of formal authority structures, centralised control and circulating memoranda shelter people inside the organisation from the outside world, which is not controlled in the same convenient way. The outside is, however, a hard and urgent reality for the organisation, so that those who can cope

with the demands of the environment in which the organisation operates are those towards whom political power tends to flow (Salancik and Pfeffer, 1977). It is the uncertainty of the demands from outside that gives political influence to those who confront them, and anyone dealing with organisational affairs that are uncertain acquires some power.

Michel Crozier (1964, p. 154) studied the work of plants in France where tobacco was processed and commented on the extraordinary power that was wielded by the maintenance engineers. The entire process was highly mechanised and predictable, so that the activities of every member were in a smooth routine. The only thing that could go wrong was for a machine to break down, yet that caused a complete disruption to the system. Because of this the only people who could put the machinery right (the maintenance engineers) wielded power out of proportion to their formal status.

This sort of power fluctuates. When the office photocopier breaks down the service engineers are much reviled, because of not being there. When they arrive they are greeted with warm smiles and cups of tea for this brief time of glory. When the photocopier works once more they are quickly forgotten or asked to move their car as it is blocking the car park. Small wonder that they seem to move so slowly in actually conducting the repair. The greatest worry for those who specialise in being able to cope with uncertainty is the fear of not being able to do it. The service engineer who has brought the wrong tools or cannot diagnose the fault suffers all the horrors of the fallen idol.

REVIEW TOPIC 18.2

We have listed eight techniques to obtain power. Which have you used and which others do you think you will use in the future?

Manipulation

The idea of manipulating other people is generally offensive, with its overtones of puppets and strings. It is, however, an ancient art and does not always arouse disapproval. For most of recorded history the young have indulged in courtship, the result of which is sometimes tears, sometimes frustration, but often a reasonable degree of mutual satisfaction, yet the process of courtship is one of manipulating emotions and cajoling a person to change his or her mind. This is all done against a background of uncertainty about motives. Are the intentions honourable or not?

In the everyday life of organisations consent is often won by manipulation. Leavitt (1978, pp. 157–60) summarises the process like this:

1. A is the manipulator; B is the person to be manipulated.
2. A's motives are not fully known to B.

3. The relationship between A and B is either established or developed by A to provide a basis of influence: getting B to do what A wants.
4. A exploits the dependency of B in the relationship.
5. Dependency of B is increased by using emotions such as approval, support, recognition.
6. Influence develops incrementally, by adding bits and pieces as dependency increases.

Described thus, manipulation sounds no more than a confidence trick, but there are many circumstances in which it can be necessary or appropriate. One of the main bases of training is reinforcement through praising the faltering attempts of the trainee in the early stages. This is manipulative in that the trainer is trying to influence the behaviour of the trainee by exploiting the trainee's dependence, using the trainee's need for reassurance. Part of any manager's responsibility is to get others to do things they would not have done otherwise. So a manager will often use manipulation to obtain compliance from someone else towards organisational objectives. The manager who manipulates others simply to advance personal objectives is much more reprehensible.

One form of manipulation is propaganda, which is attempting to build a favourable image by appealing to a large number of people. The methods of public relations are too specialised to have a place in this book, but we can include some comments about public speaking that is designed to win people round to a particular point of view. To be persuasive the public speaker has to be seen as having some expert knowledge and good intentions. His or her effectiveness will be enhanced by enthusiasm or conviction, and will connect a state of emotional preparedness – engendered at the beginning of the address – with some course of action advocated towards the end of the address. It is important that members of the audience should easily see the connection between the emotional feeling and the prescribed action. This can be helped by graphic illustration and examples.

Argyle and Trower (1979, p. 101) suggest that a propagandist should present the case in a certain order:

(a) Make amiable remarks to establish rapport with the audience.
(b) Arouse guilt, concern or anxiety.
(c) Present a strong, positive case, showing how the feeling aroused can be resolved by the recommended behaviour.
(d) Deal with any obvious objections.
(e) Draw explicit conclusions and make recommendations for action.

Persuasion

Persuasion is talking someone round to your point of view, using the force of argument and the logic of evidence that is deployed to support the argument. This is straightforward and dignified without the worrying suggestions of being devious, as with manipulation, or aggressive, as with assertiveness. It also has the attraction that the outcome will be 'right' as it will depend on the cogency of the argument and people will not comply if not convinced. Personal factors none the less make some people more persuasive than others. Persuaders are likely to be successful only when they are regarded as credible, having some track record of effectiveness. Employees find it hard to see a company management as credible if it is not successful in running the business. The persuader must also be expert, which is a more precise quality than credibility. It can be attested by qualifications, position or experience, but is a sign of having special knowledge that is seen as relevant and greater than that of the person being persuaded. Trustworthiness is important because of the feeling of helplessness that can come from dealing with an expert. The wisdom of the expert makes the person being persuaded conscious of their own ignorance and the need to place themselves 'in the hands' of the expert. So the expert must be trustworthy. The persuader who is objective adds strength to the case by being able to see both sides of a question, so that the person being persuaded is able to weigh both and decide. The opposite case has at least been set out, even if it is peremptorily dismissed.

Maintaining balance

In closing this chapter we revert to the problem that was posed at the beginning: how can we advocate behaviours that are so obviously devious and unattractive? Also, how can we set discussion about political behaviour alongside the widely canvassed behaviours of openness that are the basis of much contemporary management development?

The answer is that neither politics nor openness are the total solution. An appreciation of organisational politics is an essential part of managerial effectiveness and some political behaviour is required of every manager. When the Polaris missile system was developed in the United States it was hailed as a remarkable achievement for rational management techniques. PERT was devised and has subsequently been used in many other applications. Harvey Sapolsky (1972) studied the project as a case history of success and came to the conclusion that PERT was as effective technically as rain dancing (p. 246) but that it was effective politically because of the reputation it gave the special projects office for efficiency, and that overall Polaris was a political rather than a technical achievement in management terms:

> The success of the Polaris program depended on the ability of its proponents to promote and protect Polaris. Competitors had to be eliminated; reviewing agencies had to be outmanoeuvred; congressmen, admirals, newspapermen and academicians had to be co-opted. Politics is a system requirement. What

distinguishes programs in government is not that some play politics and others do not, but rather, that some are better at it than others.

(Sapolsky, 1972, p. 244)

Extremes of 'politicking' are destructive, as well as distasteful, and openness can mitigate such extremes. We must not overlook, however, that power is what the French political scientist Maurice Duverger has called 'Janus-faced'. Janus was the Roman god of doorways and passages, who was always depicted as facing both ways. Power is essential to the process of social integration, yet it divides people and produces conflict. For an organisation to work at all there has to be a distribution of power within the structure to get things done. Yet that very distribution is divisive and produces stress on the structure and members of the organisation. It is when that stress becomes too great that effectiveness declines.

Finally, how can one judge whether an individual manager is going too far in political behaviour? A useful test is to think back to the distinction mentioned in Chapter 3 between setting agendas for action and using networks to implement the agendas. Political behaviour is potentially useful when it is deployed to put agendas into action. It is counterproductive when it is deployed only to build and maintain networks.

Too much network and not enough agenda is associated with the type of person who is more concerned with being a manager rather than getting on with the job. The manager who under-emphasises networks and concentrates on agendas can be inward-looking and fail to take politics seriously, but we have found more examples of managers who spend so much of their time 'networking' that they forget to do the job. We recently found an example in a very large multinational company where a manager dealing with a major customer relied on a gentleman's agreement rather than on a contract, with serious results.

SUMMARY PROPOSITIONS

18.1 Power is an inescapable part of management in organisations.

18.2 Four aspects of power are resources, skill, motivation and costs.

18.3 Techniques used by individuals and groups to obtain power include alliances, lobbying, doing favours, being present, cornering resources, being indispensable, reciprocal support for a patron, and being able to cope with uncertainty.

18.4 Openness, as advocated in most management development programmes, can mitigate the extremes of political behaviour which would otherwise become destructive.

PUTTING IT INTO PRACTICE

Make a list of the various parts of your job. Which would you consider has a political aspect? Which has little political content? Make a list of the techniques to obtain power. Beside each, list the advantages of using it, for oneself and for the organisation as a whole. Now list the disadvantages of each for oneself and for the rest of the organisation.

References

Argyle, M. and Trower, P., 1979, *Person to Person*, Harper & Row, London.
Block, P., 1987, *The Empowered Manager: Positive Political Skills at Work*, Jossey-Bass, San Francisco.
Crozier, M., 1964, *The Bureaucratic Phenomenon*, Tavistock, London.
Dahl, R., 1970, *Modern Political Analysis*, 2nd edn, Prentice Hall, Englewood Cliffs, New Jersey.
Dalton, M., 1959, *Men who Manage*, John Wiley, New York.
Jennings, E. C., 1967, *The Mobile Manager*, University of Michigan Press.
Kanter, R. M., 1989, *When Giants Learn to Dance*, Unwin, London.
Kotter, J. P., 1978, Power success and organization effectiveness, *Organization Dynamics*, Winter.
Leavitt, H. J., 1978, *Managerial Psychology*, 4th edn, University of Chicago Press.
Machiavelli, N., 1981, *The Prince*, Penguin Books, Harmondsworth, Middlesex.
Neustadt, R. E., 1960, *Presidential Power: the Politics of Leadership*, John Wiley, New York.
Peter, L. J., 1969, *The Peter Principle*, Morrow, New York.
Pfeffer, J., 1981, *Power in Organizations*, Pitman, Marshfield, Mass.
Salancik, G. R. and Pfeffer J., 1977, Who gets power, and how they hold on to it, *Organizational Dynamics*, Winter.
Sapolsky, H. M., 1972, *The Polaris System Development*, Harvard University Press, Cambridge, Mass.
Simon, H. A., 1974, Authority, in *Human Relations in Administration*, ed. Dubin, R., 4th edn, Prentice Hall, Englewood Cliffs, New Jersey.
Stewart, R., 1976, *Contrasts in Management*, McGraw-Hill, Maidenhead, Berkshire.

Chapter 19

Authority, leadership and autonomy

Organisational structure and culture are ways of getting things done; authority, leadership and autonomy are also ways of getting things done. When the structure is just as it should be and the culture is carefully aligned to the mission, the people and the context, then the work actually has to be done. Management work can be seen as getting things done through people, in the broad sense of the GROUP analogy set out in our opening chapter. Any particular manager is likely to get things done largely on the basis of their personal authority, leadership and autonomy. Often managers lack confidence in this aspect of their work more than any other, and seek the endorsement of more senior, powerful people or for clear-cut procedural and policy guidelines. However important these may be, they are no more than a background in front of which the manager stands alone, with a distinctive style, personality and approach. The performance of the manager will be improved by understanding how the features of authority, leadership and autonomy mesh together.

Our previous chapter on organisational politics dealt with the nature of power in organisations and how managers can increase and manipulate the power available to them. This chapter deals with a specific aspect of how individuals deploy power in relation to subordinates: power made legitimate by expertise or hierarchical position. The three words in the chapter title describe the combination which managers need for effectiveness. Being in authority is a right to control and judge the actions of others. Leadership is the exercise of the power conferred by that right in such a way as to win a willing and positive, rather than grudging and negative, response. Autonomy is that freedom of action which subordinates see as being necessary and reasonable if they are themselves to be effective in their roles.

Authority

One of the problems of managers being in authority is that their frame of reference is different from that of their subordinates. Partly this is a simple matter of individual difference and partly it is difference in role. After the Allied invasion of Normandy in 1944, there was widespread criticism among senior service officers and politicians of how Field Marshal Montgomery was conducting the fighting round the city of Caen. Supreme Commander Eisenhower came under pressure either to dismiss Montgomery or to issue direct instructions that would require Montgomery to act against his own better judgement. Eisenhower refused, because of his practice of always delegating authority to subordinates and giving them fullest support. Even in an operation that had such detailed planning and extensive information available, Eisenhower realised the importance of being on the spot.

> [Eisenhower] did not have Montgomery's feel of the battle as a two-sided encounter in which he kept the initiative by actions which put the enemy at a disadvantage and kept him at an advantage. Eisenhower did not see that by the fighting round Caen the enemy was placing himself in a position from which he would not be able to recover. . . . Eisenhower had rightly delegated command of the land battle to Montgomery: he had wider tasks.
>
> (Sixsmith, 1973, p. 158)

On a more general level there is often a difference in objectives over work. The manager is looking for efficiency, return on capital and trouble-free coordination of employee effort, while the subordinate is seeking an agreeable, dignified way of life within the confines of the employment contract. This perennial dissonance between the points of view can be seen as early as the eighteenth century in England, when workers could appeal to the local Justice of the Peace if they considered their rate of pay unfair.

> The buyers in the labour market operated on the principle of buying in the cheapest market and selling in the dearest. . . . But the sellers were not normally asking for the maximum wage which the traffic would bear and offering in return the minimum quantity of labour they could get away with. They were trying to earn a decent living as human beings . . . they were engaged in human life rather than in economic transaction.
>
> (Hobsbawm, 1975, p. 222)

Taylorism at the beginning of the twentieth century changed that general wage/employment relationship to a specific cash nexus with a concentration on what would be paid for each of a range of human actions. This was a shift of power as employees lost their control of discretionary knowledge in order to centralise control in the hands of the managers. The long-standing refusal of skilled craftsmen and professionals to accept time study and 'the tyranny of the stop watch' has maintained for them a degree of autonomy that is jealously guarded.

The ideas of F. W. Taylor continue to suffuse much of management thinking but have had overlaid upon them the doctrine of human cooperation advanced by Elton Mayo over forty years. This depends on well-knit human groups and the development of social as well as technical skills.

> Social skill shows itself as a capacity to receive communications from others, and to respond to the attitudes and ideas of others in such fashions as to promote congenial participation in a common task. (Mayo, 1975, p. 12)

In considering managerial authority, the juxtaposition of these two innovations is usually misunderstood. Taylor's scientific management is often regarded as the tough but fair way of the old days that was very good as control, but which has now become impracticable; while Mayo's human relations thinking is wishy-washy, undermines managerial authority and leads to dubious practices like underlings addressing managers by their Christian names. In fact scientific management and the cash nexus may well tie down employees to organisational demands as a whole, but can deprive individual managers of effective power over subordinates. The control lies not with the individual manager but with the payment system, so that the employee who has filled the daily quota or who is 'ahead of the clock' may feel under little obligation to the supervisor. The dominance of the control system detracts from the legitimacy of the individual manager's authority. When the style changes to 'congenial participation in a common task', that common task is assigned to the working group by an individual manager, and the need for collaboration with other groups in the organisation who are congenially participating in an over-arching common task makes individual group members dependent on a controlling figure to communicate, explain and protect. The manager may resent being called Les (or, in other situations, have to tolerate being pushed away from the social group so that Les is no longer used) but gains, rather than loses, authority in an organisation where social skills are demanded. There is again the problem about different frames of reference. Subordinates look to the manager for authority on which they can rely to act on their behalf, solve problems and offer guidance, while the managers may be looking for deference to them as superior kinds of people.

The majority of the initiatives to develop or alter organisational culture seek to increase the individual's sense of responsibility and involvement by chipping away at unnecessary status differentials like that of 'manager and subordinate', so that the clear distinction between managers and the managed is seldom a valid description of employment categories. Few of us are now either managers or subordinates; increasingly we are both. Every member of the management hierarchy has a boss or superordinate who can prevent or help the manager get things done, and few members of an organisation do not have to get some things done by other people. So we are not here splitting people into categories but discussing two aspects of everyone's role: getting things done through people and people getting things done through you.

| REVIEW TOPIC 19.1 |

Some managers complain that they have responsibility without authority. Where this happens, what are the consequences?

Obedience

The authority of managers is underpinned by a predilection to obedience that we all have. Stanley Milgram (1974) carried out a startling series of experiments in the United States, which showed this predilection in a way that many people found disconcerting. Male volunteers were led to believe that they were taking part in a study of memory and learning. They had to administer electric shocks to learners when the learners made mistakes in answering simple questions. The electric shocks became progressively more severe with each incorrect answer. If the volunteer questioned the procedure with the experimenter, who was in charge, he was simply told that he should continue. The range of instructions began as 'Please continue' and went up to 'You have no other choice: you must go on'.

Eighteen different experiments were conducted with over 1,000 volunteers, but no matter how the variables were altered the volunteers did as they were told even when administering shocks of 450 volts to a victim begging for release. Some were unwilling to continue, but the majority continued all the way through to the end. It is not quite as bad as it sounds. The shocks were not really being given, the learner was an actor pretending to be on the point of collapse, but the volunteers thought the shocks were real and carried on 'doing their job'. Two samples:

Mr Batta:
'The scene is brutal and depressing: his hard, impassive face shows total indifference as he subdues the screaming learner and gives him shocks. He seems to derive no pleasure from the act itself, only quiet satisfaction at doing his job properly.'

Mr Gino, speaking at the end of the experiment:
'Well, I faithfully believed the man was dead until we opened the door. When I saw him, I said "Great, this is great." But it didn't bother me even to find that he was dead. I did my job.'   (Milgram, 1974, pp. 46 and 88)

Readers of this book will probably not want their subordinates to electrocute their colleagues, but the importance of this study is that it demonstrates a remarkable readiness to obey. Milgram explains this by saying that when people enter a hierarchical system ('someone else is in charge'), those people then see themselves as agents carrying out the wishes of others and put themselves in what he calls an 'agentic state'. Others take the responsibility, so that compliance is not only easy but also the criterion of satisfaction.

Milgram explains the willingness with which people adopt the agentic state by reference to a series of experiences which virtually everyone undergoes.

1. *Parental regulation.* This is the experience of almost everyone when young, as parents remorsely issue instructions on a range of matters concerning every department of an infant's life – eating, sleeping, washing, keeping quiet and so on. The one common element in all of these is the implicit 'obey me'.
2. *The institutional setting.* The child emerges from the cocoon of the family into an institutional setting. At school the child is always subordinate, although gradually acquiring seniority in relation to other subordinates. At college and in the early years at work they always have to do things prescribed by others.
3. *Rewards.* These are given to those who comply with authority and the disobedient are frequently punished.
4. *Normative support.* Authority is normatively supported as any group or institution is expected, by its members, to have a socially controlling figure.
5. *Justifying ideology.* There is a justifying ideology that supports, or legitimates, the authority of the individual controlling figure. In Milgram's experiments the volunteers came to a university to take part in scientific investigations about learning. Science and education are two powerful sources of legitimacy. Other obvious sources are religious belief and patriotism. Others again are service to the customer, the general good of the organisation and the well-being of the employees.

The explanations above have been used to explain such things as the willingness of ordinary people to participate in the slaughter of Jews in Nazi Germany or the massacre of villagers in Vietnam, but political philosophers have long debated the idea that the majority of people want to be subservient to a dominant figure or group, who will look after them. This argument runs that people have a choice as humans between freedom and happiness. Freedom involves being responsible and making decisions and judgements. Happiness relieves a person of those 'burdens' as others decide what is right and wrong, what should be done and what should not, so that the individual enjoys freedom from responsibility and the contentment of someone else doing the organisation and making all the difficult decisions. However cynical this sounds it is a recurring theme in art and literature. On a practical level in everyday life we seem to mix issues between those where we want to make our own choices and those where we are happy to leave the choice to others and obey their instructions. The person who campaigns vigorously against government policy on nuclear weapons one day will probably comply unquestioningly with medical treatment for a sore throat the following day. Our willingness to comply varies from individual to individual, but it is there within all of us. A commentary on this phenomenon is by D. H. Wrong (1979).

Whatever the reasons for obedience, the important lesson for managers is that there is a predilection for those in organisations to comply with instructions from those in authority within the organisational framework. That is the authority of those *in* authority. This can be immeasurably enhanced by those who are also *an* authority, who have some aspect of expertise to make their instructions convincing and welcome. French and Raven (1959) suggest that there are five main bases of power to influence others.

1. A (the person wishing to exercise power) has the ability to control the *rewards* of B (the person to be influenced). Managers control promotions, pay rises, some aspects of fringe benefits, etc., and are important potential sources of praise.
2. A has the ability to *coerce* B by providing punishments. Praise can be withheld; unattractive duties can be assigned to B, who may be rebuked and eventually dismissed.
3. A may have *legitimate* influence because of role. The quality assurance official has the right to examine the work done by others, just as customs officers have the right to open suitcases at national frontiers.
4. *Referent* power is where B wishes to identify with A. An extreme form is seen in the clamorous followers of popular singers, but managers tend to attract a following in organisations, even though the followers may not express themselves with such exuberance.
5. Finally A has authority in relation to B when A has *expertise* which B acknowledges and wants to use. An example we used in the discussion on organisational politics was of the maintenance engineer who can work the miracle of restarting the machine that has stopped, but there are many such examples in every organisation, and this is an authority base that does not depend on hierarchical position. Another example is of the young legal adviser in a large international company, who told the members of the main board of her company that they could not go ahead with the planned sale of a subsidiary for legal reasons. In the hierarchy she ranked low, but her technical expertise was not queried.

From our discussion so far in this chapter it may seem that managers should have no problem in getting others to do things; if people generally are predisposed to obey, then presumably all that managers need to do is to issue instructions and wait for them to be carried out.

Life, of course, is not so easy. The general predisposition to compliance is something of which all managers have to be reminded, but it is not sufficient. Although the majority of Milgram's volunteers complied, 35% did not; also they were being required to carry out a routine task rather than one depending on enthusiasm, imagination or some other quality that cannot be conjured up by simple command. How many managers could tolerate a situation in which they operated by simple decree? The fear is that the result would be the corruption of themselves by the power they wield.

Leadership

The implication behind the notion of leadership is that there is a combination of personal qualities and skills that enables some people to elicit from their subordinates a response that is enthusiastic, cohesive and effective, while other people in the same situation cannot achieve such results. There are two problems about that type of view. First it is often bad for the leaders, who grow an inflated view of their own importance, believing that success lies in who they are rather than what they do. Secondly, it limits the number of people who can safely be put in charge of sections, departments and operations because it emphasises relatively rare qualities of social dominance. It is significant that qualities of leadership are a greater preoccupation among potential leaders than among potential followers. 'I know how to get the best out of them' is heard more frequently than 'They know how to get the best out of us'. The 'great person' theory of leadership was summed up by the post-war American president Harry Truman:

> I wonder how far Moses would have gone if he had taken a poll in Egypt? What would Jesus Christ have preached if he had taken a poll in Israel? Where would the Reformation have gone if Martin Luther had taken a poll? It isn't polls or public opinion of the moment that counts. It is right and wrong and leadership – men with fortitude, honesty and a belief in the right that makes epochs in the history of the world.   (*Wall Street Journal*, 16 December 1980, p. 2)

Studies of effective leaders in order to identify the traits of leadership have failed to provide clear-cut results and it is now appreciated that there are other factors of comparable or greater significance in explaining leader effectiveness. A review by Davies (1972) shows there to be four general traits related to leadership success, although they do little more than confirm common sense.

1. *Intelligence.* Leaders usually have a slightly higher level of general intelligence than the average among their followers.
2. *Social maturity.* Having self-assurance and self-respect, leaders are mature and able to handle a wide variety of social situations.
3. *Achievement drive.* Leaders have a strong drive to get things done.

4. *Human relations attitudes.* Knowing that they rely on other people to get things done, leaders are interested in their subordinates and work at developing subordinate response.

A popular distinction between leaders is that made by Burns (1978) who distinguished between *transactional leaders*, who use styles and techniques to clarify task requirements and ensure that there are appropriate rewards; and *transformational* leaders who articulate a mission and create and maintain a positive image in followers and superiors. A more comprehensive understanding requires a consideration of the needs that a particular group of people have of their leader, and of the situation in which the led task is performed.

In 1902 the Scottish dramatist J. M. Barrie wrote a play, *The Admirable Crichton*, in which an English aristocratic family is shipwrecked on a desert island. The authority of the head of the family rapidly disintegrates in this situation and the role of leader is gradually assumed by the one person in the party who has the skills and experience necessary: Crichton, the family butler. Previously his ability and resourcefulness have been recognised with the patronising term 'admirable'; suddenly they become essential. Not born great, Crichton has greatness thrust upon him. On the desert island, his leadership was unchallenged. When the party was rescued, the crew of the ship that found them immediately re-established the norms and values of Edwardian England, so Crichton resumed his tailcoat and served his master an excellent breakfast in bed.

As with so many areas of social science investigation, much of the work on leadership over the last thirty years has been to present slightly different versions of explanatory models that are basically very similar but express differing emphasis according to the values of their proponents. So we shall describe just three of these explanations which are mutually consistent; the second depends partly on the explanations in the first.

Fiedler (1967) has developed a contingency model of leadership effectiveness in which he argues that any leadership style may be effective, depending on the situation, so that the leader has to be adaptive. We thus have a clear difference between this approach and that of the trait theorists, as we are talking of leaders adapting their style to the situation. He also appreciates that it is very difficult for individuals to change their style of leadership as these styles are relatively inflexible: the autocrat will remain autocratic and the freewheeling *laissez-faire* advocate will remain freewheeling. As no single style is appropriate for all situations, effectiveness can be achieved either by changing the manager to fit the situation or by altering the situation to suit the manager. Three factors will determine the leader's effectiveness:

1. *Leader–member relations.* How well is the leader accepted by the subordinates?

2. *Task structure* Are the jobs of subordinates routine and precise or vague and undefined?
3. *Position power.* What formal authority does the leader's position confer?

Fiedler then devised a novel device for measuring leadership style. It was a scale that indicated the degree to which a person described favourably or unfavourably their least-preferred co-worker (LPC):

> A person who describes his least-preferred co-workers in a relatively favorable manner tends to be permissive, human relations oriented and considerate of the feelings of his men. But a person who describes his least-preferred co-worker in an unfavorable manner – who has what we have come to call a low LPC rating – tends to be managing, task-controlling and less concerned with the human relations aspects of the job.   (Fiedler, 1967)

Fiedler then argues that high LPC managers will want to have close ties with their subordinates and regard these as an important contributor to their effectiveness, while low LPC managers will be much more concerned with getting the job done and less interested in the reactions of subordinates. It is then possible to combine all these elements to show how the style of leadership that is effective varies with the situation in which it is exercised. Table 19.1 shows the result of 800 studies which Fiedler carried out, using eight categories of leadership situations and two types of leaders.

High LPC leaders were likely to be most effective in situations where relations with subordinates are good but task structure is low and position power weak. They do reasonably well when they have poor relationships with their subordinates but there is high task structure and strong position power. Both of these are moderately favourable combinations of circumstance. Low LPC leaders are more effective at the ends of the spectrum, when they have either a favourable combination or an unfavourable combination of factors in the situation.

The value of Fiedler's work is that it concentrates on effectiveness as its yardstick and demonstrates the fallacy of believing that there is a single best way to lead in all situations. It is interesting that the majority of situations he describes appear to call for a generally less attractive type of person as leader, but we should remember that he was examining a range of situations for the purpose of explanation, and that situations which are at the extremes of his continuum may not be very frequent in organisational life. Although this remains the most widely accepted analysis of the leadership process, some people have found rather depressing Fiedler's accompanying argument that individual leaders have little chance of adopting a style which is more appropriate to their situation, so that it is more important to match available managers to a situation than to try changing the individual manager's style. An alternative is to tinker with the situation: modifying the task structure, varying the formal authority or changing the subordinates. The last is the

Table 19.1 Leadership performance in different conditions

Condition	Leader–member relations	Task structure	Position power	
1	Good	High	Strong	Low LPC leader more effective
2	Good	High	Weak	Low LPC leader more effective
3	Good	Low	Strong	Low LPC leader more effective
4	Good	Low	Weak	High LPC leader more effective
5	Poor	High	Strong	High LPC leader more effective
6	Poor	High	Weak	Similar effectiveness
7	Poor	Low	Strong	Low LPC leader more effective
8	Poor	Low	Weak	Low LPC leader more effective

(From Fiedler, 1976, p. 11)

most drastic and is only possible to any significant extent in very few situations. It could, however, transform condition 8 to condition 4.

| REVIEW TOPIC 19.2 |

There is great interest among managers in leadership ideas. Is this solely to justify their idea of their own importance as people deserving larger salaries and bigger cars?

Some people, especially those concerned with training, cannot believe in the degree of inflexibility that Fiedler found. One person whose ideas on training have been widely influential in the United Kingdom is John Adair. Adair produces a picture of leadership by arguing that people in working groups have three sets of needs, two of which are shared with all group members, the third being related to each individual.

1. The task to be accomplished together.
2. Maintaining the social cohesion of the group.
3. Individual needs of team members.

These three sets of needs are interdependent:

> If a group fails in its task this will intensify the disintegrative tendencies present in the group and raise a diminished satisfaction for its individual members. If there is a lack of unity or harmonious relationships in the group this will affect performance on the job and also individual needs (*cf.* A. H. Maslow's *Social Needs*). And obviously an individual who feels frustrated and

unhappy in a particular work environment will not make his maximum contribution to either the common task or the life of the group.

(Adair, 1982, p. 9)

Figure 19.1 shows these three sets of needs, or leadership functions, expressed as three overlapping circles. This emphasises the essential unity of leadership, so that a single action by a leader may have influence in all three areas.

This was used by Adair to develop leadership at the Royal Military Academy, Sandhurst, but the methods have been adopted in a wide variety of organisations. They are set out in detail in Adair (1982).

A well-tried device for identifying leadership style of the individual is the *managerial grid* used as an exercise in management development to decide one's leadership style, with the hope that it can be modified at least slightly to become more appropriate to the situation in which one is working. The managerial grid was developed by Blake and Mouton (1969) and identifies concern for production and concern for people as the two axes of a grid, illustrated in Figure 19.2. At the lower left-hand corner is a 1.1 management style which is the style of managers who have a low concern for both people and production, try to stay out of trouble and simply do as they are told. In the upper left-hand corner is the 1.9 style of high concern for people but low concern for production, and so on. The 9.9 style of high concern with both people and production is the obvious goal.

Grid training requires team members to identify their own management style, as they perceive it themselves, and then as it is perceived by others, so there is an element of sensitivity training in the approach. It is possible to identify the management style composition of any team and either alter team membership to increase effectiveness or enable individual team

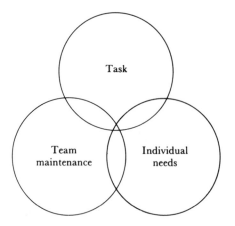

Figure 19.1 Adair's three-circle model of leadership.

members to modify their personal style. This emphasis on style rather than personal characteristics is probably the secret of the success that grid methods have enjoyed, as it provides useful criticism of the type that most of us can live with and can hope to modify.

The British writers Wright and Taylor (1984) point out the importance of leaders acting skilfully in day-to-day working relationships with people in different roles. Concentrating on the individual leader trying to improve the working performance of a subordinate, they have produced the checklist shown in Table 19.2. This makes the issue of leadership practical rather than philosophical and provides managers with methods of improving their performance.

Autonomy

Research and discussion about authority and leadership tend to centre on the role and personality or on the needs of groups to have a leadership function exercised on their behalf. These emphases tend to overlook the need of organisation members for autonomy, and the complementary need of organisations to have members who are autonomous.

From the point of view of the individual employee, there is a life cycle theory of leadership (Hersey and Blanchard, 1969) which points out that people at work need lessening task structure as they mature in an organisation, as well as during their maturation as human beings. Most forty-year-olds will find close supervision and direction as irksome as most sixteen-year-olds will find it necessary. From the point of view of the employing organisation, close supervision is time-consuming and expensive, as we saw in the discussion about the optimum span of control. Also many tasks in contemporary organisations cannot be done well without the job holder having full range for personal imagination and responsibility. Bob Ramsey retired in 1981 from the position of Industrial Relations Director at Ford of Great Britain. This is not a company renowned for its weakness and inefficiency, yet Ramsey frequently spoke of employees looking for a better service from management. The main work of organisations is done by engineers and salesmen, by designers and analysts, and by many other people with some acquired skill that the organisation needs. Managers enable those employees to do well by the management service they provide in support of the autonomy that is needed for effective individual performance.

The Moss quadrants

In our research into the management and organisation of secondary schools (Torrington and Weightman, 1989) we found that schools that cope well with their various demands and challenges are not always similar. A model

Table 19.2   A checklist for improving work performance

1. What is the problem in behavioural terms? What precisely is the individual doing or not doing which is adversely influencing his or her performance?
2. Is the problem really serious enough to spend time and effort on?
3. What reasons might there be for the performance problem? (See column 1.)
4. What actions might be taken to improve the situation? (See column 2.)
5. Do you have sufficient information to select the most appropriate solution(s)? If not, collect the information required, e.g. consult records, observe work behaviour, talk to person concerned.
6. Select most appropriate solution(s).
7. Is the solution worthwhile in cost–benefit terms?
   (a) If so, implement it.
   (b) If not, work through the checklist again, or relocate the individual, or reorganise the department/organisation, or live with the problem.
8. Could you have handled the problem better? If so, review own performance. If not, and the problem is solved, reward yourself and tackle next problem.

Possible reasons for performance problem	Possible solutions
Goal clarity Is the person fully aware of the job requirements?	Give guidance concerning expected goals and standards. Set targets
Ability Does the person have the capacity to do the job well?	Provide formal training, on the job coaching, practice, secondment, etc.
Task difficulty Does the person find the task too demanding?	Simplify task, reduce work load, reduce time pressures, etc.
Intrinsic motivation Does the person find the task rewarding in itself?	Redesign job to match job-holder's needs
Extrinsic motivation Is good performance rewarded by others?	Arrange positive consequences for good performance and zero or negative consequences for poor performance
Feedback Does the person receive adequate feedback about his/her performance?	Provide or arrange feedback
Resources Does the person have adequate resources for satisfactory task performance?	Provide staff, equipment, raw materials as appropriate
Working conditions Do working conditions, physical or social, interfere with performance?	Improve light, noise, heat, layout, remove distractions, etc. as appropriate

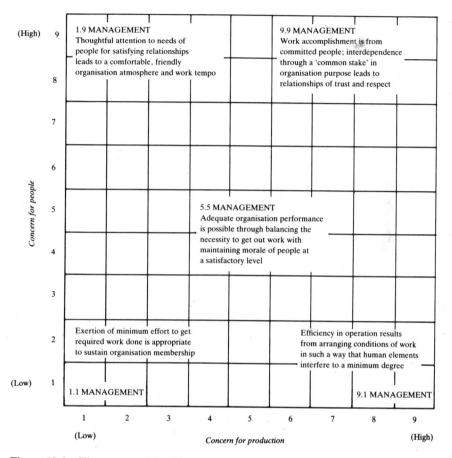

Figure 19.2 The managerial grid.

we have developed, that is applicable to all sorts of organisations, which explores the tensions of managing is given in Figure 19.3.

The horizontal dimension represents the tension between the degree of tight control on the one hand and the degree of group or individual autonomy on the other. This illustrates the range of ways that organisations deal with, and who decides, such structural things as resources, finance, staffing, job descriptions and work methods. An organisation in which all these matters are dealt with centrally would be located towards the right-hand side, but that could move progressively left as the number of matters and the nature of choice was moved out of the hands of the few at the centre and into the hands of more members of staff.

The vertical dimension represents a different tension, between values of consensus and relationships of high trust at one extreme, contrasted with

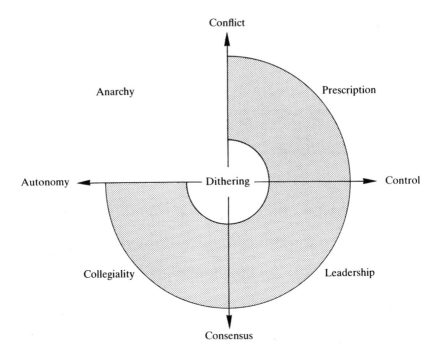

Figure 19.3 Effect management can be found in any of the shaded areas.

low trust and conflicting interests at the other. This tells us something about the culture of the organisation and represents both the assumptions people make and the behaviour in which they engage. If a significant number of people, or a small number with significant power, believe the organisation to be staffed by members of different groups whose interests conflict, then they will also believe that the main management and organisation task is to deal with this conflict and their behaviour will reflect that belief. If the prevailing belief is that there are teams within the organisation who work together to the same ends, with the management and organisation task being to nurture this consensus, then behaviour will follow that assumption.

Putting these two dimensions together produces four quadrants labelled prescription, leadership, collegiality and anarchy, known as the Moss quadrants, which represent the dominant management and organisational style operating. The prescription style is likely where there is a felt need for a lot of control mechanisms to manage conflict within the organisation; the leadership style is more likely when a similar felt need to control is linked with a strong consensus supporting initiatives of the senior management team; the collegiality style emphasises collaboration and team work enabling each member to contribute where there is a sufficiently mature staff to deliver this; the anarchic style permits the individual rights of self expression but it becomes increasingly difficult to persuade anyone else that this is an effective organisation.

We contend that none of the styles can be pursued to its extreme without creating serious organisational difficulties. Equally we argue that dithering in the centre with no clear view leads to loss of identity, direction and confidence. Each of the three main styles is appropriate for particular situations. Prescription is appropriate where consistency is important, for example in a hamburger chain. Leadership is helpful when there is uncertainty that can and should be dealt with quickly, for example when there are poor press reports. Collegiality is useful where the full commitment of individuals is necessary, for example when the situation is novel and everyone needs to deliver the service, such as in schools faced with a new national curriculum. All organisations have all of these in different proportions at different times. The balance between them is the clever art of finding the appropriate management and organisation for the particular organisation.

Authority, leadership and the manager

The basic job of getting people to obey orders is not as problematical as many managers believe, and little skill or personal charm is needed. The reason, however, for the abiding interest of managers in ideas of leadership, motivation and influence is that managers usually seek to do more than bring about simple obedience – they are trying to win a performance. They are trying to enable the members of the group, team or department to produce a workaday contribution to the organisation in commitment, collaboration, imagination, persistence and forbearance. The type of leadership that is effective varies with the situation in which it is exercised, just as the behaviour of team members varies according to the scope which their jobs offer. As with so many other aspects of management, there is no single best way of being in charge of a group of people, but in an increasing range of working situations it seems as if the successful manager is the one who is most thorough in ensuring that the team members have the correct facilities and environment to work. Skilled individuals know what to do, and need appropriate autonomy and services to perform.

| REVIEW TOPIC 19.3 |

Is the autonomy of individual workers incompatible with the power implicit in organisations?

| SUMMARY PROPOSITIONS |

19.1 The authority of managers is underpinned by a general human predilection to obey commands from those holding higher rank in the hierarchy of which they are members.

19.2 Tight control of employee performance by incentive payment schemes reduces rather than enhances the personal authority of individual managers in relation to employees.

19.3 Effective leadership depends on the situations in which it is exercised; the main variables are leader–member relations, task structure and position power of the leader.

19.4 A convenient way of understanding what is involved in the leadership of a group is to consider three overlapping needs: the needs of group members to accomplish a task together, the need to maintain the social cohesion of the group, and the needs of the individual group members.

19.5 Increasingly employees – especially those with skills or specialised knowledge – need a style of leadership that acknowledges their need for autonomy in order to make their optimum contribution.

| PUTTING IT INTO PRACTICE |

When delegating work to someone else, ask yourself:

Am I allowing them to make decisions about this?
Can they decide whether to do it or not?
Can they decide what to do or not?
Can they decide how to do it or not?
Are there any variations that they cannot decide to opt for?

In meetings do you ask for everyone's opinion? How do you hear the views of the quiet members of the group?

References

Adair, J., 1982, *Action-Centred Leadership*, Gower, Aldershot, Hampshire.

Blake, R. R. and Mouton, J. S., 1969, *Building a Dynamic Organization through Grid Organization Development*, Gull, Houston, Texas.

Burns, J. M., 1978, *Leadership*, Harper & Row, New York.

Davies, K., 1972, *Human Behaviour at Work*, 4th edn, McGraw-Hill, New York.

Fiedler, F. E., 1967, *A Theory of Leadership Effectiveness*, McGraw-Hill, New York.

Fiedler, F. E., 1976, The leadership game: matching the man to the situation, *Organizational Dynamics*, Winter.

French, W. L. and Raven, S., 1959, The bases of social power, in *Studies in Social Power*, ed. Cartwright, D., Row Peterson, New York.

Hersey, P. and Blanchard, K. H., 1969, Life cycle theory of leadership, *Training and Development Journal*, May, pp. 226–34.

Hobsbawm, E. J., 1975, *The Age of Capital*, Weidenfeld & Nicolson, London.

Mayo, E., 1975, *The Social Problems of Industrial Civilisation*, Routledge & Kegan Paul, London.

Milgram, S., 1974, *Obedience to Authority*, Tavistock, London.

Sixsmith, E. K. G., 1973, *Eisenhower as Military Commander*, Batsford, London.

Torrington, D. P. and Weightman, J. B., 1989, *The Reality of School Management*, Blackwell, Oxford.

Wright, P. L. and Taylor, D. S., 1984, *Improving Leadership Performance*, Prentice Hall International, Hemel Hempstead, Hertfordshire.

Wrong, D. H., 1979, *Power: Its Forms, Bases and Uses*, Blackwell, Oxford.

Readers may also like to read Chapter 5 in Book V of *The Brothers Karamazov* by Fyodor Dostoevsky, which is available in many imprints, including that of the Everyman Library, J. M. Dent, London, 1947.

Chapter 20

Motivation and influence

Much managerial time is spent in winning people round. This is not the same as using power, as was discussed in our chapter on organisational politics, nor is it the exercise of authority in 'the line' as in the last chapter. It is the ability to persuade and to influence, very similar to the art of selling. It is not the manipulation of resources and setting up situations which gives others little choice but to agree, and it is not the working relationship between superior and subordinate behind which there is the implicit assumption that the superior can command the obedience of the subordinate. It is a separate, specialised aspect of managerial work that enables things to get done; an extension of understanding other people and how they are motivated.

Other people do not necessarily see things in the same way that we do. Few comments can be more obviously true. Yet the behaviour and conversation of most individuals suggest that it is a truth we do not readily follow in our everyday lives. We find it difficult to understand how anyone can vote for a political party whose policies are opposed to those of the party we voted for. In industrial relations negotiations it is unusual for the protagonists to see, let alone appreciate, the opposing point of view. Those conducting selection interviews need constantly to remind themselves of the difference in perspective and understanding between themselves and those they interview.

The reason we find it so difficult to adopt a different perspective is that we all need a set of operating assumptions to conduct our daily affairs, and the one we find most comforting is that others see the world around them in the same way as we see the world around us. Recruiting for large organisations, especially recruiting for the management ranks, often follows a routine that selects those who are similar to those already employed. The operating assumption of a common view of the world is then safe. It is further consolidated by induction and training. Those entering the police force have attitudes about authority that are similar and which are reinforced by the process of training in the service. Not everyone outside the police force shares those views. In the electronics company Hewlett Packard there is constant reference to 'The Hewlett Packard way'. This is known, felt and understood by those in the company, without being made explicit.

There are still many examples of organisations that seek to employ only those who conform to a particular set of values and behaviour, with that conformity being assessed in recruitment, emphasised in induction and confirmed in promotion. Managers in such organisations need to understand individual differences sufficiently for them to identify those who fit the pattern and to avoid those who do not.

A much stronger reason for understanding how individuals differ is the impracticability of any manager seeking to work only with the like-minded. If managers could surround themselves with clones they would get standardised, sycophantic responses to all their initiatives. Different managers may have surrounded themselves with clones of a different type and it is not feasible to people an entire organisation with carbon copies of the model organisation person. Organisations deal with a clientele and the only thing the clients will have in common will be an interest in the organisation's products. As people they will vary enormously. Furthermore the remaking of organisations in their own image is a practice that can lead to criticism of unreasonable discrimination against other, worthy applicants who do not fit neatly into the mould.

Managers spend a large part of their time talking to others and trying to get others to do things. The more they can understand the nature of individual differences, the more effectively they can work with a variety of people. Managers are also likely to be more influential if they understand the differences between people.

Everyone has a different view

We all work with an image of people in our heads when we seek to understand others. We behave towards them in line with our beliefs and expect their behaviour to be predictable. The problem is that their model may not be the same as ours. Those who know what their model is are more likely to recognise the occasion when someone else is using a different model. Such recognition not only reduces the likelihood of talking at cross-purposes but also increases the likelihood of being able to understand the reasoning behind whatever the other is saying.

Schein (1970) and McGregor (1960) have looked at the models used by managers. Schein (pp. 55–76) describes four models that managers use to explain the behaviour of subordinates. Managers holding the *rational–economic* model assume that people are primarily motivated by rational appraisal of personal economic needs. The *social* model assumes that people are motivated by social needs, wanting rewarding on-the-job relationships and that they are more responsive to work group pressures than to management control. The *self-actualising* model sees people as both wanting to be, and able to be, mature independent people responsible for their own work. *Complex* man assumes that people cannot be slotted into any of the above categories but have various and complex desires that include all the above and some other needs, not all of which can be met at work.

As usual management thinkers want the best of all possible worlds and advocate the adoption of the fourth model as it includes the other three and rules out any one of them from being taken as the single explanation. Managers believing in rational–economic people can be baffled when they put up wages only to find that labour turnover rises or output falls. Other managers, who adhere to social thinking, are aggrieved when an employee applies for a better paid job elsewhere, despite the manager's efforts to be nice.

| REVIEW TOPIC 20.1 |

Which are you?

1. Rational–economic.
2. Social.
3. Self-actualising.
4. Complex.

Now ask a friend which you are.

McGregor produced what is probably the best-known theory about management attitudes to subordinates when he propounded his profoundly simple idea of the theory X manager and the theory Y manager. He believed that prevailing assumptions among managers about the typical worker were outdated as they did not take account of the education level and psychological maturity of the workforce. What McGregor saw as the prevailing assumption was summed up by theory X, which emphasised direction and control in organisations with rigid structures and management styles. In contrast a theory Y manager will give people greater freedom, will consult about methods and objectives and will delegate more authority. These theories are summarised in Figure 20.1.

McGregor was widely misconstrued as people, seeking the one right answer to all their problems, interpreted his analysis as replacing an old model with a new one. Theory X was wrong: therefore theory Y was right. They fell into the trap of believing that there could be only one model, whereas McGregor was demonstrating the range of models that could be appropriate and freeing management from the narrow-minded orthodoxy that he found all around him in the 1950s.

Theory X

1. The average human being has an inherent dislike of work and will avoid it if they can.
2. Because of the human characteristic dislike of work, most people must be coerced, controlled, directed, threatened with punishment, to get them to put forth adequate effort towards the achievement of organisational objectives.
3. The average human being prefers to be directed, wishes to avoid responsibility, has relatively little ambition, wants security above all.

Theory Y

1. The expenditure of physical and mental effort is as natural as play or rest.
2. External control and the threat of punishment are not the only means of bringing about effort towards organisational objectives. People will exercise self-direction and self-control in the service of objectives to which they are committed.
3. Commitment to objectives is a function of the rewards associated with their achievement.
4. The average human being learns, under proper conditions, not only to accept but to seek responsibility.
5. The capacity to exercise a relatively high degree of imagination, ingenuity, and creativity in the solution of organisational problems is widely, not narrowly, distributed in the population.
6. Under the condition of modern industrial life, the intellectual potentialities of the average human being are only partially utilised.

Figure 20.1   Theory X and theory Y (McGregor, 1960, pp. 47–8).

Motivation theories

To some extent employees are in control of their behaviour, as are customers, suppliers, shareholders and other managers. Much of their behaviour will thus be motivated as they consciously seek to attain certain goals. Internal motives cause people to seek specific outcomes that will satisfy their needs.

Needs or motives can be divided into two general categories. Primary needs are those relating to basic animal drives such as hunger, thirst, sleep, sex, pain avoidance, recovery from fatigue, and safety. Their influence on behaviour is obvious and easy to identify. Secondary needs are acquired through experience and vary greatly according to culture as well as the particular experiences of the individual. They are the desires for power, achievement, social affiliation, status and a feeling of personal competence. Satisfying a primary need diminishes or temporarily extinguishes the drive. A hungry person does not feel hungry immediately after a large meal. Secondary needs are not satisfied in quite the same way; meeting a need for, say, recognition is likely to produce a desire for further recognition.

Maslow (1954) grouped needs into a five-step hierarchy, illustrated in Figure 20.2. The primary needs were physiological and safety. Secondary

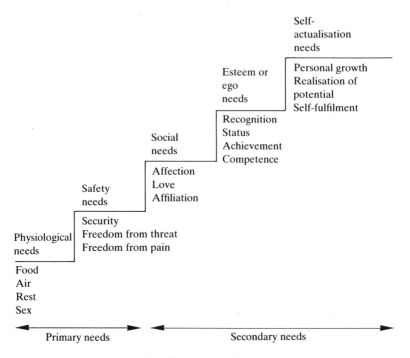

Figure 20.2   Maslow's hierarchy of human needs.

needs, dealing with the psychological aspects of man, were in three categories: social needs, esteem needs and self-actualisation needs. Maslow contended that individuals tended to move up the hierarchy of needs, and would occasionally move down for brief periods. More significant was that sets of needs came into consideration in sequence, so that until the lowest-order needs were satisfied, others were relatively unimportant, but once the lower order needs are satisfied, they lose their potency. A severe headache needs to be relieved before the desire for friendship and affection becomes strong, but once the pain is relieved, then friendship may become important.

Employees in Western societies generally have their primary needs met (although those unemployed may not) so managers are interested in the secondary needs. Some managers try to eliminate chatting between employees at work on the grounds that it distracts their attention from what they are doing. This can, however, cause output to go down rather than up because this type of social contact is a means of coping with tedious work.

The esteem or ego needs can be met at work because of the opportunities that are provided for doing relatively well when compared with others. Ego needs are interpreted in relative rather than absolute terms. The need can be satisfied by the employee feeling a degree of recognition or status that others have not achieved, or that is now achieved so that comparison is possible with others who have already reached that level.

Athletes raising their arms triumphantly above their heads are asserting their achievement in the feat which they have just accomplished. In organisational life there are innumerable ways in which status is marked. Some people have secretaries, while others do not; some wear white coats, while others wear grey; some carry skilled-status union cards, while others do not. Management strategy in relation to these indicators varies. In some organisations much effort goes into eliminating such status dividers, by ensuring that all eat in the same cafeteria, wear the same uniform and address each other only by their first names. In other organisations the status indicators are cultivated to recognise the way employees are making progress. The McDonald's chain of fast-food shops provide their staff with name badges carrying space for four stars according to the range of tasks the person can undertake, so that this recognition is not only given to the individual to compare with the position of other employees, but is also seen by the customer.

Self-actualisation is the highest order of needs in Maslow's hierarchy as it represents the restless urge to self-fulfilment that the humanist psychologists believe we all have. This is not seeking after doing better, or as well as, someone else, but satisfying oneself that one is doing all one can. Recognition and status needs are met by someone else saying 'Well done!'. Self-actualisation needs are met when one can say 'Well done!' to oneself. Organisations provide potential satisfaction of these needs in the demanding and challenging work that can be found in most management and scientific positions. Employees may, however, be deprived of this sort of potential need satisfaction in jobs which are routine and thus give no scope for initiative. Other jobs may not be routine, but can still lack this type of need satisfaction because of limits that are placed on the scope of the job and the denial of creativity. This is often a problem of over-specialisation in management ranks: jobs are chopped up so small that few people are able to complete an assignment and have to pass it on for completion by someone else.

The ranking of these five sets of needs in a hierarchy is based on two important assumptions: first, that a satisfied need is not a motivator, and second, that as one set of needs becomes satisfied, then the next set of needs becomes dominant. The implications of this for managers are obvious. It is not worth trying to provide means for employees to satisfy self-actualisation needs if lower-level needs have not yet been met. Also it is pointless trying to 'motivate' employees by considering their lower-order needs if these are already satisfied. A further dimension is that the level of need satisfaction can vary. A group of managers who assemble for a two-day course, never having met each other before, will initially be much more concerned about the accommodation and catering arrangements than they will be later in the course, when social needs will become dominant, rapidly followed by esteem needs.

Herzberg (1968) developed the Maslow idea of the hierarchy by making a stronger distinction between lower- and higher-order needs. He described the lower-order needs as potential dissatisfiers, or hygiene factors, and only the higher-order needs were potential satisfiers or motivators. He contended that those managing organisations had to get the hygiene factors right, just as an operating theatre has to be clean and a kitchen well-scrubbed. Without those basic satisfactory conditions employees would be dissatisfied. Once the organisation was 'clean', further attention to lower order needs would not enhance employee performance. They can hamper when they are not properly met, but they cannot motivate beyond the level of basic satisfaction. Herzberg listed specific hygiene factors for life in organisations as including:

Company policy and administration
Supervision
Working conditions
Salary
Relationship with peers
Personal life
Relationship with subordinates
Status
Security

Most of these have in common the fact that they are extrinsic, coming from outside the person. Herzberg's list of satisfiers or motivators was shorter:

Achievement
Recognition
Work itself
Responsibility
Advancement
Growth

These are generally intrinsic, coming from the inside of the person, and are not so easily satisfied. The person who achieves something then wants more achievement; the person who has challenging, interesting work wants more of it to do. This has proved a most popular theory with managers, as it has provided a practical basis for management action: give people scope for achievement, recognition, enriched jobs, etc., and they will work harder, be more content and appreciate the goodness of the manager who made it all happen.

Despite the popularity of Herzberg, based on Maslow, there are some words of caution. Herzberg's research was mainly among engineers and accountants – well-educated, middle-class Americans, and other people may have quite different needs and attitudes. Contemporary with Herzberg, a study in a British car manufacturing plant described the instrumental orientation of those whose attitudes were examined:

> The workers were particularly motivated to increase their power as consumers and their domestic standard of living, rather than their satisfaction as producers and the degree of self-fulfilment in their work.
>
> (Goldthorpe *et al.*, 1968, p. 38)

In other words, work for these workers was mainly a means towards another end rather than having intrinsic merit. The attempts by some enthusiasts to revolutionise the quality of working life by introducing motivators to jobs where they have been traditionally absent have usually failed after a brief honeymoon period. Maslow can be criticised for the precision of his stratified hierarchy of secondary needs, as human beings are not as consistent as that, and Herzberg made extravagant claims for the universal applicability of his theory, which have not been borne out in practice for all groups of workers. Despite these reservations, a careful consideration of what both Maslow and Herzberg say provides a very helpful framework for understanding general aspects of motivation.

REVIEW TOPIC 20.2

The French writer and hostess Madame de Stael (1766–1817) is alleged to have written 'To be totally understanding makes one very indulgent . . .' (*Tout comprendre, c'est tout pardonner*).

As managers try to understand their subordinates are they likely to become indulgent?

Two theories which add important dimensions to Maslow and Herzberg are those of Lewin and Vroom. Lewin's field theory (Lewin, 1952) emphasises that individuals operate in a field of forces that represent subjective perceptions about the environment, the importance of a goal and the psychological distance of the goal. Lewin uses it to try to account for the difference of motivation in people at different times. For example, you and I might both want to meet the Wimbledon Tennis Champions. I see the circumstances as far too difficult; the goal of seeing them is not compelling enough to overcome the psychological distance to make any effort worth while. You, however, may be in more favourable circumstances, may want to see them enough to overcome the psychological distance between you.

Vroom's expectancy theory (Vroom and Deci, 1974) proposes that motivation is a product of the value that individuals place on the possible results of their actions and the expectation that their goal will be achieved. The importance of this approach is that it emphasises the individuality and variability of motivation rather than the generalisations of Maslow and Herzberg.

Those wanting to delve further into this area are recommended to see the work of Steers and Porter (1987) for a detailed assessment of the relevance of this research and theorising to organisations. A more general text is Arnold *et al.* (1991).

Stereotyping

In trying to understand other people we all, instinctively, use a short-cut method known as stereotyping. This is an essential aspect of dealing with others but can also be a straitjacket if we do not use it carefully. If you have lost your way in a foreign city and decide to ask someone for directions, you do not stop the first person you see; you pick out someone from the surrounding crowd who looks to you a potential source of good information. You probably look for someone who is not in a hurry, neither too young nor too old, appearing intelligent and sympathetic. You have a working stereotype of who would be an appropriate person to ask. At work we carry round in our heads a series of stereotypes which influence all our dealings with other people. Some of these are carried over from our general experiences and prejudices, for example:

Scots are careful with money.
Small women are assertive.
Men with long hair are unreliable.

Others are linked to working experience and values:

Shop stewards are bloody-minded.
All engineers think clearly.
Accountants are dull.
Women make good secretaries.

There is seldom time in all working situations to abandon stereotyping as a way of approaching matters, especially in emergencies, where some sort of working hypothesis is needed immediately. The danger of stereotyping is, of course, that people are not treated and understood as individuals but as categories. This is unreasonable to them (and can be unlawful) and it limits the ability of the person who is over-dependent on stereotypes to work with others to the full extent of their abilities. A special form of this is the halo effect, where individuals are judged according to an imaginary halo above their heads. Someone, for instance, who is never late may be pointed out as an admirable employee even though the quality of the work is poor.

Stereotyping often occurs between departments in organisations, so that marketing people are often regarded by others as superficial, flashily dressed and not really doing anything, while production people are seen as earnest, harassed and socially ill at ease.

Here is a brief summary of suggestions made by Zalkind and Costello (1962) for improving one's ability to perceive others accurately.

1. The better we know ourselves, the easier it is to see others accurately.
2. One's own character affects what one sees in others.
3. The accuracy of our own perceptions depends on our sensitivity to the differences between people.

Valuing: consideration, delegation and participation

Another aspect of influencing people and getting the best from them is staff morale. Most organisations are suffering from innovation overload, just at a time when staff morale is lower than it has been for years because of redundancies and a general levelling of status differentials. Staff are responding to this in different ways: some by withholding commitment (see Scase and Goffee, 1989), some by withdrawing from extra work, some by increased militancy; some by reduced militancy; some simply bow their heads and resolve to work harder – again – like Boxer the horse in *Animal Farm*. In our research in secondary schools (Torrington and Weightman, 1989) we identified four ways adults could value each other which could assist the improvement of staff morale. It is a complex social interaction to value someone else, which has something to do with them as a person as well as the job which they do. Four types of valuing need to be examined: consideration, feedback, delegation and consultation.

Consideration

One teacher said to us 'No-one supports me here. No-one talks to you in the staff room. It is not friendly with folk across departments. I'd rather go and read a book.' People tend to feel a lack of consideration from their colleagues when the organisation culture is one of keeping to oneself rather than talking to colleagues, even at the level of simple things such as eye contact in the corridors, good mornings, smiling and the everyday courtesies of the working day. Our evidence suggests that most people would welcome more of these small gestures at work. Lack of consideration may be one of Herzberg's dissatisfiers.

Feedback

The second type of valuing is concerned with feedback, evaluation and appraisal. All too often the enormous contribution and exhausting effort that people put into their jobs seems to lack any perceptible output. People need feedback from their colleagues. This can be formal performance appraisal: see Chapter 11. But it can also be informally taking an interest in what each other is doing. It is not hierarchy bound; a junior saying 'That's great! How do you do it?' can be very pleasing.

Delegation

Members of staff are valued when responsibility is delegated to them, but this involves delegating real responsibility down the hierarchy, not just giving poeple jobs to do. Individuals must be trusted to make decisions about whether, what and how to do things, not just given the work of completing tasks. Also responsibility cannot be delegated and then taken away without devaluing their confidence and future effectiveness.

Consultation and participation

In view of the innovation overload referred to already, it is difficult to create the conditions in which people will respond to change with enthusiasm. However, if they wish to respond with commitment rather than mere stoical compliance, there is scope for a participative style of implementation that creates a sense of ownership of the 'how' of innovation even if there is no sense of the 'what'. Consultation makes the earlier stages of innovation slower but the later stages are quicker and more effective. The nature of consultation and participation is affected by structures (see Chapter 14), by process (see Chapter 15) and by the consultative performance of people in key positions (see Chapter 3).

Assertiveness

Assertiveness training is currently popular with women's groups; it is designed to develop people's confidence to control their own affairs and involves breaking minor 'rules' of polite behaviour.

Assertiveness training was initially developed in psychotherapy to help people who feel inadequate in their dealings with other people because they are afraid to speak up for what they believe and are not willing to resist when others appear to take advantage of them. Managers are not likely to suffer that degree of social handicap, but the techniques can be useful to develop self-confidence to deal with unfamiliar situations. The method is to work, with a friend or colleague, to identify the type of situations in which one is passive or diffident and then to think out some assertive responses for such a situation, which are practised with a friend and then gradually tried out in real life. This type of role-playing has been a familiar part of many management training courses without ever being dignified with the term assertiveness training. Trainee sales representatives often role-play with trainers playing the part of difficult customers, and personnel specialists frequently carry out dummy negotiations with tough shop stewards.

There are many situations which few people enjoy dealing with, for example:

1. People talking in the row behind you in the theatre.
2. People who jump the queue.
3. Complaining in a shop about the quality of something you have bought.
4. Going to a party where you do not know anyone.

In organisational life other worries are experienced:

1. Being criticised by a superior.
2. Criticising a subordinate.
3. Advocating an unpopular point of view at a meeting.
4. Being asked to do something you do not feel capable of doing.
5. Asking subordinates to do something that you think they will resent.

The reluctance to criticise underlies the widespread ineffectiveness of performance appraisal, which has been described as 'a good idea gone wrong'. Managers chafe at the chore of filling in forms, but they also resist having to be specific in explaining to subordinates the extent to which their performance is not satisfactory. Apprehension about giving unpopular instructions is probably the most common managerial nightmare and is why managers so often dread situations in which their authority is not clear-cut. What would happen if the subordinate would not comply? In practice the confidence to say 'no' is much more difficult to find and hold to than the confidence to say 'do as I say'.

| REVIEW TOPIC 20.3 |

Identify one or two situations at work in which you typically feel diffident and think out some assertive responses or initiatives to use in them.

Bargaining and exchange

Call it bargaining, negotiating – even cajoling or bribing in some situations. A agrees with B to give something in return for desired behaviour. Sweets to a child, tips to the dustman, promotion to the executive are obvious examples. Less obvious, but perhaps more common, are friendship and favour, inclusion in a group, approval and status. Exchange methods can follow from any power source, depending on what is offered, but resource and position are the most frequent bases. (Handy, 1981, p. 123)

Bargaining covers the explicit as well as the implicit. Occasionally there is an explicit deal, with offer and consideration: 'If you can get the machine repaired by Friday, I'll put your departmental budget higher on the agenda for next week's meeting'. But these are infrequent in transactions within the organisation, as they put on an informal and unofficial basis that which should not require any extra arrangement beyond straightforward request.

More common is the implicit offering of friendship, approval or gratitude if something can be done.

'I really have a problem, can you possibly help me . . .?'
'Be a pal and . . .'
'You are the only person who could possibly do this.'
'I always believe in asking the experts.'

A similar version of this is to do favours to others, so that there is a scattering of IOUs that can be called in, the biblical bread upon the waters. The problems with this type of dealing are first that the 'rewards' offered may have to increase to maintain their value, but also that the exchanges depend on both parties being able to reward the other. Offering approval loses its value if your approval is not wanted, so that bargaining works best when the parties to the bargain are roughly equal in their power to reward each other:

> Perceptions of power inequality undermine trust, inhibit dialogue and decrease the likelihood of a constructive outcome. . . . Inequality tends to undermine trust on both ends of the imbalanced relationship, directly affecting both the person with the perceived power inferiority and the one with the perceived superiority.   (Walton, 1969, p. 98)

The process of reciprocal reward takes a slightly different form when it becomes social exchange in a continuing working relationship between people. Homans (1958) studied the 'traffic patterns' of interaction in groups and concluded:

(a) The more often people interact with each other, the more favourable will be their mutual feelings.
(b) People who interact with each other frequently are more likely to adopt similar practices than people who interact less frequently.

Collaborative influence

When it is important to people to believe in what they have to do, that belief will probably only be reached by participating in the process of deciding what should be done: they will support that which they have helped to create. There is a series of ways to do this, varying in the degree of participation. Full participation is the process whereby there is free and spontaneous discussion among members of a group, with the minimum of agenda, so that a collective will emerges from the discussion that will be supported by all members because of the full and frank exchange of opinions that produced the consensus view. This is not a denial of leadership, as there is a need for summarising, clarification and – ultimately

– action, which has to be focused. It is, however, a process which makes the leader answerable to the group.

Consultation is a process in which the leader or manager retains the responsibility for deciding what should be done, but seeks a strategy that the responding individual or group will accept. Not always do the respondents have full commitment to such decisions, because they are accepting strategy but do not have responsibility for the decision that is reached.

A different form is élite corps involvement, where members of the organisation are involved in making a decision, but their involvement is based on them being members of an élite group, called in for consultation. As they are specially selected, they are flattered and may commit themselves fully to a course of action whether their involvement is by full participation, consultation or simply being told before other people.

Collaborative influence is often achieved in the most informal ways without any calculation.

'What do you think . . .?'
'Any ideas?'
'I'd like to have a word with you about . . .'
'I'm thinking of . . . but I'm not at all sure that it's right.'

It is also not the sole preserve of those high in the hierarchy winning round those who are lower: it is just as frequently used by those seeking the backing of their organisational superiors.

Miscellaneous aspects of influencing technique

There are one or two aspects of social technique that everybody uses in conversation that can be identified and practised. The practitioner can then become more adept in social exchanges and more successful in winning people round.

1. *Reinforcement.* In our relationships with others we reward some behaviours that they produce, smiling, nodding, making agreeing noises or
   saying things that convey agreement, pleasure or wonder at the wisdom
   that is being offered. The effect of this is to reinforce the behaviour that
   is being rewarded. Equally the withdrawal of rewards prevents behaviours being reinforced. Frowning, not paying attention, yawning,
   shaking the head or saying things that express disagreement, annoyance
   or dismay tend to inhibit the behaviour with which they are associated.
   The general effect of reinforcement is to increase the amount of the
   behaviour that is being reinforced, so that a man rewarded by his wife for
   taking an interest in the children will continue taking an interest in them,
   and a trainee rewarded by the instructor for producing good work will
   produce more good work. Despite the general usefulness of this

technique, there are two reservations. First, those who are insecure, or anxious, may be so keen on rewards that they will suspend judgement to obtain them, so that the reinforcer is rewarding sycophancy. Secondly, reinforcement is most effective when provided by someone whose acceptance is worth having, so that its effect will not be great unless the personality of the reinforcer or the relationship between the reinforcer and the rewarded person is appropriate.

2. *Reward.* An aspect of manipulative style that is more pervasive than simple reinforcement. It is described by Argyle (1972, p. 74) as rewardingness, and deals with the way in which a person becomes relatively popular and influential on the opinions of others. The manager rewards others by being responsive to their needs and interests, responding quickly to requests for information, return telephone calls and assistance. Explanations of why certain things are needed can be a reward, as can suggesting how problems could be overcome and inviting comments on proposals that are being put forward. This is not quite the same as being permissive or *laissez-faire*, as some core of direction is usually needed. In deciding policy directions, for instance, the manager working with a group of others will not want to direct at the beginning of a discussion as it is important to generate as many ideas and alternatives as possible, so they will do no more than start the conversational ball rolling. Later, however, there will be a need to pull strands of argument together, find a small number of choices for further discussion, and focus thinking on those. Later still it will be necessary to adopt a stricter style when discussion moves through decision-making to action.

The essence of being rewarding in one's behaviour is to be warm and friendly towards other people, but the way in which the rewards are offered will vary between individuals, as will the way in which they are received. Cheerful exuberance may be interpreted as overbearing; congratulation may be construed as being unctuous; an attempt not to embarrass may be regarded as coldness. Managers also have to exercise control, as they cannot always respond in the rewarding way that the other would like.

In these situations the manager should look for an alternative. The young person in the policy discussion who is advocating a line of action that others regard as haywire will not get the proposal discussed further, but has to be kept 'in play' to redirect their attention constructively towards the other ideas that are being considered. The person has to be rewarded by some alternative such as an agreement to look at the proposal again in three months' time, or a frank acknowledgement that the proposal is very well regarded but too risky for over-cautious colleagues.

3. *Participation by the other.* A cumbersome phrase to encompass a range of ways in which one sees a matter from the point of view of the other

person and so both rewards that person and participates with them in deciding what to do. The main aspect of this is the understanding of a different frame of reference, which is a sociological term to describe a set of basic assumptions that determines behaviour and attitude. This is most relevant on a large scale, and there is the regular example of managers and politicians failing to understand the apparent bloody-mindedness of people who take industrial action at a time when that action will clearly imperil the jobs that the action is intended to protect. The reason is that the people taking the action have a quite different frame of reference, leading to different expectations, priorities and objectives. To them their action is logical and only the management are bloody-minded. Similar differences of view affect what is called 'cashless pay'.

Ray Hughes has worked in a clothing factory for 37 years. On Thursday evenings he receives his weekly wages, paid in cash, of approximately £150 after deduction of income tax and national insurance. On the way home he deposits £20 in his Post Office savings account and puts £30 in his back pocket to cover his personal expenditure for the week. He then gives £100 to his wife, who deals with all the household expenditure. He and his working colleagues are resisting a proposal by the management of their factory that they should be paid by cheque. Not only does this involve the inconvenience of cashing the cheque, but it brings nearer the day when a major principle would be lost. Mrs Hughes might find out exactly how much her husband gets paid, and in many families that is a jealously preserved confidence. The management persist in wanting to pay by cheque to overcome the time and expense of handling large amounts of cash, which pose a serious security risk. They point out all the advantages of having a bank account to Ray Hughes and his friends, but the fundamental difference in their frames of reference makes their exchanges a dialogue of the deaf.

On a one-to-one level managers need to think themselves into the position of the person with whom they are talking, to see the topic as clearly as possible from the other point of view in order to make the most of the exchange.

In this chapter we have reviewed some of the ways in which individual managers can get their own way and get things done without having the dubious benefit of formal authority to issue orders. All the comments centre round two aspects of style: first, the confidence of the manager in setting out what is wanted, being sure, clear and precise; and secondly, the ability of that manager to work with the responses and needs of the other person, rewarding, and understanding the other point of view. To be effective, the manager needs not only to understand but also to practise. What we have described here are things that all of us do to some extent every day of our lives, as part of being a member of the human race interacting with others of our species. If we can understand that interactive process better, we can then practise our behaviours and improve our performance.

SUMMARY PROPOSITIONS

20.1 People have primary needs and secondary needs. Secondary needs are those which have the greatest influence on working behaviour.

20.2 Stereotyping is a necessary mode of behaviour to cope with novel situations but limits a manager's scope for getting the best from themselves and others working together.

20.3 Winning consent without having authority is becoming more important to managers because of the increasing number of situations in which they have no authority, their formal authority is curbed or they have limited expertise.

20.4 To win consent managers need to understand themselves, the other person in the interaction and the interaction itself.

20.5 Methods of approaching particular situations include assertiveness, manipulation and persuasion.

20.6 Aspects of style leading to influence include reinforcement, reward, and participation by the other.

PUTTING IT INTO PRACTICE

Next time you want to influence someone, make a list of what is in it for them. Try to think of at least three reasons, from their point of view, for doing it.

Next time you are feeling aggrieved because someone has mistreated or misunderstood you, write down what it is they have misunderstood. Now think what you could have done or said to make their job of understanding you easier. They may of course continue to misunderstand you!

References

Argyle, M., 1972, *The Psychology of Interpersonal Behaviour*, Penguin Books, Harmondsworth, Middlesex.

Arnold, J., Robertson, I. T. and Cooper, C. L., 1991, *Work Psychology: Understanding Human Behaviour in the Workplace*, Pitman, London.

Goldthorpe, J. H., Lockwood, D., Bechhofer, N. and Platt, J., 1968, *The Affluent Worker: Industrial Attitudes and Behaviour*, Cambridge University Press.

Handy, C. B., 1981, *Understanding Organisations*, Penguin Books, Harmondsworth, Middlesex.

Herzberg, F., 1968, One more time: how do you motivate employees?, *Harvard Business Review*, Jan/Feb.

Homans, G. C., 1958, Social behaviour as exchange, *American Journal of Sociology*, vol. 62, pp. 597–606.

Lewin, K., 1952, in *Field Theory in Social Science*, ed. Cartwright, D., Tavistock, London.

Maslow, A. H., 1954, *Motivation and Personality*, Harper & Row, New York.

McGregor, D., 1960, *The Human Side of Enterprise*, McGraw-Hill, New York.

Scase, R. and Goffee, R., 1989, *Reluctant Managers: Their Work and Lifestyles*, Unwin Hyman, London.

Schein, E. H., 1970, *Organizational Psychology*, 2nd edn, Prentice Hall, Englewood Cliffs, New Jersey.

Steers, R. W. and Porter, L. W. (eds), 1987, *Motivation and Work Behaviour*, 4th edn, McGraw-Hill, New York.

Torrington, D. P. and Weightman, J. B., 1989, *The Reality of School Management*, Blackwell, Oxford.

Vroom, V. and Deci, E., 1974, *Management and Motivation*, Penguin Books, London.

Walton, R. E., 1969, *Interpersonal Peacemaking: Third Party Consultations*, Addison Wesley, Reading, Mass.

Zalkind, S. S. and Costello, T. W., 1962, Perception: some recent research and implications for administrators, *Administrative Science Quarterly*, no. 7, pp. 218–35.

Chapter 21

Interpersonal communication

In face-to-face situations you speak, you listen and you question. This chapter is about the skills involved in all those activities, but especially the second and third. First there is a model of the communications process, then a section on listening skills and finally a series of questioning and associated methods for dealing with the range of situations that occur in interpersonal contacts.

Politicians who say in television interviews, 'I would like to make it perfectly clear . . .' may be doing more to clarify their own thoughts to themselves than to increase the accuracy of the message received by the audience. They risk over-emphasising what they want to say rather than what is being heard and understood by the audience. In contrast, the manager who concentrates on feedback and listening will be clear to the audience, as the feedback and listening constantly monitor the accuracy of the picture being put together in the minds of the audience. A well-tried way of illustrating this is to use the analogy of telecommunications.

The communications model

Figure 21.1 shows that a person with an abstract idea to get across to someone else begins by encoding it. The idea is translated into speech patterns and actions to substitute for, or embellish, what is to be said. The signal is then transmitted by the words or actions being produced. The receivers pick up the message with some or all of their senses and decode it. That decoding is not a simple mechanical process but an interpretation, and the code book used is that of the receiver's personal experience, expectation, trust, initial level of understanding and all the other factors that make for individual difference in perception. It is clearly in the encoding/decoding process that error will occur. The sender of the message will try to use a code that is appropriate to the receiver who will decode the message in its context. After decoding there is the final loop that closes the circuit of

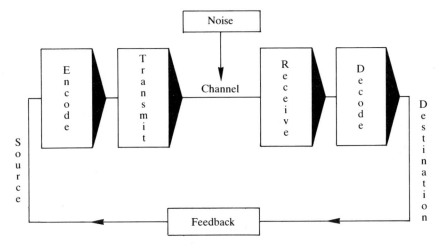

Figure 21.1 The communications model.

communication: feedback. The receiver gives some indication to the transmitter that the message has been received, and the nature of the response will usually indicate something of the quality of understanding.

Communication is therefore both mutual and circular, and feedback offers the opportunity for correction or reshaping of the original message. The sender can add to or alter the first message in order to clarify it and the receiver can test the decoding to make sure that the message registered is the message that the sender intended.

An example might be the thirsty man who approaches a bar. He encodes his thought by saying, 'A glass of beer, please'. His preoccupation with his own thirst is such that he provides little information apart from the bare necessity of beer. The bartender has little initial difficulty as people constantly come into the bar asking for beer. It is only the person asking for a glass of water who might be required to repeat the question. However, there are different sizes of glass and different types of beer, so there is a range of responses that will seek clarification of the original message:

Looking puzzled, to show that the message is insufficient
Offering a choice – 'half or a pint?'
Making a suggestion – 'a pint of best bitter?'
Seeking confirmation of a guess – 'a half of your usual?'

Each of these will lead to the feedback loop being completed by the bartender pouring what is required.

A further component of the communications process is 'noise'. That is anything that interferes with the quality of the message transmitted and received. We are all familiar with the experience of tuning a radio set to a signal in such a way as to avoid 'static'. In face-to-face communication the idea of noise can be used to cover all manner of things from the obvious problem of making yourself heard and understood above the sound of the pneumatic drill in the road outside, to the less obvious minor distractions of inattention, a familiar perfume that you cannot quite identify, or wondering where he bought those shoes.

The competent manager gives careful attention to speaking, or transmission, making sure that the initial message is complete and couched in terms suitable to the receiver. This is not simply articulating clearly; it is also remembering who the receiver is and what the context is, including the problems of stereotyping, cognitive dissonance and the frame of reference.

| REVIEW TOPIC 21.1 |

Tomorrow make a mental note of incidents during the day when someone else does not immediately understand what you say, or interprets you incorrectly. In the evening review each incident to work out what went wrong and how you could have avoided the problem.

Listening

To transmit effectively we have to listen carefully, because of the mutual and circular process that communication comprises. We have to be on the lookout for signals and willing to spend the time needed to listen and build understanding, deliberately holding back our own thoughts, which would divert or compete with the other. This is unusual. If you eavesdrop on conversations, you usually hear two people competing with each other to speak rather than to listen. They are putting on a display, using the other person rather like a punch-bag. Careful and patient listeners are able to build on what the other is saying by planting their own ideas in the seed bed of what the other is interested in, or concerned about, and able to understand.

> Unfortunately, few people are good listeners. Even at the purely informational level researchers claim that 75 per cent of oral communication is ignored, misunderstood or quickly forgotten. Rarer still is the ability to listen for the deepest meanings in what people say.   (Bolton, 1987, p. 30)

This ability to extract the real message from all the mass of material that is expressed has been called 'listening with the third ear' (Reik, 1948) and is almost the opposite of the example of the man in the bar who provided too little information. Many people provide too much, largely by being bound up with their own preoccupations, and the third ear enables the listener to pick out the significant elements and to discard the remainder.

We spend a great deal of time listening. Maude (1977) cites studies showing that dieticians spend up to 63% of the time listening and 22%

talking, while adult employees generally spend 42% of their time listening and 32% talking. Too often, however, our listening is passive, as we simply wait for the other person to finish. Sproston and Sutcliffe (1990) provide excellent guidance on how to listen effectively. Here are some features of listening skill.

Tone of voice

Different feelings express themselves in different voice characteristics. An American counselling expert suggests the following probable meanings for various characteristics:

Characteristic	*Probable meaning*
Monotone voice	Boredom
Slow speed, low pitch	Depression
High voice, emphasis	Enthusiasm
Ascending tone	Astonishment
Abrupt speech	Defensiveness
Terse speed, loud tone	Anger
High pitch, drawn-out speech	Disbelief

Giving attention

We listen best by giving attention to what the other person is saying. Inclining the body towards the other person is a signal of attentiveness, so we need to remember our posture, which should be inclined forward and facing the other squarely with an open posture: folded arms can be inhibiting.

Eye contact is crucial to good listening, but is a subtle art:

> Effective eye contact expresses interest and a desire to listen. It involves focusing one's eyes softly on the speaker and occasionally shifting the gaze from his face to other parts of the body, to a gesturing hand, for example, and then back to the face and then to eye contact once again. Poor eye contact occurs when a listener repeatedly looks away from the speaker, stares at him constantly or blankly, or looks away as soon as the speaker looks at the listener. (Bolton, 1987, p. 36)

The distinction between 'focusing one's eyes softly' and staring is vital, though difficult to describe, and competence in eye contact is never easy to establish. It is one of the most intimate ways of relating to a person and many managers fear that the relationship may become too close. Even if you are happy with it. you may find that the other person is uncomfortable with you looking through the 'window' of their eyes.

We also show physical responses in our attentiveness. First we have to avoid distracting the other person by physical behaviour that is unrelated to what is being said: fiddling with a pen, playing with car keys, scrutinising your fingernails, wringing your hands, brushing specks of dust off your sleeves are a few typical behaviours that indicate inattention. Skilled listeners not only suppress these, they also develop minor gestures and posture variants that are directly responsive to what the other is saying.

Silence

Being silent helps you to listen by providing space for incoming messages, but it also provides opportunities to observe the other person and to think about what is being said. Most people are uncomfortable with silence and try to fill it with inconsequential chat, but this interferes with listening. Being silent, and deliberately leaving verbal lulls in face-to-face situations, provides the opportunity for the other person to say more – perhaps more than was initially intended.

Silence still has to be attentive and the longer the silence, the harder it is to be attentive: think of the last lecture you attended and how hard it was to maintain attentiveness.

Silence may be necessary while someone processes a new thought. A question posed in performance appraisal, for instance, may be greeted with initial silence. The unwise interviewer will fret about having disconcerted the respondent and will fill the silence by suggesting the answer, or rewording the question, when in fact the respondent needs the silence to produce a considered answer. Mayerson (1979, p. 37) suggests that thirty seconds is not too long to leave a silence:

> . . . it is more helpful at first to let the silence happen. There is a temptation to fill it up as if it were an empty basket. This has negative effects, especially if the silence is a productive one or one of great feeling... The length of time one should let silence alone is arbitrary. It depends on the cues one is getting and one's own comfort with the situation. A very general rule of thumb is 30 seconds. That is a long time. More than 30 seconds lets everyone forget what was happening, and takes the participants away from the emphasis or the subject.

REVIEW TOPIC 21.2

Consider the following sayings:
'The audience were on the edge of their seats.'
'She gave me the cold shoulder.'
'He remained poker-faced throughout.'
'Speech is silver; silence golden.'
'She is down in the mouth today.'
'He was all ears.'
'She is a stuck-up person.'
'He is on his high horse.'
'Her face lit up . . .'
What do these suggest to you about effective and ineffective listening?

Reflection

In reflection, the listener picks up and restates the content of what has just been said. Beveridge provides an excellent summary of its use in counselling situations:

> . . . a selective form of listening in which the listener picks out the emotional overtones of a statement and 'reflects' these back to the respondent without any attempt to evaluate them. This means that the interviewer expresses neither approval nor disapproval, neither sympathy nor condemnation.
>
> (Beveridge, 1968, p. 72)

At a more prosaic level, reflection provides indication of listening. This indicates that you are attending to what the other person is saying, you have understood it and you are providing the opportunity for any misunderstanding to be pointed out. The standard method is paraphrasing, by which the listener states the essence of what has been said. This is done concisely and gives the speaker a chance to review what has been said.

Mayerson (1979) describes a similar tactic as empathic feedback. An example of how this would be done is in the following exchange:

> Respondent: 'Seniority does not count for as much as it should in this company'.
> Reflection: 'You feel there is not enough acknowledgement of loyalty and long service?'

Alternative reactions would have a different effect, for example:

> 'You sound like someone who has been passed over for promotion', or 'Oh, I don't know about that'.

Both alternatives push the respondent on to the defensive, expecting a justification of what has been said. Another alternative:

> 'Well, I think seniority has been over-emphasised in the past'

stifles the opinion before it has been fully expressed. The respondent who is diffident will not develop the feeling further, so the matter cannot be resolved. There is also the danger that any one of these evaluative reactions could evoke a comeback from the respondent which complies with the view suggested by the interviewer. This is the same problem as that of the leading question, which is dealt with shortly.

Questioning and associated methods

We now consider specific aspects of method in communication by setting out a number of ploys, grouped into five categories – opening, questioning, feedback, braking and closing, and general – that can be used to handle different stages of interpersonal communication.

1. Opening

Interactions usually open with a degree of skirmishing as each party assesses the other and tunes in. This is followed by more subtle behaviours to support the relationship and maintain the credibility of the attitudes that were demonstrated at the beginning.

RAPPORT

Enabling the participants in an interpersonal exchange to interact effectively.

This is the sort of thing most people do quite instinctively a dozen times a day. 'Hello, how are you today?'. 'Can't complain. How are you?'. 'Not so bad for the time of year, I suppose. Be better by five o'clock'. 'Ha, won't we all! Well, see you later'. 'Right, cheers'. That type of ritual conversation takes place on staircases and in changing rooms regularly, and the same pair of people will say much the same things to each other day after day, but they have 'bonded' at the beginning of a new day and the fact that their exchange is always the same has a certain reassurance about it. In interviews and committees, however, there is greater formality in the exchanges which make this stage of the proceedings more important than in casual encounters, especially when strangers are meeting for the first time, as in most employment interviews and much selling.

All parties will have an interest in setting up rapport, but in the more formal situations it is the duty of the clear controlling figure – the selection interviewer, the appraiser, the mentor – to take the initiative. Candidates do not expect to have to put selectors at their ease. Here are some of the standard methods.

(a) *Small talk*

The staple component is small talk that does not matter in substance. Most common is to discuss the weather, so that the participants can use an innocuous topic to exchange words and sounds while assessing the other's personality, and beginning to relax in the presence of their counterpart.

(b) *Friendly, easy manner*

This is much easier to advocate than to produce. In many of the situations the person not directing the interaction will be wary or ill at ease. Allaying that suspicion will nearly always help the conduct of the meeting, so that exchanges become more frank and informative. The first step is to show friendliness in the opening display, but that will have to register with the receiver as friendliness and not as condescension, falseness or casual indifference. This is difficult to do and most problems occur with people who try too hard and come across as insincere.

(c) *Calm attention*

The interviewer who is able to project a feeling of calm and quiet will win a response from the other person more quickly and constructively than the interviewer who deliberately or unwittingly conveys an atmosphere of busyness and preoccupation. The manager who can create an unhurried atmosphere will complete the encounter more quickly than the person who emphasises that only a few minutes are available. Paying attention to what is being said will focus the thinking and responses of the other person.

(d) *Explaining the procedure*

In any interaction the respondent will be uncertain about what is to happen, through being dependent on the other to direct proceedings. The interviewer can build rapport by explaining aspects of the process – how long the conversation is likely to take and what the interviewer would like to accomplish are useful here. If the respondent is to take an initiative at any stage, this is usefully signalled now: '. . . there will obviously be questions that you want to ask, and there will be plenty of time for that later on'.

We must ensure that establishing rapport is not mechanical, but a ritual that is used to make the interaction work. Examples of falseness in rapport exchanges are the health service administrator who opened each selection interview with a question about the candidate's journey. As each person replied with one of the normal variations of 'Very nice, thank you', he reacted with a standard, hearty 'Splendid!'. Unfortunately he produced the same 'Splendid!' when one candidate told him that she had had a puncture and arrived ten minutes late. An earnest interviewer of school-leavers applying for jobs in a well-known bank always exchanged pleasantries for three minutes with a strained smile before changing expression to one of pained disapproval and saying, 'Well, I think we've established rapport, so I will proceed with the questions'.

REWARD

Sustaining the smooth interaction between the participants in an exchange.

Rapport does not take too long or it becomes laboured. After a very few minutes the conversation moves to the substance that the two people have come together to discuss. It is important, however, that the interviewer does not leave behind the warm and responsive behaviour displayed at the beginning: that has to be maintained throughout the encounter. Some of the conventional methods are given here.

(a) *Interest*

We all respond positively when a listener is interested in what we are saying, so the manager will encourage and draw out the respondent by showing interest in what is being said. If it is possible also to agree with what is being said, the reinforcement of the respondent will be greater.

(b) *Affirmation*

A talker is always looking for the affirmation of the listener in order to complete the feedback loop in the communication circuit. The most common form is the head nod, and many public speakers look for head nods as a way of judging the supportive mood of the audience. Other ways of affirming are the use of the eyes. These are too subtle and individual to describe, but we each have a repertoire of signals to indicate such reactions as encouragement, surprise and understanding. When the eyes are part of a smile, there will be stronger reward to the talker. There are also words and phrases, 'Really?', 'Go on . . .', 'Yes . . .', 'Of course . . .', 'My word . . .', 'You were saying . . .'.

(c) *Noises*

Conversation contains a variety of noises that are ways of rewarding the other party. They are impossible to reproduce in words but are usually variations on a theme of 'Mmm . . .' and they form a part of the conversation that is inarticulate yet meaningful, and keep things going without being interruptions.

EXPLODING
Bringing into the open feelings that are latent, but being suppressed.

This last, melodramatically named opening ploy is for use in those specialised situations where there is some pent-up feeling that the interviewer believes should be expressed early in order to clear the way for subsequent discussion. It is used in discipline or grievance settlement on occasions, but is less common in other encounters.

(a) *Letting off steam*

Many managers ignore signals of frustration in respondents because they do not want to get into a difficult or contentious situation, and the warning signals are disregarded. If, however, a respondent is showing obvious signs of anger or distress at the start of an encounter, it can be helpful to encourage the blow-up and the rush of feeling that follows. It will not solve the problem, but it will at least make the rest of the conversation more constructive.

(b) *Digging*

Sometimes the anxiety or disappointment in the respondent is latent, but not pent up to the extent that the lid will blow off the head of steam. There may still be the need to bring the disquiet to the surface in an attempt to prevent further festering. The signals are harder to read and will probably only be seen by someone who knows the respondent well, who may then try a sally like 'There seems to be something on your mind?'.

2. Questioning

Questioning is obviously a large part of interpersonal communication, but the competent manager is able to classify questions into different types and work out the appropriate way to use each type.

CLOSED QUESTIONS
Questions that seek precise, terse information.

When we want precise, factual information we close the question to control the answer:

'Is it Clarke with an e, or without?'
'Who is in charge?'

These are useful when you want clear, straightforward data, and most encounters feature closed questioning at some point.

OPEN-ENDED QUESTIONS
Questions avoiding terse replies, and inviting respondents to develop their opinions.

Here the respondent is invited to speak without having the interviewer prescribe what the answer should be. The question does little more than introduce a topic to talk about:

'How are you getting on?'
'What does your present job entail?'
'What are your future plans?'

Open-ended questions often come at the beginning of an encounter as a means of developing the rapport. It makes things easy for the respondent, who is given latitude to decide what to talk about, with the opportunity to relax and get going. Their main purpose, however, is to obtain the type of deeper information that the closed question misses, as the shape of the answer is not predetermined by the questioner. You are informed not simply by the content of the answers, but by what is selected and emphasised.

DIRECT QUESTIONS
Questions 'insisting' on a reply.

Now the manager is asserting his or her authority and the 'right to know'. Direct questions use the prescriptive style of the closed question but seek fuller information of the type that open-ended questions usually deliver, unless the respondent is being evasive:

'Did you take the money?'
'Why did you leave that job?'
'Did you, or did you not, clock Charlie Miller in yesterday?'

INDIRECT QUESTIONS
Questions taking an indirect approach on a difficult matter.

These have the same general objective as direct questions but take an indirect approach. Higham illustrates how an indirect question can be a more effective approach than the direct alternative:

> 'What were your colleagues like in that job?' is preferable to 'Did you get on all right with the rest of the office?'. But the virtues of the indirect question go further still. A blunt 'Did you like that job?' almost suggests you didn't, or at least raises the suspicion that the interviewer thinks you didn't! Put indirectly as 'What gave you the most satisfaction in that job?', it has the merit of concentrating on the work rather than the person . . .   (Higham, 1979, p. 134)

PROBES
Questioning to obtain information that the other person is trying to conceal.

This is not so much a style of questioning as a tactical sequence to deal with those situations in which supportive and encouraging interviewers can be deflected by respondents who are not to be cajoled, by the winning ways of reward and open-ended questions, into divulging information they prefer to conceal. When this happens the questioner has to make an important, and perhaps difficult decision: do you respect the respondent's unwillingness and let the matter rest, or do you persist with the enquiry? Reluctance is quite common in disciplinary and grievance interviews, where someone may be reluctant to criticise a colleague, and in employment interviews there may be an aspect of the recent employment history that the candidate wishes to gloss over. The most common sequence for the probe takes the following form.

(a) *Direct questions*
    Open-ended questions give too much latitude to the respondent, so direct questioning is needed. Careful phrasing may avoid a defensive reply.

(b) *Supplementaries*
    If the first direct question produces only evasion, then a supplementary will be needed, reiterating the first with different phrasing.

(c) *Closing*
    If the probe is used when the rapport is well established, it stands the best chance of being successful, but it then needs to be closed skilfully. If the information has been wrenched out like a bad tooth and the interviewer looks horrified or sits in stunned silence, then the respondent will feel put down beyond redemption. The interviewer needs to make the divulged secret less awful than the respondent had feared, so that the encounter can proceed with reasonable confidence. For example:

> 'Yes, well you must be glad to have that behind you'.

There is a dirty trick that can be used as an alternative method of probing. Although no reader of this book would ever dream of using this tactic, it is described below so that you can see it coming if anyone tries it on you.

(d) *Overstatement*

If a suggestion is put that implies a reason for the reluctance that is more grave than the real reason, then the respondent will rush to correct the false impression.

Q. 'There appears to be a gap in the employment history at the beginning of last year. You weren't in prison or anything, were you?'.

A. 'Good heavens, no. I was having treatment for . . . er . . . well, for alcoholism, actually'.

A thoroughly dirty trick, but effective.

PROPOSING QUESTION
A question used to put forward an idea.

This is for feeling a way out of an impasse, and is to be found in negotiation, brainstorming and other situations where there is difficulty in pulling people together. It is a ploy to test for consensus without being so positive that it then has to be defended if consensus does not emerge:

'Well, now that we have the consultant's report we must clearly accept Helen's earlier suggestion'.

This is either a tactic for the acknowledged leader in a group, or it is a bid for leadership by one member challenging the rest to disagree.

RHETORICAL QUESTION
A question forbidding disagreement.

This is really a way of making a statement, as it is putting a question in such a way that the answer is too obvious to state. Replying to a mixture of allegations about incompetent behaviour, a manager might ask:

'How can we be slack on purchasing procedures and too strict on reorder levels, both at the same time?'.

3. Feedback

There is one ploy to be mentioned under this general heading, although some of the main behaviours have already been described under reflection, rapport and reward.

SUMMARY *and* RERUN
Drawing together in summary various points from the other person and
obtaining confirmation that you have understood correctly.

The respondent will produce lots of information in an interview and you
will be selecting that which is to be retained and understood. From time to
time you interject a summary sentence or two with an interrogative
inflection:

> 'You did take the wallet out of his locker, then, but this was because he
> had asked you to fetch it for him so that he could repay Charlie his
> fiver?'.
> 'So the difficulty in meeting the sales target has been more to do with
> production problems than with customer demand?'.

This tactic serves several useful purposes. It shows the interviewer is
listening, gives the respondent the chance to correct any false impressions
and reinforces the key points that are being retained. It is also a useful way
of making progress, as the interjection is easily followed by another
open-ended question – 'Now perhaps we can turn to . . .'.

| REVIEW TOPIC 21.3 |

Recall a recent face-to-face situation in which you were involved – an
interview, a discussion, a *tête-à-tête*, a lesson, an argument. Identify three ways
in which the other person was especially effective, and analyse why. Then
think of three things about your own performance that did not seem to be
effective. Why was that?

---

4. Braking and closing

Most of the suggestions so far have been to encourage a response, but it is
easy to nod and smile your way into a situation of such cosy relaxation that
the respondent talks on and on . . . and on, rather like lying back in a warm
bath. Also, there are a surprising number of interviewers who can begin an
interview smoothly but have great difficulty closing, so there are two ploys
to suggest.

BRAKING
Slowing the rate of talking by the other person.

You may eventually need to become peevish with the over-talkative
respondent, but braking provides a sequence of less drastic techniques to
shut people up. You will seldom need to go beyond the first two or three,

but five are offered in case you have to deal with a really tough case, like a university lecturer or someone selling you double glazing.

(a) *Closed questions*

It has already been pointed out that closed questions invite terse replies. One or two interjected to clarify specific points may stem the tide.

(b) *Facial expression*

The brow is furrowed to indicate mild disagreement, lack of understanding or professional anxiety. The reassuring nods stop and the generally encouraging, supportive behaviours of reward are withdrawn.

(c) *Abstraction*

If the respondent does not notice the change of facial expression, the next step is for the eyes to glaze over, showing that they belong to a person whose attention has now shifted away from the respondent and towards lunch or last night's football match.

(d) *Looking away*

To look at one's watch during a conversation is a very strong signal indeed, as it clearly indicates that time is running out. Most people are very reluctant to do it and often an interviewer will take the watch off beforehand so as to be able to look at it discreetly during the interview. An alternative is to keep it on your wrist so that you can look at it more obviously and so slow down a verbose respondent. Other, milder, ways of looking away are looking for matches or glasses, looking at your notes or looking at the aircraft making a noise outside the window. A rather brutal variant is to allow your attention to be caught by something the respondent is wearing – a lapel badge, a tie, a ring or piece of jewellery, maybe. Putting on your glasses to see it more clearly is really rather unsporting!

(e) *Interruption*

The most blunt of methods. Most people avoid it at all costs, but in the end you have no choice.

CLOSING

Finishing the exchange without 'losing' the respondent.

In closing an interview future action is either clarified or confirmed. Also, respondents take a collection of attitudes away with them, and these can be influenced by the way the encounter is closed, particularly after counselling or disciplinary interviews. There is a simple procedure:

(a) *First signal, verbal plus papers*

The interviewer uses a phrase to indicate that the interview is nearing its end:

'Well now, I think we have covered the ground, don't you?'.
'I don't think there is anything more I want to ask you. Is there anything further you want from me?'.

In this way you signal the impending close at the same time as obtaining the respondent's confirmation. There is additional emphasis provided by some paper play. A small collection of notes can be gathered together and stacked neatly, or a notebook can be closed.

(b) *Second signal, explaining the next step*
The interviewer confirms what will happen next:

> 'Can we meet again next week, to see how things are proceeding?'.
> 'There are still one or two people to see, but we will write to you no later than the end of the week'.

(c) *Closing signal, stand up*
As the ground has been prepared, all that is now required is the decisive act to make the close. By standing up the interviewer forces the respondent to stand as well and there remain only the odds and ends of handshakes and parting smiles.

5. General points

Some common behaviours can produce an effect that is different from what is intended, so here are some approaches to avoid.

LEADING QUESTIONS
Questions that imply what the 'correct' answer is.

They will not necessarily produce an answer which is informative, what they will produce is an answer in line with the lead that has been given:

> 'Would you agree with me that . . .'.
> 'I believe in strict control of expenditure and firm handling of debtors: what about you?'.

Unless you are really using the question rhetorically, leaders are of little value, and can be misleading in the replies they produce.

UNREASONABLE EXHORTATION
Expecting a change in the emotional state of someone else as a result of complying with an instruction.

This is a commonplace which does more for the person doing the exhorting than for the person who is exhorted because the change that is sought is rarely a simple matter of will:

> 'Stop crying'.
> 'Relax'.
> 'Cheer up'.

MULTIPLE QUESTIONS
Questions that give the other person too many inputs at one time.

This is sometimes found in interviewers who are trying very hard to efface themselves and let the respondent get on with the talking, so there is an occasional attempt to put a number of questions together. The idea is to provide the respondent with a stock to draw on when ready:

'Well, can you just tell me why Fred threw the spanner at you, if it really was Fred, what you did when you saw it on the floor and what on earth the start of all this silly horseplay was?'.

However helpful the interviewer intends to be, the effect is that the respondent will usually forget the later parts of the question, feel disconcerted and ask, 'What was the last part of the question?'. By this time the interviewer has also forgotten, so they are both embarrassed.

TABOO QUESTIONS
Questions that infringe the reasonable personal privacy of the person to whom they are put.

Though there is a proper place for the probe, there are some questions that have to be avoided, usually in selection interviews, as they could be interpreted as discriminatory. It is at least potentially discriminatory in selection, for instance, to ask women how many children they have and what their husbands do for a living. Questions about religion or place of birth are also to be avoided.

Also some questions may do no more than satisfy the idle curiosity of the questioner. If there is no point in asking them, they should not be put.

MECHANICAL BEHAVIOUR
Routine questions that never vary, with contrived, stilted reactions to the respondents' replies.

Mechanical behaviour is suitable for some situations, where carefully phrased closed questions, developed over years of experience, efficiently produce precise information. This is appropriate, for instance, for those registering births and deaths, or for the initial stages of many medical investigations. Most managerial encounters need to go further than this because there is a working relationship to be created, sustained or repaired.

Transactional analysis

To conclude this chapter there is an account of a specialised understanding of the exchanges between people.

The theory propounded by Eric Berne (1966) as the basis for transactional analysis is that there are three ego states of the individual. The parent ego state is one of authority and superiority, and a person acting in this state is typically dominant and scolding. It is the state in which all our value judgements are stored and the state of a person every time he acts in a way learned from his parents. The child ego state contains all the impulses that are natural to an infant. There is all the unpredictability of tantrum and charm, obedience and defiance, tears and laughter, sulks and joy. The parent acts in a way he was taught; the child acts in the way he feels, impulsive and uncensored. The adult ego state is objective and rational. No matter what prejudices or emotions were communicated by parents, someone in the adult state deals objectively with reality, analysing situations as realistically as possible: processing data, estimating probabilities and making decisions. It is not prejudiced by the values of the parent nor by the natural urges of the child. These labels have nothing to do with age, nor do individuals fit into only one of the three categories. All of us have all three states and spend each day moving from one to another. The manager trying to win people round will discern the ego state of the other person and respond appropriately. Choosing the appropriate response requires an understanding of the three basic types of transaction: complementary, crossed and ulterior.

A *complementary transaction* is:

> . . . appropriate and expected and follows the natural order of healthy human
> relationship.   (Berne, 1966, p. 29)

They take place between any two ego states, where the transactors are in the ego state appropriate to the transaction. Figure 21.2 shows first a diagram of a transaction where both parties are in the adult state and secondly a transaction where one is in parent and the other in child. Both are complementary, with the lines of transaction running in parallel, understanding and appropriate action being achieved.

Crossed transactions are those in which the opening statement elicits an inappropriate response. Complementary transaction can continue indefinitely with communication and understanding being sustained. Crossed transactions cause an interruption. Either there is no communication or the subject is changed. Figure 21.3 shows two crossed transactions, first one in which the manager produces an inappropriate response and secondly one producing an inappropriate response from the subordinate.

Ulterior transactions are more complex as they always involve more than two ego states. The most common form is where a real message is disguised under an explicit, but socially more acceptable, transaction. The communication is not straightforward as there is always an ulterior motive: a game is being played. In Figure 21.4 we see an opening statement by a manager who wants a member of his staff to accept a move out of marketing into public relations because he feels it will be a good career move, but he

Subordinate:

'Will we be working overtime on Saturday?'

Ⓟ Ⓟ Manager:

Ⓐ ⟺ Ⓐ 'As far as I know at the moment, yes we will.'

ⓒ ⓒ

Subordinate:

'I've got a splitting headache. Do you think I could go home?'

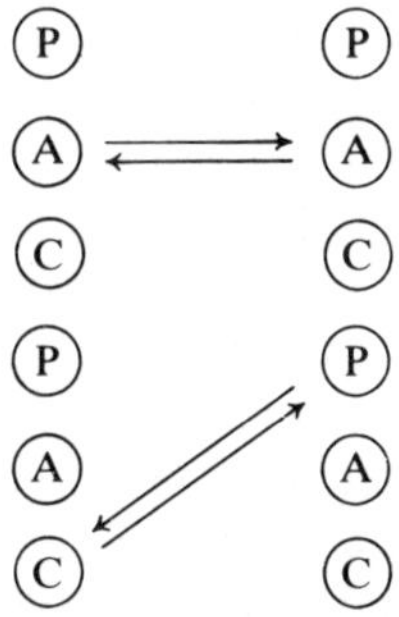

Ⓟ Ⓟ Manager:

Ⓐ Ⓐ 'Yes, you get home to bed. It'll be all right.'

ⓒ ⓒ

Figure 21.2 Complementary transactions.

Subordinate:

'I haven't had my copy of the new works handbook. Have you got a spare?'

Ⓟ Ⓟ Manager:

Ⓐ ⟶ Ⓐ 'Surely you can see I'm busy. Can't you pick one up at the office on your way home?'

ⓒ ⓒ

Manager:

'According to the rota, it's your turn to stay behind and clean up.'

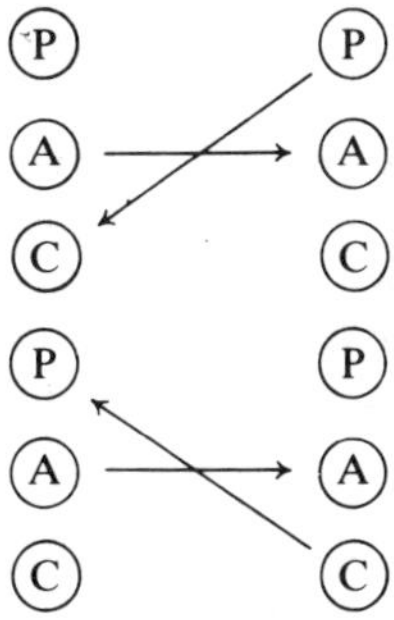

Ⓟ Ⓟ Subordinate:

Ⓐ ⟶ Ⓐ 'Oh no. I'm going out tonight. Can't you get someone else to do it?'

ⓒ ⓒ

Figure 21.3 Crossed transactions.

Manager:

'They have an interesting vacancy in PR, but I'm not sure you're ready for it.'

('Go on. Pick up the challenge.')

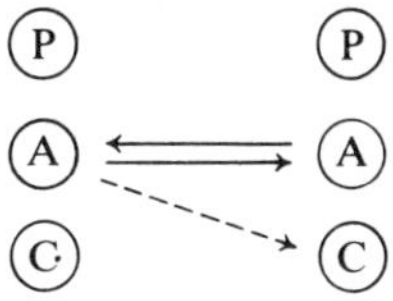

Ⓟ Ⓟ Subordinate:

Ⓐ ⟺ Ⓐ 'No, I suppose I had better get a bit more experience before I try for a move.'

ⓒ ⤑ ⓒ

Outcome: the manager loses the game.

Manager:

'They have an interesting vacancy in PR, but I'm not sure you're ready for it.'

('Go on. Pick up the challenge.')

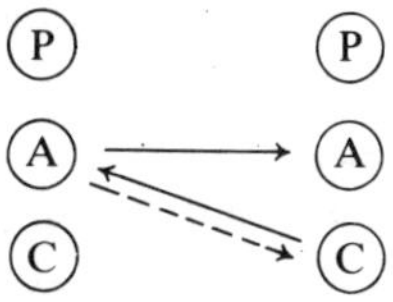

Ⓟ Ⓟ Subordinate:

Ⓐ ⟺ Ⓐ 'Why not? I think I stand as good a chance as anybody else, and I'd certainly like to give it a try.'

ⓒ ⤑ ⓒ

Outcome: the manager loses the game.

Figure 21.4 Ulterior transactions.

also believes that the member of staff will not be keen to make the change. The solid arrow in the drawing shows the explicit adult–adult message and the dotted line shows the implicit adult–child message. The response is either what the manager wanted (child–adult) so that the game has been won by the manager, or it is a simple response to the adult–adult explicit message and the manager has lost.

In most situations the ideal transaction is adult–adult, but any complementary transaction is better than any crossed transaction. If two people are both in the child state and start shouting at each other, they will not resolve their problems, but they will cope with the situation better than if one were in a different ego state.

Central to transactional analysis is the concept of stroking, the idea that we all need attention, recognition and approval. This influences much of our early life and influences our dominant ego state throughout later life:

> . . . infants require physical strokes for survival: unless babies are touched, they will die. As we grow older, our need for physical touching diminishes, though it never disappears. We learn to survive on non-physical strokes, to substitute any kind of attention for the physical strokes we still want and need. Negative attention will do if we can not get positive attention.
>
> (Wagner, 1981, p. 35)

Stroking can therefore be either positive or negative. There are three kinds. Positive conditional strokes are those bestowed on behaviour that is approved, with the assumption that the stroking will continue as long as the behaviour continues: 'That programme was just what we needed', 'I am very pleased with your progress'. Positive unconditional strokes are bestowed for some aspect of what you are rather than what you have done: 'I like you', or 'What do you think?'. Perhaps the most common is the smile.

A negative conditional stroke is given to behaviour that is disapproved, with the implication that the disapproval would be lifted if the behaviour were to change: 'You are still making too many mistakes', or 'This is the third time you have arrived late this week'. All of these have a useful place in transactions. A fourth has no useful place at all. The negative unconditional stroke is a bleak disapproval of the other person: 'I don't like you', or 'You make me sick'. There are also certain dismissive behaviours under this heading, such as taking no notice when someone speaks or interrupting them in the middle of a sentence.

As long as managers realise the nature of the three ego states and work within them, they are able to analyse what is being said and how they should respond. The manager who can build a strong adult ego state, and encourage others to do the same, is able to conduct transactions in a forthright and objective manner. He will concentrate on complementary transactions, use ulterior transactions sparingly and avoid negative conditional strokes at the same time as developing his use of the other three.

21.1 The analogy with telecommunications helps us understand how to be effective in interpersonal communications.

21.2 The effective communicator must be a skilful listener, as listening is just as important as expressing.

21.3 Although questioning is a natural human skill, managers need to realise and practise different types of questioning according to the nature of the situation they are attempting to manage.

┤ PUTTING IT INTO PRACTICE ├

Try the following with a friend or colleague.

1. *Listening, summary and rerun*
   a. You both spend two minutes preparing a brief statement on different controversial topics.
   b. Make your statement to your partner.
   c. Your partner restates what you have said, reflecting and summarising it as accurately as possible.
   d. You make whatever corrections are necessary until you are satisfied that your partner has summarised your point of view accurately.
   e. Change roles and repeat the exercise.

2. *Asking open-ended/follow-up questions*
   a. You both prepare one or two open-ended questions about a similar topic, such as how things are done in each other's organisations, what you did over Christmas, or what sort of house you would ideally like to own.
   b. You put an open-ended question to your partner and develop the reply with follow-up questions.
   c. Change roles and repeat the exercise.

References

Berne, E., 1966, *Games People Play*, André Deutsch, London.

Beveridge, W. E., 1968, *Problem-Solving Interviews*, Allen & Unwin, London.

Bolton, R., 1987, *People Skills*, Simon & Schuster, Australia.

Higham, M., 1979, *The ABC of Interviewing*, Institute of Personnel Management, London.

Maude, B., 1977, *Communication at Work*, Business Books, London.

Mayerson, E. W., 1979, *Shoptalk: Foundations of Managerial Communication*, Saunders, Philadelphia.

Reik, T., 1948, *Listening with the Third Ear*, Grove Press, New York.

Sproston, C. and Sutcliffe, G., 1990, *Twenty Training Workshops for Listening Skills*, Gower, Farnborough.

Wagner, A., 1981, *The Transactional Manager*, Prentice Hall, Englewood Cliffs, New Jersey.

Part VI

People

We have all heard a thousand times some version of the statement, 'An organisation is only as good as the people in it.' It may be a cliché, but it remains a truth.

Managers work with and through other people and every manager has a host of responsibilities that affect people's jobs, careers and whole lives. This section of the book deals with those matters that are typically found in books on personnel management, but you cannot leave them all to the personnel manager. Managers who can select all the members of their team are extremely fortunate; most have to manage a team that has come together already and whose members are on the lookout for a single false step by the newly-appointed manager, but there are always selections to be made and always training and development needs to be met.

Managers have to understand the dynamics of teams so that people working together can achieve more than those same people working independently, and the way in which people are employed is a feature of management undergoing fundamental change. Tomorrow will you have a contract *of* employment or a contract *for* performance? Which would you prefer, for yourself and for the people who work with you?

G R O U P

Chapter 22

Selecting team members

Few managers are able to pick their own team. A manager moving into a new post is the newcomer surrounded by people who are already established. Except in rare circumstances it is either unethical, unlawful, too expensive, impractical or simply foolish to discard those who are established and replace them with one's own nominees. Selecting team members is, therefore, a quite different activity for the individual manager than it is for the personnel specialist, who is recruiting people for the organisation as a whole.

The personnel specialist has to consider the broad issues such as equality of opportunity, promotion prospects, pension entitlement and the degree to which the potential recruit is likely to 'fit' the corporate culture; one development of the late 1980s was the move to selecting people initially on the basis of an assessment of their potential commitment instead of seeking to develop commitment after appointment. In contrast the individual manager is an occasional selector only, and is concerned much more with the internal dynamics of the working team and the nature of the working relationship with the person appointed. All those concerned in the selection decision – personnel specialist, individual manager and potential recruit – are concerned that there should be a good match between people appointed and the situation in which they will be working, but each has a different perspective. This chapter is about the decision-making of the individual manager trying to develop and maintain a balanced working team.

The manager selects a few members of the team either single-handedly or in consultation with others, but tolerates the vagaries of many others. One could almost say that picking one's own people is an abdication of management, a part of the art being to organise and coordinate the contribution of different types of people, including those one does not get on with. This involves managers adapting their style and approach to the varied expectations and needs of others, rather than being able to work only with kindred spirits, hand-picked for their compatibility.

Daniel Greensmith had founded and developed a small printing business, working closely with three colleagues who helped him start the company and who 'grew' with it. When the proprietor of a nearby, slightly larger printing company retired for health reasons, Daniel Greensmith bought the business. The move was welcomed by the managers and staff of the taken-over company, as Greensmith was known and well regarded. To avoid any misunderstanding, a consultant was engaged to advise on the management structure of the combined business and how the senior positions should be filled. Greensmith told the consultant what he was looking for and the consultant advised him about which members of the two companies fitted his specifications. The three loyal lieutenants were appointed to three of the top four posts reporting to Greensmith. Within six months the business was in difficulty, and Greensmith had enough self-knowledge to see why. He explained it to one of the authors as follows:

> I only knew one way to run a business and the three lads who had been with me from the beginning knew no more than I did: they were really just extensions of me. When the merger came along I hired a consultant because I wanted everything to be done fairly, without any feeling of favouritism, but I hired a personnel consultant instead of a business consultant. He was very good at finding out and describing what I wanted, but he was not the right person to tell me what the business needed. I appointed the people I knew and felt comfortable with, but we were ignorant of the subtleties of the company we had taken over. What I needed was strong, articulate opposition to my new ideas from people who knew what they were talking about so that the good ideas would have been made better and the nonsense filtered out. What I got was a bunch of yes men.

| REVIEW TOPIC 22.1 |

In what sense is picking one's own people an abdication of management?

Picking one's own team is a luxury few managers are able to enjoy and it can be a dangerous privilege, leading to the appointment of sycophants instead of creating a robust, balanced group of individuals, working with rather than for the person in charge.

The employment contract

Notwithstanding the warning of the last paragraph, managers have some part to play in selecting those who join the working team, and this chapter deals with that selection activity. The approach to selection is to appreciate that selecting people for jobs is a process of setting up an employment contract between the individual employee and the employing organisation. This is much more than the legally binding contract of employment which summarises the rights and obligations of the two parties; it is matching two sets of needs and expectations (Schein, 1979; Mumford, 1972; Torrington and Hall, 1991). It is natural to think in terms of what contribution to organisational success will be made by the employee, although this is seldom thought out very clearly and often centres round narrow, personal preferences of the manager in charge of the section where the appointment is to be made. It is also accepted that individual employees expect certain satisfactions from their employment, but frequently these two sets of requirements are seen as being satisfied independently of each other: the employee gets a salary, some holiday and contributions to a pension scheme in exchange for which personal interest and achievement are set aside in order to accommodate the routine requirements of the employer. Satisfactions for either party are likely to be mainly at the expense of the other.

In reaction against this there are some employment situations where too much is done to satisfy the employee, in such a way that the attempt is self-defeating. The conditions of work are enhanced – more money, longer holidays, free meals, flexible working hours – but nothing is done about the work, which remains an irksome necessity to be tolerated with as much restraint and dignity as possible. The result is often inefficiency, slackness, and employees who are not only dissatisfied with their work, but also feel guilty about their dissatisfaction with the paraphernalia of good conditions that surrounds them.

The essence of the employment contract idea is simply that the two sets of needs are not independent but complementary; the employee seeks satisfaction in the work done as well as from the circumstances in which it is done, and employees satisfied with their work will be more secure, more creative, more responsive to customers, more reliable and more efficient. The personnel department can do no more than clear away some of the possible impediments to a good employment contract. It is the individual manager who clarifies the needs of the organisation and integrates those with the needs of the employee, so that both are satisfied by the same processes.

The importance of this approach is that the manager selecting team members has to think just as much about what the appointee is looking for as about what the job requirements are. Both selector and appointee are choosing and it is important to both that each makes a sound decision.

Attracting team members

People, working groups and departments acquire reputations and one aspect of those reputations is to influence the number and type of people who want to join the group. All managers are interested in the reputation that they and their departments enjoy. 'A really first-class, very enthusiastic bunch of people' is the sort of label that is likely to attract people seeking that sort of working environment, whereas 'It is very well run and the manager is scrupulously fair' conveys a different image that will appeal to different people.

Reputations can be reliable indicators within an organisation, where the grapevine will do its work, but are much less useful as indicators to those outside the organisation, who may be influenced more by stereotypes. One local government official grumbled to us about the difficulty of recruiting people other than those who were looking for 'a safe billet'. She felt that local government had a popular image of being comfortable but dull and that this image became a self-fulfilling prophecy, as applicants came either because that was what they wanted or because they could not find anything else and thought themselves into the model they expected.

The reputation of the employing organisation in the labour markets is mainly a job for the personnel manager, but other managers can ensure that they are people worth working with and their departments worth working in. They can, however, do little to alter the truth. So they need to declare and embody what they actually are and how they really work, rather than generate some artificial picture of what they think will make them 'attractive'.

Managers are attracting potential team members in two ways. First, they are attracting the person who is looking for an internal move or awaiting their new posting. In this context reputation can be vitally important. If there is a loosely structured method of career advance, wherein individuals apply for jobs that appeal to them, managers are traders on the internal labour market and will want to create a climate of opinion about who would fit into their department before specific vacancies occur. If movement is centrally controlled, so that individuals are moved between jobs, then the reputation of an individual manager or department will affect the attitude and expectations of the new arrival.

Secondly, managers are attracting potential members by creating recommendations. Existing employees ask if there may be a vacancy for their next-door neighbour, cousin, son, or someone with whom they have worked previously. This remains the dominant way in which new employees are recruited. It is also the way in which organisations perpetuate the existing make-up of the workforce because new recruits tend to be 'made in the same image' as those who recommend them. This can stultify the development of a group of employees with contrasted abilities and perspectives, as well as perhaps denying employment opportunities to certain social groups. A further disconcerting tendency is the development of ghettos. There are still some examples of the 'all-black' night shift, for example, as a result of recruitment being left to the supervisor.

Information supporting selection decisions

The reputation of candidates and of departments and organisations in which candidates seek openings spreads informally. There are other sources of information, some of which will be available in any selection process.

Application forms

These are nearly always available for scrutiny. Either the candidate is from outside and is completing one with the vacancy in view, or is an insider who completed a form some time previously. The value of this document is that it sets out systematically the basic information about the person being considered. Because of this orderly display it is also the common basis for the selection interview.

Surveying application forms from candidates enables one quickly to pick up and compare a few key points about a number of applicants, such as age, qualifications, current post, salary and location. It is the easiest and most effective method of producing a short list. The way in which information about candidates is displayed in it provides a logical sequence for the selection, or employment, interview. The information is presented in biographical sequence so as to provide a pattern for questioning that is fruitful for the interviewer and coherent to the respondent. Some forms also provide space by each entry for the interviewers to make their own comments.

Curricula vitae

A long-standing practice, which is now becoming more widespread, is for candidates to submit a curriculum vitae (CV). This is often attractive to those who are articulate and experienced, as it enables them to tell their story in their own way, with the degree of detail and emphasis which gives the most positive picture of their track record and potential. It can appeal to recruiters as well, because the style and approach of the CV gives a number of individual clues about the candidate which are obscured by the standardised method of the application form.

The shortcomings of the CV are that systematic comparison is difficult and judgements are likely to be based on the more intangible aspects of the application, and on the style rather than the substance of the candidate ('I like the look of this one'). The CV writer necessarily uses a grapeshot approach, making every possible point in a very general way rather than tailoring the information to the vacancy.

Letters

Another tactic is to ask candidates to fill in a form but also to write a letter of application, with the form setting out the biographical information systematically and the letter making the case for that particular person being fitted to the specific vacancy. This approach requires clear advice to candidates on what the letter should contain; otherwise there is the likelihood that the letter restates what is in the form together with self-aggrandising assertions of little value and at varying levels of self-consciousness.

Job descriptions

Descriptions of the post may be available in detailed documents, or simply be a picture in the mind of the selector. Usually the written job description is preferred as it sets out what candidates want to know about the job for which they are applying, and summarises for selectors the points against which they are matching those interviewed. It is also argued that the process of producing the job description clarifies for the selector the details of the job to be done.

Candidate specifications

Profiles of the ideal candidate, prepared beforehand on the basis of the job description, may also be available. This too may be just a picture in the mind of the selector, or it may be a written profile that specifies requirements in terms of qualifications, length and type of working experience, aptitudes, skills and intelligence. The advantage of this is mainly in the short-listing of candidates, comparing application form details with points in the specification. It then has a later role in the examination of the ways in which preferred candidates do not quite meet the specification and in deciding which requirements are the most important.

Job descriptions and candidate specifications are the product of job analysis, extensively described in many books about organisational psychology and personnel management. Pearn and Kandola (1988, pp. 81–94) provide an excellent review.

Test scores

These are sometimes available in larger organisations, or where external candidates are being put forward for consideration by consultants. The easiest to deal with is a test of skill or proficiency, such as typing or a driving test, which indicates a level of competence by a generally acknowledged yardstick.

Tests of intelligence are not so easy to use. They measure some of a person's abilities against a standardised indicator, such as intelligence quotient (IQ) or quartiles of the general population, but there is often resistance from candidates to taking such tests, especially if they are well established in their careers and feel that undertaking such tests is like testing Giotto to see if he knows how to hold a paint brush. A test of this type that is widely used is the Graduate Management Admission Test, which is administered by the University of Princeton and used by business schools in many countries to decide whether or not candidates will be able to cope with their master's programmes. More specialised are tests of aptitude, like those used to select prospective trainees for aircrew duties or recruits for engineering apprenticeships. They assess not skill but the potential to develop a skill that depends on some aspect of natural aptitude like manual dexterity or spatial judgement. Potential recruits to the fire services, for instance, are tested for their ability to deal with heights and to deal with confined spaces, as well as their physical stamina.

The most controversial tests are those of personality, which claim to produce profiles of human traits and motivation, so that selectors can have a prediction about a candidate's potential for a post that goes beyond an assessment of existing skills, intelligence and aptitudes. Some authorities question this type of testing on the basis that personality cannot be measured and others because of contrasting views on how personality is constructed. This is especially difficult because of a bias within tests towards some cultural norms but not others.

> . . . widely-used tests will inevitably incorporate an element of bias . . . where it is found that the use of selection tests appears adversely to affect minority ethnic applicants and women . . . then it could well be that culture bias is a factor. (Straw, 1989, p. 76)

A minor practical problem is that the tests rely on candidates answering questions honestly, yet many are tempted to write an answer that they see as being socially acceptable. Wills (1984) makes the case in favour of personality testing for management jobs, while Swinburne (1985) argues that few personality tests are suitable for occupational use.

References

References provided by previous employers, family friends and Justices of the Peace are notoriously unhelpful and often misleading, but they are still extensively used. They are supposed to provide evidence of character, but the self-selecting nature of their nomination by candidates makes their objectivity questionable. Candidates choose reference writers because they think they will provide a 'good' reference, and 'bad' references are extremely rare.

There appears to be a set of coded messages conveyed by the concluding sentence of reference letters, which will usually be one of the following:

> 'I am delighted to commend Bloggins to you without any reservation . . .'
> 'I strongly recommend Bloggins as a very well qualified candidate for the vacancy.'
> 'I recommend Bloggins to you for serious consideration.'

Those three standard recommendations then have the personal embroidery that succeeds in making them difficult to interpret. 'I am delighted . . .' becomes 'I am honoured . . . or 'I am very happy . . .'. This sounds a flippant comment, but any regular attender at selection panels where references are being considered will notice the tendency for battle-weary members of the panel to look at the end of the reference first. If the remainder is read at all, it is interpreted in the light of that key, closing sentence. References may give an insight into the character of the person writing them, but they tell you little about the person on whose behalf the letter has been written.

Occasionally candidates are damned, but seldom explicitly, as reference writers seem unwilling to put in writing their reasons for saying that Bloggins is awful. Rare, but potent, is for a referee to decline the invitation to write a reference at all. More common is for the written reference to add an invitation to discuss the matter further by telephone.

Other methods of selection in current use include bio-data analysis, which is a systematic examination of the life history of the applicant and scoring certain key features to produce a profile of likely candidates. Graphology, palmistry and astrology are still used in some organisations, although there is no evidence to support their effectiveness. Larger companies increasingly use assessment centres, whereby a number of shortlisted candidates undergo a range of selection methods, including group exercises. This has the value that a variety of evidence is collected and a balanced assessment is possible.

The selection interview

Every time someone is selected to join a team, there will be an interview to precede the appointment. Mainly this is for the selector to decide whether the candidate is suitable, but candidates will also be making up their minds whether the move is one that they wish to make or not. Some selection processes seek to rule out the possibility of the candidate deciding against the job as a result of the interview, on the grounds that candidates should have made up their minds firmly and should not waste the time of the interviewers with interviews that may not be needed. Sometimes candidates are asked to declare at the beginning of the interview that they are firm applicants. In other situations travelling expenses are not paid to candidates who do not accept an offer of employment.

This is part of the ritual of the selection interview and the importance of ritual in the selection process, which is partly an initiation rite, should never be underestimated. Candidates arrive in their best clothes and are expected to show deference to the interviewers and great keenness to be employed, whilst the selectors are unlikely to wear their best clothes, sometimes demonstrate their superiority by being late or preoccupied with other things, and will never show enthusiasm to employ the candidate – willingness maybe: enthusiasm never.

Write a reference for someone applying for your job, avoiding outright condemnation or unequivocal enthusiasm. Then show it to a friend and ask if they would be disposed to employ or not to employ the person on the basis of the reference, with their reasons.

Although these ritual elements are inevitable in the selection situation, the purpose of the interview goes much further and has as its main objective the ability of the selector to decide whether the candidate is appropriate or inappropriate for the post under consideration. How can this be done effectively? The remaining pages of this chapter seek to offer general advice for the occasional interviewer. More detailed guidance is available in, for instance, Lewis (1985) or Torrington (1991).

The interview setting

This should be one that is appropriate for a private conversation, so that the exchanges will be frank and constructive. Many people also feel that the setting should reduce the status barriers between interviewer and respondent on the grounds that the interviewer is in the socially superior position of having a job to offer, or not, while the respondent is in the inferior position of wanting the job and being disposed to propitiate the interviewer in order to get it. If the seating arrangements underplay that distinction, then candidates will be more relaxed and more open in what they say. This status reduction can be done by avoiding direct, face-to-face interviewing across a desk and moving to a situation where both participants are sitting at the same height, not directly opposed and without any obvious advantage to the interviewer.

There is a danger in the setting becoming too informal and thus destroying rather than mitigating the ritual elements. The friendly chat over a drink in a local pub may be pleasantly relaxed and the candidate will probably (eventually) become very loquacious, but it is a difficult 'interview' to structure and may disconcert the candidate, who is expecting something more businesslike.

The plan of the interview

This is most easily taken from the sequence of the application form particulars. The development of the questioning is then one that builds logically in the mind of the selector and can be followed constructively by candidates, who can see how the interview is progressing, rather than feeling that there is some hidden agenda that they do not understand and which consequently worries them.

There is one preliminary: setting up rapport. At the opening of the interview candidate and selector assess each other and tune in to each other. It is usually done by exchanging words about trivia (some people believe that it rains frequently in Britain simply to provide a topic of conversation at the opening of interviews), explaining procedure and plenty of nods and smiles. It also gives the selector an opportunity to sketch out what is to happen and where the interview fits in with the rest of the decision-making process.

After the pleasantries of rapport, there is a change of pace as the interview moves to information exchange, and we need to remember that the information is moving both ways, not only towards the selector. If the candidates are from inside the organisation they will know most of the things they need to make up their minds about the post and will probably have just one or two check questions as well as a keen interest in the type of person the selector is. Candidates do not have the benefit of application forms, test scores or candidate specifications of the people with whom they will be working, but they are still keenly interested and try to understand as much as they can during the brief encounter of the interview. The external candidate will have a wider range of uncertainty and more gaps in understanding to fill in; again the interview is the opportunity. Convention says, however, that candidates do not ask selectors questions about their qualifications and ambitions, so they rely on clues and information conveyed unwittingly by interviewers.

The selector has the advantage of being able to structure the encounter, as candidates expect to have to respond to initiatives, rather than take initiatives themselves. The first question is important in setting both the tone and direction of the exchange. Consider this very common opening question:

'Tell me, why have you applied for this job?'.

Despite its extensive use, it is an ineffective way to begin, as it puts the candidate on the defensive, feeling the need to say the right thing, whether it is true or not. It is also a very difficult question to answer, as the reasons for seeking a move are probably varied and hard to summarise. Also some of the common reasons – more money, dislike of present boss, easier travel, more holidays, more security – are the sort of reasons that candidates often feel inappropriate to mention, especially at the beginning, so they speak vaguely about challenge and unfulfilled potential. The interview thus gets underway as a form of verbal fencing, with the candidate wary of the next question. Now consider this, alternative, opening question:

'Could you give me a general outline of your present responsibilities?'.

This has a number of advantages. First, the candidate will know the answer and that answer will be full of relevant, valuable information as it relates to what the candidate can do rather than to any subjective evaluation of motives. Secondly, it is not likely to be regarded with suspicion by the candidate trying to guess what the question is 'really after'. Thirdly, it will provide an admirable starting point as there will be a number of aspects that could usefully be developed further. This is not to suggest that all selection interviews should start with this particular question, but to suggest that questions that are about real facts and events are more sensible and useful than questions that require candidates to speculate or which make them uneasy.

A further development on the interview plan is to take a step back in time to an earlier point in the candidate's career and then move forward to the present, reviewing various developments on the way. This should be done with no more than one backwards move, if possible, as it is much easier to explain something and to understand something if it is examined as it developed rather than in reverse. Selectors get quite bewildered and candidates become incoherent when asked to explain their choice of degree, then their choice of 'A' levels, and then their 'O' level or GCSE performance.

Selectors may find it useful to note key issues and check points. Key issues will be two or three features of information from the application form that stand out as needing clarification or elaboration. A particular episode of previous employment may need to be explored to see the range of responsibilities held, the difficulty of the circumstances or the number of subordinates. There may be key issues in the educational record, overseas experience or work in a specific industry that needs to be discussed. Check points are details that need to be confirmed, like grades in an examination or dates of appointment.

All of this has to be done in a framework and atmosphere that is not a sceptical cross-examination of an evasive witness, but a meeting in which the candidates are enabled (not just allowed) to talk about themselves fully, frankly and with relevance to the vacant post. As long as the selector organises and leads the interview, the information flow from the candidate will be much more useful and informative than if the candidate is required only to provide clipped replies to a list of predetermined questions.

Deciding the appointment

The job of deciding who should be offered the appointment is simple to describe, but less easy to accomplish. It involves deciding first whether there is a good match between the person being considered and the job that has to be done, and secondly whether there is a good match between the group of people among whom the work will be done and the person being considered.

The first of these decisions is the more straightforward and can be based on the systematic matching by the selector of the job description and candidate specification on the one hand and the information obtained about the candidate on the other. A systematic approach on the basis of good documentation should decide whether someone is appointable or not. The best known aids to this type of decision-making are those of Rodger (1952) and Fraser (1978), still in use despite their age.

Deciding whether or not the candidate would fit socially is more problematic as it raises all the risks of appointing only 'clones', and the risk of being unlawfully discriminatory. Seear (1983) provides comments on keeping within the law. There may be helpful advice from the personnel department if they have run personality tests, but the likelihood of a good match between the prospective new recruit and the other members of the working team is mainly a matter for the selector's judgement.

Consultation with team members can help. The more people who meet the candidate, the more opinions there will be about suitability and the greater willingness to make the match effective, even if individual opinions have been overruled. Information to the candidates can also help. The more frankly they have had problems and opportunities discussed with them, the more prepared they are to make their contribution to a constructive working relationship. Finally, a group of people working together apathetically, poorly organised and critical of their leaders, can undermine the effectiveness of even the most enthusiastic new recruit. A robust, well-organised team of confident people who work well together with mutual respect will be able to assimilate some inappropriate appointees without serious trouble. Whereabouts in that spectrum does your team stand?

Induction

Whether new team members come from outside the organisation or from within, the first few days and weeks are an important period of 'reciprocal moulding' as they are fitted into the structure and into the formal framework of relationships. Wise selections are made to work by sensible induction and even unwise selections can be made tolerable by hard work in the early stages of the working relationship.

─┤ SUMMARY PROPOSITIONS ├──────────────────

22.1 Deciding the types of skill and experience required in a new appointment is more important than pondering the personal qualities of applicants.

22.2 In selection processes both the selector and the appointee are making choices and decisions; it is important to both that the other gets what they are looking for.

22.3 The selection interview is partly an initiation rite and the importance of the ritual elements should not be underestimated.

22.4 The most logical and helpful sequence for the selection interview is to review the biography of the candidate.

Interaction guide for the selection interview

1. *Before the interview*

Review	(a) Job description
	(b) Candidate specification
	(c) Application forms
Note	(a) Key issues
	(b) Check points
Check	(a) Timetable
	(b) Interview setting

2. *During the interview*

Begin with	(a) Welcome
	(b) Rapport, through the discussion of trivia, explaining procedure and adopting a relaxed, friendly manner.
Exchange	(a) Questioning, e.g. 'Could you give me an information outline of your present duties?'
by	(b) Logical sequence, such as working chronologically through the application form
	(c) Listening and observing
	(d) Enabling the candidate to be frank and informative
	(e) Remembering key issues and check points
At all times	(a) Maintain rapport
	(b) Keep notes
	(c) Control the interview

3. *After the interview*

Consider the person/job match	(a) By reviewing the job information:
	(i) Job description
	(ii) Candidate specification
	(b) By reviewing the candidate information
	(i) Application form
	(ii) Interview notes
	(iii) Test scores (if any)
	(iv) References (if any)
	(c) Deciding whether there is a good match or not, and the significance of any 'poor fitting'
Consider the person/group match	(a) By reviewing results of personality tests (if any)
	(b) By consulting with team members
	(c) Guard against unlawful discrimination
Decide	(a) To whom the job offer should be made
	(b) The terms of the offer
Notify	(After job offer has been accepted) the unsuccessful candidates.

Drill for recruitment

The following drill is based on The IPM Recruitment Code, Institute of Personnel Management, London, August 1980.

Recruiters	*Applicants*
1. Job advertisements will state clearly the form of reply desired (for example, curriculum vitae, telephone for application form, completed application form) and any preference for handwritten applications.	1. Advertisements will be answered in the way requested.
2. An acknowledgement or reply will be made promptly to each applicant by the employing organisation or its agent.	2. Appointments and other arrangements will be kept, or the recruiter will be informed promptly if the candidate discovers an agreed meeting cannot take place.
3. Candidates will be informed of the progress of the selection procedure, what this will be, the time likely to be involved and the policy regarding expenses.	3. The recruiter will be informed as soon as a candidate decides not to proceed with the application.
4. Detailed personal information (for example, religion, medical history, place of birth, family background) will not be asked for unless and until it is relevant to the selection process.	4. Only accurate information will be given in applications and in reply to recruiter's questions.
5. Before applying for references, potential employers will obtain the permission of the applicant.	5. Information given by a prospective employer will be treated as confidential, if so requested.
6. Applications will be treated as confidential.	

Drill for selection decisions

The five-fold framework for selection decisions shown below was devised by John Munro Fraser. It is used extensively in companies as a basis for selecting between candidates.

For each candidate score A, B, C, D or E in each box, with A indicating much above average and E indicating much below average for the category. The selector uses this as a way of organising thinking about candidates and then weighs the significance of the scores for the particular vacancy.

Categories of personal qualities	Names of candidates Adams Brown Clark Davis Evans
1. Impact on others, or the kind of response an individual's appearance, speech and manner calls out from others	
2. Qualifications and experience, or the knowledge and skill different types of work require	
3. Innate abilities, or how quickly and accurately an individual's mind works	
4. Motivation, or the kind of work that appeals to an individual and how much effort he is prepared to apply to it	
5. Emotional adjustment, or the amount of stress involved in living and working with other people	

References

Fraser, J. M., 1978, *Employment Interviewing*, 5th edn, Macdonald & Evans, London.

Lewis, C., 1985, *Employee Selection*, Hutchinson, London.

Mumford, E., 1972, Job satisfaction: a method of analysis, *Personnel Review*, Summer.

Pearn, M. and Kandola, R., 1988, *Job Analysis: A Practical Guide for Managers*, Institute of Personnel Management, London.

Rodger, A., 1952, *The Seven Point Plan*, paper no. 1, National Institute of Industrial Psychology, London.

Schein, E. H., 1979, *Organizational Psychology*, 3rd edn, Prentice Hall, Englewood Cliffs, New Jersey.

Seear, B. N., 1988, Non discrimination in employment, in *Corporate Personnel Management*, ed. Livy, B., Pitman, London.

Straw, J., 1989, *Equal Opportunities: The Way Ahead*, Institute of Personnel Management, London.

Swinburne, P., 1985, 'A comparison of the OPQ and 16PF in relation to their occupational application, *Personnel Review*, vol. 14, no. 4, pp. 29–33.

Torrington, D. P., 1991, *Management Face to Face*, Prentice Hall International, Hemel Hempstead, Hertfordshire.

Torrington, D. P. and Hall, L.A., 1991, *Personnel Management: A New Approach*, Prentice Hall International, Hemel Hempstead, Hertfordshire.

Wills, Q., 1984, Managerial research and management development, *Journal of Management Development*, vol. 3, no. 1.

Chapter 23

Staff development

As change becomes more rapid in our lives we all have to learn new things. For example we have learned in the last fifteen years to get money out of the wall at banks, serve ourselves at petrol stations, buy train and parking tickets from machines, programme the video recorder, and leave messages on answering machines. All of these have required some form of self-development where we accept responsibility for our own learning.

Kanter (1989, p. 321) has argued that in the future job security will not be based on working for the same organisation all our working life but on our employability.

> If security no longer comes from being employed, then it must come from being employable.

> In a post-entrepreneurial era in which corporations need flexibility to change and restructuring is a fact of life, the promise of very long-term employment security would be the wrong one to expect employers to make. But employability security – the knowledge that today's work will enhance the person's value in terms of future opportunities – that is a promise that can be made and kept. Employability security comes from the chance to accumulate human capital – skills and reputation – that can be invested in new opportunities as they arise.

This means constantly keeping up to date with skills and knowledge and learning to learn. Organisations will need employees who can take on new ideas, techniques and situations and match them with the core activities of the organisation.

Training and development

The term 'training' is frequently used to refer to the teaching of technical skills to non-managerial personnel, whereas 'staff development' has been used for white collar and management programmes. 'Staff development' is now used in organisations to mean the whole process of identifying training needs, conducting training where necessary, examining individual performance and looking at career development. Some of these are dealt with in this chapter which is largely about how to decide what to train and the next chapter which is about how to do the training. But staff development is part of the whole way an organisation manages its people. Differences in recruitment, structures, employment practice and the whole range of Human Resource Management will encourage or discourage different sorts of staff development. So it is also worth looking at Chapter 11 on performance management, Chapter 14 on structure and organisation, and Chapter 19 on authority, leadership and autonomy. When a manager has a specific problem to unravel, ideas from a range of areas can be applied, whereas books are written in discrete chapters.

Development is making learning happen, whereas training is the planned process to achieve effective performance. Without developing, staff effectiveness will suffer as staff become jaded and outdated in their skills.

The difference in the use of the terms training and development is not always clear and there is an obvious overlap; for example, a popular book in this area by Reid *et al.* (1992) has both words in the title. Perhaps it is best to say that training has more specific objectives, methods and learning than development and is related to a specific time and context. So learning about SIMs (School Information Management computer programme) would count as training whereas learning about school management could include a variety of experiences and would count as development.

| REVIEW TOPIC 23.1 |

Justify, in terms of the development and training which may take place, the expense of sending the senior staff of your organisation away for a week's skiing or winter sun.

The national scene

Since the mid-eighties an enormous amount of time, energy and money has been spent on the issue of training by the British government and other organisations. This has been due in part to pressure from the European Community to do so. But there are also four main issues which it is hoped will improve with a better training of the British workforce. They are:

1. A relatively declining economic position.
2. The rapid change in technologies.
3. Changing patterns of employment and consequently unemployment.
4. Education being seen as not providing suitably skilled workers for employers.

NATIONAL EDUCATION AND TRAINING TARGETS

FOUNDATION LEARNING

● By 1997, 80% of young people to reach NVQ II (or equivalent)

● Training and education to NVQ III (or equivalent) available to all young people who can benefit

● By 2000, 50% of young people to reach NVQ III (or equivalent)

● Education and training provision to develop self-reliance, flexibility and breadth

NATIONAL EDUCATION AND TRAINING TARGETS

LIFETIME LEARNING

● By 1996, all employees should take part in training or development activities

● By 1996, 50% of the workforce aiming for NVQs or units towards them

● By 2000, 50% of the workforce qualified to at least NVQ III (or equivalent)

● By 1996, 50% of medium to larger organisations to be 'Investors in People'

Figure 23.1 National Education and Training Targets (NETTs).

For these and other reasons there have been a large number of training and training-related initiatives with various initials and abbreviations. Perhaps the most important for general management purposes are NETTs, NVQs, and TECs and LECs.

National Education and Training Targets (NETTs) are targets for young people and adults to reach by the year 2000: see Figure 23.1. It is assumed that employers will play a large part in this and are encouraged to do so through the government-sponsored initiative 'Investors in People'.

National Vocational Qualifications (NVQs) range from level 1, basic, to level 5, professional and managerial. They cover a wide variety of vocations and professions and are given by a large number of organisations who have been validated by the National Vocational Council. The aim is to make them the main vocational qualifications, with professional and craft qualifications tied into the system.

Training and Enterprise Councils (TECs) and Local Enterprise Councils in Scotland (LECs) were set up by the Department of Employment to involve local employers in improving the skill base in their area. The boards are made up from local chief executives of commercial firms and a few public sector stake holders such as Further and Higher Education. The TECs and LECs are also charged with managing various government initiatives such as youth and adult training.

REVIEW TOPIC 23.2

What geographical area does your local TEC or LEC cover? How does this fit in with Local Authority boundaries and Chambers of Commerce?

Despite the sometimes religious fervour of people working in these areas, the results have not so far always been as widespread as was hoped. Reid *et al.* (1992, p. 51) suggest that on the whole training in British industry can best be described as follows:

- Only rarely integrated with mainstream operations
- Has a low operational priority
- Does not normally appear amongst strategic plans
- Is a peripheral activity for most line management
- Usually functions via *ad hoc*, unrelated events
- Not normally mentioned as part of new capital projects, product launches, reorganisation plans, etc.
- Viewed as an expense not an investment.

The purposes of training

With all this national pressure to get involved with training, what is in it for organisations? Why should they spend time, effort amd money on training? As long ago as 1982, before the main drive for training, Tyson and York (p. 178) gave a useful list:

1. Maximising productivity and output.
2. Developing the versatility and employability of human resources.
3. Developing the cohesiveness of the whole organisation and its sub-groups.
4. Increasing job satisfaction, motivation and morale.
5. Developing a consciousness of the importance of safety at work and improving standards.
6. Making the best use of available material, resources, equipment, and methods.
7. Standardising organisational practices and procedures.

Any or all of these may concern a particular department, manager or job holder at any particular time. The training personnel in large organisations will be concerned with trying to integrate these into the overall policies of the organisation. This is a time-consuming job and takes longer to achieve than many expect. The current development of Human Resource Management in the personnel field tries to integrate training and development with a whole range of other aspects of managing people in the workplace; see, for example, Keep (1989).

Defining what performance is wanted

The increasing speed of change in organisations means that most employees find their jobs changing around them. They frequently lose certainty about what they should be doing, why and how. With a plethora of possible jobs to do, is it any wonder that some people get overloaded and feel overworked? In some this can lead to symptoms of stress, illness and absenteeism. Others feel bewildered that their efforts have not been recognised by the obvious signs of money, time, resources or thanks – nor have they effected change. All of this, in some cases, leads to embittered staff who become destructive and 'switched off'. Others feel they are running around getting nowhere. This may be because they have a mismatched jumble of jobs that it does not make sense for one person to be doing. How can these people make sense of it all and ask for help?

In most employing organisations it is the responsibilty of management to ensure that the work is distributed in suitable chunks, with appropriate materials and resources, to suitably selected and trained people. Required performance is communicated to individuals in several ways. Everyone is supposed to have a contract of employment that outlines their basic duties and conditions of work. In addition most organisations have formal rule books, job descriptions, training manuals, standards and procedures. Expectations are also communicated more informally through briefing meetings, training sessions, meetings and individually. There may be problems in any of these. For example the descriptions, procedures and standards may be poorly thought out, inappropriate or out of date. We cover these topics in more detail elsewhere in this book. Even if the prescriptions are paragons of perfection, they are useless if they are poorly communicated. See Chapter 15 for further discussion about problems with communication.

Aspects of the organisation that are outside the individual's control can lead to individuals performing badly. Usually this is because the work is in some way not suitably organised. It may be resolved by new or clearer instructions and training or a rethink about the job itself. Areas to consider are given below.

Assignment and job   Sometimes individuals simply do not know what is expected of them. They may have been away when the new instructions were given, or have arrived recently. The job may be impossible for one person to do or so badly thought out that it is only possible to do it in this 'poor' way.

Job changed   The actual work that people do is changed because of new technologies, practice and products introduced. In addition the whole job may be reorganised to fit in with new ideas about the department or section. Where this does not make sense to the individual because of lack of communication or disagreement, they are less likely to work well.

Pay If the pay is felt to be too low then the work is likely to suffer. If there is a felt unfairness this is likely to affect the work done. The poor administration of pay, such as late payment, wrong deductions etc., can make people less willing to contribute their best.

Investment in equipment Although we say 'a poor workman blames his tools', there is very little a worker can do if there are not enough of the right materials and tools to work.

Physical conditions If people are too hot, cold, wet, hungry, tired, deafened, cramped or in some other way irritated or made uncomfortable by their environment, they will be distracted from work.

Location and transport When companies relocate there are obvious implications for the employees. Sometimes employees feel this has been a deliberate ploy used by management to test loyalty and reduce manpower. Reorganisation of shifts and work times can lead to problems where public transport timetables have not been considered.

Planning Poor work can result from lack of suitable plans. They may be too idealistic, too constrained, out of touch with reality, not enough, or out of date. With planning goes some degree of improvisation. This may have become too frequent, or not frequent enough, so the individual does not know what they are trying to do.

Training There may be difficulties where the wrong training has been given, the training has been given in the wrong way, there has not been enough training or it is out of date.

Discipline Different groups develop their own rules about what is seen as appropriate behaviour. Where a group runs on self-discipline normally there may not be enough formal processes to tell the poor performer about their work. Equally incompatible is the person in another group who finds they are irritated by the strict procedures being used for small errors. There may be an inappropriate permissiveness.

Management There may be poor management. This may be a particular individual manager, such as an immediate boss, who has not acted appropriately. It may be the whole management system that is causing problems, such as when managers become too keen on being managers rather than getting on with doing the job of management.

Group dynamics It may be that a person does not fit in with the group and has become the butt of complaints. It may be that even if their work is adequate the rest of the group will not believe it. A self-fulfilling prophesy may be at work.

Approaches to training

There is a wide range of different ways of training. Some have a theoretical base such as experiential training methods, based on the model of Kolb (1984): see next chapter. In this sort of training some sort of experience is provided as the starting point of the training. This might be a contrived role play, an outdoor adventure, exchanging days with a colleague or going on assignment to some other section of the organisation. After the experience the other three stages of Kolb's cycle of reflecting, generalising and testing are systematically explored using the material from the experience.

Other approaches can have an in-built logic to them, such as the so-called systematic training cycle advocated by the Department of Employment: see Figure 23.2. In this approach the identification of training needs is carefully analysed before the training is planned; the training is then carried out and the whole process evaluated. This requires time and careful monitoring, so presumes in practice that a training department exists to carry this out.

The two important considerations, whichever approach one chooses, are first how to decide what to train, and second how to go about doing the training.

Competence

The most popular current approach to training and development is to develop lists of competences which individuals need in order to be effective and then to train or develop these. The current interest in competences was

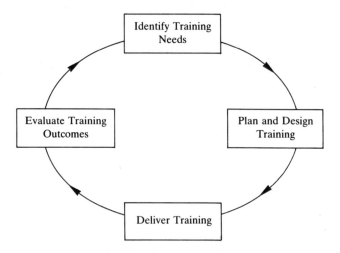

Figure 23.2 The systematic training cycle. Crown Copyright; reproduced by arrangement with the Employment Department from the Training and Development Lead Body's *National Standards for Training and Development*, 1992.

1. Competences pertaining to dealing with *people*
    1.1. Those for whom one has responsibility
        1.1.1. Selecting
        1.1.2. Enabling
        1.1.3. Guiding
        1.1.4. Directing
    1.2. Peers, clients and customers
    1.3. Those to whom one reports

2. Competences concerned with *managing activities*
    2.4. Financial activities
    2.5. Systems control
    2.6. Techniques
    2.7. Functional activities

3. Competences reflecting a sensitivity to *environment and external factors*
    3.8. Customer expectations and needs
    3.9. Legal considerations
    3.10. Organisational, social, economic and political environment, including technological change

4. Competences reflecting *personal effectiveness*
    4.11. Communication
    4.12. Numeracy and numerical technique
    4.13. People orientation
    4.14. Results orientation
    4.15. Self-awareness and development

Figure 23.3 Management competences.

developed by Boyatzis (1982) and the term includes not only skills but also mind sets and personal attributes. The lists are usually generated by committees of experienced trainers and practitioners debating what should be included. Figure 23.3 shows a short list of management competences generated by the Training Agency in 1989; each of these sections is then broken down into its component parts. Another list of management competences is given in Chapter 2 – the MCI standards.

The job composite model of competences

Although competence-based training has become the received wisdom on approaches to management training, all the lists we have seen have been difficult to use in practice, mainly due to an understandable attempt to be precise or over-inclusive.

Torrington, Waite and Weightman (1992) developed a composite model to describe the work of personnel specialists working in the health service. We are therefore presenting a crude model here as a framework which could be applied to other groups of jobs. It is crude because the boundaries must be blurred: ambiguity is essential if we are to make sense.

Our analysis starts from this point, by considering not whether a person is able to do a job, but what skills are required in order to be able to do a job: not 'this is how you do recruitment', but 'these are the skills you need in order to do recruitment excellently'. This is the approach of competence analysis, distinguishing between the competent performance of a job and the competences required in order to perform a job excellently.

The basis of this model is an analysis of the jobs that need doing by personnel managers. The following list we feel encompasses the main areas of expertise that a large NHS personnel department could need to have. The composite is based on eight facets of the personnel operational role:

1. The personnel manager as SELECTOR
2. The personnel manager as PAYMASTER
3. The personnel manager as NEGOTIATOR
4. The personnel manager as PERFORMANCE MONITOR
5. The personnel manager as WELFARE WORKER
6. The personnel manager as HUMAN RESOURCE PLANNER
7. The personnel manager as TRAINER
8. The personnel manager as COMMUNICATOR

Every mainstream personnel management job consists of one or more of these roles. Selector and Trainer are those most commonly found to comprise a complete job. Some combination of two or three is usual. All the roles are highly interdependent.

Figure 23.4 summarises the main areas of expertise or *professional competence* that are comprehended by each professional role. There is also a list of generic competences which are more general competences used in at least two, and sometimes more, of the professional roles.

The idea of the Job Composite Model, therefore, is that each individual's job will be a composite of activities drawn from the professional list and from the shorter list of *generic competences*. Job-specific individual training needs can then be derived by using our self-assessment questionnaire, which is a more detailed version of Figure 23.4 developed from these two lists of competences.

There have been many criticisms of the type of analysis we are putting forward here, not least of which is the belief that a competence-based approach cannot take into account individual differences.

> Users of competency-based assessment should be aware that it provides one relatively partial view of performance. Its strong emphasis on the need for scientific rigour tends to lead to a rather narrow perspective which, on its own, is barely capable of reflecting the rich and often paradoxical nature of human behaviour.   Jacobs (1989)

One way around this problem is to construct competence analysis in terms of self-assessment, enabling staff at all levels and varying from tyro to past master to assess their own training needs.

Our research has demonstrated the need for this approach caused by the wide differences in practice between parts of the organisation, which make it quite inappropriate to have an 'ideal' model of, for example, a personnel department. These are some of the main differences we found between Health Service Districts:

- The different levels of funding received.
- The different skills and experience of the people.
- The differing hierarchical position of personnel, including the relationship to the general manager.
- The differing relationships with Region.
- Differing perceptions of the personnel role held by personnel directors, their staff and their colleagues.
- The differing nature of the districts themselves: size, labour markets, medical specialisms, and so forth.

Below we give some hypothetical examples of the sort of competences, both professional and generic, that particular job holders might conclude were necessary for them to do their work. These lists might be arrived at by the job holder alone or in consultation with their boss and/or colleagues.

A pay strategy post

Appropriate professional competences:

1 Job analysis
1 Job evaluation
2 Pay determination
2 Employee benefits
2 Performance-related pay
2 Salary administration
2 Salary structures
2 Pensions/sick pay
2 Taxation and National Insurance
3 Consultation
3 Employee involvement
3 Negotiating bodies
3 Agreement and procedures
6 Planning
6 Computer analysis

Appropriate generic competences:

9 Personal organisation
9 Interpersonal communication
9 Problem-solving and decision-making
9 Report-writing

Name .... Date ....

Current post ....

Using the job composite model of personnel competences, complete the following checklist by assessing your present expertise in each of the identified competences as either A, B, C, D or E, indicating:

A Little or no expertise;
B Some expertise, but a need for further development or updating now;
C Expert;
D Considerable expertise, but some further development or updating necessary soon;
E Not relevant to the present post.

Professional competences

1. The PM as selector
.... Vacancy identification
.... Job analysis
.... Recruitment advertising
.... Selection process
.... Psychometric testing
.... Selection decision-making
.... Letters of offer
.... Contracts of employment
.... Employee records
.... Induction/socialisation

2. The PM as paymaster
.... Job evaluation
.... Pay determination
.... Employee benefits
.... Performance-related pay
.... Salary administration
.... Salary structures
.... Pensions and sick pay
.... Taxation and National Insurance

3. The PM as negotiator
.... Consultation
.... Employee involvement
.... Negotiating bodies
.... Trade union recognition
.... Agreements and procedures
.... Grievance and discipline
.... Redundancy and dismissal
.... Industrial tribunals

4. The PM as performance monitor
.... Appraisal/assessment
.... Attendance management
.... Management of poor performance

5. The PM as welfare officer
.... Health and safety
.... Counselling services
.... Occupational health
.... Health and safety legislation

6. The PM as human resource planner
.... Supply and demand forecasting
.... Modelling and extrapolation
.... Manpower utilisation
.... Planning
.... Statistical method
.... Computer analysis

7. The PM as trainer
.... Identification of training needs
.... Design of training
.... Delivery of training
.... Evaluation of training

8. The PM as communicator
.... Bulletins
.... Community relations
.... Team briefing
.... In-house magazines

Figure 23.4 The self-assessment questionnaire.

Note: PM = Personnel Manager

Generic competences

9. Managing oneself
. . . . Personal organisation
. . . . Time management
. . . . Interpersonal communication
. . . . Assertiveness
. . . . Problem-solving and decision-
making
. . . . Report writing
. . . . Reading
. . . . Presentations
. . . . Managing stress

10. Working in the organisation
. . . . Networking
. . . . Working in groups
. . . . Power and authority
. . . . Influencing
. . . . Negotiating

11. Getting things done
. . . . Setting objectives
. . . . Goal planning and target setting
. . . . Managing external consultants
. . . . Using statistics
. . . . Information technology literacy
. . . . Keyboard skills
. . . . Minute-taking
. . . . Record-keeping
. . . . Setting up systems and procedures

12. Working with people
. . . . Interviewing
. . . . Listening
. . . . Counselling
. . . . Conducting and participating in
meetings
. . . . Team-building

Figure 23.4 *contd.*

9 Making presentations
10 Networking
10 Influencing
11 Statistics
11 Information technology literacy
11 Setting up systems and procedures
12 Conducting and participating in meetings

Most of the other competences listed would probably be scored E (no current or foreseeable need for competence in this area). Of the competences listed which are needed, some no doubt will have been scored A or B, suggesting some difficulty. These then need prioritising.

A recruitment officer post

Appropriate professional competences:

1 Vacancy identification
1 Job analysis
1 Recruitment advertising
1 Selection process
1 Selection decision-making
1 Letters of offer
1 Contracts of employment

1 Induction socialisation
3 Agreements and procedures
6 Supply and demand forecasting

Appropriate generic competences:

9 Managing oneself
9 Time management
9 Interpersonal communication
12 Interviewing

| REVIEW TOPIC 23.3 |

How many of the generic competences listed in Figure 23.4 are common to most jobs?

Deciding what to train

If we see training as the process of bringing someone to a level of competence, we have to know what is required. In most large organisations there is a training department or training officer who has the organisational responsibility for this sort of activity and most managers need no more than a passing understanding of the process that is involved.

As a training objective, for instance, the manager will want the trainee to understand the task to be performed and what is required to reach a level of competence. So the manager has to decide how much understanding is needed at the outset in order to provide a satisfactory basis for the training. There are two aspects to this: assessing training needs associated with the job and assessing those associated with the individual.

Job analysis can be done in several different ways. This can be a comprehensive analysis of all the skills and understanding required to do a job. This would involve a detailed study of everthing involved over a full cycle of the job. Or it may be appropriate to look at a part of the job where there are problems, it is critical or where new approaches are needed. More detailed explanations of these methods can be found in specialised books; see, for example, Reid *et al.* (1992). This analysis leads to a job specification which gives details of the mental and physical activities of the job and the environment where the job is done. The skills and knowledge required to do this are then listed.

Individual analysis, which is the assessment of a person's competence at doing the tasks, can also be done in several ways. This might include self-analysis or assessment centres where experts evaluate performance on set tasks. The most usual way, however, is as part of the performance appraisal process described in Chapter 11. This might involve systematic observations of the individual at work, collecting evidence of their perform-ance or the informal understanding of daily working together.

A comparison can then be made between the job analysis and the individual analysis and the difference will lead to a diagnosis of training need. It may be that new techniques are being introduced, it may be that old skills have faded or that there has never been sufficient understanding to do the job superbly. See the section earlier in this chapter, on defining what performance is wanted, for areas that can be considered if the difference between performance required and performance given is too wide a gap.

This systematic approach is now widely accepted in training departments, but it should always be remembered that the whole process is dependent on judgement at various points and so appropriately should involve managers outside the training department.

Continuous development

Continuous development is currently widely advocated as a way of coping with rapid changes. It is about encouraging learning at all times. The argument is that the more an individual learns, the more confident they become at doing so, they learn to learn, and are likely to want to learn some more. Reid *et al.* (1992) summarise the process in a continuous development spiral: see Figure 23.5.

This learning can take place in all sorts of settings, both formal and informal. It does not necessarily occur only in formal training sessions. Mumford (1989) gives a useful list (see Figure 23.6) of learning opportuni-ties which exist for managers in the real environment. This list has situations, people and processes that are available and cover a wide range of different styles of learning. Looking at this list one can see that the active learner could maximise their skills and understanding of the organisation whereas the timid would concentrate merely on their own current perform-ance.

REVIEW TOPIC 23.4

Look through Figure 23.6 and find one situation and one person that you could use in the next week to actively learn from. Did you manage to do so?

Careers

Managers have to learn how to manage talent and this includes developing staff so they develop careers to suit themselves. This is increasingly important if the comments given at the beginning of this chapter by Kanter are true. All of us need opportunities to develop skills and a reputation. This involves ensuring that subordinates get a variety of opportunities and

People

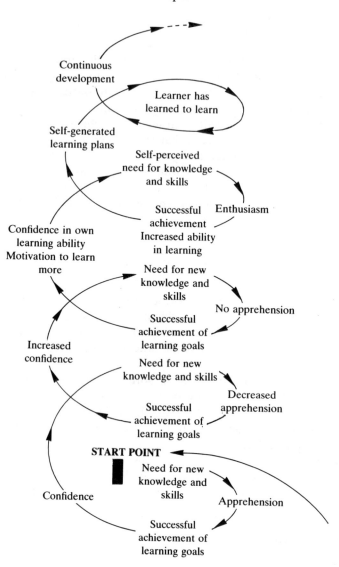

Figure 23.5 The continuous development spiral.

experiences as well as being assessed. As Handy puts it, managers have to be:

> teacher, counsellor and friend, as much or more than he or she is commander, inspector and judge . . .   (Handy, 1989, p. 104)

Our colleague Valmai Bowden, looking at the careers of bench scientists, has pointed out that this nurturing of people's careers can be compared to

Situations within the organisation

Meetings	Modelling
Task – familiar	Problem-solving
– unfamiliar	Observing
Task force	Questioning
Customer visit	Reading
Visit to plant/office	Negotiating
Managing a change	Mentoring
Social occasions	Public speaking
Foreign travel	Reviewing/auditing
Acquisitions/mergers	Clarifying responsibilities
Closing something down	Walking the floor
	Visioning
Situations outside your organisation	Strategic planning
	Problem diagnosis
Charity	Decision-making
Domestic life	Selling
Industry committee	
Professional meetings	**People**
Sports club	
	Boss
Processes	Mentor
	Network contacts
Coaching	Peers
Counselling	Consultants
Listening	Subordinates

The opportunities identified here are not necessarily separate. You may, for example, think of something first in terms of something happening at a meeting – or you may think of the way in which one of your colleagues achieved success at a meeting.

Figure 23.6 Learning opportunities (from Mumford, 1989).

parenting. Some managers are very strict and dogmatic ('do it like me') while others are more facilitating and encourage self-direction and assessment. Those who are lucky enough to have good parenting are likely to develop into the confident, learning, self-developing individuals who are more likely to have rewarding careers. Those who feel ignored and rejected can become embittered.

Most managers now realise that they must take responsibility for their own careers. As Stewart (1991, p. 193) points out, managers' careers look very different now from the traditional progress up the ladder. The important issues are getting relevant experience and whether the CV will look good to other employers. This may be achieved by changing jobs within an organisation or between organisations.

Do most people only have a career in retrospect? Or is planning a career something useful for a twenty-year-old to do?

The changes which have occurred in jobs and careers in the eighties and nineties have major implications for individuals. Rosemary Stewart (1991, pp. 196–201) suggests the following advantages and disadvantages of these changes:

Advantages

Changes in jobs –
  More responsibility and autonomy

Changes in careers –
  More control of your destiny
  A better match for one's abilities
  More variety and interest
  More flexibility in the pattern of work
  More choice of working environment

Disadvantages

Harder work and greater pressure
Less security
Less opportunity for promotion
Loneliness
Problems of dual careers

Inevitably, individuals will respond to these changes in different ways. But it is quite likely that more people will try to balance their life between work and home in different ways from those adopted in the past. This is partly because of the increase in women working but also because of the restructuring of careers; see, for example, Scase and Goffee (1989) for detailed descriptions of reluctant managers.

SUMMARY PROPOSITIONS

23.1 There are a lot of government initiatives on training for work. This is felt to help the economic position of Britain as there will be a more skilled workforce.

23.2 Staff development is not just about training; it includes organisation structures, performance management and the culture of the organisation – in other words, the whole range of Human Resource Management.

23.3 Training is the process of bringing someone to a level of competence.

23.4 Competence-based training for personnel staff can be based on a job composite model incorporating features of both professional and generic competence.

23.5 A systematic approach to training is to identify the competences necessary to do the job and the competences of the individual to do these; this gives the training needs.

23.6 Individual careers are less likely to be spent and developed within one organisation now than they were in the past. This requires people to develop their own careers which will depend on skills and reputation.

| PUTTING IT INTO PRACTICE |

Alan was appearing as the main witness for his company in a court case brought by his company. They were taking one of their suppliers to court over the quality of the material. The events in question took place several years ago and involved Alan in a lot of preparation beforehand. The court case was at the High Court in London and involved Alan being away from home and the office for over two weeks. He was in the witness box for five days being cross-examined.

What approach would you take to ensure he was suitably prepared and competent for this event?

References

Boyatzis, R. E., 1982, *The Competent Manager: A Model for Effective Performance*, John Wiley and Sons, Chichester.

Handy, C., 1989, *The Age of Unreason*, Business Books, London.

Jacobs, R., 1989, Getting the measure of management competence, *Personnel Management*, June, pp. 32–8.

Kanter, R. M., 1989, *When Giants Learn to Dance*, Unwin, London.

Keep, E., 1989, A training scandal?, in *Personnel Management in Britain*, ed. Sisson, K., Blackwell, Oxford.

Kolb, D., 1984, *Experiential Learning: Experience as the Source of Learning and Development*, Prentice Hall, Englewood Cliffs, New Jersey.

Mumford, A., 1989, *Management Developments: Strategies for Action*, Institute of Personnel Management, London.

Reid, M. A., Barrington, H. and Kenney, J., 1992, *Training Interventions: Managing Employee Development*, 3rd edn, Institute of Personnel Management, London.

Scase, R. and Goffee, R., 1989, *Reluctant Managers: Their Work and Lifestyles*, Unwin Hyman, London.

Stewart, R., 1991, *Managing Today and Tomorrow*, Macmillan, Basingstoke, Hampshire.

Torrington, D., Waite, D. and Weightman, J., 1992, A continuous development approach to training Health Service personnel specialists, *Journal of European Industrial Training*, vol. 16, no. 3, pp. 3–12.

Tyson, S. and York, A., 1982, *Personnel Management Made Simple*, Heinemann, London.

Chapter 24

Training

Rugby players talk of going training on damp Tuesday evenings, minor royal figures talk of their personal trainers, many of us have attended compulsory Health and Safety training days and McDonald's serving staff have gold stars on their lapels to indicate which training procedures they have completed satisfactorily. So what is all this training?

Perhaps the most useful way to think of training is as the planned learning process to achieve effective performance. So the Rugby player is trying to perfect the tackle, the royal figure perfect poise, the compulsory course to instill safe practice and McDonald's to present a uniform service. All of these require an understanding of how we learn and the differences between sorts of learning situations.

How people learn

As learning is intrinsic to both training and development, we need to understand something of the process whereby people learn. It is a subject that has attracted much attention in the training field as well as in schoolteaching. The traditional distinction between cognitive learning, learning skills and developing attitudes was based on the proposition that these were not only three different types of objective but also three different types of process. This has been refined for practical application in adult learning by the CRAMP taxonomy (ITRU, 1976) based on the work of Eunice and Meredith Belbin (1972).

CRAMP divides learning into five basic types.

1. *Comprehension.* Where the learning involves theoretical subject matter, knowing how, why and when certain things happen. Examples would be most of mathematics, the elements of computer programming or the theories of economics. Learning of this type is best approached by methods that teach the whole subject as an entity, rather than splitting it

up into pieces and taking one at a time. The lecture is the time-honoured method of doing this.

2. *Reflex learning.* Where the trainee is acquiring skilled movements or perceptual capacities. Effectiveness requires practice as well as knowing what to do, and speed is usually important so that the learning process involves constant repetition to develop the necessary synchronisation and coordination. An obvious, but extreme, example is juggling, but there are many more common examples, like machining, inspection on an assembly line or computer input.

3. *Attitude development.* Concerned with enabling people to alter their attitudes and social skills. This has been very popular in management development and centres on the understanding trainees have of themselves. Group methods are typically used for this purpose as attitudes are very difficult to influence and change permanently through instruction, although many – like politicians – find it difficult to believe that conversion cannot be achieved by exposition. Socialisation seems more effective.

4. *Memory training.* This obviously deals with people learning information, like the periodic table of chemical elements, and is usually done in the same way as reflex learning with trainees learning parts of the information at a time and then proceeding to the next stage.

5. *Procedural learning.* Very similar to memorisation except that the drill to be followed does not have to be memorised: it has to be located and understood. A lawyer does not have to learn all the statutes and cases, but does need to know where to locate them. If a process plant is run down once a year for annual maintenance, the engineers do not have to memorise the rundown procedure, but they have to know where it is and to be able to understand all its stages when it is required.

In practice most forms of training involve more than one type of learning, so that the trainee motor mechanic will need to understand how the car works (comprehensive) as well as practising the skill of tuning an engine (reflex). The car driver needs to practise the skill of coordinating hands, feet and eyes in driving as well as knowing the procedure to follow if it breaks down, but the CRAMP analysis helps us to identify the type of learning that is predominating in any particular situation.

Gagne (1975) has examined all processes of learning and identified a chain of eight events which take place:

1. *Motivation.* The learner has to want to learn, and that requires that they want to achieve the product of this learning. A person will be motivated to practise five-finger exercises on the piano because of wanting to achieve the ability to play a Beethoven sonata, which would be the end-product of this learning.

2. *Perception.* The matter to be learned has to be identified and separated

from other matters around it, so that it becomes a clear and specific objective.

3. *Acquisition.* The matter being learned is made sense of by being related to other things known by the trainee.

4. *Retention.* The material or skill acquired is retained in the long-term memory and/or the short-term memory. The two-stage process of human learning comprises first the short-term memory in which one holds, for instance, the name of a person to whom one has just been introduced. Secondly, there is the long-term memory to which one transfers those names which one wishes to store permanently. This is an important distinction in learning as some material goes into short-term memory only to aid understanding at the time and then should not be transferred to long-term. An example is the joke in the lecture, which may be remembered at the expense of the point it was illustrating.

5. *Recall.* The learner has to be able to summon up items from memory when they are needed.

6. *Generalisation.* This is the ability to apply what has been learned to a wide variety of situations other than the specific situation in which learning has taken place. The skilled motor mechanic will be able to apply the essence of what has been learned to the maintenance of a new model of car that was not produced at the time of training.

7. *Performance.* That which has been learned is now done: the trainee pianist plays the piano, the student writes the examination script, or the embryo salesperson goes out and sells something.

8. *Feedback on performance.* The learner receives some feedback on whether the performance was satisfactory or not. To some extent this lies in the obvious quality of the performance. If the task is to mend a fuse, success or failure is clear, but with most learners some degree of approbation and comment is needed from the coach or trainer, as this can not only incorporate varying degrees of satisfaction and encouragement but also be analytical: what went wrong, how it could have been avoided, what aspect needs more practice, what to do next and so forth.

REVIEW TOPIC 24.1

Throughout the book we have these review topics. Which one of Gagne's eight events are they trying to help?

A failure in learning can be because of difficulties at any of these eight stages and this sequence applies to all learning, whether of the relatively formal type that is found in training for industrial skills or in an activity like coaching, where the learning may be incidental to some other activity.

A third model of learning which has been widely used in training is the experiential learning model (Kolb *et al.*, 1974): see Figure 24.1. Kolb argues that to be effective a learner needs to be able to do each of the four

This model suggests that the learning process is a cycle of the following stages.

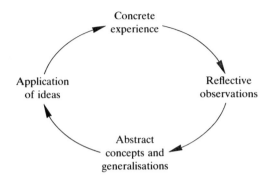

(Source: Kolb et al. 1974)

This is a particularly useful model for devising coaching and learning experiences on the job.

Figure 24.1 Kolb's experiential learning model.

processes: experience, observe and reflect, theorise and conceptualise, and test and experiment. He felt that most people preferred one mode to the others. This led Honey and Mumford (1992) to define four learning styles: activist, reflector, theorist, pragmatist.

Deciding how to do the training

In designing the training programme, how much should the task to be performed be broken down into components or subroutines to aid learning? When Clive Sinclair introduced the personal computer for use in the home, arrangements had to be made for users to learn computer operation and programming at a distance. What had to be learned was divided up into small packets of information that could be both understood and practised in sequence. Each packet of information, set out in an instruction manual, could be understood by reference either to its own content or to what had already been covered. The sequence was as follows:

1. The computer and setting it up	2½ pages
2. The keyboard	3 pages
3. Numbers, letters and the computer as a calculator	3 pages
4. Some simple commands	2 pages
5. Simple programming	3½ pages
6. Using the cassette recorder	3½ pages
7. Colours	1½ pages
8. Sound	1 page
9. What's inside the case	1½ pages

(Vickers and Bradbeer, 1982)

Trainee typists learn subroutines for each hand before combining them into subroutines for both hands together, as they use their hands in ways that are relatively independent of each other, with the left always typing 'q' and the right always typing 'p', so that coordination of the hands is needed only to sequence the actions. A further aspect of learning to type is to practise short letter sequences that occur frequently, such as 'and', 'the', 'ing' and 'ion'. This sort of practice enables actions to become both automatic and reliable. The amateur typist will often transpose letters or hit the wrong key, writing 'rwong' instead of 'wrong' or 'hte' instead of 'the'. The properly-trained typist will rarely do this because the repeated drills will have made the subroutines automatic and therefore usually correct.

Every person training others has to provide feedback, so that the trainee can compare their performance with the required standard and can see the progress being made. The characteristics of good feedback are immediacy and precision. If feedback comes immediately after the action, then the trainee has the best chance of associating an error with that part of the performance that caused it, whereas delay will emphasise what was wrong, but the memory of what happened will have faded. Precision in feedback requires the information conveyed to be as accurate as possible and related to what the trainee has done, rather than to the results of this action, so that the trainee is able to pinpoint the action that needs to be remedied and how it can be altered. In teaching someone to drive a car, you may well have the alarming experience of the car lurching forward from a stationary position and then stopping dead. The comment to the trainee driver 'not smooth enough' is unhelpful as it makes an obvious statement about what the car has done instead of a comment on what the driver did wrong. 'Too quick on the clutch' focuses on what the driver did, but probably in language that will be imprecise to the listener. Something like 'You brought the clutch pedal up too quickly with the left foot' would be precise feedback.

Feedback and reinforcement are important. This is praising and underpinning satisfactory performance by encouraging trainees with plenty of positive comment and reward, like giving lumps of sugar to a well-behaved horse. Although this is a useful general rule, it is not a complete explanation of how people learn:

> Learning is not fundamentally a matter of gradually strengthening connections but rather an all-or-none event. Thus most modem theorists tend to favour the idea that the individual connection is acquired on a single occasion . . . The effects of repetition may be to recruit more and more single connections, but each one is learned or not learned.   (Gagne, 1975, p. 44)

Training methods

Recent preoccupation with training methods may have led some people to the conclusion that training would be effective providing that the correct

Type of learning	Typical training methods
Comprehension	Lecture
	Seminar or discussion
	Film, film strip or video
Reflex	Task
	Split up into steps
	Simplification
Attitude	Experiential methods
Memory	Mnemonics
	Jingles
Procedural	Rules or routines
Varied	Assignments
	Distance learning

Figure 24.2   Types of learning and training methods.

method was selected for a given application. This chapter has already suggested that group methods, for instance, are the most appropriate way of developing attitudes, but that the lecture will be more appropriate for training which involves comprehension as its main purpose. There has, however, developed some reaction against too great a concern about method at the expense of substance. A study conducted among 64 students taught by different modes and tested both immediately after the teaching session and again one month later showed no difference in the results achieved by lecturing, case studies and role play or other experiential methods, with the following conclusion:

> It appears trainees can learn effectively in a variety of modes, perhaps indeed finding as much or more satisfaction from what they are learning than the way in which they are trained. (Gale *et al.*, 1982, p. 16)

In the generally vague area of management development there is perhaps need for more attention to what it is appropriate for managers to learn.

Despite this cautionary note the method of training still has to be appropriate for the purpose to be served. Figure 24.2 summarises the methods most suitable for the five sections of the CRAMP listing.

Here is a brief description of some of the more common methods of training, with some of their advantages and disadvantages.

Lecture.   A talk given without much participation by the trainees. Suitable for large audiences where the information to be got over can be worked out precisely in advance. There is little opportunity for feedback, so some may not get the point. It requires careful preparation and should not be longer than forty minutes.

Talk. A talk allowing participation by the trainees, by asking questions of them or by them. Useful for getting over a new way of looking at things which requires some abstraction, for example some management ideas or view of the future. It is suitable for giving information to up to twenty people. It can only work where people are willing or able to participate. Where people do not want to participate it becomes a lecture.

Skill instruction. The trainee is told how to do it, shown how to do it, does it under supervision. This is suitable for putting across skills as long as the task is broken into suitable parts. The breaking down of tasks into suitable parts will vary with the task and the person to receive the training. This form of training is not appropriate for all skills as some tasks are best learnt as a whole.

On the job. Here trainees work in the real environment with support from a skilled person. This gives the trainee real practice and it does not involve expensive new equipment. However, not all skilled people are skilled trainers. The essential ingredients are briefing, feedback and support that help the individual to achieve the objectives in a structured way. See the later section on coaching.

Audiovisual presentations. This includes slides, films and video, which now is by far the most common. This technique is similar to a lecture in what it can achieve, but video has the additional advantage over a lecture that you can stop and start it as you want.

Programmed instruction. Also called computer assisted learning, or CAL. Trainees work at their own pace using a book or computer program which has a series of tasks and tests geared to teaching something systematically. It is suitable for learning logical skills and knowledge. It does not allow discussion with others. This might be important where the application may be debatable.

Discussion. Knowledge, ideas and opinions on a subject are exchanged between trainees and trainer. This is particularly suitable where the application is a matter of opinion, for changing attitudes and finding out how knowledge is going to be applied. The technique requires skill on the part of the trainer as it can be difficult to keep discussion focused and useful.

Role play. Trainees are asked to act the role they, or someone else, would play at work. It is used particularly for face-to-face situations. It is suitable for near to real life work, where criticism would be useful. The difficulties are that trainees can be embarrassed and its usefulness is very dependent on the quality of the feedback.

Case study. This is where a history of some event is given and the trainees are invited to analyse the causes of a problem or to find a solution. This provides an opportunity for a cool look at problems and for the exchange of ideas about possible solutions. However, trainees may not realise that the real world is not quite the same as the training session.

Exercise. Trainees do a particular task, in a particular way, to get a particular result. This is suitable when trainees need practice in following a procedure or formula to reach a required objective. The exercise must be realistic.

Project. Similar to an exercise but with greater freedom to display initiative and creative ideas. Projects provide feedback on a range of personal qualities. They need the full interest and cooperation of the trainee and specific terms of reference.

Group dynamics. Trainees are put into situations where the behaviour of the individuals and the group is examined. The task given to the group usually requires them to cooperate before they can achieve the objective. Observers collect information about how the trainees go about this and then feedback to the group and individuals after the task is completed. Trainees learn about the effect they have on others. This may be threatening and anxieties need to be resolved before the end of the session. Again this is very dependent on the quality of the trainer and can be dangerous if entered too casually.

Secondment. Organising a placement in an alternative department or organisation for the achievement of a specific goal. Often used for management and professional development. The individual may of course choose not to come back!

Job rotation. By setting up flexible working patterns within the organisation an individual can broaden their experience and skill. See Chapter 16 for more details.

Acting up. Doing a more senior job temporarily to cover for absence or vacancy, for example maternity cover. In a similar manner to the above an individual can broaden their experience and skill within a position of greater responsibility.

Action learning. The linking of a structured task and action within the learning process, using Action Learning Sets, which are groups of people who discuss the problems with an identified facilitator. It is difficult to keep on the task and to complete the task as individuals develop, but the method is found to be very useful by chief executives who can feel very isolated.

Distance learning. Involves the individual utilising a range of teaching materials outside the traditional course environment. The Open University and Linguaphone Language courses are probably the most well-known examples. This is the ultimate in self-learning and can be difficult to sustain in isolation.

Coaching

Coaching and training are both intended to improve a person's working performance, but each involves a different working relationship. The coach is trying to improve the performance of someone who is already competent, while the trainer is trying to bring someone to the level of competence. The most accomplished tennis player needs a coach from whom to receive guidance, criticism and analysis of performance, and that can come from someone who is a less accomplished performer. The child learning to play tennis for the first time has to be trained in the basic techniques and methods of the game, and the accomplishment of the trainer is fundamental to successful instruction.

Both activities are concerned with how people learn, but the nature of the authority required in the coach is not the same as that needed in the trainer. Because of that difference, the approach of the coach is different from that of the trainer and the dependence of the trainee is much greater than that of the person being coached. Although it has received scant attention in the management literature, coaching seems an important activity to discuss in a management book as it is so difficult to isolate what makes a good manager.

Effectiveness lies much with individual style, confidence and personality, just as effectiveness in sport lies much with such qualities as touch, timing and a good eye. None of these can be taught to people, but coaching may be able to develop them in people.

There is a distinction to be drawn between coaching and counselling. Lopez (1968, p. 112) points out the danger:

> The supervisor's function is to coach, not counsel. The proper object of coaching is to improve present job performance; the proper job of counselling is the realisation of potential. The former emphasises doing, the latter, becoming. If the supervisor attempts to counsel rather than coach, he will indeed do exactly what some critics accuse him of doing: 'play God'.

The counselling relationship involves a great deal of trust and a concern in the counsellor for the wellbeing and personal growth of the client above all else. The manager acting as coach cannot claim that degree of altruism and the person being coached will not be likely to share with the manager all their personal concerns about the future. Coaching is centred on performance in the job now.

In the opening of this section we distinguished between coaching and training by describing coaching as improving the performance of someone who is already competent rather than establishing competence in the first place. Further aspects of coaching are that it is usually on a one-to-one basis, is set in the everyday working situation and is a continuing activity. It is gently nudging people to improve their performance, to develop their skills and to increase their self-confidence so that they can take more responsibility for their own work and develop their career prospects. Most coaching is done by people with their own subordinates, but the subordinate position of the person coached is by no means a prerequisite. What is essential is that the coach should have qualities of expertise, judgement and experience that make it possible for the person coached to follow the guidance.

Examples of coaching incidents are the head of a fashion section in a department store chatting about new lines while putting out the stock with a member of staff, or the foreman working alongside an engineer while changing a gearbox. The coaching process was implicit in the much-maligned 'sitting next to Nellie' method of industrial training, whereby a new recruit worked alongside an experienced hand in order to pick up the way of working. This is a valid criticism when used as a method of initial training, as the learner is not able to discriminate between what can be used and what can be disregarded in the performance observed. It is only appropriate when the learner is in a position to make detailed and subtle changes in their own performance: they have the necessary basic skill and knowledge and are merely adding to their repertoire of skills.

Early moves in the United States to integrate black workers in previously all-white workshops used the buddy system of attaching the newly recruited black to an experienced, established white worker to act as the buddy during the early days of employment.

| REVIEW TOPIC 24.2 |

How can a performer be coached by someone who is not as skilled as the performer?

It is what is said and how the discussion develops that can turn these pleasant exchanges into constructive coaching sessions. As with most aspects of managerial activity there is no standard method of coaching as the focus of the activity is the person being coached, whose needs and capacities will be so varied. One way managers differ has been described by Schein (1980) when he advanced his theory of the career anchor, arguing that every manager has some aspect of their attachment to work that will not be abandoned and which will act as the dominant guiding force in their life.

Examples are autonomy, creativity, organisational security, managerial competence and technical competence. If a manager is anchored to the importance of their technical ability, a coach would need to emphasise that and support it while perhaps looking for some modification to another activity like becoming more managerially competent. The coach would never succeed if they were to denigrate the importance of the technical and emphasise the managerial instead.

One of the most difficult judgements in coaching a manager is to distinguish between those aspects of performance that are essential and those that are just a matter of style. Much management training has foundered on the belief of a manager training subordinates that this way of doing things was the only way they could be done.

Stewart and Marshall (1982) have found that managers often reject much of management training as they believe that their own situation is unique and does not fit the generalised analysis of behavioural research. If this applies, then it not only requires a development approach that is specific to the individual, but also makes coaching a particularly apt method.

The essence of coaching is in two activities, delegation and discussion, neither of which will work very well unless accompanied by the other.

1. *Delegation.*   One of the least understood words in the management vocabulary. It is not giving people jobs to do; it is giving people scope, responsibility and authority. When the legendary James Bond says to a barman, 'A medium dry Vodka Martini – with a slice of lemon peel, no ice, shaken and not stirred; with either Polish or Russian Vodka', he is giving the barman a job to do with no scope for initiative, only the opportunity to perform a skilled task to a precise specification. When Bond's boss, M, says, 'Your assignment, Bond, is to stop Blofeld by any means you know how', he is delegating to James Bond considerable responsibility and authority.

   The question we have to ask about delegation is how much scope it gives to individuals to test their own ideas, develop understanding and confidence, and flex some muscles. The more specific the instructions and terms of reference, the less learning will be managed as a result of that activity. With the assignment delegated, the individual then starts work with the initiative also of seeking guidance and discussion on progress from the coaching manager, so that action is always in their own hands rather than in the hands of the coach, who will have to exercise a nice judgement on the degree of intervention. Too many interventions and the person being coached leans on the coach and becomes dependent. Too few interventions and the person being coached makes mistakes and loses confidence.

   An example of this is the 'shadowing' of hospital consultants by qualified, but junior, hospital doctors and medical students. Initially the junior observes and discusses the case only, but later takes the major role, with the consultant observing and discussing the case. Another example is 'handover time' when a person about to leave a post and the successor are both in the post together for a short time. This period is useful for discussing major issues, for introductions and for demonstrating procedures. It should not be too long a period or the person taking over is less likely to try new methods; they will have become too convinced of the unchallengeable correctness of what exists.

   A systematic use of job exchange for training, an extension of the coaching idea, has been developed by Revans (1971) who argues that groups of about six senior managers from a variety of settings can learn a great deal by tackling a particular problem that is currently being faced by one member of the group. Each group member works in one of the other organisations to find a solution to the problem, while all group members meet regularly to discuss their progress – an example of coaching by peers.

2. *Discussion.* Effective coaching discussion depends on a sound working relationship with the coach, whose comments are welcomed rather than resented or mistrusted. The coach can assist by analysing problems and helping to work out alternatives from which choices are to be made. As far as possible criticism is based on facts and not on opinion, and aimed at positive, constructive improvement of the job, not denigration of the job holder. Even reinforcing by praise has to be specific, otherwise it produces a warm glow (and perhaps intensifies a feeling of adoration for the coach) but the warm glow will fade and the praised person is not left with anything on which to build.

The delegation that is involved in coaching involves taking risks:

> No man can be certain that his subordinates will perform well, but the act of giving responsibility should imply confidence that the task set will be achieved. It is unreasonable to expect a man to give of his best if he suspects that his boss, because of his behaviour, does not really expect him to succeed and is only waiting for him to fail before doing the job himself.   (Singer, 1974, p. 63)

Evaluation and validation of training

If work organisations are to spend resources on training it is important to evaluate whether the training really proves useful. Validation is the word used to describe the process of seeing whether the training achieved its objectives. Evaluation is used to describe the process of ascertaining whether the training has affected the performance of the job. It may be that an outward bound course on leadership meets all the course objectives, the validation, but we cannot see any changes in performance at work, the evaluation. Evaluation is much more difficult to do because of the problems of deciding, defining and measuring performance. This is particularly difficult with abstract performances such as management.

Hamblin (1974) suggests five levels on which evaluation could take place:

Reaction.   The training is subjectively evaluated by the trainees on completion. They give their personal views and impressions of the value of the training.

Learning.   Measure the amount of learning that has taken place in the training reliably and validly. This is what we have called validation.

Job behaviour.   Assessing how much of the training has affected the work performance about six to nine months later.

Organisation.   The impact of training on the whole organisation is measured using criteria such as productivity, time taken to do work, waste material, absenteeism, labour turnover, and running costs.

Ultimate level.   Trying to assess the effect of training on profitability and growth. For example some of the training in customer care in the service industries in the 1980s may account for increased profitability in this sector.

SUMMARY PROPOSITIONS

24.1 There are five basic types of learning: comprehension, reflex learning, attitude development, memory, and procedural learning.
24.2 All learning has a chain of eight events: motivation, perception, acquisition, retention, recall, generalisation, performance, and feedback.
24.3 The appropriateness of training methods varies with the type of learning.
24.4 Coaching is an appropriate training method for the competent performer and does not require the coach to be more competent than the coached.

PUTTING IT INTO PRACTICE

Write a training programme for a friend or relative:

1. Cooking your favourite meal.
2. Looking after your house in your absence.
3. Washing your favourite sweater.

References

Belbin, E. and Belbin, R. M., 1972, *Problems in Adult Retraining*, Heinemann, London.

Gagne, R. M., 1975, *Essentials of Learning for Instruction*, Holt, Rinehart & Winston, New York.

Gale, J., Das, H. and Miner, R., 1982, Training methods compared, *Leadership and Organisation Behaviour Journal*, vol. 3, no. 3, pp. 13–17.

Hamblin, A., 1974, *Evaluation and Control and Training*, McGraw-Hill, London.

Honey, P. and Mumford, A., 1992, *Manual of Learning Styles*, 3rd edn, McGraw-Hill, Maidenhead, Berkshire.

ITRU (Industrial Training Research Unit), 1976, *Choose an Effective Style: a Self Instructional Approach to the Teaching of Skills*, ITRU, Cambridge.

Kolb, D. A., Rubin, I. M. and McIntyre, J. M., 1974, *Organizational Psychology: An Experiential Approach*, Prentice Hall, Englewood Cliffs, New Jersey.

Lopez, F. M. Jr, 1968, *Evaluating Enployee Performance*, Public Personnel Association, Chicago.

Revans, R. W., 1971, *Developing Effective Managers*, Longmans, London.

Schein, E. H., 1980, *Organizational Psychology*, 3rd edn, Prentice Hall, Englewood Cliffs, New Jersey.

Singer, E. J., 1974, *Effective Management Coaching*, Institute of Personnel Management, London.

Stewart, R. and Marshall, J., 1982, Managerial beliefs about managing, *Personnel Review*, vol. 11, no. 2, pp. 21–5.

Vickers, S. and Bradbeer, R., 1982, *Sinclair Spectrum Introduction*, Sinclair Research Ltd, Cambridge.

Chapter 25

Team working

The teams of people at work are varied in the degree of involvement with each other that team members have. The members of a choir or a team of dancers have to work together with split-second precision, subordinating all aspects of their own personality to a tightly controlled, collective activity. Those working on machine-paced production lines have equally specific and inflexible operations to perform, but with less skill and variety being offered in the routine they follow. A group of sales representatives introducing a new brand of photocopier all follow a similar selling routine and are selling an identical product, yet they spend most of their time alone and are physically dispersed from each other. The people running a hotel have duties that interrelate closely, but with very different skills and conventions. However varied the nature of working teams, the one thing they have in common is a desire by all members that the team should succeed. The desire of an individual to succeed personally at the expense of team success is dangerous.

[It is unrealistic always to seek team spirit and commitment to management objectives. Some groups of working people may mistrust or not accept management objectives, yet will still be able to make the specific contribution that managers require of them.] Studies of conflict demonstrate that groups whose interests diverge can still find an accommodation that will satisfy both, just as throughout the later stages of the Cold War the Russians were able to purchase large quantities of surplus North American grain to supplement the poor yield of their own harvests at the same time as vigorously opposing the economic system that produced the abundance. Guirdham (1990, p. 374) offers the following as the characteristics of a fully effective team:

> Team objectives are clearly understood by all members.
> All members are committed to the objectives.
> Mutual trust is high.
> Support for one another is high.

Communications are open and reliable, not guarded and cautious.
Team members listen to one another, understanding and being understood.
The team is self-controlling.
Conflicts are accepted and worked through.
Members' abilities, knowledge and experience are fully used by the team.

The reasons for working in teams

Working via a group of people rather than via individuals has many problems. Groups tend to work slowly and present the difficulty of producing compromise solutions that may be too timid for the problem they are designed to tackle, but managers and administrators persist in convening new groups or working parties. Reorganisation is a commonplace of industrial and commercial life, as well as throughout the public sector, and the essence of this activity is regrouping of individuals and the reallocation of managerial responsibilities. Whatever the reservations, the way in which groups operate and the way in which group membership is set up are both obviously regarded as crucial to management and organisational effectiveness. There are three reasons for this.

First, a group approach is usually best when the problem to be faced is unfamiliar and difficult or risky, without a clear procedural basis for action. Secondly, a group approach is needed when a range of skills and understanding has to be deployed in concerted endeavour, individual skill being insufficient. Thirdly, there is the shrewd view that 'people will support that which they have helped to create'. If action is to follow decision, then action will be taken more accurately and more willingly by those who have participated in shaping the decision.

| REVIEW TOPIC 25.1 |

Company reorganisation usually has the changing of working teams at its centre. What does this tell us about the importance to managers of these teams? What does it tell us about the importance to individuals of these teams?

An advertising campaign will be created by imaginative individuals having brainwaves, but underpinning those creative leaps are a series of meetings and conferences at which ideas are swapped, derided, developed and improved. A clever turn of phrase by a copywriter is turned into a sketch by an artist and sight of the sketch triggers off a further development of the initial idea. The operating theatre of a hospital has in it a group of people all of whom have varying levels and types of skill. The surgeon is at the centre, controlling the operation, but the surgeon cannot complete the operation without the effective and swift coordination of all the other skilled people present. When a company is to introduce a new product, the launch is usually preceded by a sales conference at which all those involved in sales promotion, marketing, face-to-face selling and (perhaps) distribution come together to learn what is involved and to generate enthusiasm about the new venture. Many of the traditional problems of tension and disagreement between production and marketing in companies can be traced to the fact that the production people (who were not invited to the sales conference in Majorca) see a new product as a series of headaches while marketing people see it as a golden opportunity. A time-honoured way of overcoming this problem is reorganising employees into product groups, so that the focus of selected marketing and production experts is made the product rather than the function. Taking *everyone* to Majorca is so expensive.

There may be advantages to management interest in team working, but why should individual employees want to work in this way? Although we vary in the degree of our willingness to work closely with others, we each have an in-built need to belong to groups with which we can identify and in which we can compare ourselves with other individuals. These needs are not met completely by family and out-of-work friendship groups; there is a need for work group attachment as well. This can operate at the level of attachment to the industry ('I am in engineering'), to an occupation ('I am an electrical engineer'), to an organisation ('I am with XYZ and Co.'), to a small group ('I am on the design team'), or to a role ('I am the electronics specialist on the design team'). For some people all those attachments will be important, but for most one will dominate the others, and a few people will have very low attachment. It is difficult, for instance, to imagine Beethoven wanting to identify with any working group, yet he was remarkably productive. Every organisation has its share of minor Beethovens.

Katz and Kahn (1978) advocate groups as being an important arena for individuals to find a sense of accomplishment and completion of a task, particularly in those work settings where this cannot be experienced individually, as in many manufacturing processes. This is the main argument behind the movement for autonomous work groups and for quality circles in factories.

> By being part of something beyond the physical self, the individual can achieve a sense of belongingness and can participate in accomplishments beyond individual powers. (Katz and Kahn, 1978, p. 374)

Teams at work

An initial distinction that has to be made about working in teams is between the task that the group has to achieve and the processes by which the team members operate. We are here concerned mainly with the processes but only by completing the task satisfactorily is there any justification for considering the process. There is always a danger that the activity of being in the team, with all those other nice people, can be emphasised at the expense of the task, but there is some evidence that a significant basis for the satisfaction of individual team members with their membership is the sense of achievement in producing results. At the same time it is necessary for the team to maintain cohesion while being unsuccessful. Most teams experience failure as well as success and the test of effectiveness may well be the ability to get through the bad times without disintegrating.

Teams differ according to their purpose. The working party, or task force, is a short-term grouping while the work group is fairly permanent, and those who are members of the first will also be members of the second, although, maybe, not the other way round. Some teams, such as the board of directors in a company, have decision-making as their prime task; while others, such as autonomous work groups, have the objective of making things by cooperative effort.

One of the most common teams currently is concerned with quality. The Total Quality Concept (TQM) that is so widely adopted has grown out of the earlier use of quality circles, which were small, informal groups set up to discuss means towards quality improvement. These were developed by the Japanese Kaoru Ishikawa, as described by Mohr and Mohr (1983). A group of seven to ten employees from a unit meet together for about one hour a week to identify, analyse and make recommendations about problems of quality or productivity in their unit.

A similar development is the autonomous work group or self-managed team. Hackman and Oldham (1980) define these as having three essential characteristics:

1. They are *real*, in that they are intact, identifiable social systems, even if small or temporary.
2. They are *work* groups that have to do a specified piece of work that results in a product, service or decision, whose acceptability is measurable.
3. They are *self-managing* groups whose members have the authority to manage their own task and interpersonal processes as they carry out their work.

A rigorous, three-year study of the application of this approach showed that it produced major economic benefits for the employer (Wall *et al.*, 1986).

Characteristics of teams

Tuckman (1965) suggests that there are clear stages in the growth of relationships in groups of people working together, as shown in Table 25.1, of forming, storming, norming and performing. People come together and conflict develops between members as they assess each other before they

Table 25.1 Stages in the growth of group cohesion and performance

Stage of development	Process	Outcome
1. Forming	There is anxiety, dependence on leader, testing to find out the nature of the situation and what behaviour is acceptable	Members find out what the task is, what the rules are and what methods are appropriate
2. Storming	Conflict between sub-groups, rebellion against leader, opinions are polarised, resistance to control by group	Emotional resistance to demands of task
3. Norming	Development of group cohesion, norms emerge, resistance is overcome and conflicts patched up; mutual support and sense of group identity	Open exchange of views and feelings; cooperation develops
4. Performing	Interpersonal problems are resolved; interpersonal structure becomes the means of getting things done; roles are flexible and functional	Solutions to problems emerge; there are constructive attempts to complete tasks and energy is now available for effective work

(Based on Tuckman, 1965)

move to the third stage of finding a way of working together. Finally they work well and produce results.

The length of time required for this process varies. For a team that is to be together for a long time, it may take many months because the degree of investment required from each member is so high and the personal risks of failure so great. If the team is convening as a short-term, part-time activity – like the group that is arranging the office party at Christmas – then the individual investment is less, the risks fewer and the mutual tolerance greater, so that the process is easily truncated. Individual tolerance of the process varies, so that there is always at least one person who will quickly make a comment like 'If we don't get something settled soon, we will be here all night'.

A number of experimental studies have attempted to establish which method of communication within a team is the most appropriate. The classic study was that of Leavitt (1951), which is summarised in Figure 25.1. For experimental purposes members of a small group were given tasks which involved communicating with each other, but they were required to

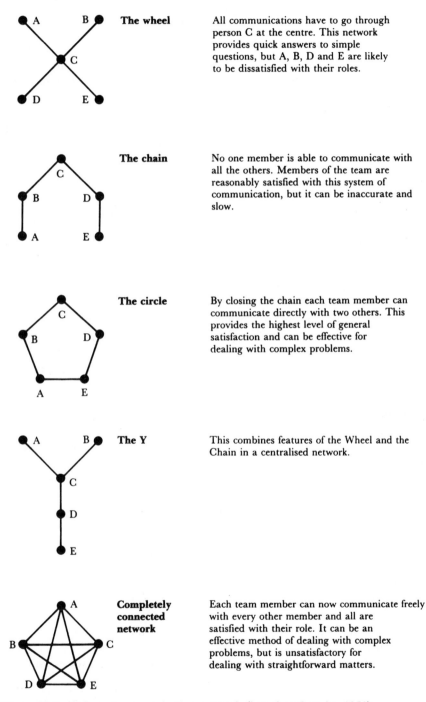

The wheel — All communications have to go through person C at the centre. This network provides quick answers to simple questions, but A, B, D and E are likely to be dissatisfied with their roles.

The chain — No one member is able to communicate with all the others. Members of the team are reasonably satisfied with this system of communication, but it can be inaccurate and slow.

The circle — By closing the chain each team member can communicate directly with two others. This provides the highest level of general satisfaction and can be effective for dealing with complex problems.

The Y — This combines features of the Wheel and the Chain in a centralised network.

Completely connected network — Each team member can now communicate freely with every other member and all are satisfied with their role. It can be an effective method of dealing with complex problems, but is unsatisfactory for dealing with straightforward matters.

Figure 25.1 Types of communication network (based on Leavitt, 1951).

communicate in differing, specific ways. The Wheel and Y networks had a central controlling person in the system, while the others were decentralised with varying degrees of limitation on the freedom with which group members exchanged information. Centralised networks were best for getting simple jobs done and decentralised networks produced better solutions to difficult problems. Centralisation was highly satisfying to person C at the centre, but frustrating for others.

The patterns illustrated each represent a typical situation found in working life. The Wheel is like a regional sales team with four members reporting to a regional manager. The Chain is like a department with two executives, B and D, each reporting to a manager C and having personal assistants A and E. The Y is similar to an orthodox chain of command with one person B who is outside and who communicates only with C, as in the case of a key supplier or customer. The Circle and the Completely Connected Network are like discussion groups, with the Circle being an unusual form which is more important from the experimental point of view than because of the frequency with which it is found.

The most effective teams are those which can vary their mode of operation between, say, the Wheel and the Completely Connected Network in line with task requirements. Managers who try to centralise all com-munication will find resistance from team members, who will lack any sense of involvement in what is taking place. Managers who decentralise every-thing will miss opportunities through wasting time, and team members will come to regard the process as one of all talk and no action. Managers who can achieve a shrewd balance and have thorough, decentralised considera-tion of matters which can only be dealt with in that way will then find that their team members readily acknowledge the right and necessity of the managers operating in a centralised way for the majority of straightforward decisions and information.

Another classic study was that of Rice (1958). It is interesting that this was conducted in an Indian textile factory; not all our evidence comes from North America. Rice had four main conclusions (pp. 37–9):

1. The most productive group, and the one most satisfactory to its members, is the pair; then groups of six to twelve, with eight as the optimum.
2. Group stability is more easily maintained when the range of skills is such that all members can comprehend each others' skills; that is, they could aspire to acquire them.
3. The fewer differences in prestige and status within the group, the more stable it is.
4. When individual members of a work group become disaffected and no longer fit in, they should be able to move elsewhere.

Group size is particularly important for teams who need to exchange ideas, as too few people are not able to generate sufficient richness of ideas, but too many can lead either to a baffling excess of suggestions or to some more cautious members being inhibited.

Team roles

R. F. Bales (1950) developed a series of observation categories for studying the process of interaction in small groups. These are shown in Figure 25.2. He found that groups needed both members who were effective in the task area and those who were effective in the social and emotional area. Team members who were task oriented were the most influential and those who were social–emotional oriented were the best liked, but both were necessary for the continuing effectiveness of the group. Bales also differentiated between behaviour in the group that was emotionally positive and that which was emotionally negative.

There are always the conciliators, the antagonists and the neurotics, working alongside the questioners, clarifiers and directors. Neither can succeed without the other and each group member will be partly task oriented and partly social–emotional oriented, with one orientation typically dominant.

Belbin *et al.* (1976) carried out a systematic study of management teams and concluded that six roles were needed in effective management teams apart from specialist and functional roles.

His six were subsequently expanded to eight roles (Belbin, 1981):

1. Company worker, who keeps the interests of the organisation to the fore at all times.
2. Chairman, who ensures that the views of all participants are heard and who keeps things moving.
3. Shaper, who follows particular lines of argument and blends together elements of the contributions from several other members.
4. Ideas person, who contributes novel suggestions.
5. Resource investigator, who assesses the feasibility of contributions and finds out where and how to obtain the required resources.
6. Monitor/evaluator, who evaluates the relevance of the contributions being made and the extent to which the team is meeting its objectives.
7. Team worker, who maintains the social cohesion of the group and the discussion process by joking and agreeing with others.
8. Completer/finisher, who looks for conclusions and tries to get things done.

Here again we see the importance of task orientation as well as the social–emotional area or team maintenance, but a related aspect of the roles which team members assume is the way in which conflict can develop within the general mode of cooperative team working. As with conflict between

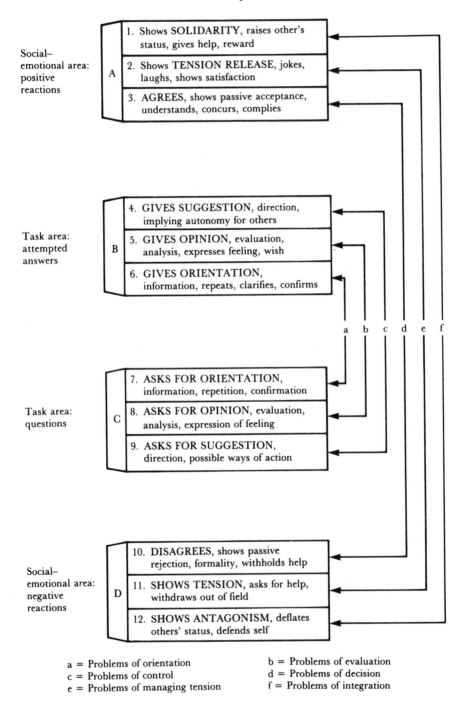

Figure 25.2 Interaction process categories (from Bales, 1950).

management and a collective of employees, this can be constructive or destructive. John Hunt (1979, pp. 90–1) summarises the possibilities:

Conflict may:
Introduce different solutions to the problem,
Clearly define the power relationship within the group,
Encourage creativity and brainstorming activity,
Focus on individual contributions rather than group decisions,
Bring emotive, non-rational arguments into the open,
Provide for catharsis, release of interdepartmental or interpersonal conflicts of long standing.

Conversely, if conflict is destructive, it may:
Dislocate the entire group and produce polarisations,
Subvert the objectives in favour of sub-goals,
Lead people to defensive and blocking behaviour in their group,
Result in the disintegration of the entire group,
Stimulate win–lose conflicts, where reason is secondary to emotion.

The team leader is always vigilant for the level of conflict in the team. Although the comments of Hunt, above, are directed towards behaviour in face-to-face groups, there is a similar problem with the general, long-term working relationships between team members. They are all to some extent in competition with each other, all likely to feel that they are being left out of important meetings and all likely to mistrust the manoeuvres of their colleagues. This can keep people on their toes and ensure a keen level of contribution, but there is always the risk that the conflict can become destructive and the manager will need then to confront the problem. This is not a favourite job for managers, as it can involve unpleasantness and the outcome is hard to predict. The best guide for dealing with such problems is a publication on interpersonal problem-solving by Richard Walton (1969).

| REVIEW TOPIC 25.2 |

Think of a group you were with within the last few days, for example:

a business meeting,
a lunch group,
a sports team,
a seminar, or
a dinner party.

1. Who spoke most?
2. Who spoke least?
3. Who gave most task-oriented conversation?
4. Who gave most group-oriented conversation?
5. Did you find it a satisfying experience? Why, or why not?

Team development

Understanding the ways in which teams work is the best way to working effectively with and through them, as most people have to find a way of working with what there is rather than being able to make changes. For managers, however, who are able to take initiatives to improve their teams, some techniques have been evolved for assisting this process.

Sensitivity training

A controversial method of developing in people an awareness of their impact on others. It is potentially useful to develop an ability of individuals to work in teams and uses group methods to achieve its objectives. The idea is that all of us dissemble in our everyday dealings with others; we smile at people we dislike and restrain critical comments about others, either because we fear retaliation or because it is not accepted behaviour. Sensitivity training forces trainees to be more open in their behaviour towards others and, in the process, become more sensitive to the feelings and attitudes of others. The method is basically to put a group of eight to twelve people in a room without any agenda or programme and leave them there for long periods. The lack of structure provides a void which group members try to fill and their comments gradually become more frank. As there is nothing to talk about, they inevitably talk about their relationship with each other. Those who are task oriented or social–emotionally oriented become apparent and everyone comes to a deeper understanding of how they relate to others. The value of this method can be considerable, but the risks are also great. It encourages people to be more open and honest with each other, but has the following drawbacks:

1. It forces many individuals to undergo a personality-humiliating and anxiety-provoking experience from which they might not recover.
2. It strips some people of defenses they badly need and provides them with nothing to replace those defenses.
3. It encourages behavioral modes that are acceptable in the laboratory but unacceptable in most organizational settings.
4. Any benefits accrued from the experience are so short-lived as to make the experience a waste of time and money.
5. It encourages and subtly coerces individuals into revealing aspects about themselves that constitute an invasion of privacy, thus harboring later resentment in participants. (du Brin, 1974, p. 424)

Against such a catalogue of drawbacks it is remarkable that the sensitivity training method was used so extensively. It is described here because elements of the method are to be found in many other training approaches, even though they are rarely described as sensitivity training.

Organisation development

A term that has been applied to many different approaches, but one of them is to use an Organisation Development (OD) consultant to work with a group of people to improve their collective performance. The group consists of people who do work together and the discussion is based on what they have to say rather than on any 'instruction' from the consultant, who is usually described as a change agent because this method has so often been used to make working teams more effective at innovation. There will be an agenda, with items such as:

1. Are we each clear about our duties and responsibilities?
2. Are there any areas of overlap? Anything missing?
3. In what ways do we communicate well with each other? In what ways badly?
4. How can we communicate with each other better?

The role of the consultant is to direct the discussion to the agenda and to ensure that it is kept to the way the job is done rather than attacks on individuals and their personal characteristics. This produces candour and constructive discussion, but deflects the behaviours that could be destructive.

This is not a speedy process and it will probably take a number of meetings before all participants are convinced that there will be an improvement. Ideally some everyday working experience is interspersed with the training sessions to put into practice some of the proposals in order to re-examine, in the everyday situation, some of what has been said in discussion. One method is to start with a weekend of discussion and then have two or three follow-up sessions after a few weeks back in the workplace. The consultant should be phased out towards the end of the training period.

Committee operations

Committees operate in a relatively formal way. There is invariably someone taking the chair and usually minutes are kept. These may be drafted by a secretary during and after the meeting, but eventually they have to be accepted by all members at the next meeting. The person in the chair has considerable scope for determining the way in which proceedings are recorded and emphasised, but there is less scope for determining decisions, unless the committee is remarkably compliant. Before a decision is reached it will be framed with some precision, even though it may not be put as a formal motion. Either the chairperson will frame it in a leading way – 'Are we all agreed then, that we offer the post to Smith?' – or it will be put to the meeting as a motion from committee members. The wording is likely to be clarified and tidied up before the committee as a whole votes on it.

One determinant of effectiveness will be the size of the committee. What is appropriate depends on the committee's main purpose. Hare (1981) produces evidence that a membership between six and ten is preferred for problem-solving and making decisions. Fewer members means that there may be insufficient input of information and ideas. More people leads to unwieldly discussion, diverse information input and the inhibiting of the less confident members of the committee. Schwartz (1980, p. 342) makes the following suggestions:

Relatively large committees are desired when:
- A principal purpose of the committee is to inform the members who comprise it.
- Widely differing talents and experience are needed to make the recommendation or decision.
- The scope of the committee's activities is very broad. In these cases, however, it may be wise to divide the work into sub-committees.

Relatively small committees are desired when:
- Speedy action is needed.
- The matter assigned to the committee must be kept confidential. Obviously, the more persons serving on a committee, the greater the chance of information leaks.

Committee effectiveness is also influenced by the nature of the membership. There are nearly always some ineffective members who hold their place for political reasons or even as a form of punishment. They are likely to delay, confuse or demoralise the committee as a whole. One of the important matters to be resolved is whether an individual is essential or 'possibly useful'; only the essential should be recruited. The ideal committee member should be interested in its purpose, with relevant knowledge and experience and sufficient time to attend and prepare for meetings. Finally the ideal member should be psychologically equipped for the committee process: able to compromise after reasoned argument, listening as well as talking, but sufficiently resolute to persist in trying to persuade other members to their point of view. In this way the contribution is made and used by the group as a whole in the search for consensus.

The method of the committee discussion is basically the exchange of information followed by working on hypotheses. On each issue or item on the agenda members first seek out the facts, even if those facts do not necessarily support their personal cause. This search for information may be aided by information being provided by the chairman or secretary for study beforehand. Nearly all committees have some preliminary documentation of this type, but it will be expanded by verbal contributions from committee members. This will add to what is written or provide interpretation. A committee deciding whether to install gas- or oil-fired central heating will be provided with the comparative cost estimates, but individual members will have a myriad of questions to put to the various interested members, which could not all be anticipated beforehand. As more and more information is exchanged the committee members build up a shared information base that makes ultimate consensus possible.

Once committee members find answers to all their questions they are reaching a point where decisions could be made, and this decision-making is expedited by exploring hypotheses. The nature of contributions changes. In information exchange the contributions are mainly question and answer, with questions like the following:

'Do we know how long it would take?'
'Could Fred tell us . . .?'
'Will the suppliers provide . . .?'

When discussion on a topic moves to hypotheses, the questions become leading:

'It seems to me that we have only one course to follow'
'Does this mean that we have to . . .?'
'Would anyone agree with me that . . .?'

REVIEW TOPIC 25.3

The Roman poet Ovid (49 BC–AD 17) made the comment 'You will go most safely in the middle . . .' (*medio tutissimus ibis*).

Does decision-making by committee increase or decrease the desire for safety?

As working on competing hypotheses develops, the person in the chair will be looking for the most acceptable hypothesis in order to single it out for the committee's consent. When topics are extremely complex, the committee may divide up the work between subgroups of themselves, so that a series of working hypotheses is developed and the committee reconvenes to find a viable amalgam of the contributed part-decisions.

SUMMARY PROPOSITIONS

25.1 The working team is the fundamental unit of organisation and many organisational tasks cannot be achieved by other means.

25.2 All employees can achieve a degree of satisfaction in team working that they cannot achieve by other means.

25.3 A distinction can be drawn between the task of a group and the processes whereby the group deals with the task. Teams need contributions that are both task oriented and social–emotionally oriented.

25.4 Committees formalise the act of group working. This is fundamental to the working of any organisation.

25.5 Committees are semi-permanent bodies whose main purposes are to make decisions and diffuse information.

25.6 Although decisions by committee may be less cost-effective than those made by individuals, they may be bolder, and a committee decision starts life with all the members committed to its success.

25.7 Members of committees compete with each other as well as cooperate. When controlled from the chair, this improves the quality of the committee's work.

25.8 The main operating method of committees is the exchange of information, working on hypotheses and achieving consensus.

PUTTING IT INTO PRACTICE

Team leaders can make their teams more effective by analysing the roles that team members fill, to see what contributions are being made and what is being left out. This can also provide the basis of developing the contributions and career prospects of individual team members.

Use the matrix in Figure 25.3 to record incidents of team members' behaviour that you observe in any aspect of team working. The types of

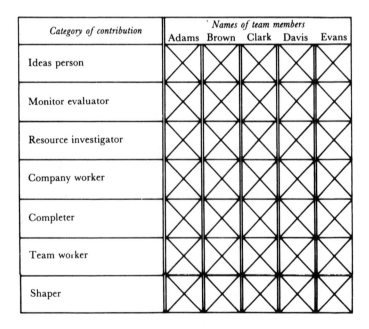

Figure 25.3 Matrix for analysing team members' roles.

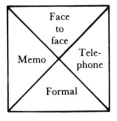

Figure 25.4   Incidents in team working (based on Belbin *et al.*, 1976).

activity will vary between teams and the situations in which they are working, but the most common are as follows:

1. Face-to-face (informal).
2. Memorandum.
3. Telephone.
4. Formal meeting.

The matrix is set out with seven roles identified by Belbin and referred to in this chapter. These are on the vertical axis with columns for each team member arranged horizontally. Each of the resulting boxes is divided into four sections, so that the behaviours can be tallied with strokes to record each incident. The sections are as shown in Figure 25.4.

Incidents should be recorded over a week and at the end of the week you can see both the emphasis of the contributions being made by individual team members and the team roles which are being filled and those which are not. Most people make contributions in a variety of roles but you should also find some who consistently make more contributions in one particular area.

Are there any roles not being filled? Should they be? Who might be encouraged to fill them? (For example, someone who makes an occasional contribution in this area, or yourself?)

This method of analysis is the one we regard as most appropriate for management teams, but some people prefer the Role Analysis Process (RAP) described in French and Bell (1990).

References

Bales, R. F., 1950, *Interaction Process Analysis*, Addison-Wesley, Reading, Mass.

Belbin, R. M., 1981, *Management Teams*, Heinemann, London.

Belbin, R. M., Aston, B. R. and Mottram, R. D., 1976, Building effective management teams, *Journal of General Management*, vol. 2, pp. 23–9.

du Brin, A., 1974, *Fundamentals of Organization Behaviour*, Pergamon, New York.

French, W. L. and Bell, C. H., 1990, *Organization Development*, 4th edn, Prentice Hall, Englewood Cliffs, New Jersey.

Guirdham, M., 1990, *Interpersonal Skills at Work*, Prentice Hall, Hemel Hempstead.

Hackman, J. R. and Oldham, G., 1980, *Work Redesign*, Addison-Wesley, Reading, Mass.

Hare, A. P., 1981, in Borgatta, E. F. and Baker, P. M., Symposia on small groups, *American Behavioral Scientist*, May/June.

Hunt, J., 1979, *Managing People at Work*, Pan Books, London.

Katz, D. and Kahn, R.L., 1978, *The Social Psychology of Organizations*, 2nd edn, John Wiley, New York.

Leavitt, H. J., 1951, Some aspects of certain communication patterns on group performance, *Journal of Abnormal and Social Psychology*, vol. 45, pp. 38–50.

Mohr, W. L. and Mohr, H., 1983, *Quality Circles*, Addison-Wesley, Reading, Mass., p. 13.

Rice, A K., 1958, *Productivity and Social Organisation*, Tavistock, London.

Schwartz, D., 1980, *Introduction to Management: Principles, Practices and Processes*, Harcourt Brace Jovanovich, New York.

Tuckman, B. W., 1965, Development sequences in small groups, *Psychological Bulletin*, vol. 63, pp. 384–99.

Wall, T. D., Kemp, N. J., Jackson, P. R. and Clegg, C. W., 1986, Outcomes of autonomous work groups: a long-term field experiment, *Academy of Management Journal*, vol. 29, pp. 280–304.

Walton, R. E., 1969, *Interpersonal Peacemaking: Third Party Consultations*, Addison-Wesley, Reading, Mass.

Chapter 26

Differing patterns of employment

Working life for many people is surprisingly rigid: nine till five for five days a week with a few individual days' holiday at religious festivals and three or four weeks' annual holiday, which must be taken within a twelve-month period. That is the popular view of 'a proper job'. It is relatively secure and predictable and you set up your life around that pattern, with work fitting into a predetermined slot in the annual/weekly cycle.

Patterns of employment are changing, with many variations on that basic theme emerging towards the close of the century. There are two points of view about the changes. One is that employers are denying people reasonable security and predictability: the ideal should be a permanent, full-time job for everyone. The opposing view is that changing patterns enable people to break out of that rigidity and find a more personalised mode. The stimulus towards this has included the desire of some employees with extended families in other countries to spend lengthy periods of leave abroad, and the interest of some potential employees in working part-time, although the mould-breaking development was the introduction of flexible working hours during the early 1970s. This simple practice enables people to vary their actual hours of attendance at work marginally at the beginning and end of the day and is now widespread in clerical and administrative work.

Organisations adopt employment strategies in response to prevailing labour market conditions. Such strategies are shaped by economic, technological, political and social factors.

In this chapter we shall examine different employment strategies and policies, including increased labour flexibility, the development of a segmented labour market, and the growing use of subcontractors and external agencies. We shall then go on to review recent political and demographic changes in Britain and Europe, and consider their likely impact on employment strategy in the 1990s.

REVIEW TOPIC 26.1

Apart from the money and the implicit security, would you prefer 'a proper job', as defined in the opening paragraph, or something different? What is the reason for your preference?

Flexible employment strategies of the 1980s

The recession of the late 1970s, together with a number of other factors including: increased overseas competition, technological change and reduction in working time, caused a number of companies in the early 1980s to review their employment policies.

A key consideration was 'flexibility'. In order to survive after the recession, organisations needed to become much more flexible in their response to external influences. This in turn required them to be more flexible in their internal organisation, including the deployment of personnel. By changing the way work was organised companies hoped to increase the flexibility of their operation. Research by John Atkinson of the IMS (Atkinson, 1984) suggested that these employer initiatives could be incorporated into a new employment model which moved away from the traditional, hierarchical structure of organisations. Atkinson termed this model 'the flexible firm'.

Such a firm consists of three groups of workers:

Core workers comprise the primary labour market. They conduct the key, company-specific activities. If the nature of the operation changes these workers will be expected to learn new skills and accept lateral transfer, often outside their normal skill environment – functional flexibility. Core workers are full-time, permanent, career employees, mainly in managerial, professional and skilled technical positions.

Peripheral workers comprise the secondary labour market. These jobs are not company-specific and tend either to be less skilled, requiring little training, or generally-skilled, in that the skill can be readily applied in a number of different working situations, such as a driver or systems analyst. Peripheral workers enjoy a lower level of job security and have less access to career opportunities. This encourages a high level of labour turnover. In some cases an organisation may supplement the flexibility of the first peripheral group with a second peripheral group. These workers are hired on contracts which permit easy adjustment of numbers, such as part-timers, job sharers and temporary workers – numerical flexibility.

External workers the division of labour into core and non-core tasks highlights the potential role of contractors, agencies and self-employed workers for undertaking both routine and specialist jobs, for example catering, cleaning, road transport, security, public relations and market research. Benefits to the employer of subcontracting include improved flexibility and productivity, reduced employment costs, increased resources available for main business activities, and enhanced job security for core employees (Evans and Walker, 1986). However, there are also a number of disadvantages in the widespread use of contract staff (Cross, 1986):

Cost although contract workers may allow short-term savings to be made, long-term costs may well exceed those of employing an equivalent number of permanent staff, if the contract workers are engaged at premium rates.

Quality and reliability it is more difficult to monitor work and safety standards of contract staff. Peter Jordan was a building contractor, who obtained a lucrative contract to erect two and a half miles of security fencing. One of the contract conditions was that the concrete posts should be dug in three feet below the surface. Through shortage of permanent staff he employed a team of twelve from a subcontractor, only to receive a complaint from his customer that the posts had been sunk only eighteen inches into the ground. The cost of putting the error right turned a small operating profit for the year into a substantial loss. There was no recovery possible from the subcontractor, as he had 'moved away'.

Employee relations how will the use of contract workers affect relations with permanent staff and trade unions? There may well be different levels of weekly or monthly pay, and those on 'permanent' contracts will not always appreciate the value of those contracts compared with the higher-paid insecurity of those hired in from an agency.

Another issue is the increasing practice of 'contracting out'. Employers shed employees in order to trim headcounts, and then re-engage them as self-employed independent contractors, thereby retaining their valuable skills and background knowledge. This allows greater flexibility for both employer and contract worker – organisations are able to deal more effectively with fluctuating business requirements, and workers are able to offer their services to a number of companies (Clutterbuck, 1986).

┤ REVIEW TOPIC 26.2 ├──────────────────────────

Are you a core, peripheral or external worker? Would you rather be one of the others? Which would you most like to avoid?

The consequences of the above employment strategies for workers are considerable. Whilst core employees are afforded permanent, full-time, secure employment, the position for peripheral workers is not as favourable. Peripheral jobs tend to require low-level skills with little training, investment or promotion opportunities. Such workers, particularly part-timers, are also at a disadvantage as regards non-pay benefits and employment rights.

However, whilst the labour surpluses of the 1980s may have facilitated such working arrangements, political and demographic changes may force employers to develop more varied policies in order to meet current employee demands and expectations.

| REVIEW TOPIC 26.3 |

a. What are the advantages and disadvantages of using contract staff?
b. What steps can organisations take to incorporate numerical and functional flexibility into their work systems?

Demographic issues

There are four major demographic issues facing employers in the 1990s in relation to the external labour market (Atkinson, 1989):

Labour shortages: In 1971 there were approximately 900,000 live births in the UK. By 1975, it was less than 700,000 and has remained below 800,000 per annum to date. Thus, although the workforce is growing, it is not expanding quickly enough to meet any demand for labour, if we continue with traditional approaches to employment. The 1990s could be characterised by skill shortages, in the same way as the 1980s were characterised by labour surplus.

Age composition: The impact of the above population statistics has been highlighted in a report on 'Young People and the Labour Market' (NEDO, 1988):

> Over the next five years the number of 16–24-year-olds in the labour force will fall by 1.2 million, a decline of one fifth – with a decline of 23 per cent in the 16–19-year-old age group. Employers are going to find it much more difficult to recruit sufficient numbers in the future.

Companies that rely on young people in certain jobs, or as trainees for specific career plans, will experience particular problems. However, it is likely that the majority of employers will be forced to review policy as regards the preferred age of new recruits.

Sex composition: Due to the decline in population growth, employers will have to rely more on increasing the readiness of all individuals to work. For example, it is estimated that 90% of the expected increase in labour supply to 2000 will be among women. By 2000, women will comprise 44% of the labour force.

Skill shortages: Demand for labour in manual and unskilled jobs is likely to continue to contract during the 1990s. However, demand for skilled people, particularly professional, scientific and technical workers, is predicted to increase.

It is predicted that demographic factors and educational policy will lead to a drop in the number of students attending university from 124,000 in 1992 to 113,000 in 1998 (Curnow, 1989). The 1992 Autumn Statement by the British Chancellor of the Exchequer introduced changes in the funding of teaching in universities that will curb the growth in student numbers that had been seen until that year. The numbers were capped and the fee that universities could charge for students of the humanities and social sciences was reduced by a third. This may have the effect of deflecting students away from the burgeoning business studies and social science areas, but the rapid growth of the 1989–1992 period has been halted. In addition, there is evidence to suggest that with regard to new graduates and skilled staff, implementation of the Single European Market in 1992 will produce a net worsening of supply in the UK, as more potential recruits seek employment overseas (Pearson and Pike, 1989). Indeed, the increased willingness of graduates to work abroad is reflected in the success of recent European job fairs (Hall, 1990).

At the time of writing (spring 1993) it is very difficult to see signs of labour shortage, but there are certainly clear signs of differing patterns of employment contract being developed.

REVIEW TOPIC 26.4

What effect can you see now of the changing composition of the workforce and the social and political context of work?

A response to demographic change

Overall, these demographic and labour supply factors could cause a tightening of labour markets in all parts of the country. What would exacerbate the situation is the failure of employers to devise and implement suitable responses. Atkinson (1989) has suggested a sequential response by firms to the predicted demographic downturn. His model outlines a progression from short-term to more long-term responses, and from an external labour market perspective back to an internal one.

Responses to a tightening labour market include:

Intensifying recruitment efforts through advertising campaigns and posters, targeting distant markets, encouraging relocation/travel, etc.
Strengthening liaison with schools, colleges and universities by introducing work experience and YTS schemes or open-days for local youngsters. Poole (1989) suggests that firms should offer 'rewards' such as spon-

sorships, donations, prizes, etc. to schools and colleges which provide recruits.

Increasing pay. This will have a spiralling effect, as an increase introduced by one company will be undermined by the same response from competitors.

Eventually, organisations will find that the growing cost of competing for the available labour will lead them on to find *substitute* workers, i.e. to target non-traditional sectors of the labour force.

Employers will finally come full circle, back to their present labour force. Policy initiatives here include the *creation* of enhanced job opportunities and improved worker performance:

- increased training and retraining
- improved deployment of labour through job restructuring/multiskilling (see Hendry and Pettigrew, 1988)
- development of career programmes and improved promotion opportunities
- moves towards greater employee participation through team building, profit sharing, etc.
- company incentives (loyalty bonuses, non-contributory pension schemes).

Women

In an attempt to attract women recruits, many organisations are introducing new flexible working arrangements. By targeting recruits who do not fit into the traditional 'nine- to-five' work patterns, companies are able first to select from a wider labour pool and, secondly to provide a closer match between working hours and business requirements (such as late night/weekend opening).

A problem facing many employers wishing to attract women returners is the issue of childcare facilities. Most women are reluctant to return to work after maternity leave, without childcare they can both trust and afford. Current provisions fall well short of demand – recent estimates place only 3,000 children in workplace nurseries, whilst 250,000 attend childminders.

For many employers, particularly small firms, the cost of establishing a workplace nursery is prohibitive. Only 9% of employers currently offer childcare facilities. One solution is the pooling of resources with local councils and other employers to set up nurseries:

> Islington Council aims to set up a 40-place staff nursery in partnership with another employer . . . The council will reserve a number of places for staff in hard-to-fill jobs such as teachers. The nursery will be highlighted in advertisements for such jobs. (Hall, 1990)

Alternative options include vouchers or cash allowances. If childcare facilities in Britain are to be improved, input is required not only from employers, but also from the Government. In April 1990, the Chancellor made the move of removing the tax employees must pay on employers' provision of workplace nurseries. However, this concession applies only to nurseries run by employers jointly with other employers, voluntary bodies or local authorities. It is therefore likely to have only a limited effect on the spread of childcare and the return of mothers to work.

| REVIEW TOPIC 26.5 |
---

   a. I don't think employers do enough to help working parents. Provision of child care facilities should be a legal obligation.'

   b. It is an inappropriate use of company money to set up creches and will only be done by companies with surplus cash. Furthermore it is unsuitable for the child, who becomes dependent on the continuing ability of the company to provide the facility.'

Older workers

Over the next two decades the population of the UK and the rest of Europe will age. It is predicted that by the year 2000, the over-65s will make up 15–16% of the UK population (Goetschin, 1987). Coupled with a decline in the number of youngsters entering the labour market, these statistics have important consequences for employers.

At present, there are over ten million pensioners in the UK, together with large numbers of workers who have taken early retirement. For employers faced with a diminishing workforce, the over-50s have become a target recruitment group. The most publicised schemes are those introduced by the large retail chains:

> Two years ago Tesco targeted older people in Crawley with a local advertising campaign. It filled all its vacancies within a week. The success of this campaign encouraged the company to develop a mature entrant programme – life begins at 55 – recruiting up to the age of 69 . . .   (Finn, 1990, p. 37)

For many mature employees, work provides a necessary social focus, part-time hours being most attractive. Although such recruits may require longer training and a more democratic style of management, the benefits of improved customer service, high staff motivation and reduced turnover outweigh any drawbacks.

A few companies are also considering flexible forms of retirement as a means of retaining the valuable skills and experience of their older employees. For example, older managers can be re-employed as external consultants or assigned to project work. One problem with these schemes is the rigidity of current pension arrangements. However, reforms allowing for 'phased' retirement and part-pension options would encourage the development of flexible retirement. Such policies are of particular relevance in the light of predicted demographic trends.

Factors influencing employment strategy in the 1990s

The Single European Act (1986)

Improvement and harmonisation of living and working conditions throughout the European Community has been part of the Common Market since the EEC Treaty (sometimes called the Treaty of Rome) of 1957, which sets out the principles and framework for achieving a single European market. (Mill, 1990)

The Single European Act rejuvenated the original theme of the Treaty of Rome in the form of some 279 measures deemed necessary to achieve a single market in Europe. Such a market will provide Europe with a unique industrial and commercial opportunity, in addition to strengthening political links within the Community. The Act identified 31 December 1992 as a final date by which time all measures should have been adopted.

The move towards the single market led to the idea of a 'social dimension'. It was the European Commission's thesis that employees in the Community would not willingly accept the impact of the economic measures involved in building a single market unless they saw that there was also a social dimension to the process, which guaranteed that employment and social rights would be maintained and, indeed, gradually harmonised upwards across the Community.

Pursuing the objective of giving concrete expression to the 'social dimension', the Commission lost no time in drawing up a 'Community Charter of Fundamental Social Rights of Workers'. A preliminary draft of the social charter was issued by the Commission in May 1989. The final text of the charter was endorsed during the Strasbourg summit in December 1989. It sets out a range of basic employment rights under twelve headings:

1. The free movement of workers within the EC
2. 'Fair remuneration' for employment
3. The improvement and approximation of conditions of employment
4. Social security
5. Freedom of association and collective bargaining
6. Vocational training
7. Equal treatment for men and women
8. Information, consultation and participation arrangements
9. Health and safety at the workplace
10. Young people
11. Retired people
12. Disabled people

Employment strategy and the Single European Market

The British position on the social charter has always been hostile, and the Maastricht Treaty of 1991 eventually resulted in a British opt-out. However, it is likely, together with the Single European Act, to have a considerable influence on employment practices in the UK over the next decade. A pre-Maastricht review of the likely impact of 1992 was given by Underwood (1989):

Recruitment: Although employers have been free to recruit in Europe for several years, a number of problems – language difficulties, choice of advertising media, recognition of qualifications, assessment of work experience – have limited employee movement. However, it is anticipated that the advent of the Single Market, together with greater European awareness, will prompt an increase in labour movement. UK recruiters will then be forced to compete in a wider market.

Health and Safety: The European Commission has drawn up a framework setting out employers' responsibilities as regards health and safety. Many of these recommendations are already covered by the Health and Safety at Work Act (1974) – thus British employers may not have to review as many practices as some other member states. However, a proactive approach should be taken and any new legislation incorporated into current policies.

Employee relations: Within Europe, attitudes to employer–employee relations are developing, and new issues such as the protection of part-time and temporary workers are being discussed. UK employers must therefore face the possibility of some changes in the terms and conditions of their employees.

Training: In order to compete in a European market, organisations will need to provide increased vocational training and also language skills for employees.

Pay: At present UK salaries are generally below European levels. This has obvious implications for remuneration packages, particularly if companies are recruiting outside the UK.

Over the next decade employers will need to adopt an overall employment strategy for Europe, compatible with cultural variations, but flexible enough to meet individual needs.

Eastern Europe

A final consideration is the political changes in Eastern Europe, including the reunification of Germany. Although a few British companies have been trading for some years in the Eastern Bloc, these countries represent a largely untapped source of business and labour – the total population of the eight Eastern Bloc states being 43% of that of the twelve member states of the EC. Already there are reports of companies looking to the East in order to fill technical and other vacancies (see *Personnel Today*, July 1990). The 'opening up' of this market, together with the increased mobility of Eastern Bloc workers, will undoubtedly affect employment conditions in the rest of Europe.

Changing approaches to the contract of employment

Within this overall framework, employers are using an increasing variety of approaches to the contract of employment.

Flexible working hours

The first, and easiest, move away from the concept of fixed daily or weekly hours is to flex the hours.

The concept of flexible working hours (FWH) was introduced into Britain in the early 1970s and today approximately two million people in Britain work on this type of contract, the majority being white-collar workers. The arrangement has proved popular with both employers and employees.

The basic principles of FWH are simple:

> They involve the abolition of fixed working hours and the exercise of choice by the individual employee over his starting and finishing times. Given that he is contracted to work a certain number of hours in a day (or a week, or a month) it is up to him when he attends the place of work, within limits set down by the employer. (IDS, 1983a, p. 2)

The general features of FWH schemes are the following:

(i) There are agreed hours between which the employee may work, for example 8.00 am to 6.00 pm. This is known as the 'bandwidth'.
(ii) There is a time of day when all employees must be present, the 'core time'. Typically schemes have a core time of at least two hours in the morning and two hours in the afternoon, although in retailing the core time is more likely to be around lunchtime.
(iii) The periods of time between the bandwidth and the core time constitute 'flexible bands'. It is during these periods at the beginning and the end of the day that employees may choose to work. They must ensure that all contracted hours are completed by adding from the flexible bands enough hours to those in the core to complete the total for which they are contracted. Exactly when these hours are worked has to be agreed with the supervisor, who will ensure a reasonable distribution to cover business requirements throughout the day.

(iv) Each scheme's rules also have a settlement or accounting period for hours:

> The settlement period is the time in which employees must complete their contractual hours. For example, if an employee is contracted to work a 35 hour week, in a 4 weekly accounting period he will have to clock up 140 hours on the FWH scheme.   (IDS, 1983a, p. 2)

(v) Employees may be able to build up credit hours in order to take time off during core time. For example, if they have worked enough hours in one period (normally seven or eight) they may be allowed to take a day off in the following period. Most schemes place a limit on the number of these 'flexi-days' (usually one or two) that can be taken in any one period.

In order for a FWH scheme to be seen to be fair and accurate, opportunities for abuse must be kept to a minimum. This is normally achieved through the use of efficient time-recording and monitoring systems. The four types of system in use are manual systems, clocking systems, time recorders and computer systems. For many white-collar employees time-keeping is a matter of trust rather than control. Staff may therefore resent the introduction of new machinery for recording their working hours. However, the lack of such a system may give rise to suspicions of favouritism or that some individuals are not putting in their full complement of hours.

Many employers regard FWH as an employee benefit and have introduced these schemes as a method of attracting and retaining staff. For a full review of the advantages and disadvantages of FWH for both employers and employees, see IDS (1983a).

Compressed hours

Compressed hours arrangements enable people to work for four and a half or fewer days a week by extending the time spent on each day. In some British Aerospace plants a thirteen-hour shift, three-day week has been introduced for some operations and has proved to be an operational benefit as well as very being popular among those doing the work. A further variant is to contract to provide a specified number of hours a year (usually 1,700–1,750), while the individual enjoys considerable latitude in deciding when to work those hours. This can lead to some working intensively for several months in order to enjoy six or seven weeks' uninterrupted break, whilst being paid on a regular, unvarying basis. This approach has been useful in a number of different types of employment, such as continuous process and retailing, and is especially appropriate in work where there is a cyclical or seasonal demand, such as tourism, where the employer can concentrate hours into the busy periods. It is an interesting way in which flexibility can be developed in line with business demand.

Part-time working

The part-time contract is growing rapidly and Syrett (1983) gives a guide to different methods, including an analysis of how the costs vary between the employment of part-timers and full-timers. It remains debatable as to what proportion of the part-timers are working in this way simply because there is no alternative and what proportion prefer this mode. The great majority of part-timers are women.

A specialised form of working part-time is 'moonlighting'. Originally this term was used to describe the practice of doing a part-time job as well as a full-time job. This still applies, for instance, to the large number of people who work part-time in public houses for two or three evenings a week in addition to five days a week in the day job, but the increase in part-time working means that some people will put together a couple of part-time jobs. Charles Handy has advanced his theory of portfolio working, where we put together a range of different activities to comprise a rich variety:

> My own portfolio, as a professional man in his Third Age, is as follows: 150 days fee work (at varying rates and including provision for administration, paperwork and abortive meetings with clients); 50 days gift work (for various associations, societies and groups); 75 days study (essential to keep up to date in my work); 90 days homework and leisure (it is hard to distinguish between the two). (Handy, 1989, p. 152)

| REVIEW TOPIC 26.6 |

'Portfolio living is fine for people like Professor Handy, who are well qualified and experienced and able to pick and choose between opportunities. Most people are much more limited in what they can do and are dependent on employers providing proper jobs.'

What would you say on that point?

Job sharing

After a slow start, there is now growing use of job sharing, where two people share between them the demands of a full-time contract, so that the employer has the benefit of a full-time commitment and the employees have the flexibility and reduced hours that they prefer.

Job sharing potentially gives access to higher status, better paid jobs than were traditionally available to part-timers. How a job is shared depends on the needs of the job, the employer, colleagues and the job sharers themselves. For example, some jobs require a hand-over period of a few hours each week to enable sharers to exchange information. Other posts may require only a minimal briefing, often in the form of a telephone call or note. The most common arrangement is for each sharer to work two and a half days a week; variations include mornings/afternoons, alternate weeks or months.

Advantages of job sharing cited by employers include increased flexibility, peak period cover, reduced absenteeism, continuity during holidays and sick leave, promotion of equal opportunities and the availability of a wider range of skills and experience brought to bear on one job. Many employers also believe that job sharing improves staff retention and recruitment. Possible disadvantages may include increased administration/recruitment costs, communication problems and additional supervision.

From the employees' perspective, job sharing provides a flexible alternative to full-time working, the sharers retaining the status and promotion prospects of equivalent full-time staff. Many of these people are unable to work full-time. Job sharing offers them the opportunity to pursue a career whilst they raise a family or develop another interest. If a job sharer leaves it is common practice to offer the post to the remaining sharer. Many part-time jobs have reverted to full-time status in this way. Alternatively, the employer may advertise for another sharer – few have difficulty in filling these posts, since there is an increasing demand for part-time work. Indeed, a survey of job sharing in the London boroughs (New Ways to Work, 1990a) found that 84% of London boroughs have formal job share policies, an increase of 34% since 1987.

Term-time working

Term-time working is an arrangement whereby employees are given unpaid leave of absence during school holidays, while retaining the same conditions of service as permanently contracted full- and part-time staff. This form of flexible working has long been used by local authorities (see New Ways to Work, 1990b) and is now being taken up by private companies, in order to encourage women with older children to return to work.

In 1989 the Alliance and Leicester Building Society introduced term-time working for parents of school-age children:

> Under the scheme, parents of children aged from five to fourteen can work during school terms only. Staff taking this option are given 10 weeks unpaid leave each year to take during the school holidays, on top of which they are expected to take at least four weeks of their annual holiday entitlement (from three to six weeks depending on seniority and service) during the school holidays. This minimum of 14 weeks holiday amply covers the summer, Easter and Christmas breaks. (Spencer, 1990, p. 32)

The holiday periods are covered either by rescheduling work or by taking on casual labour. Although the Alliance and Leicester was not experiencing recruitment problems at the time, this scheme is part of a long-term initiative to improve recruitment and retention of staff.

Term-time working provides a flexible option for many working parents. Indeed, it is noticeable that many of the schemes have been taken up by both working fathers and mothers. It is also of particular assistance to single parents who may not have a partner available to assist in taking and collecting children to and from school.

Career breaks

Career breaks allow an employee to take an unpaid break from work, generally between two to five years, whilst remaining in touch with the company (for example, through training/refresher courses, newsletters, annual reports, or working for short periods). On returning, employees are guaranteed a job at the level of their original post, plus adequate retraining.

Career breaks were first introduced by the high street banks to encourage women to return to work after having a family. The National Westminster Bank introduced its career break scheme in 1981. This allows both men and women, at any level, to take up to five years off to care for children.

The use of similar schemes is now spreading in both the private and public sectors: ICI and Norwich Union have introduced five-year career break schemes; in July 1990 the NHS announced a career break scheme for all categories of workers. However, take-up figures for current schemes suggest that the legal implications of a break in service with regard to continuity of employment and statutory rights may be deterring employees from requesting career breaks (see Lucas, 1990). Employers may therefore be forced to review schemes if staff are to be encouraged to take up career breaks.

Sabbaticals

Sabbaticals are extended periods of leave, usually seen as a reward for long service and generally intended to allow the employee an opportunity to pursue outside interests, such as holiday, voluntary work, or further education. They can last anything from four weeks to a year and can be paid or unpaid. Sabbaticals were originally introduced in the USA, where one in six employers now offer them. Although they are still fairly novel in the UK, a number of companies are considering schemes. May (1985) provides a full review of the sabbatical programme currently operated by the John Lewis Partnership.

Homeworking

At present there are estimated to be over two million people in the UK working at or from home. Homeworking is not an easy or cheap option. It requires the recruitment of suitable workers, effective communication channels and remuneration policies, together with the development of progressive training and promotion structures (Rothwell, 1987).

Examples of homeworking projects operating in the UK include those run by IBM (UK), Digital Equipment Co., Rank Xerox and Texaco. One of the earliest schemes was established by F-International, a computer software company. Approximately 75% of the workforce is self-employed and work from home; 90% are women. Employees are recruited to work on particular projects for which an hourly rate is paid. On average individuals work 20–25 hours per week. The scheme requires close supervision and effective communication channels.

Advantages of this and other homeworking schemes include increased flexibility, job satisfaction and productivity (average gains 20%), widening of the labour pool to include homebound workers, improved retention levels and reduced overheads (Kelly, 1985).

Successful homeworking requires attitudinal changes on the part of both workers and managers. As Stanworth and Stanworth (1989) explain, homeworkers need not only technical knowledge but also psychological preparation – the ability to 'self start', to use small business and time management skills, and to cope with isolation. Many such workers fear that being home-based will result in reduced promotion prospects and marginalisation from the social and political life of the workplace. Personality is also an important factor; an extrovert with high affiliation needs may not easily adapt to home-based work.

Homeworking requires a shift from traditional management methods, often characterised by close supervision of the work process, to a more open style of management whereby workers are given greater autonomy and flexibility. Managers need to develop delegational skills, together with the abilty to set joint objectives/targets and to assess individual performance on results.

Autonomy is a key feature of the ways in which differing working patterns appeal to individual people at work, but there is a general, slow move in that direction by other means as well. Although hierarchy remains a standard feature of organisation, its form is being gradually modified to give greater emphasis to networking and individual responsibility. The personal organiser loose-leaf notebook that has become so popular is a symbol of the greater self-sufficiency that many people now find in their jobs.

The orientation of the job has also changed so that it is more outward-looking. There have been a number of exercises to train staff in social skills, which have had the effect of orienting people away from preoccupation with doing what they are told, heavily reliant on supervision, towards being more individually and personally responsive to other people.

SUMMARY PROPOSITIONS

26.1 The norm of a regular job with regular hours is undergoing radical change as a result of increased overseas competition, technological change, pressure on margins and reductions in the normal weekly hours of work.

26.2 The main general change in ways of working is brought about by employers thinking of workers in three categories: core, peripheral and external.

26.3 The possibility of labour or skill shortage has caused some employers to make the return to work of women and older employees easier.

26.4 The differing patterns of working that have been introduced include flexible working hours, compressed hours, part-time working, job sharing, term-time working, career breaks, sabbaticals and homeworking.

PUTTING IT INTO PRACTICE

The following is a checklist to use before introducing flexible working arrangements.

Forms of flexible working

1. What type of flexible working schemes would be particularly relevant to your organisation?
2. Are there any jobs that would not be suited to flexible working? Give examples and explain why.

Communication and consultation

1. Have all proposed changes been discussed with employees and trade unions?
2. How important is flexible working to your employees? Would a survey or questionnaire be helpful?
3. Devise ways of communicating and promoting new working patterns to employees: team briefings, poster campaigns, newsletters.

Management commitment

1. Explain the reasons behind the introduction of flexible working. Is it related to: market and customer needs, internal efficiency/productivity, development in new technology, availability of labour? What are the cost benefits?
2. Have all line managers been briefed on the implications of flexible working?
3. What management problems, if any, do you envisage (e.g. supervision, timekeeping)? How can they be solved?

Employee rights

1. Are flexible working options open to all employees?
2. Do flexible working options offer the same conditions of service and promotion/training opportunities as traditional full-time employment? If not, explain why.

References

Atkinson, J., 1984, Manpower strategies for flexible organisations, *Personnel Management*, August, pp. 28–31.

Atkinson, J., 1989, Four stages of adjustment to the demographic downturn, *Personnel Management*, August, pp. 20–4.

Clutterbuck, D., 1986, *New Patterns of Work*, Gower, Aldershot, Hampshire.

Cross, M., 1986, Flexible manning, in *New Patterns of Work*, ed. Clutterbuck, D., Gower, Aldershot, Hampshire.

Curnow, B, 1989, Recruit, retrain, retain: personnel management and the three Rs, *Personnel Management*, November, pp. 40–7.

Evans, A. and Walker, L., 1986, Sub-contracting, in *Flexible Patterns of Work*, ed. Curson, C., Institute of Personnel Management, London.

Finn, W., 1990, Grey matters, *Personnel Today*, April, pp. 37–8.

Goetschin, P., 1987, Re-shaping work for the older population, *Personnel Management*, June, pp. 39–41.

Hall, L., 1990, Firm links for kids, *Personnel Today*, April, p. 3.

Handy, C., 1989, *The Age of Unreason*, Business Books, London.

Hendry, C. and Pettigrew, A. M., 1988, Multi-skilling in the round, *Personnel Management*, April, pp. 36–43.

Incomes Data Services, 1983a, *Flexible Working Hours*, IDS Study 301, Incomes Data Services, London.

Incomes Data Services, 1983b, *The Job Splitting Scheme*, IDS Study 289, Incomes Data Services, London.

Kelly, M., 1985, The next workplace revolution: telecommuting, *Supervisory Management*, October, pp. 2–7.

Lucas, D., 1990, Breaking up is hard to do, *Personnel Today*, July, pp. 41–2.

May, S., 1985, Sabbaticals: the John Lewis experience, in *New Patterns of Work*, ed. Clutterbuck, D., Gower, Aldershot, Hampshire.

Mill, C., 1990, How the European Community works, *Personnel Management Plus*, July, p. 17.

NEDO, 1988, *Young People and the Labour Market*, National Economic Development Office, London.

New Ways to Work, 1990a, *Job Sharing and Flexible Working in the London Boroughs*, April, London.

New Ways to Work, 1990b, *Newsletter*, vol. 6, no. 1, London.

Pearson, R. and Pike, G., 1989, *The Graduate Labour Market in the 1990s*, Falmer, East Sussex.

Poole, M., 1989, Time to tackle the labour supply problem, *Personnel Management*, July, p. 79.

Rothwell, S., 1987, How to manage from a distance, *Personnel Management*, September, pp. 22–6.

Spencer, L., 1990, Parent Power, *Personnel Today*, April, pp. 32–3.

Stanworth, J. and Stanworth, C., 1989, Home truths about teleworking, *Personnel Management*, November, pp. 48–52.

Syrett, M., 1983, *Employing Jobsharers, Part-timers and Temporary Staff*, Institute of Personnel Management, London.

Underwood, R., 1989, New frontiers: new horizons, *Personnel Management*, February, pp. 34–7.

Chapter 27

The future and the professional manager

Few aspects of understanding are sought more eagerly than a look into the future. For centuries people all round the Mediterranean consulted the oracle at Delphi before embarking on any major enterprise. The tragedy of Macbeth is heightened by his reliance on the prophecy of the three witches. Today large segments of national newspapers are taken up with predictions based on the position of the stars and planets, and whether it will rain before breakfast. Having heard our favourite prediction, we then do not exactly ignore it; we interpret it in the way that suits us.

In concluding this book with some thoughts about the future, we do so realising that we are probably wrong and that whatever we say readers will interpret it in the way that suits them, emphasising and remembering what they like and ignoring what they dislike. We also realise that some people, browsing in bookshops and libraries, will glance at only this chapter before putting the book back on the shelf. So, with some misgivings, here we go.

Decentralisation and autonomy

The trend towards decentralisation of organisations and individual autonomy will continue. Operational units will be smaller and more manageable by having more scope delegated to them from the centre and less emphasis on conformity to a single pattern. This is not always possible, especially where consumer preference is important. Retail banks cannot vary their operational patterns much, as their interconnection is a major feature of their working, but gradually operational units of all types are gaining more independence for their operations. This provides more managers with more scope. Just as management by objectives was a popular attempt to isolate the activities of individual managers so that they could see their performance in isolation from collective performance, so there is growing a more real independence as accountability, responsibility and autonomy are made more feasible through managers being required to conform to organisation-wide norms on a relatively narrow range of activities only but with considerable scope to run the undertaking in their own way.

The decentralisation trend could lead to more people having senior management responsibilities and opportunities. This type of professional autonomy makes the idea of the professional manager, with skills suitable for a number of different situations, a more feasible proposition for the future than it has been in the past. Accountancy and marketing skills have become professionalised and transferable, but managerial skills have been more organisation-dependent due to the 'middleness' of most managers. That could now be changing.

Two widely-publicised reports (Handy, 1987; Constable and McCormick, 1987) advocated professional qualifications for all managers, and moves are currently establishing specific management competences against which preparation for management posts can be assessed. It is interesting that these developments, by the Management Charter Initiative, have worked on the basis of classifying some competences as appropriate for supervisory posts, some for the middle and others again for senior positions. That classification is one which we find difficult, as our observations in many organisations show that work done by a senior manager in one will be done by a junior manager in another.

This decentralisation is accompanied by an expectation of greater autonomy among those who do not see themselves as managers. Autonomous work groups received great publicity and scrutiny because they broke the mould of supervision. The pre-existing assumption had been that people at work needed supervision to keep them from idleness and to avoid their individual efforts being uncoordinated. By the basically simple tactic of getting (or letting?) work groups to organise themselves and exercise their own responsibility without the yoke of close supervision, it was demonstrated that tight control is not always necessary. Although the speed of movement varies, the general development of autonomy is growing apace, so that the professional manager will be increasingly concerned with a management team or departmental team of other professionals or quasi-professionals, wanting to know what is required of them and then wanting to be left alone to get on with it.

There is a cautionary note to be sounded, what Keith Sisson has called 'the tyranny of the strategic business unit'. The delegation of authority can be so narrowly prescribed that the strategic business unit is only an operational unit, with closely defined, short-term objectives and lacking any scope for strategic decision and action. In this situation the strategic control of the business is in the hands of a small number of head office strategists and those in the operational units have relatively little range to their activities. This is a part of the management style whereby strategy is conceived as acquisition and divestment rather than investment.

Managerial élite

In many ways managers as a social grouping are growing apart from those with whom they work. It is not their social origins, upbringing or schooling that makes the difference, but the approach to the job. Most people at work find their weekly hours slowly reducing, their annual days of holiday increasing and their age of retirement dropping. Paid employment may still be the central organising feature of our society and occupation may still be the main determinant of social status, but for many people work is not as focal as it was and some of our human needs are now met not through work but through the twin anodynes of television and do-it-yourself. If even slightly fewer needs depend on paid employment for their satisfaction, then employees become marginally more amenable and less prickly because it means less to them. Also the growing number of people who are retired and the significant number of people who are unemployed mean that 'working' is not the universal activity that it once was.

For managers it is different. There is a continuing preoccupation with correct dress and correct manners. Smart suits and hand-painted or self-coloured ties are still *de rigueur* for men, and women maintain a distinctive convention of dress, even if they are not quite so hidebound. Manners or styles of behaviour are also distinctive, so that some outside observers regard management as being no more than games-playing and posturing. Although this is an exaggeration in most instances, and is much reduced by decentralisation and autonomy, one of the conventional behaviours is 'commitment'. Managers are expected to be enthusiastic and thoroughly committed to their careers in a way that would nowadays seem slightly odd in many other occupational groups. This, of course, is a standard attribute of the professional in other fields. For managers it involves a willingness to travel considerably, day-by-day or week-by-week, so that it must be possible on one day to take the 6.30 am train to London, returning at midnight and on another day to fly to Bahrain for a week. Domestic commitments and family responsibilities do not fit easily into that sort of operating style. For most managers it also involves mobility, which presents a different set of domestic difficulties.

REVIEW TOPIC 27.1

Few managers appear relaxed and their lives are characterised by constant bustle, as we saw in Part I of this book, with hectic travelling a familiar feature of the managerial life style. To what extent do you think this is:

1. Setting a pace for everyone else to follow?
2. Inevitable due to the demands of the business?
3. Putting on a show, to convince people (and themselves) that they deserve to be well paid?
4. Unnecessary?

5. Harmful to their businesses because it is a distraction from what they really should be doing?
6. A result of management appealing mainly to people who are hyperactive?
7. Changing?

Total preoccupation of this type is relatively easy and attractive to the young and independent. It is tolerable to the married, but problematic for those with families – especially women. Women at the professional managerial level in business have found much improved opportunities in the last decade and have fared better than semi-skilled and clerical women, but for many of them success is gained at the expense of family life. The 28-year-old woman manager who is wondering whether or not to have a baby for the first time will realise that her neighbours who are doctors, barristers, schoolteachers, civil servants, lecturers and solicitors will find it much easier to return to their professional careers as young mothers than would she. It seems to be easier for those who bear their children while they are in their late teens or early twenties and who then begin the assault on the male-dominated bastions of management in their later twenties.

Age

Managers will respond to two different challenges relating to age. First will be the age of the customers. The decline in the fertility rate in Western countries has been accompanied by steadily growing life expectancy so that the mean age of the population is rising. Managers supplying goods and services have already exploited the adolescent market and, more recently, the market among the 'mature young' in their twenties and thirties but without family commitments (the dual-income-no-kids-yet or 'dinkies'). An expanding market will be among those of advancing years.

Within organisations, however, the situation is different. At the beginning of this chapter we suggested that decentralisation and autonomy could lead to more managers requiring senior management rather than middle manage-ment skills. We have also referred to the shake-out of employment among those who are older. In our interviews with managers while preparing this book we have been struck by how young managers are. This is not just a version of the hoary old comment about policemen getting younger as you get older, it appears to be a clear trend of significant management responsibility to come to younger people.

Partly this is a result of early retirement and similar shake-out strategies. If the 'old' people in the organisation are in their late fifties instead of in their early sixties, then the age balance shifts, so that the 'middle aged' are 40 instead of 48 and the 'young' are 25 instead of 30. Another reason is the growing significance of new technology, especially the computer, which seems to be best understood and developed by those in their teens and early twenties. Also the need to be committed, that we have mentioned, seems easier to sustain while young.

The idea of giving real responsibility to young people has been a commonplace for decades, even though it has not often been seen in practice. Now it is becoming more common, but what happens to older managers? In times of expansion the answer is easy: the organisation grows and more people are constantly needed to feed growth. If organisations are getting smaller, or remaining small, that answer will not work. The alternative is that managers move down the hierarchy as well as up. At the moment that sort of move is almost unknown, partly because of the concern with status and partly because of the concern with income level and pension level. The manager at forty is anxious to maximise earnings because of family responsibilities with children and ageing parents. The manager at fifty plus develops an anxiety to maximise his or her final salary, so as to boost the pension. This can produce a number of undesirable effects. One is the managers who are 'counting the days' until retirement but have to cling grimly to jobs they no longer really want to do, just to maintain the pension. Another possibility is the department or business that stagnates for years because the person in charge is in the run-up to retirement and does not want any innovation or change. A third problem is that of the managers who keep going at full throttle in the closing stages of employment, only to find the sudden change to the different pace of retirement very hard to take.

REVIEW TOPIC 27.2

Do you find managers getting younger where you work? If you do, do you think this makes things better or worse? If not, what advantages do you think would come from younger people holding positions of real responsibility?

It is unrealistic to think simply of moving people out of the organisation as they get older. First, this can be extremely expensive, and secondly, it reduces the all-round capability of the management, which needs the contribution of older people as well as those who are younger. Those who are older are likely to take a more measured view of proceedings and some companies, as we saw in our chapter on different patterns of working, have positively sought out older people as new recruits.

The computer

One great uncertainty is the influence of the computer. We have plenty of predictions, mostly prophecies of what the computer and the microprocessor can do which are logically developed to produce a picture of what will happen; manufacturing will progressively be taken over by robots, rapid transfer and manipulation of data, the paperless office, people working from home instead of coming into a centre, and so forth: the golden age of the post-industrial society. Our questions about this are first the extent to which the possible will become reality and secondly to wonder what will be done to make up what the computer will take from us.

Managers have long had the opportunity to spend more of their time, and make more of their decisions, by rational planning and operational research methods than in fact they do. There continues to be a preference among managers to spend their time talking with people and to make their decisions as a result of discussion and shrewd judgement. Will managers now begin to eschew face-to-face discussion in favour of face-to-terminal decision-making, or will they continue to confer and keep busy while others feed to them an ever-increasing flow of processed information requiring interpretation, evaluation and further discussion? Research findings suggest that managers work the way they do at least partly because they like it that way.

> The manager actually seems to prefer brevity and interruption in his work.
> Superficiality is an occupational hazard of the manager's job. Very current
> information (gossip, hearsay, speculation) is favoured; routine reports are not.
> The manager clearly favours the . . . verbal media, spending most of his time
> in verbal contact.   (Mintzberg, 1973, pp. 51–2)

The date and male gender of that quotation may be significant. Most of the studies of managerial work have been of men, and of men and women, working in a male-dominated culture. It may be that the increasing proportion of managerial jobs done by women will alter the stereotype. How significantly will managers allow this pattern of working to change and how great will the influence of the computer on managerial work actually become?

Apart from managers, there is then the question about how everyone else will make up for what the computer takes away. If there is a general tendency for people to work at home, taking their terminal with them, how popular will that turn out to be? It is over a century since the household ceased to be the central productive unit and the men, and later the women, began to spend a large part of their waking hours at a different social centre – the factory, shop or office. To be housebound has become a blight. We can see how it used to be:

> In 1810 the common productive unit in New England was still the rural
> household. Processing and preserving of food, candlemaking, soap-making,
> spinning, weaving, shoemaking, quilting, rug-making, the keeping of small
> animals and gardens, all took place on domestic premises. Although money
> income might be obtained by the household through the sale of produce, and
> additional money be earned through occasional wages to its members, the
> United States household was overwhelmingly self-sufficient. . . . Women were
> as active in the creation of domestic self-sufficiency as were men.
>   (Illich, 1981, pp. 111–12)

Since that time we have dismantled, or allowed to wither, all the social mechanisms that supported that self-sufficiency, and developed the social institution of the workplace as the arena for many of our human needs, like affiliation, interaction, team working and competition. It really seems most unlikely that the move away from working in the household will be reversed. In every country of the world roads and railways are jammed with people going to work at the beginning of the day or returning at the end.

The computer revolution may not turn everyone into a homeworker, but it is still having a significant impact. There is the slightly isolating nature of the work that computerisation produces. The individual employee is not one of many in a crowded workshop, but one of a few scattered around a mass of busy machines. The clerical employee spends more time gazing at a computer terminal and less talking to colleagues. What employee behaviour will this engender and what attitudes will be associated with that behaviour? As more people become able to use the computer, especially for word processing, there will be a net loss of jobs. This has been seen in its most dramatic form in the publishing of newspapers, where typesetting has been eliminated through journalists typing their copy directly at a computer terminal. The first book we wrote together in 1984 was composed initially in a series of handwritten and manually typed drafts, which were then cut, edited and pasted up for a professional secretary to produce the final typescript. This book has been composed, edited and a final typescript produced by the authors using two word-processors.

---| REVIEW TOPIC 27.3 |----------------------------------

What difference has the computer made to your working life so far? What further effect do you expect it to have in the next five years?

Worldwide regional management?

We considered in Chapter 10 some of the international developments that are likely, and the challenge of the global business seems quite mind-boggling. There may be an intermediate stage between national management and international management, and that is a form of management that is generally applicable in one of the main regions of the globe. Most international companies are originally either North American, West European or Japanese. In 1985 Kenichi Ohmae described this as the Triad, three regions with 600 million residents:

> . . . whose academic backgrounds, income levels, life style, use of leisure time and aspirations are quite similar. In these democratic countries, the national infrastructure, in terms of highways, telephone systems, sewage disposal, power transmission, and governmental systems, is also very similar.
>
> (Ohmae, 1985, p. 37)

Despite the similarities, we have seen how markedly different management methods often are. Also the decade since the remarks were made has seen the inexorable rise of the South-east Asian countries.

Canada, Mexico and the United States are making moves to harmonise the nature of their employment legislation, there are moves towards harmonisation among the ASEAN (Association of South East Asian Nations) countries, and the development of the European Community is slowly continuing.

In Britain most of the writing about *international* management is in fact about management across Europe, and the evolution of Community legislation is gradually bringing together the legal framework within which employment is managed. In the ASEAN countries there is a similar degree of common features, despite the marked difference in economic health of the constituent countries. These common features derive from the legacy of colonialism, the high level of unemployment and illegal migration between member countries, the prominent role of trade unions in achieving political independence, and the fact that many of the workers are illiterate and therefore require a great degree of protection from unscrupulous employers (Torrington and Tan Chwee Huat, 1993, Chapter 21).

With this type of economic and social cooperation, there may be a stage at which it is possible to recognise regional management as a stage between national and international, with national gradually being superseded by its regional version.

Regional industrial relations?

By the 1960s trade unions had become a feature of almost every industrial country of the world and personnel managers always had the industrial relations portfolio as a key part of their role. Trade unions, however, varied greatly between different countries in their ways of operating. In some they were the vehicle of fundamental political change, especially in the overthrow of colonial rule. In some they were the vehicle for the intended achievement of a Communist government; in others they became a part of the mainstream political movements. They grew in power and influence, but then the tide turned against them in the West.

Unions in the United States lost popularity because of allegations of corruption and a disenchantment with their methods. The elected leaders of the new post-colonial powers felt that unions were useful when in opposition, but an encumbrance when in government. The Communist Party failed to achieve government in the countries of Western Europe and one of the most popular stories in the United Kingdom of the decline of Communism in Eastern Europe was the rise of Lech Wałesa and the trade union Solidarity to bring about the collapse of a Communist government under the inspiration of the Roman Catholic Church. By 1985 the percentage of employees who were trade union members had sunk to 17% in both France and the United States, 29% in Japan and 52% in the United Kingdom (Dowling and Schuler, 1990, p. 142).

In the age of human resource management, industrial relations and trade union negotiation has nothing like the prominence it had, and practice is extremely varied:

> . . . industrial relations phenomena are a very faithful expression of the society in which they operate, of its characteristic features and of the power relations between different interest groups. Industrial relations can not be understood without an understanding . . . of the society concerned.   (Schregle, 1981, p. 27)

These variations are often solidified in a legal framework that was elaborately constructed at a time when governments saw unions as a threat to social stability.

This diversity means that there is little scope for a coordinated global industrial relations strategy for any business. There may be a strong case for a regional strategy.

International social responsibility

The international dimension of the social responsibility question has still to be developed. During the latter half of 1992 several powerful Western countries suffered serious economic problems because of speculation against their currencies, much of which was at the hands of major banks. Logging operations in South America are ravaging the rain forests, which are essential to life continuing on the planet. Error, or neglect, in the management of manufacturing processes can produce a tragedy like that of Bhopal in India, Chernobyl in the Ukraine or the various discharges of crude oil that have occurred all over the world. Since the first formal warning by the American Surgeon General about the risks of smoking, tobacco consumption has been falling in Western countries, so the tobacco companies have increased their marketing in less developed countries.

Ethical standards vary. The Recruit affair was a major Japanese scandal involving allegations of corruption among the country's most senior politicians. In the aftermath there was much American criticism of Japanese business practices and a flurry of righteous indignation in Western newspapers about the need to use 'slush funds' in various countries to obtain business. Becker and Fritzsche (1987) carried out a study of different ethical perceptions between American, French and German executives: 39% of the Americans said that paying money for business favours was unethical, but only 12% of the French and none of the Germans agreed. In the United States Japanese companies have been accused of avoiding the employment of ethnic minority groups by the careful location of their factories (Cole and Deskins, 1988, pp. 17–19). On the other hand Japanese standards on employee health and safety are as high as anywhere in the world (Wokutch, 1990). In South-east Asia the contrast in prosperity between countries like Malaysia and Singapore on the one hand and Indonesia and the Philippines on the other means that there are ethical questions about the employment of illegal immigrants that are superficially similar to those of Cubans and Mexicans in the United States, but which do not occur in other parts of the world (Torrington and Tan Chwee Huat, 1993, Chapter 3). There is the continuing legacy of apartheid in South Africa, very low wages and long working hours in China, and in Europe the British government refuses to accept the social chapter of the Maastricht Treaty harmonising employment conditions across the European Community.

The disparate nature of ethical standards between countries will be one of the key issues to be addressed by managers operating in the international arena in the future. There will gradually be a growing together of national practice on working hours, but it will take a lot longer for rates of pay to harmonise. One can visualise common standards on health and safety developing much more quickly than equality of opportunity between the sexes and across ethnic divisions. How readily will consumers in country A pay more for their goods in order to improve the quality of life for workers in country B?

There seem to be games being played between governments and multinational companies:

> Corporations in the international arena . . . have no real desire to seek international rules and regulations . . . that would erode the differential competitive advantage which accrues as a consequence of astute locational decisions. Indeed the strategies are centred on endless negotiations, or the ability to play off the offer from one nation against that of another. . . . Examples of this strategy can be found in the recent negotiations over CFC restrictions, ozone depletion and the preservation of the Amazon rain forest.
>
> (McGowan and Mahon, 1992, p. 172)

Conclusion

We hear frequent references to the way in which the world is becoming a global village, with Armani clothes, Levi jeans, Pepsi-Cola drinks, Glaxo pharmaceuticals and Sony compact discs to be found everywhere. World-wide telecommunications are instant, 747s with Rolls Royce engines are everywhere and Michael Jackson can be seen by a thousand million people at a single performance. Amongst all this is the practice of management. Whether companies internationalise, multinationalise, globalise or trans-nationalise, management will remain largely a national activity, bounded by culture, geography and legislative systems.

The development of computer usage will make redundant more and more jobs without succeeding in getting us all to work at home. Managers will be more set apart from other workers by their shared conventions of dress and lifestyle, concentrated among people in their late twenties to late forties. There will be more decentralisation and autonomy, but in some circumstances that autonomy may be severely limited.

In this concluding chapter we have suggested a few possibilities for the future. They are offered here as they sustain our belief that managers progressively need to develop a personal survival kit that will enable them to be effective in a wide variety of situations, becoming less organisationally dependent and more self-sufficient.

We see the stereotype of the future manager as being younger, better-paid and more autonomous than those of today. To succeed they will need to be mobile and bright. More of them will be women and most will have a strong specialist skill in either accountancy, marketing or a technological area. All of them will need organisational knowledge and a set of operational managerial skills of the type that we have described in these pages. Above all they will need individual flair, imagination and application. Management is a science: successful management is an art.

Good luck!

References

Becker, H. and Fritzsche, D. J., 1987, A comparison of the ethical behavior of American, French and German Managers, *Columbia Journal of World Business*, Winter, pp. 87–95.

Cole, R. E. and Deskins, D. R., 1988, Racial factors in site location and employment patterns of Japanese auto firms in America, *California Management Review*, Fall, p. 11.

Constable, J. and McCormick, R., 1987, *The Making of British Managers*, British Institute of Management, Corby, Northamptonshire.

Dowling, P. J. and Schuler, R. S., 1990, *International Dimensions of Human Resource Management*, PWS-Kent, Boston, Mass.

Handy, C. B., 1987, *The Making of Managers*, National Economic Development Office, London.

Illich, I., 1981, *Shadow Work*, Marion Boyars, London.

McGowan, R. A. and Mahon, J. F., 1992, Multiple games, multiple levels: gamesmanship and strategic corporate responses to environmental issues, *Business and the Contemporary World*, vol. 14, no. 4, pp. 162–77.

Mintzberg, H., 1973, *The Nature of Managerial Work*, Harper & Row, London.

Ohmae, K. 1985, *Triad Power, The Coming Shape of Global Competition*, Macmillan, London.

Schregle, J., 1981, Comparative industrial relations: pitfalls and potential, *International Labour Review*, vol. 120, no. 1, pp. 15–30.

Torrington, D. P. and Tan Chwee Huat, 1993, *Human Resource Management for South East Asia*, Simon & Schuster, Singapore.

Wokutch, R. E., 1990, Corporate social responsibility, Japanese style, *Academy of Management Executive*, May, pp. 56–72.

Author index

Subject index